The Clinton Legacy

The Clinton Legacy

edited by

**Colin Campbell and
Bert A. Rockman**

CHATHAM HOUSE PUBLISHERS

SEVEN BRIDGES PRESS, LLC

NEW YORK • LONDON

SEVEN BRIDGES PRESS, LLC
135 FIFTH AVENUE, NEW YORK, NEW YORK 10010

Publisher: Robert J. Gormley
Managing Editor: Katharine Miller
Production Services: *TIPS* Technical Publishing, Inc.
Project Manager: Robert Kern
Composition: Bright Path Solutions
Cover Design: Timothy Hsu
Cover Photo: Rick Friedman/Black Star/PNI
Printing and Binding: R.R. Donnelley & Sons Company

Library of Congress Cataloging-in-Publication Data

The Clinton Legacy/edited by Colin Campbell and Bert A. Rockman.
     p. cm.
   Includes bibliographical references (p.) and index.
   ISBN 1-889119-14-8
   1. Clinton, Bill, 1946– 2. Politics and government—1993– I. Campbell, Colin, 1943– II. Rockman, Bert A.
   E886.C576 2000
   973.929'092—dc21

                                        99-6299
                                           CIP

Manufactured in the United States of America
10   9   8   7   6   5   4   3   2   1

To the memory of our cherished friend, Ed Artinian,
whose legacy will never be in doubt

Contents

Introduction
Colin Campbell and Bert A. Rockman ix

1: The Partisan Legacy: Are there any New Democrats?
(And by the way, was there a Republican Revolution?)
Byron E. Shafer 1

2: Campaigning Is Not Governing: Bill Clinton's Rhetorical
Presidency
George C. Edwards III 33

3: Demotion? Has Clinton Turned the Bully Pulpit into a Lectern?
Colin Campbell 48

4: The President as Legislative Leader
Barbara Sinclair 70

5: Judicial Legacies: The Clinton Presidency and the Courts
David M. O'Brien 96

6: A Reinvented Government, or the Same Old Government?
Joel D. Aberbach 118

7: Clinton and Organized Interests: Splitting Friends, Unifying Enemies
Mark A. Peterson 140

8: Race, Gender, and the Clinton Presidency
Virginia Sapiro and David T. Canon 169

9: Clinton's Domestic Policy: The Lessons of a "New Democrat"
Paul J. Quirk and William Cunion 200

10: Engaging the World: First Impressions of the Clinton Foreign Policy Legacy
Emily O. Goldman and Larry Berman 226

11: Clinton in Comparative Perspective
Graham K. Wilson 254

12: Cutting *With* the Grain: Is There a Clinton Leadership Legacy?
Bert A. Rockman 274

Notes 295

Index 335

About the Contributors 345

Introduction

COLIN CAMPBELL AND BERT A. ROCKMAN

In a book we edited and published in 1995 dealing with the initial two years of President Bill Clinton's first term, we observed that despite the Republican landslide victory of 1994 and Clinton's less than soaring public standing, he could bounce back and be reelected.[1] And he did. His approval ratings for the job he has been doing as president have remained buoyant through most of his second term. Now the authors of this volume have a different task—less to assess what happened and its short- to medium-term implications and more to focus on what Clinton's presidency might mean over the longer run. *What, in other words, is Clinton's legacy?* The authors of this volume try to assess his legacy—and, indeed, whether he will actually leave one—from a variety of angles, among them politics, policy, institutions, as well as leadership and societal context.

Legacies are a complicated business to deal with. How long a period of time are we talking about? To whom is the legacy bequeathed? And by whom is it interpreted? The more distant the time period, the less a presidency will stand out unless it has been associated with disastrous turns of fortune or with perceptions of strong and effective leadership, which are sporadically made possible by the presence of crises or, more rarely, by big congressional majorities associated with the president's party. Crises *force* presidents to do things; big congressional majorities *allow* them to do things. But these conditions are uncommon.

Except for the scarlet letter of impeachment, Clinton's presidency is not particularly likely to stand out because the times in which he governed denied much opportunity to make a bold mark. Politically he began with shrunken majorities that soon thereafter turned into minorities. And economic good times carried with them no sense of urgency for government to do much of anything. Thus, his resources and his opportunities were few. Nevertheless, because times were good, his presidency, on the whole, received good marks from the public. The good times might have provided Clinton with slack to resurrect some of his earlier projects. But now, not only did he no longer have the congressional majorities to have even an outside chance at carrying the day, he also effectively delegitimized any semblance of his original agenda by disowning it. Presumably, Clinton concluded that it was better that the passengers (especially the ones in steerage) go down rather than the ship's captain.

What lay within Clinton's capacity to be effective will certainly fuel debate mainly because it is unknowable. Was he a shrewd realist or simply an expedient opportunist? Notably, Clinton's overused metaphor about building a bridge to the twenty-first century is remarkably devoid of any image as to what should lie on the other side. Much like all of the "new" Nixons who were in a near constant state of reinvention by the old one, Clinton has been a politician in transition, seemingly devoted more to turning losing into winning than to defining an objective for which winning would be relevant. Paradoxically, the longer he served as president, the more Clinton's latitude for bold strokes seemed to constrict despite his benefiting from the halo effect associated with economic good times. Clinton's presidency has been more defined by the times in which he has presided than the times have been redefined by his presidency. That is, of course, a joint function of Clinton's limited opportunities and his opportunism.

Clinton may have made a real impact in the nature of partisan politics, especially in regard to the identity of the Democratic Party—a point, we hasten to add, that the authors of the chapters in this volume debate. Has Clinton helped create a new Democratic Party or merely found the median between the parties to be a convenient and pragmatic positioning point? Has Clinton altered the fault lines of American politics, or do older political cleavages still dominate? Has Clinton maneuvered his way around the zone of acceptance with adroitness, probing as to where he could effectively apply pressure? Or did he simply fail to take any risk, thus locking himself and his options into a logic of foregone conclusions? Whatever the case, as president, Clinton clearly has been a practitioner of the art of the possible rather than a leader who attempts to stretch the boundaries of the possible.

Confronted with divided government and budget constraints (which Clinton bought into), there was not much a traditional Democrat could do in the way of social democratic programs. Clinton found that out with his health care reform proposal even before the Democrats lost control of Congress. So, he became a practitioner of "acupuncture politics"—seeking to alleviate some of the pressure points when that seemed possible and popular and, perhaps, it seemed possible precisely because it was popular. After the great health care debacle, he pushed health insurance portability, health coverage for children, and a patients' bill of rights. Though these proposals were popular, some conflicted with the interests of Republican constituencies or the doctrines of Republican politicians. Where Clinton could not get a policy, he was able, along with his party, to get an issue. Traditional liberal Democrats, however, saw Clinton as caving time and again to the conservative Republican agenda on matters such as welfare reform, civil liberties, immigration, and immigrants' rights (which were essentially discarded). Liberal Democrats are not notably popular in the country, despite the fact that their programmatic legacy—Social Security, Medicare, Medicaid, and so on—is wildly popular. Republicans had the upper hand numerically and also from the standpoint of the relative popularity of their policy positions on the matters on which Clinton more or less (a meaningful distinction in this case) assimilated the Republican position.[2]

How one views Clinton in the longer run may depend upon whether it is perceived that he did the best that was possible, merely the possible, or that he sacrificed policy for political advantage. Some, especially Republicans, are likely to view Clinton as an unsavory and untrustworthy politician who opportunistically took the ground from beneath the Republican platform except on matters in which the Republican position was unpopular, such as anti-choice on abortion, or tinkering with Social Security and Medicare. From a less politically impassioned perspective, Clinton may be seen as a president who enabled the system to work even though he could not coax it to work *his* will. As with any president, how Clinton is seen will be determined by the beholder. But Clinton's is a more complicated case than most.

Part of the complication of Clinton's case lies in his character and, as a result, also in the institutional legacy of the Clinton presidency. Clinton began his presidency amid questions about his character—was he an inveterate womanizer? Was he duplicitous and slick? Was he shady in his business and campaign practices? These questions, except possibly the last one, are no longer in doubt. Clinton's long drawn-out struggle with Independent Counsel Kenneth Starr did even more damage to Starr than to Clinton. But the damage was different. Starr's operation showed him to be in monomaniacal pursuit of Bill Clinton. It demonstrated his lack of proportionality and it revealed to most Americans what they *really* have to fear from the state. But Clinton's response to the pressures, however legit-

Colin Campbell and Bert A. Rockman

imate or illegitimate, that Starr's investigation placed on him brought him into personal ill-repute, even as many Americans separated his personal defects from his conduct of the presidency. Clinton did manage to demonstrate without much doubt that his word was worthless, that lying came easy to him, and that his behavior and lack of self-control toward women left him a perpetual adolescent.

Jimmy Carter, whose character was never in doubt, demonstrated how little character counted for the way people viewed him as a president.[3] Ironically, Bill Clinton also showed that his considerably less virtuous character counted less than people's views that he has been a competent president during prosperous times. In the longer run, however, Jimmy Carter's post-presidential good deeds may be more meaningful to his reputation than his ill-regarded presidency. Clinton's presidency, too, may be subsequently viewed in the light of his character—his affair with Monica Lewinsky, his lies to the public and to his associates about it, and his stonewalling of his pursuers. It is plausible that Clinton's political opportunism and flawed character will be thought of as part of the same witches' brew.

Kenneth Starr's lengthy and relentless pursuit of Clinton, whatever else it has yielded, has had an institutional legacy, as much the result of Clinton's behavior as of Starr's. As David O'Brien shows in his chapter for this book, the no-yield legal strategy of the Clinton White House challenged the courts to take the bait. Both the Clinton White House and those seeking to bring Clinton down (or to justice), whether the Paula Jones foundation–funded attorneys or Starr's prosecutorial team, used the courts as the venue for their battles. The courts almost always bit, and by ruling against Clinton's claims, weakened the implicit prerogatives of the presidency, much as had happened in the later stages of the Nixon presidency. The process began with the bizarre Supreme Court decision that Paula Jones—whom Clinton either harassed or by whom he was being harassed—could sue Clinton for civil damages during his presidency on the premise that this would not much interfere with his conduct of the presidency. Subsequently, Starr convinced the courts to rule against the president's efforts to keep White House aides from testifying to the grand jury by invoking executive privilege and also to force the White House Secret Service detail to testify before the grand jury.

Future presidents will step into an office that by legal precedent is now a weaker one than Clinton came to. Clinton bears much of the responsibility for its weakening; so do Starr and the Paula Jones attorneys. Ultimately, of course, the judicial branch has opened up a can of worms by ruling on matters over which it

xii

has limited competency and, strictly speaking, jurisdiction. Certainly, Hillary Clinton's initial outburst about a right-wing conspiracy in hot pursuit of her man was *well founded*. Right-wing foundations came to the aid of Paula Jones in their effort to topple or weaken Clinton. She was a vehicle for their cause; in the end, however, Clinton had no one to blame but himself. His irresponsible behavior occasioned the juridical attack on the presidency. Neither Nixon nor Clinton served well the office they inhabited, whatever their other virtues and vices.

In sum, the Clinton presidency may cast a minuscule shadow insofar as a policy legacy is concerned. The lowlights of Clinton's presidency will be the office's weakening, which he unintentionally helped produce, and his character flaws, different from, but as deep as, Richard Nixon's. The highlights will be Clinton's personal and political resiliency, especially his political aptitude. Although he failed to push forward a national agenda to the satisfaction of New Deal–style Democrats, he did prove himself wondrously adept at political survival, and he both accomplished and blocked enough to be a force in policymaking. He may not have been able to work miracles, but he did better than one could reasonably expect with what fate had dealt him. His friends will see Clinton as a president who brought moderation to an environment hyped with political zealotry, thus reclaiming the center in American political life. Those less friendly toward him will see Clinton as an unprincipled scoundrel who reinforced the public's view of politicians as untrustworthy and contemptible. The fact is that Clinton has been *all* of these things. This contributes to bafflement concerning an enduring Clinton legacy precisely because no one can be sure just exactly what his legacy might be (except possibly for his damage to the office itself) if, indeed, there is to be one at all.

Despite the uncertainty surrounding Clinton's achievements, the authors of the succeeding chapters try to unravel the mysteries of the Clinton presidency and what, if anything, the eight years of his presidency will mean after he leaves.

Since Clinton touted himself to be a "New Democrat," Byron Shafer, in his chapter, "The Partisan Legacy: Are there any New Democrats? (And by the way, was there a Republican Revolution?)," asks whether Clinton actually shifted political cleavages in the U.S. or whether such changes actually helped Clinton find his wings. Such changes, Shafer concludes, have been only on a superficial level, whereas partisan continuities are more fundamental and are still essentially based along the fault lines of an era of divided government going back at least to 1968 and, in some ways, even to the New Deal politics of the 1930s. From this perspective, Clinton's political legacy is shallow indeed.

George Edwards, in his chapter, "Campaigning Is Not Governing: Bill Clinton's Rhetorical Presidency," emphasizes the counterproductive influences of Clinton's hyper-political style of governing. Clinton was filled with aspirations but little strategy. Adopting campaign techniques for governing backfired, as Clinton seemed unable to focus and develop a strategy for pushing ahead until his main role came to be primarily that of pushing aside Republican initiatives.

Colin Campbell deals with this theme in a different way in his chapter, "Demotion? Has Clinton Turned the Bully Pulpit into a Lectern?" As does Edwards, Campbell concludes that Clinton's presidency has lacked focus and message. But Campbell also argues that when the choices availed themselves, Clinton failed to use moral suasion as part of the presidential tool kit, thus reducing the bully pulpit to a lectern. In essence, Campbell argues, by essentially acceding to the Gingrich agenda and by failing to articulate its own, the Clinton presidency only succeeded in widening what he terms "the governability gap."

In her chapter, "The President as Legislative Leader," Barbara Sinclair notes the complexity of Clinton's situation as a legislative leader and asks whether he has been effective in that role. She contends that the incentives of the Clinton administration were in generating a record that required compromise with the Republican majority. The incentives of the Democratic minority in Congress, however, were to oust the Republican majority by making them look bad. Sinclair distinguishes different conceptions of the president as legislative leader. In its maximum conception, she clearly thinks that Clinton failed, though that may well be for reasons outside of any president's control. But in its minimalist conception, Clinton succeeded in keeping his opponents off balance and their agenda from coming to full legislative fruition.

David O'Brien's wide-ranging chapter on Clinton's "Judicial Legacies: The Clinton Presidency and the Courts" sees Clinton's own imperiled presidency, under continuous investigation and ultimately the threat of his removal from office, as connected to his judicial legacy and the institutional weakening of the presidency. Continuous investigation, abetted by the White House strategy of contesting investigatory demands through court battles, eroded formerly uncontested, if ambiguous, presidential prerogatives and discretion. This legal shadow, and the Republican control of the Senate after 1994, also curtailed Clinton's ability to use the courts and judicial appointments as a presidential lever—not that Clinton at any time showed much interest in using judicial appointments as an ideological aid to his presidency. Consequently, Clinton's impact on the judiciary has been slighter than those of the Reagan-Bush presidencies.

If Clinton seemed reluctant to use judicial appointments as a political tool, there was no such reluctance on the part of the administration to try to work its will through the executive branch when Congress was a barrier. In his chapter, "A Reinvented Government, or the Same Old Government?" Joel Aberbach demonstrates that the administrative presidency is alive and well in the Clinton administration. Faced with divided government, the Clinton presidency has resorted to tactics similar to its Republican predecessors, namely, using administrative means to do what cannot be done through legislative means. Aberbach also inquires into the much-heralded plans for governmental reinvention launched under Vice-President Al Gore. While he does note that the reinvention agenda will generate controversy and debate among aficionados of government management, it is not likely to be high on the list of things for which the Clinton administration will be remembered.

Clinton's tendency to build political coalitions from the middle, in the view of Mark Peterson, proved to be an unworkable formula. In his chapter, "Clinton and Organized Interests: Splitting Friends, Unifying Enemies," Peterson observes that Clinton was better at unifying opposition to him than at generating unified support on his behalf. Creating an expanded interest group base was part of Clinton's New Democrat strategy. While this strategy has sporadically worked in areas that are neither traditionally identified with Democratic policies nor at the federal level (crime control, for example), on the big federal issues associated with the Democratic agenda, building coalitions from the middle has mainly failed to produce the expected support. Why? Peterson notes that passion leads to mobilization, and a passionate center is in scant supply. And this may be why a political strategy of the center has great difficulty building a sustainable base, although it can have ad hoc successes.

Virginia Sapiro and David Canon focus on Clinton's supporting groups in their chapter, "Race, Gender, and the Clinton Presidency." Most prominent among Clinton's political support coalition were African Americans and women. The authors ask why these groups remained so steadfast in their support, especially inasmuch as some of Clinton's behavior, whether calculated or otherwise, could be construed as offensive to these core constituencies. For the most part, however, Clinton cultivated these constituencies through symbolic politics, appointments, and policies. When he was down, they came to his aid. A part of their attraction to Clinton was not only what he did to cultivate them, it was also what the Republicans did to repel them, a lesson that Republicans may now be in the process of absorbing.

Continuing with the theme of building a centrist political and policy strategy, Paul Quirk and William Cunion, in their chapter on "Clinton's Domestic Policy: The Lessons of a 'New Democrat,'" ask what happens when a "centrist president attempts to lead a deeply divided, or *polarized*, Congress?" What happened is that the centrist president often got the upper hand politically over the Republicans. From a policy standpoint, however, much depends upon whether the centrist positions stem from principles or political opportunism. The authors believe the latter produces bad public policy, dependent upon fluctuations in public taste. They suggest that Clinton's centrist stance has had more to do with political opportunism than with principles.

In their chapter, "Engaging the World: First Impressions of the Clinton Foreign Policy Legacy," Emily O. Goldman and Larry Berman ask whether Clinton has "left a legacy others can build upon, develop more fully, articulate more clearly, and implement more effectively?" They note that "articulating a coherent foreign policy vision at this historic moment is fraught with difficulty" and that this problem is not exclusively endemic to the United States or to Clinton. The old certainties are gone. Providing conceptual traction for the present and future is a formidable task. On some matters, especially but not exclusively those of international financial management, Clinton leaves a positive legacy. On others, especially those likely to engage U.S. military involvement and the relationship between force and political objectives, clarity and decisiveness (but apparently not luck) appear to be lacking.

Judging "Clinton in Comparative Perspective," Graham Wilson asks what will "Clinton's *political* legacy be to the repertoire of leadership strategies in advanced democracies?" Clinton and Tony Blair, the "New Labour" Party prime minister in Britain, have been advocates of "the third way," defined as the space between big-state welfare commitments and protections and an unmerciful capitalism. The old way, for sure, meant that there was no way these political leaders could be elected. There is both uniqueness and portability in the Clinton style of perpetual campaigning, positioning, and spinning. Two conditions, the necessity of a lengthy period of right-wing leadership to incubate the "new" photogenic and articulate centrist leaders of "old" left parties and institutions that give prominence to a central executive leader, limit the portability of the Clinton style to only a few countries, most notably to Britain. Still, governing in an age of constraints, according to Wilson, makes centrist positions more attractive because increased public commitments are perceived to be unfeasible.

Finally, in his chapter, "Cutting *With* the Grain: Is There a Clinton Leadership Legacy?" Bert Rockman asks what Clinton's options really were and whether his leadership will leave a legacy. Rockman notes that Clinton was inclined to cut *with* the grain rather than against it. His legacy, if there is one, is likely to be less in policy than in politics. Clinton has been an agile, skilled political leader. The main question is, given these qualities, has he fended better for himself than for his policy agenda? Given that he was dealt a weak hand, how well did he play it? And could he have played it differently? With what consequences?

Clinton already has achieved a certain dubious repute thanks to Ken Starr, Henry Hyde and the House Judiciary Committee Republicans, and, of course, to his own scandalous behavior. That legacy is not the one Clinton wanted to leave, but it is likely to be the matter for which his presidency will be most noted. Clinton faced an uphill climb to make his mark. Political tacticians, even ones as keen as Clinton, get us through the moment and then slip from memory. What did Clinton stand for? What was, as James Carville liked to put it, "his sacred ground"? Did he have any other than political survival? Political pragmatists tend to go easily into history, leaving only faint traces behind. We often prefer the heroic gesture as worthy of a legacy. Good times, however, do not make for grand gestures. Clinton presided over good times, and that may be his legacy. One could ask for worse things.

But one also could ask for better things. No doubt, the Clinton administration deserved praise for bringing a balanced agenda of greater fiscal responsibility on both the revenue and expenditure sides, and possibly as well for signing on to the Republicans' balanced budget proposal. At least psychologically, these factors are among those that have helped sustain growth, prosperity, low unemployment, and low inflation. But the Clinton administration did little to address the needs of those on the bottom rungs of society who had become unfashionable and thereby dispensable. The New Democrats knew the votes were with the broad middle-class base of society, and that, understandably, is where Clinton and his key strategists went hunting. It is conceivable that the real legacy of the eight years of Clinton's presidency is that the Democrats and Clinton managed to become presidential winners by sacrificing society's losers.

On the other hand, the conditions of general prosperity have been relatively kind to the disadvantaged, and that in turn provides the fault lines for debate within the Democratic Party. Traditional liberal Democrats *talked* about doing things for the poor and, indeed, frequently did do them. But in so doing, they made themselves unpopular. Clinton, by contrast, has thrown the unfortunate to the wolves when occasion demanded—and on matters such as welfare reform he was followed by many of his party's traditional liberals as well. Ironically though, Clinton's policies, some of which have generated little fanfare, such as the Earned Income Tax Credit and the conditions of full employment that have benevolently wrapped themselves around his administration, have helped those in the lifeboats without drawing attention to them as a special interest of the Democratic Party. This, too, may be a distinctive contribution of the Clinton years and Clinton's effort to reformulate the Democratic Party. This effort has been remarkable for not losing its core constituencies at the polls while gaining the support of newer middle-class interests at least temporarily turned off by the moralizing appeals (with their antilibertarian implications) of much current Republicanism. For the short term, Clinton and the Democrats have found a winning formula. That can only be good for Clinton's reputation. But Clinton's reputation, beyond impeachment, is likely to have—as most presidential reputations have—only a short shelf life.

The Clinton Legacy

1

The Partisan Legacy:
Are there any New Democrats?
(And by the way, was there a Republican Revolution?)

BYRON E. SHAFER

We offer our people a new choice based on old values. We offer opportunity. We demand responsibility. We will build an American community again. The choice we offer is not conservative or liberal. In many ways it's not even Republican or Democratic. It's different. It's new. And it will work.

— Bill Clinton, Acceptance Speech, Democratic Convention, 16 July 1992

What is ultimately at stake in our current environment is literally the future of American civilization as it has existed for the last several hundred years. I'm a history teacher by background, and I would assert and defend on any campus in this country that it is impossible to maintain civilization with twelve-year-olds having babies, fifteen-year-olds killing each other, with seventeen-year-olds dying of AIDS, and with eighteen-year-olds ending up with diplomas they can't even read. What is at issue is literally not Republican or Democrat or liberal or conservative, but the question of whether or not our civilization will survive. . . .

— Newt Gingrich, Washington Research Group Symposium, 11 November 1994

The Clinton years were nothing if not a period characterized by *claims* about major partisan change. Two of these changes, however, crowd out all the others. The first involved the coming of the New Democrats, self-described. The second involved a putative Republican Revolution. Both were on the grand scale, in terms of their purported impact. Each only gained emphasis from the fact that it ran directly opposite to the other. If either was true, it defined the partisan legacy of the Clinton Presidency. If neither was accurate, the Clinton presidency was, in partisan terms, a period of structural drift and opportunistic response—a time when no one could find the key to shaping an era, or when the nature of that era did not permit systematic success.

The Clinton years suffered no lack of further, superficially compelling, individual partisan events. Yet, in order for such events to have any lasting partisan effect, they needed to register in one of two ways. They needed to shift the *social coalitions* associated with the two main political parties. Or they needed to shift the *programmatic positions* that party candidates offered the general public. These two elements are normally united in a more or less seamless fashion in practical politicking; they can be separated, however, for analytic purposes, and, in fact, the two main claims about a partisan legacy for the Clinton years did speak explicitly to both.

The first of these claims involved the ascension to national leadership of the "New Democrats." That monicker was intended to distinguish them from party predecessors, and in both critical regards. From one side, they were to offer a new programmatic focus, one more attuned to contemporary fiscal constraints and one more connected—or in their view, reconnected—to public values. From the other side, they were to champion a new social constituency in the form (in their rhetoric) of "the forgotten middle class." The fate of Bill Clinton was intertwined with these goals well before his actual election. Because he was elected and, especially, reelected using precisely these campaign thematics, his fortunes put the issue of the existence, content, and consequence of a New Democracy at the center of any Clinton legacy in partisan affairs. In European terms, Bill Clinton was cast as the key party "modernizer" of his time. The question is whether he succeeded.

Yet the fortunes of a putative New Democracy were not alone at the contentious center of any Clinton legacy. Indeed, right beside them, jostling for legacy status, was a development on the opposite side of the partisan aisle. For the first time in either forty or seventy years, depending on how you count, the Republicans resumed control of Congress at the first midterm election of the Clinton presidency. And they too asserted both critical elements of a lasting partisan change. Programmatically, they promised to reconfigure existing policies in line with modern fiscal reality, while turning governmental machinery to the active support of public values. Coalitionally, they were less pointed than the Democrats, but that was because what they really promised was that even more of the broad and amorphous American middle class would find its natural home in the newly invigorated Republican Party. Otherwise, they were even less abashed in proclaiming a change. Newt Gingrich, the Georgia congressman who would become Speaker of the newly Republican House, heralded their arrival as nothing short of a "Republican Revolution."

The Old Order and the New Politics

I was born in a little town called Hope, Arkansas, three months after my father died. I remember that old two-story house where I lived with my grandparents—they had very limited income. It was in 1963 that I went to Washington and met President Kennedy, at the Boys Nation program. And I remember just thinking what an incredible country this was, that somebody like me, you know, had no money or anything, would be given the opportunity to meet the President. That's when I decided that I could really do public service, 'cause I cared so much about people. I worked my way through law school, with part-time jobs, anything I could find. And after I graduated, I really didn't care about making a lot of money. I just wanted to go home and see if I could make a difference. We've worked hard in education, in health care, to create jobs, and we've made real progress. Now it's exhilarating to me to think that as President, I could help to change all our people's lives for the better, and bring hope back to the American dream.

— Text of Democratic commercial from the 1992 general election campaign

The party system within which these competing claims surfaced, and which they had to transform in order to prove accurate, had been in existence for sixty years by the time Bill Clinton was elected president. Indeed, the course of his life is a reasonable introduction to critical moments in this "New Deal party system." Clinton was born on 19 August 1946, only weeks before the first serious challenge to it, when Republicans first reseized control of Congress and announced their aspirations for bringing the system to an end. They failed, and the New Deal era was to run for another generation. By the time this era finally ended, in 1968, Clinton was in college, preparing to enter politics. He did, and one of his initial tasks was thus—presciently—to adapt the local Democratic Party to an emerging new politics, in a new period known nationally as the Era of Divided Government. Twenty years further on, he would acknowledge the same goals and trumpet the same skills for a potential Clinton presidency.

But that is getting ahead of the story. The New Deal era, the old order into which Clinton was born, had been sparked by the market crash of 1929, fanned by the Roosevelt landslide of 1932, and fed by the New Deal *program* that followed. The great and dominating substantive concerns of this era were economics and social welfare, as befitted an agenda called into being by economic catastrophe. By the time Clinton was born, the policy content of this dominant economic/welfare dimension included all the hallmark programs of the Rooseveltian New Deal: unemployment compensation, Social Security, industrial recovery, farm price supports, labor-management regulation, rural electrification, and on and on. In the years after Clinton's birth, the policy content of the same dimension was to expand to include full employment plus the "missing pieces" of the original New Deal agenda: health care, housing assistance, poverty amelioration, higher education, and, last but not least, civil rights. The staying power of these programs, as items for partisan conflict, would prove remarkable.[1]

The great and continuing secondary concern of this period was foreign affairs, again befitting an era forced within a painfully few years to confront the catastrophe of total war. In the years before Clinton's birth, this involved a huge build-up of defense manpower and industry to pursue victory in World War II. In the years after, the "Cold War" followed with its mixture of international alliances, military support, and conventional foreign aid. The United States had been drawn reluctantly into the worldwide conflicts capped by the Second World War; it was to be a principal architect of the succeeding international environment. Both tasks would belong largely to the Democratic Party.

As ever, there were social coalitions to go with these programmatic directions, coalitions that were in fact integral to them. By 1946, two of these, robustly constructed, dominated the political landscape. Both were built principally on social class, unlike the geographic basis of the previous party system, albeit with important ethnic and regional twists. The larger was a blue-collar coalition, aligned with the national Democratic Party, that featured working-class Americans generally, plus key ethnic minorities (especially Jews and blacks), the poor, and the entire (the "solid") South. The smaller was a white-collar coalition, aligned with the national Republican Party and confined essentially to middle-class Americans, plus farmers, outside the South.

These coalitions were then crucially buttressed by the main division among the interest groups of the time, essentially a business-labor divide. In this, organized labor became an increasingly important adjunct to the Democratic Party, first in legislative and then in electoral politics. By contrast, while corporate management did provide some funding and the occasional "blue-ribbon" candidate for the Republicans, it was really small business—the Chamber of Commerce, not the National Association of Manufacturers—that carried the load for the Republican Party among the organized interests.[2]

Policy positions and social coalitions were then knit together, and connected up to the institutions of national government by the political parties. Already by 1946, however, these were not just mirror images within the party system of the late New Deal; they had become parties different in organizational kind. The Democrats were an amalgam of urban machines in the North, court-house rings in the South, and volunteer activist branches scattered throughout the country. New Deal programs had actually helped extend the life of the organized (the "regular") Democratic Party within this mix. The Republicans, still paying a high price for incumbency when the Great Depression hit, had moved earlier to become the kind of organizationally amorphous, activist-based political party that both parties would become in the second postwar era, each relying on ideology and issues to motivate party workers. For the Republican Party, in truth, this was not so much modernization as simple survival.

There was, finally, a diagnostic partisan dynamic to go with this mix of policy conflicts, social coalitions, and partisan intermediaries, a distinctive character to party competition in the long-running New Deal era. Seen by way of ongoing policy conflicts, the party on the left, the Democratic Party, was widely perceived as more in tune with public preferences on social welfare. By contrast, the party on the right, the Republicans, was widely perceived as more in tune with public preferences on foreign affairs. The crucial fact, then, was just that the public ordinarily gave a much higher priority to social welfare.

Seen by way of ongoing social coalitions instead, the dominant fact of partisan politicking from 1932 through 1968 was that the unity and vitality of the Democratic coalition remained the central story of electoral *and* institutional politics. After 1946, however, Republicans could win, if Democratic policy assets were devalued and if Republicans had special assets of their own, as they would in 1952 with Dwight Eisenhower as their nominee. Eisenhower brought remarkable personal assets to help produce the one great exception to Democratic dominance in this era. When he did, the Republicans, too, were entitled to assume unified partisan control of American national government.[3]

The New Deal era then came to an end in 1968, but the New Deal party system continued on—and in that distinction lay much of the story of partisan politics from 1968 through the arrival of Bill Clinton as president in 1992. At the time of the 1968 presidential election, Clinton was consolidating an interest in politics while dramatically broadening his social horizons. As a Rhodes Scholar at Oxford University, he was old enough to engage seriously with the political currents and social trends of his time, some of which would return to haunt him as lesser issues when he ultimately ran for president. He would return to pick up a law degree and then go back to enter politics in Arkansas, where he would inevitably have to adapt to the changes producing a new political era.

Few observers at the time failed to notice the extensive anomalies of the year 1968, anomalies, that is, when viewed within the confines of the old order. Race riots, campus unrest, Vietnam protest, political assassinations, the implosion of the national Democratic Party in convention: all these led to the narrow election of Richard Nixon as president, while the Democratic Party retained solid—overwhelming, really—control of both houses of Congress. Within that context, it was still reasonable to believe that the American political sequence might feature a Nixon interregnum, as it had earlier featured an Eisenhower interregnum, followed by restoration of unified Democratic control of national government. But in fact, the constituent elements of a new era and order, especially their programmatic divisions and social coalitions, were all incipiently present.

As it arrived, the substantive break-up of the old era was easiest to recognize in foreign affairs, where the Cold War consensus disintegrated. Now, there were nationalists who continued to support the containment of communism, opposed by accommodationists who felt that containment was an increasingly sterile doctrine. The Vietnam War gave this division its cutting edge, and Bill Clinton's relationship to it was to put him on one side—and haunt him—a generation later. Yet a panoply of further security issues, from arms control to defense budgeting, would be available to keep this division alive. More to the point, Vietnam *protest* was a key route into the rest of a newly augmented set of valuational conflicts, within which foreign affairs was to be only one large but supporting element.[4]

Anti-war protest as behavior was borrowed, most centrally, from civil rights protest. And anti-war protest was to lead on to a general round of reform agitation in politics. But protest was linked from the start in the public mind to other, essentially cultural divisions: over crime, for example, where the question was whether criminal behavior was a socioeconomic product to be understood (the progressive position) or a moral breakdown to be countervailed (the traditional view). Vietnam protesters themselves often underlined this link, by insisting that they were part of a "counterculture." This was as good an introduction as any to that larger valuational division, eventually to include the public role of religion, community prerogatives, patriotism and national integration, deference and responsibility, educational orientations, public deportment, family structure, even the proper attitude toward human life, especially at its beginning and at its end.

The social coalitions that were to go with these substantive divisions — the social coalitions to go with *dual* concerns, for social welfare and, now, cultural values — had long been incipiently available. Or at least, it had long been known that economic liberals, those most concerned with the welfare essence of the New Deal program, were often social conservatives, emphasizing family, neighborhood, community, and country. Just as it had long been known that economic conservatives, especially the highly educated, occupationally prestigious, and financially well-off among them, were often cultural liberals, emphasizing personal choice and the individual construction of social life. These background alignments were not themselves new. What had changed was merely the relative importance—the "weight"—of this second set of (essentially cultural) concerns.[5]

Yet while this was occurring, the political parties had also changed in their basic structure. Accordingly, it was to be the interaction of this changing party structure with changing public issues and changing social coalitions that would institutionalize a new partisan dynamic. At bottom, both political parties now shared the dominant characteristics of the immediate postwar Republicans. That is, both were now effectively networks of issue-oriented activists, not individuals for whom partisan solidarity displaced ideology, much less individuals for whom patronage or pecuniary concerns explained their willingness to do the work of the party. Gone was the reliable party "machinery," especially for the Democrats, built on control of the divisible rewards of government and buttressed by an unreformed hierarchy of party offices and by the loyalty of a New Deal generation of partisans, who were gradually passing from the scene.

In its place were the individual issue activists whose support was now essential to mounting campaigns and gaining public office: they *were* the party in the operational sense. More to the point for a new political order, they were also the key to institutionalizing a partisan connection between economic/welfare and cultural/national issues. They had hardly abandoned the old social-welfare basis of the party system. Republican activists remained very conservative, Democratic activists very liberal on these matters. What they had done was vastly to expand the foreign-affairs dimension, to cultural issues more generally, in a way that *they* found to be ideologically consistent. Republican activists were thus traditionalistic in social matters, nationalistic in foreign affairs; Democratic activists were now progressive in social matters, accommodationist in foreign affairs.[6]

Had these increasingly consequential activists not been naturally inclined to this particular combination of positions, they might well have been driven to it anyway, by the nature of the new (ideological and issue-oriented) organized interests that joined one or the other party coalition. For the Democrats, these included environmentalists, peace groups, feminists, homosexuals. For the Republicans, they included anti-abortionists, gun owners, tax reformers, religious fundamentalists. And on and on in both cases. But in truth, there was no need for "pressure" from these groups in order to secure these two opposing partisan programs. For party activists were now the natural products of membership in precisely these organizations.

There was, of course, not just a heightened interparty conflict inherent in this tension—Democrats versus Republicans—between consistent liberals and consistent conservatives. There was now a further intraparty conflict—Democrats versus Democrats and Republicans versus Republicans—*between party activists and their own rank and file*. At bottom, there were now two opposing majorities simultaneously present in the mass public: more liberal than the active Republican Party on economics and social welfare, more conservative than the active Democratic Party on culture and foreign affairs. The obvious solution in the United States, thereafter, was just to colonize one elective branch of national government with one majority and one elective branch with the other.

Split partisan control of national government was what that solution contributed practically, and in the particular historical sequence in which this new partisan dynamic arrived, it implied a Republican presidency coupled with a Democratic Congress. "Divided government" was what it came popularly to be called, and the Era of Divided Government was thus at hand. Indeed, if the one-term, idiosyncratic presidency of Democrat Jimmy Carter is chalked up to the

Watergate crisis—it is hard to imagine Carter as a plausible candidate in 1972, and he was defeated for reelection in 1980—then the entire period between the election of Richard Nixon in 1968 and the arrival of Bill Clinton in 1992 featured Republican control of the presidency and Democratic control of Congress.

The Rise of the New Democrats?

They're a new generation of Democrats, Bill Clinton and Al Gore, and they don't think the way the old Democratic Party did. They've called for an end to welfare as we know it, so welfare can be a second chance, not a way of life. They've sent a strong signal to criminals, by supporting the death penalty. And they've rejected the old tax-and-spend politics. Clinton's balanced twelve budgets, and they've proposed a new plan investing in people, detailing a hundred and forty billion dollars in spending cuts they'd make right now. Clinton-Gore. For people. For a change.

— Text of Democratic commercial from the 1992 general election campaign

The background contours of a new political order were not obvious even to its main participants at the time of its arrival. Crosscutting policy conflicts and crosscutting social coalitions, with an overlay of recurring tensions between active members and the rank and file of *both* parties: these were to become the ongoing context for electoral and institutional politics in the quarter-century after 1968. Such a context did not lack strategic imperatives, implicit advice that party leaders ignored at their peril. For the Republicans, this new political context counseled an emphasis on cultural/national issues, and neutralization of economic/welfare concerns. For the Democrats, the opposite advice applied: emphasis on economic/welfare concerns, neutralization of cultural/national issues. But because the new order was both complex and different, the strategic imperatives that came with it were only ever to be learned in a kind of trial and error.

On the other hand, the direct partisan outcomes of the new order were inescapable. Split partisan control of the institutions of national government now reliably occurred. Moreover, for almost a quarter century, this split had a further partisan patterning: Republicans captured the presidency, while Democrats captured—held, really—Congress. Divided government as an outcome was frustrating for both parties, but this further pattern also colored their thinking about how to address it. For their part, Republicans did not so much celebrate their return to the presidency, after nearly sixty years in the partisan wilderness. Instead, they resented their inability to "complete" the return, and add control of Congress. Most often, they assigned this failure to a massive superstructure of pork-barrel corruption, put in place over sixty years by way of the old divisible goods of government, the new distributive formulas of politics, and the directly personal rewards of office.

Republican dismay, however, was fully matched among Democrats, who lamented their failure, for more than a generation, to hold onto the presidency—when "nothing else had changed." Their congressional margins rose and fell, but only marginally. Only Ronald Reagan even appeared to threaten these, when he captured the Senate in 1980. Yet his gains disappeared at the end of the first full cycle for this new crop of senators, returning the Senate to Democratic control in 1986. In any case, the House of Representatives remained Democratic throughout. At the beginning of this twenty-year run, neither the initial Nixon election of 1968 nor his landslide reelection in 1972 shook this control. At the end, the House was solidly Democratic even before the Democrats regained the Senate in 1986, and it remained solidly Democratic afterward, when George Bush defeated Michael Dukakis for president, solidly, in 1988. Which is to say: year in and year out, there was a Democratic House, and year in and year out, it looked basically the same.

One of the earliest responses to the Democratic side of this puzzle was the formation, by the House Democratic Caucus after the 1980 election, of the Committee on Party Effectiveness (CPE). Jimmy Carter, incumbent Democratic president, had just been resoundingly defeated for reelection, so that it was less easy to argue that Democratic misfortunes were just, as before, some Nixonian interlude. Regardless, without a Democratic president to represent the national party and in the face of a confusing new partisan landscape, congressional Democrats felt the need to increase their influence. There was some incipient conflict behind this aspiration, since that influence was to be exercised in implicit opposition to the activist base of the party, including the Democratic National Committee, which members of Congress viewed as insufficiently attached to the practical needs of gaining and holding public office. Otherwise, however, programmatic and coalitional implications to this new committee were left intentionally vague.[7]

Both edged closer to becoming explicit with the creation of an extra-party organization, the Democratic Leadership Council (DLC), after the 1984 election.

The Reagan reelection had been disastrous for the Democrats in the same puzzling way as its predecessor. In response, the DLC aspired to be a more effective voice for successful Democratic officeholders, of whom there were still many, by moving beyond the House Democratic Caucus to include senators, governors, and other key state-level officials. In terms of a policy program, its members continued to be more likely than the active party as a whole to favor economic moderation and cultural traditionalism, and hence more likely to be moderates and conservatives than liberals. In terms of a social coalition, they continued to be more likely to be southern and western than northeastern and midwestern, more likely to come from middle-class than working-class areas, and more likely to represent suburban than urban districts. Otherwise, the new organization remained hesitant about drawing lines that would inevitably set "New Democrats" against their predecessors.

The 1988 election changed all that. Nineteen eighty-eight proved to be another disaster on the same template, despite the careful and conscious efforts of nominee Michael Dukakis to emphasize neutral competence. But this time, the outcome, so disappointing after early leads in the polls, altered the orientation of the DLC and put definition into an incipient New Democracy. Line-drawing did occur, dissident members exited, and a redrawn organization became the single clearest embodiment of what it meant to be a New Democrat. The idea was to recast the Democratic Party coalition so as to restore it to enduring majority status under changed social conditions, a general goal that could be saluted by most Democrats. But once it had to be given specifics, even the definition of "changed social conditions"—much less a changed policy program and a changed social coalition—was bound to be highly conflictual. Despite that, two key documents set out what it meant, thereafter, to reside on the New Democratic side of the line.

The first was an analysis entitled "The Politics of Evasion: Democrats and the Presidency," focusing on three alleged myths that were recurrently defeating the national party.[8] First was the Myth of Mobilization, which excused defeat through declining turnout, and suggested that victory would return if only the party worked harder. Careful statistical reanalysis, said the DLC, made this claim simply false. Second was the Myth of Liberal Fundamentalism, which argued that policy change, if any, needed to emphasize the *distance* between Democrats and Republicans. This led, in the DLC analysis, to programmatic positions wildly discordant with general public values. Third and last was the Myth of the Congressional Bastion, which argued that repeated partisan defeats were nevertheless transitory, as evidenced by the fact that Democrats continued to do well in Congress. The DLC countered that gradual destruction of this congressional advantage must follow continual loss of the presidency, with particular damage to typical DLC members.

Published in September of 1989, "The Politics of Evasion" was the most systematic analysis of the *problem* from a New Democratic perspective. The solution, and the other key substantive document in the evolution of a New Democracy, was the policy statement ratified at the DLC annual convention in May of 1991 and published as "The New American Choice: Opportunity, Responsibility, Community."[9] Its "New American Choice Resolutions" ranged widely, to include governmental structure, environmental policy, educational reform, foreign trade, military reorganization, child support, and equal opportunity. But they could be gathered into four main initiatives, two in the realm of economics and social welfare, and two in the realm of culture and foreign affairs. The economic/welfare planks were premised, first, on addressing social-welfare needs through accelerated economic growth and, second, on restoring the reputation of the party as a governing instrument by emphasizing spending cuts. The cultural/national planks were premised, first, on putting the party back on the side of "the moral and cultural values that most Americans share" and, second, on coupling this with a strong national defense for a dangerous world.

The Old Democracy, in the form of the issue activists who generated presidential campaigns and did the work of the party at state and local levels, could be characterized as strongly liberal on both of these two main dimensions of public issues and policy conflict, with a particular attachment to the newer cultural and national concerns. The New Democrats now had a counterpart position. They could be characterized as self-consciously *moderate* on both dimensions, in full understanding that cultural and national moderation would seem especially controversial within the active Democratic Party of its day. While "The New American Choice" did not set out the social coalitions that went with these programs, their framers, and active members of the DLC generally, knew their content. The party needed to escape the geographic locus of its reliable strength, the Northeast and industrial Midwest, for the growing West and South. It needed to escape the spatial locus of its reliable strength, urban America, for the growing suburbs. And it needed to escape the social locus of its reliable strength, the working class and the poor, for the growing middle class.

One other important change occurred while the DLC was abandoning its amorphous content in order to define the "New Democrat." Bill Clinton, incumbent governor of Arkansas, became its chairman in March of 1990. Clinton had thought about a presidential run in 1988, and he was thinking even more seriously about 1992. The DLC chairmanship would provide him not only with a pre-packaged program but with organizational connections around the country. His actual campaign, both for the Democratic nomination and for the general election, would thus be the first successfully national campaign by a New Democrat, strictly defined. It would also be a classic example of the way in which strategic definitions become blended with the actual events and demands of practical politics, as well as of the way in which such a blend has to conform to the larger structure of the political order around it.[10]

It was widely noted at the time that a weak field of alternative contenders for the Democratic nomination in 1992 facilitated Clinton's march to the nomination. At the point when entry decisions for the nominating contest had to be made, George Bush, an incumbent president fresh from victory in the Gulf War, looked extremely difficult to unhorse. Yet it was less widely noted that the character of this field meant that Clinton did not need to define himself diagnostically as a New Democrat, because he had no strong and serious opposition from an archetypal "Old Democrat" to overcome. Likewise, it was widely noted that the issue agenda of the campaign changed radically between the time-of-entry decisions and the time of actual delegate selection, as Gulf War victory was unceremoniously pushed aside by national economic recession. But it was again less widely noted that this led the Democratic nominating and election campaigns to look like archetypal responses to the existing—the ongoing—political order.

In his own nominating campaign, Clinton was encouraged to concentrate on economics and social welfare, and to slight cultural and national issues. From one side, the economic situation had deteriorated seriously, and *any* Democratic nominee had to demonstrate his potential for dealing with that. Yet the prominence of such a need also encouraged any potential nominee to sound very much like an Old Democrat. So did the related emergence of health care as the major social-welfare issue of the campaign. All Democrats, old and new, could be united on this, and it was quickly seized by the Clinton campaign as a central plank in its program.

From the other side, the Clinton nominating campaign was dogged by personal revelations and character attacks—these almost undid him at the start—so that the cultural dimension, when it was receiving emphasis from the environment, was doing so in a very unhelpful way. Clinton was nevertheless careful to eschew cultural progressivism, and he did offer some specific programs with strong traditional themes: his promise of a National Service Corps, for example, and the one that would come back to haunt him, his promise to "end welfare as we know it." But an emphasis on economics and social welfare, plus the risk of harm from cultural and national issues, made Bill Clinton look very much like the logical next link in a chain of Democratic nominees stretching back to 1968.

So, in essence, did the general election campaign. The Republicans needed to talk about foreign affairs in 1992, with a sitting president who had won the Gulf War (over both the Iraqis and the Democratic Congress). Just as the Republicans needed to talk about experience and character, where a sitting governor of Arkansas could not possibly match the former and had not fared well on the latter. By contrast, the Democrats needed to talk about the economy—"Stupid!"— and they did, in their televised commercials, ad nauseam. They also needed to talk about social welfare, especially health care in a year when recession was canceling job-based insurances, and they did not fail to meet that imperative either. At the end, the result looked very much like the standard product of the Era of Divided Government, in all but one of its key details, rather than as the opening embodiment of a New Democracy.

In this, Bill Clinton secured slightly less of the aggregate vote than Michael Dukakis before him: 43 percent for Clinton, 45.6 percent for Dukakis. But in a year in which Ross Perot took 18.9 percent as an independent candidate, a slight decline was sufficient to carry thirty-two states and 370 electoral votes for Clinton, versus ten states and 112 electoral votes for Dukakis. That converted painful defeat into substantial victory, so that the coming of the first self-conscious New Democrat to the White House could hardly be argued to have been constrained by the thematics of the New Democracy. On the other hand, it was hard to find much impact from those thematics in the specifics of the vote, that is, in Bill Clinton's social coalition.

Clinton did improve the Democratic presidential vote in the South, but the vote in the West was simultaneously down, and both effects were marginal. Exit polls echoed these results for the other target constituencies of the New Democracy. Thus Clinton ran a little better than Dukakis in the suburbs and small cities, and a little worse in the big cities and in rural areas. He ran a little better with the white middle class, and a little worse with the white working class. He ran a little better than Dukakis among self-described moderates, and a little worse among both conservatives and liberals. Yet these increments were tiny—one or two percentage points—and an analyst unconcerned with the New Democracy could be excused for not noticing. They might just as easily have been evidence that *any* campaign had to have some effect.[11]

The Coming of a Republican Revolution?

The Blue Danube plays in the background, under a legend proclaiming "The Clinton/McCurdy Crimefighter Follies," as rough-looking men in balletic tutus waltz with each other: "Dance lessons. Midnight basketball. New restrictive gun controls. Just some of the ways Bill Clinton and Dave McCurdy think their new thirty-billion-dollar crime bill will make our streets safer. No wonder the Oklahoma Fraternal Order of Police endorsed Jim Inhofe for Senate." Fade out around the legend "Feel Safer Yet?"

— Text of Republican commercial from the 1994 general election campaign

Overall, then, the outcome of 1992 suggested nothing so much as an Old Democratic win within an established political order, with one big practical and theoretical exception. In practical terms, the fact that Bill Clinton *did win* meant that split partisan control—formally divided government—would disappear. There would thus be unified partisan control of national government in the first Congress under President Bill Clinton. Moreover, in theoretical terms, an election in which a sitting president is defeated is almost inevitably a referendum on his tenure, not an endorsement of any defined alternative. This was true even with the coming of Franklin Roosevelt in 1932; it could only be more true with the coming of Bill Clinton sixty years later. A New Democrat as president would thus get to put meaning into the 1992 election. He would have unified partisan control of government with which to do it. And *that* would constitute the true definition of the New Democracy.

In hindsight, the fact that the practical definition of the New Democracy was destined to be hammered out in tandem with the formal definition of an alleged Republican Revolution is curious. That fact is also ironic, since it suggests that the two developments were, in some way, inherently connected. But it would be several years before this connection—and the (related) way in which an ongoing political order would constrain both initiatives—could be seen by even the most perceptive analysts. In the meantime, the opening opportunity belonged to the New Democrats, not to any putative Republican Revolutionaries. Theirs was the initial chance to shape a program that might appeal to a new social coalition. Theirs was the immediate chance to set the symbolism that would alert the general public to what a New Democracy could imply.

Which is not to deny that, as with the preceding election campaigns, there were established constraints which had to be blended into any New Democratic program. The most fundamental of these was the existing character of the congressional Democratic Party in a period of unified partisan control of Congress. These were, of course, overwhelmingly Old Democrats. A majority had been in Congress before there was a DLC. A majority even of the rest represented the preferences of the active Democratic Party: liberal on economic/welfare issues, liberal on cultural/national issues as well.

The more evanescent but temporarily intense of these constraints arose from the election itself. Bill Clinton was, after all, a minority president: 57 percent of the voting public had opted for someone else. While his minority status would quickly fade—he was now *the* president, after all—it did undercut any claims for a New Democratic mandate. More pertinent for any fresh substantive focus, Ross Perot had secured 19 percent of the vote, in a campaign focused largely on the federal budgetary deficit and deficit reduction. Within this, there were seventy-three congressional districts where Perot received more than a quarter of the total, and where successful congressmen might reasonably look upon this result as the single clearest policy mandate of the election.

Nevertheless, despite the emphasis of the Clinton campaign and the size of the Perot vote, the first act of the Clinton administration came not on economics but on culture. In his very first official action, the president began his term of office by issuing an executive order restoring the ability to conduct medical research on human fetal tissue. Moreover, if that was an obscure act for all but a narrow band of issue specialists, the opening symbolism of the new administration for the general public was set by another cultural proposal, to remove the ban on active homosexuals in the military. Argument over lifting this ban was to dominate the first two weeks of the new administration and erupt intermittently for months thereafter, generating conflict and headlines out of all proportion to any numerical impact. Along the way, major congressional figures who were also self-conscious New Democrats, most especially Sam Nunn, senator from Georgia and chairman of the Senate Foreign Relations Committee, were to be evidently embarrassed.[12] On the other hand, two major policy initiatives with great potential impact, the real legislative agenda of the early Clinton presidency, were also launched shortly thereafter—and each represented at least the temporary triumph of the established Democracy.

The first of these initiatives derived from a fiscal choice, between economic stimulus (Old Democratic) and deficit reduction (New Democratic). The second derived from a social-welfare choice, between health care (Old) and welfare reform (New). Between the first pair, the economic-stimulus package won out, and was announced immediately. Between the second, the health-care package won out and was sent to a commission under the direction of none other than the first lady. The first of these choices was justified on the grounds of campaign thematics, plus electoral demand. The second was justified on the grounds that it was nearly impossible to do two large and complex policy proposals during one Congress, and that health care, too, represented the greater electoral mandate. Though it was also true that it was much easier to develop support for health care than welfare reform out of the existing Democratic Party.

This second choice was to become a long, slow, political agony for most of the main players. The first, by contrast, ran into immediate trouble. While the economy appeared to have turned the corner, the fiscal deficit, augmented by recession, was continuing to grow. As a result, congressional supporters for this choice, of economic stimulus over deficit reduction, proved to be in short supply. Republicans had never been invited to be part of the development of either program: the congressional leadership wanted to make these packages the obvious product of unified-party control, while the new president had never known the need to consult a Republican minority. Yet a substantial minority of *Democrats* went on to insist on priority for deficit reduction, with economic stimulus (if any) to follow. As a result, a significant package for deficit reduction would emerge by summer. As a further result, a significant package for economic stimulus would never really emerge at all. As a final result, the middle-class tax cut, another rhetorical staple of the election campaign and one that might also have been taken to represent electoral demand, was sent quietly away.[13]

In any case, the new administration had, in passing, set out its policy stance for all to see: sharply liberal on cultural/national issues, clearly liberal on economic/welfare issues, too. By late summer, administration strategists had themselves come to focus on this perceived stance—their initial self-portrait—and had begun to try to turn and re-tailor it, shifting back strongly toward the New Democratic agenda. Yet at this point, the main vehicle for that shift, the North American Free Trade Agreement (NAFTA), brought difficulties of its own. NAFTA was a quintessential New Democratic program; of that there was no doubt. But ironically, the president was destined to be successful on it in ways that did not ultimately clarify the New Democratic message but did further alienate him from his own congressional party.

Despite being a classic New Democratic program, NAFTA might actually have been ducked by the new administration, had it not already acquired substantial diplomatic momentum by the time Clinton took office. Foreign trade—with its free-trade versus protectionism cleavage—had long been an issue that crosscut the two parties. Nevertheless, the New Deal had brought *free* trade into the national policy consensus, and the free-trade wing of each party had remained dominant into the 1970s. By the 1990s, each party still possessed two wings on the issue. But now, the Republicans were clearly the party of free trade, and the Democrats just as clearly the party of protectionism—to the point where most of the House leadership worked actively against the president on his own bill! In perhaps his finest leadership and lobbying effort, Clinton managed, in spite of all, to take much of the remaining Southern Democracy into a unified Republican camp and defeat a solid majority of his own party nationwide.[14]

This was the great New Democratic triumph of the first Clinton Congress. Moreover, it was a cultural/national triumph of exactly the sort that The New American Choice Resolutions had promised. Yet its symbolic role came largely as a corrective to what had preceded it on cultural/national conflicts in the Clinton administration, and its gains here were destined to be neutralized in the longer run by the fate of the Omnibus Crime Bill a year later. At the same time, a New Democratic triumph on NAFTA meant that Old Democrats, both in Congress and in the country, had not gotten the program they had desired, fiscal stimulus, but did get the one they detested, NAFTA. Finally, and even more to the partisan point, by the time Congress reconvened in the new year, there was a third, different, and clear programmatic alternative emerging—no symbolic confusion on this one—through which *Republicans* hoped, and some expected, to brush aside the New Democracy and attract the true majority coalition of the future.

This program would be a formal party product, from the Republican National Committee in coordination with the National Republican Congressional Committee. It would be aimed directly and self-consciously at the midterm election of 1994. It would intend to provide a comprehensive and consistent alternative to the Clinton program. And to that end, it would be strongly conservative on both economics and culture. But its real purpose, as much as anything else, was to suggest that the Republicans were a coherent and prepared alternative to fumbling Democratic incumbents. The document embodying all of these approaches came to be called the Contract with America, and if few members of the American public ever knew what was being contracted, all Republican candidates for the House and some of those for the Senate were at least exposed to it. A total of 367 actually signed.[15]

Surely most of these, too, thought of the Contract more as a device for symbolizing their seriousness of purpose and readiness to govern. On the other hand, for their incipient leader, Congressman Newt Gingrich of Georgia, the House minority whip, it represented substantially more. For the Contract with America represented the ascendance of Gingrich and his allies within the congressional Republican Party, and he was actually to get the chance to pursue its implementation. Indeed, if Bill Clinton was the poster boy for the New Democracy, Gingrich was to be the counterpart for any Republican Revolution. As such, the story of postwar politics might as easily have been hung upon Gingrich's career as upon Clinton's.

In programmatic terms, Gingrich was a founding member of the Conservative Opportunity Society (COS), a counterpart to the Democratic Leadership Council as a key formative influence on new Republican policy thinking. In coalitional terms, he was a central actor in the rise of a southern Republican Party, which ended the "Solid South" of the old order. He was also a committed devotee of technological developments, including the use of public-affairs television to put out a sharpened House Republican message—quintessential tactics for the new politics. Finally, he had the audacity to aspire to the House Speakership, from a time when neither the Democrats nor his own party would have seen this option as either practical or attractive. But that is a story for a different legacy.

Instead, in opposition to any Clinton legacy, the Republican Party in 1994 carefully tested a set of propositions for majority attraction and/or interest-group mobilization, and these came out as the Contract with America. Their roots in the COS program meant that this was to be, first and foremost, a sharpened message on economics and on the generalized virtues of capitalism and free enterprise. To that end, there were clear economic/welfare planks: Balanced Budget Amendment and Line-Item Veto, Tax Cuts for Families, Fairness for Senior Citizens, Roll Back Government Regulation, Create Jobs. Yet there were also clear cultural/national planks: Stop Violent Criminals, Strengthen Families and Protect Our Kids, Strong National Defense, Congressional Term Limits. And there were, of course, planks joining the two: Welfare Reform, Common Sense Legal Reforms. None would have been mistaken for anything other than the consistent conservative approach. Together, they contrasted completely with the early Clinton program.

It was, however, two other policy conflicts, real legislative conflicts with concrete policy outcomes, that then set the substantive context for the 1994 election and helped forge the choice for its voters: health care and criminal justice. Each would be disastrously unhappy for congressional Democrats, albeit in nearly opposite ways. But even for voters who missed one or the other of their policy outcomes, they would also, together, establish a "competence context." This too would not be one that an incumbent congressman desired, a situation made only worse by a large and ongoing scandal involving congressional paychecks and the congressional bank, a scandal almost inevitably focused on the majority party in Congress.

The Clinton administration hardly turned this contextual agenda over to the Republicans without a fight: the administration could read the same polls that encouraged the drafters of the Contract. In response, by the summer of 1994, it had begun a serious correction, aimed at bringing New Democratic themes back to the fore. Health care was in deep and obvious trouble, but administration strategists continued to seek compromises aimed at delivering at least some new health-care benefits to the general public. That covered the economic/welfare dimension, and if these were Old Democratic benefits, they seemed sure to prove popular. Moreover, the other issue at the center of institutional politicking was quintessentially New Democratic. Indeed, the Omnibus Crime Bill was tailored to reflect the New Democracy, overall and line by line. That covered the cultural/national dimension, and its intended thematics looked unproblematic. But this time, it was the politics of implementing them that would go badly awry.[16]

Analysts would generate whole volumes (and many of them) on the fate of the Clinton health care project. Those most sympathetic would attribute this fate to a gross imbalance in fund raising and lobbying, and gross imbalance there certainly was. Those less sympathetic would focus on Democratic ineptness: a program that could not have been passed, in its time, even in countries more inherently sympathetic than the United States, developed in a manner that built the coalition against it rather than the coalition for it. But here, the point is merely that the president gambled on securing some outcome with which to go to the American public, rather than on using the issue to attack the Republican Party. In the end, he was left with neither a policy nor an issue.

All of which might *still* have come together to produce a different electoral context overall, or at least a neutralized electoral context in partisan terms, had the Omnibus Crime Bill played out as administration strategists intended. Crime had been a leading issue with the general public throughout 1994—it topped the *New York Times* poll more often than any other—and both parties hoped to benefit from a focus on criminal justice. If much of the particular substance of the president's approach was classic New Democracy, polls suggested (and polls had already been used to test) that its main provisions had general public support. Yet, in the process of bringing it up and putting it at the center of his legislative program, Bill Clinton, rather than harvesting any latent popularity, was to be whipsawed on the issue instead.

Conservative Republicans attacked parts of the bill as too apologetic, too concerned with criminals rather than their victims. Liberal Democrats attacked parts of it as too punitive, as stigmatizing their own constituencies. And moderate Republicans refused initially to come to the aid of a proposal on which they had not been consulted. By the time a bill succeeded, with moderates wooed back on board and liberals "bought" through new divisible benefits, any impression of presidential leadership had been dissipated. And the stock Republican portrait of another Democratic bill—culturally liberal and full of pork—had been successfully painted.

The verdict in the tally that really mattered, at the general election six weeks later, was devastating. In the Senate, Republicans gained and Democrats lost a net of eight seats, swinging the balance from 56–44 Democratic to 52–48 Republican, before Richard Shelby, Democratic senator from Alabama, switched parties to make it 53–47. In the House, Republicans gained (and Democrats lost) a net of 53 seats, swinging the balance from 258–176 Democratic to 229–205 Republican.[17] The details beneath these summary numbers were even more disastrous.

To constitute their net gain of eight in the Senate, the Republicans lost no previously held seats and picked off eight previously Democratic ones. To constitute their net gain of fifty-three in the House, all 165 Republican incumbents were reelected, while the party picked up thirteen of seventeen open seats, and a further fifty-one from Democratic incumbents. All the usual subpatterns were still present in these details. That is, open seats were more likely to shift than those with incumbents; among incumbents, freshmen were more likely to lose than their seniors; among seniors, those in districts carried by the other party for president in 1992 were more likely to lose than those in own-party districts. Yet for 1994, these constituted only a modest firewall against a raging Republican conflagration.

The Era of Divided Government Redux

We're back.

— Legend on a Republican T-shirt issued after the 1994 election,
showing an elephant lumbering up the steps of the Capitol

In any case, the composite result was decisive. Recapturing the Senate would have been pleasant enough, of course. But now the House had been recaptured too, for the first time since 1952—yet really for the first time without a successful Republican president at the head of the ticket since 1946, the year of Bill Clinton's birth. On the other hand, the same rule would apply to Speaker Newt Gingrich and his Republican Congress in 1995 and 1996 as had applied to President Bill Clinton and his Democratic administration in 1993 and 1994. Which is to say: The Republican Revolution, to date, was largely a repudiation of what the New Democracy had turned out to be. Only now could it achieve its actual policy meaning, along with its appropriate social coalition, through the policy leadership that followed. Yet here, at least, there was a distinctive difference.

The New Democrats had possessed their "New American Choice Resolutions," and their unofficial leader, Bill Clinton as chairman of the DLC, had been duly elected. But the results of the 1992 election blew them otherwise off course, and the character of the Old Democracy went a long way toward keeping them there. Similarly, a huge new cohort of successful Republicans had its Contract with America, and their unofficial leader, Newt Gingrich as Speaker of the newly Republican House of Representatives, had also come to power, or at least to office. Yet the results of the 1994 election had no immediate—or rather, immediately disturbing—implications for pursuit of the Contract. Moreover, that huge influx of new, Contract-signing members joined a Republican residuum whose members had literally never had to rally behind any alternative program of their own. The result was that the Contract with America did indeed become the agenda for the 104th Congress.

At first, this fact drew analytic comment out of sheer wonder that a national policy agenda could be driven from the House of Representatives. Yet for six months, through the summer of 1995, the Contract became the single simplest summary of the agenda for national politics. By some measures, its subsequent success was also phenomenal. Each of the fifteen major bills from the Contract package achieved a floor vote in the House within the promised 100 days. All but the proposed constitutional amendment establishing term limits for congressmen actually passed, and that exception would have required a two-thirds majority. Admittedly, the Senate was more dilatory. Fewer Republican senatorial candidates had signed on initially; fewer Republican victors were new to the Senate; many senators came from states where some constituencies had voted against House candidates aligned with the Contract. The president was a still more mixed respondent. He was, for example, happy to sign the line-item veto for the budget; willing to go along with the bar on unfunded mandates; opposed to many aspects of product liability reform and to tort reform in general.

On the one hand, then, the final concrete product of this agenda, signed into law and implemented, remained much less than Republican Revolutionaries had dared to hope. On the other hand, in terms of seizing and altering the agenda for conflict in American politics, their initial triumph remained overwhelming, to the point where Bill Clinton, the President of the United States, had to remind a press conference along the way that "the Constitution gives me relevance, the power of our ideas gives me relevance. . . . The president is relevant here." Republican congressmen and senators were entitled to go home for the summer recess and look forward to completing their revolution in 1996, adding a Republican presidency to control of Congress and restoring unified government to their side of the partisan aisle.[18]

And then, after the 1995 summer recess, it all went strikingly wrong. Indeed, while the lead-up to a change in expectations contained some important preliminary events, it actually went wrong within a few weeks over Christmas and New Year's of 1995–96. The turn-around began when congressional Republicans returned to Washington and took on a committed effort to solve, not just ameliorate, the problem of the deficit. This meant that there had to be real and substantial cuts to spending. That meant that major welfare entitlement programs, especially the social insurance programs of Medicaid, Medicare, and Social Security, had to be sharply restricted in their projected growth, and ideally trimmed. To this end, Republicans were willing to draw up a federal budget that would accomplish those goals. To that end, they were willing to shut down the federal government temporarily, rather than pass a continuing resolution, if the president would not sign this or some acceptable compromise version.

The first shutdown came in November of 1995, the second came in December–January, and the line from there to the November election of 1996 ran relentlessly. The Republicans had taken a clear gamble, that these initiatives would bring them major economic/welfare credit for "fixing" the deficit, along with major competence credit for actually getting a huge job done. The Democrats, in response—and here, the president *was* the highly relevant figure—described those actions as menacing some social insurance programs directly, while menacing all indirectly through payment delays during the shutdown, simultaneously "proving" the irresponsibility of their protagonists. It may be that those who desired to complete the Republican Revolution could have survived having this gamble go wrong once. They could not survive it a second time, and presidential preference polls tell the story.[19]

Throughout 1995, the early presidential preference poll ("If the election were held today, for whom would you vote?") matched President Clinton with the Republican frontrunner, Bob Dole of Kansas, Senate majority leader. While Clinton was universally known and Dole largely unknown (in spite of a long, high-profile life in politics), Dole actually tracked Clinton closely across this period, occasionally surpassing him. Clinton then took the lead during the key period of the second governmental shutdown, in late 1995 and early 1996, and the lines diverged sharply thereafter. They were never to close again. The Republicans had once more been successfully painted, as they had throughout the New Deal era and on into the Era of Divided Government, as stiff conservatives on economics and social welfare. Though in truth, they themselves had successfully pushed that dimension—and hence that perception—to prominence.

The White House still needed to do two major things by way of a response. It needed to keep the economic/welfare dimension in the face of potential voters. And it needed to protect the president's flank on the cultural/national alternative, the one that had done his party so much damage in 1994. The latter was largely accomplished through a return to New Democratic rhetoric and themes. This included small things, such as the endorsement of putting the nation's children into school uniforms. It included large ones, such as the much-ballyhooed announcement in his State of the Union that "the era of big government is over." But it did have one major legislative element as well. In the spring of 1996, Bill Clinton signed the National Welfare Reform Act, thereby returning to the other priority of his first Congress, the road not taken when he opted for health care. The resulting bill gave more power back to the states, reduced overall spending more, and was far tougher in personal eligibility and time limits than any plan he might have signed during that first Congress, thanks to the aggressive drive of the new Republican majority. But sign it—and claim it—he nevertheless did.[20]

The Democratic election campaign then did everything it could toward—it was essentially devoted to—keeping economic/welfare concerns at the center of public discussion. In this, the president enjoyed some ironic advantages. Because Clinton had seemed so much at risk of not being reelected, during the period in 1995 when challengers within his party would have had to come forward, none did. As a result, he could spend the entire spring and summer, while the Republicans contested their nomination, doing generic advertising and then specifically attacking the Republican frontrunner, Bob Dole. Worse, Dole, as a comparative moderate, had to emphasize his conservatism on the way to the nomination, when that was what Democratic attack ads were emphasizing too. Moreover, in a final irony, where Bill Clinton had been the unpopular national leader of 1994, targeted by Republicans as their key demon, it was Newt Gingrich who assumed that mantle for 1996, targeted continually by the Democrats. Both those generic ads and the pointed attacks on emerging nominee Dole hammered away at "the Dole/Gingrich budget" and "the Dole/Gingrich Republicans," though the actual Republican ticket was to be, of course, Dole/Kemp.

In any case, the 1996 presidential outcome was remarkably parallel to—it was a near replay of—the 1992 outcome. The two-party vote in 1992, Clinton over Bush, had been 54–46. The two-party vote in 1996, Clinton over Dole, was 55–45. The electoral vote in 1992, Clinton over Bush, had been 370–168. The electoral vote in 1996, Clinton over Dole, was 379–159.[21] Yet two other things were strikingly different this time, one of them insistently evident and the second easy to miss.

The insistent fact was that the Republicans had retained control of Congress after their success of 1994, the first time they had done this since 1926–28. They did lose a net of nine seats in the House, thereby surrendering the conventional gains for a winning president, but, crucially, not surrendering enough to lose the Speakership. And they actually gained two seats in the Senate while Bill Clinton was being solidly reelected. The fact which no one emphasized at the time but which everyone would soon have cause to notice was that, unlike the situation in either 1992 or 1994, both of these partisan successes—Democrats for the presidency or Republicans for Congress—came without any alleged program for creating a new partisan majority, much less a new partisan era.

The unified Democratic control of national government that followed the elections of 1992 had swept away the surface pattern of divided government, the one which had essentially characterized the previous quarter-century: Republicans controlling the presidency, Democrats controlling Congress. It had then been replaced by the opposite model, perhaps temporarily, in 1994: Democrats controlling the presidency, Republicans controlling Congress. But the argument that this might be only a transition to unified Republican control of government, even to a Republican Revolution, had now been dealt a serious blow, by confirmation of the opposite pattern of divided government from that which had preceded the arrival of the New Democrats in the White House.

Moreover, and more to the point, neither party, this time, came (back) into office with a new program allegedly aimed at creating a new partisanship. There were no "New, Revised, American Choice Resolutions." There was no Contract with America, Part Two. There was only a campaign in which Democrats attacked Republicans on economic/welfare issues, especially protection of major (and existing) social insurance programs, and in which Republicans attacked Democrats on cultural/national issues, especially "character" and its links to drug use, sexual immorality, and, above all, personal dishonesty. Neither of these campaigns provided any basis for major programmatic initiatives, and in fact there were to be none.

That left the 1998 election to introduce any major remaining twists to the partisan legacy of the Clinton presidency. Yet what was really inherent in electoral positioning for 1998 was just a shifting restatement of familiar themes. So that what resulted, perhaps inevitably, was just a fresh embodiment of an ongoing political order. As 1998 opened, the White House announced that this would be the year when the president would rescue Social Security by putting it on a financially stable basis for an enduring period, and when he would expand health care by shifting the definitions that governed existing programs: classic economic/welfare initiatives. Republicans countered that this would be the year when *they* reformed the Internal Revenue Service in particular and then moved on to systematic tax reform in general: classic Republican ripostes on that same economic/welfare dimension.

By spring, these putative initiatives had been displaced by partisan skirmishing over regulation of the burgeoning HMO (health maintenance organization) sector, on which Republicans tried consciously not to cede a major social-welfare concern, and over regulation of smoking, especially teenage smoking, one of the main cultural issues on which Democrats already had the majority position. By summer, these too were receding from the national agenda, to be displaced by partisan conflict over the first fiscal *surplus* in more than a generation. Each side traced that surplus to its first election—of a Democratic president in 1992, of a Republican Congress in 1994—and each circled back to argue for its archetypal response: Democrats using the surplus to reinvest in Social Security, Republicans returning the surplus to its "owners" as tax cuts.

By fall, finally, all the foregoing had been displaced by White House scandal and an incipient impeachment, another cultural issue which was never a Democratic asset but brought intrinsic risks to its Republican handlers as well. With many policy questions raised but none resolved, and with a tricky moral and procedural issue on the front burner, where party combatants needed somehow to give the appearance of nonpartisanship, CNN called the election "hard to read."[22] Yet in the end, it was less obscure than indecisive, less the embodiment than the postponement of any new partisan patterns. The first two elections of the Clinton presidency, in 1992 and 1994, had been characterized by partisan upheaval and (two!) sharply divergent visions of the partisan future. The second two elections, in 1996 and now 1998, were to be characterized by a remarkable stasis instead. Or rather, what was inherent in the outcome of 1998 was that same mix of surface fluidity with stable underlying contours that had characterized the Era of Divided Government since its beginning.

In the immediate aftermath, commentators rushed to award victory to the Democrats. Part of this perception, despite inconsequential shifts in the actual vote, was the result of accidental collusion between the two political parties. Republicans had hoped for a large win and expected a moderate one; Democrats had feared a moderate loss but hoped for a small one. When the result was no change in the Senate and a Democratic *pick-up* in the House, that result confounded both expectations. Moreover, in the face of several scholarly benchmarks that had found their way into popular analysis, any gain at all was effectively magnified. These benchmarks included an alleged "six-year itch," by which the party of the president suffered substantial losses at its second midterm, along with the more reliable "surge and decline," in which that party always lost seats at the midterm by comparison to the preceding presidential election.[23]

Objectively, on the other hand, precious little happened. In the Senate, Democrats picked up three seats previously held by Republicans, and Republicans picked up three seats previously held by Democrats. The outcome, of course, was a net change of zero. In the House, Republicans lost and Democrats gained a net of five seats, an outcome tied for the second-lowest change in postwar midterms. It occasioned no shift in overall partisan control. Yet the main points for a partisan legacy from the Clinton presidency lay effectively elsewhere. From one side, this aggregate outcome meant that any Republican Revolution had certainly stalled. From the other side, its *underpinnings* represented, if anything, the resurgence of the Old Democracy.

For the Republicans, control of Congress was ultimately maintained. This meant that divided government—split partisan control—was ultimately maintained as well. If it was sixty years since an out-party had lost seats at the midterm, such a loss in 1998 was conditioned by a specific context, one wherein this party had picked up fifty-three seats at the previous midterm and surrendered only nine in the presidential election that followed. Moreover, these two putative exceptions were otherwise strikingly dissimilar. The previous exception (in 1934) was a major aftershock to the New Deal era, completing its arrival only two years before. Its current counterpart (in 1998) was a minor adjustment to the Era of Divided Government, born *thirty years* previously.

For the Democrats, their triumph, though real enough to cause House Republicans to shuffle their leadership, was actually elsewhere. As a result, so was its message. Widely expected to lose seats by means of a sharp drop in voter turnout—the usual midterm fall, compounded by an unproductive legislative session and emergent White House scandal—the party suffered neither this exaggerated decline nor its associated loss. Yet here, for a Clinton legacy, the point was that the interest groups that mobilized to support a last-minute blitz by President and Mrs. Clinton, along with the constituencies they targeted—namely, organized labor and racial minorities—were themselves mainstays of the Old Democracy. If they appeared to deserve real credit for stemming what even late polls suggested would be the expected fall, their success really harked back to the partisan world *pre-Clinton.*

Partisan Continuity and Partisan Legacies

Evidently the processes of political change proceed under the handicap of considerable friction. Pre-existing party attachments may have a durability that contributes to the lag. Men generally have a resistance to the salesmen of a new order whose tasks of indoctrination are not the work of the day. A generation or so may be required for one outlook to replace another. . . .

— V.O. Key Jr., "Secular Realignment and the Party System," 1959

In the end, the partisan situation was effectively unchanged, leaving little room for a Clinton legacy. Judged by its programmatic offerings or its social coalitions, the year 1998 could have been the year 1988 or even the year 1968. At bottom, the Era of Divided Government merely continued. This was not to deny that the Clinton presidency had been characterized—littered, really—with specific partisan events of high individual drama. It had begun with the defeat of an incumbent Republican president, the archetypal product of an existing order, by means of a self-consciously new kind of Democrat, atop the first "real" unified government in a generation. But that auspicious beginning had been swept away within one Congress. It was succeeded by an even more dramatic partisan event, in the first Republican capture of Congress for two generations. If any surprised analysts could have missed the fact, its products went on to bill themselves as revolutionaries. Yet this tide too crested within one Congress.

Already by 1996, as a result, high partisan drama had folded back into an ongoing political order. The *labels* had changed within this order. Now, a Democrat controlled the presidency, while Republicans controlled Congress. But the underlying pattern, split partisan control of national government, obviously continued. More important, the main elements underpinning its continuation were not superficial, not just labels at all. For the new politics, established in 1968, continued because the basic substantive and structural underpinnings to it continued, undisturbed in their essence. Which is to say:

- The Democratic Party continued to be the party perceived as best able to handle economic and welfare issues, and these hardly went away in the shift from an old order to a new politics.

- The Republican Party continued to be the party perceived as best able to handle cultural and national issues, and these actually achieved a substantially greater priority in the new politics than they had under the old order.

- The general public, finally, found itself sitting to the right of the active Democratic Party on cultural/national issues, to the left of the active Republican Party on economic/welfare issues.

That public had not necessarily chosen "divided government"; it merely became more comfortable with it through experience. What this public did prefer was its own modal policy positions. As long as the active members of *both* political parties were opposed to these positions, that public was destined to find split partisan control of national government to be a useful resolution, and these party activists were effectively dedicated to helping the public find it.

This continuing situation—these programmatic offerings and these social coalitions, filtered by these political parties—was essential for understanding any number of major partisan phenomena of the time. It was the very basis for split partisan control of national government, of course. But it went on to explain why, in the Era of Divided Government, unified partisan control was at best transitory, at worst the product of an actual mistake by the general public. In the aftermath of the Nixon resignation, the general public had believed that Jimmy Carter represented economic liberalism coupled with cultural conservatism. It was not an unreasonable belief, given the Democratic campaign in the aftermath of the Watergate crisis. But it was wrong. Carter was to offer only economic/welfare retrenchment and sacrifice, while running an otherwise orthodox—that is, a culturally liberal—Democratic government. He would be removed from office by the general public at its first opportunity.

Unified government did not return until Bill Clinton ran for president, when he too managed to convince the public that he was an economic liberal and a cultural conservative. This time, that perception was only half wrong. Yet when Clinton failed to deliver on the promised economic/welfare initiatives and did deliver on the (undesired) cultural/national counterparts, the public took its first available option. And the first Republican control of Congress since 1954 was the result. Note that this also goes a long way toward explaining the particular partisan balance under divided government, a phenomenon otherwise puzzling to analysts when split partisan control initially appeared. The relationship between two active parties, one uniformly conservative and one uniformly liberal, plus a general public that shared neither policy combination, was the general underpinning for divided government. Its further partisan characteristics were then dependent upon the issues of the day, and upon the stage of the electoral cycle.[24]

To say that both active parties contributed to this situation is not, however, to say that party activists desired it, much less enjoyed it. And in fact, this same continuing pattern is essential, finally, to understanding the two proposed alternatives to it during this administration. Both were conscious attempts to break the mold, change the program, alter the coalitions, shift the order, and end the Era of Divided Government. The more complex and strategic of these was the putative creation of a New Democracy, by way of the Democratic Leadership Council and by means of the Clinton presidency. The more concrete and tactical was the putative arrival of a Republican Revolution, in the form of the Contract with America and a new congressional majority. The first received its initial disconfirmation in the election of 1994. The second received *its* initial disconfirmation in the election of 1996. Neither received much support—neither was even much in evidence—by the election of 1998.

Or at least, such is the judgment that someone faced with evaluating a partisan legacy fifteen minutes after its last general election has to render. Yet history retains a proven ability to overturn the best summary judgment by way of a few well-chosen, stubborn, subsequent facts. If it should, then two other summary views of the Clinton legacy in partisan politics remain available, views whose supporters stand ready to proclaim their success, after only modest delay, if events prove kind. So perhaps it is best—fairest and safest—to close with these. One still belongs to the New Democrats, the other to the Republican Revolutionaries. Both have supporters who take the long view. Either might always triumph in the end.

New Democratic believers argue that theirs was always going to be a long march. In the absence of an agreed national crisis, one cannot reposition a decentralized and amorphous political party at a stroke. It would have been better, undeniably, if Bill Clinton had fronted new party doctrine from the start of his administration. But there were practical reasons why this was difficult, and Clinton did, after all, return to the New Democratic philosophy within months of his first midterm election. If Al Gore were to succeed Clinton, hew more decisively to the program, and thus hold it at the center of national attention for what might become *sixteen years*—two terms of Clinton, followed by two terms of Gore—then, say the believers, their philosophy might yet conquer the party, in a gradual but ineluctable fashion.[25]

Privately though, even the believers are worried. For a start, the 1996 Democratic National Convention had shown precious little of this hoped-for effect. Its delegates really hated the main successes of the Clinton presidency that were most clearly in line with the New Democracy, namely NAFTA and welfare reform. Moreover, the Clintons themselves were already arguing for a new synthesis, blending—blurring—Old and New Democrats. Even worse, Gore, their putative successor, was already using his position, as he naturally might, to woo the interest groups of the Old Democracy: organized labor most critically, but also feminists and homosexuals, added to the environmentalists for whom he had long been attractive. By the time of his success, he might as easily be seen as a classic Old Democrat for the new politics: liberal on economic/ welfare issues, liberal on cultural/national issues too.

Republican Revolutionaries have their own version of the same argument. Again, the main proposition says that the formula was right, but implementation was flawed. After forty years in the partisan wilderness, it required a dramatic figure, in the mold of Newt Gingrich, to bring the formula to national attention. Who else would have spent a generation crying aggressively in that wilderness? Yet dramatic figures inevitably add personal dynamics to a policy program, quirks that can themselves prove unpopular. Gingrich also added tactical errors, including two government shutdowns and a frontal assault on the long-run problems of key social insurance programs. Which, say the believers, have served to mask the fact that the main propositions in the Contract proved popular. There seems no reason why there might not be successor propositions—all it took the first time was determination plus polling—nor why these should not prove popular as well.[26]

On the other hand, once again, both analysts and believers have increasing reasons to doubt. For the analysts, thirty years after the 1968 election, the program is still essentially the same, and no fresh Republican majority has surfaced in its wake. Party identification, it is true, no longer means what it once did; crosscutting issue preferences and crosscutting social coalitions are increasingly the story. Yet the prospect of an extended era of unified Republican control of government in the face of those crosscutting influences and in the absence of a shift in partisan identifications appears remote. Worse, for the believers, the very fruits of Republican victory seem increasingly devoted to split partisan control. Or at least, those Republican congressmen who survived two successor elections after 1994 appear better and better at using governmental products and constituency service to maintain themselves in office, even if this runs actively counter to the need for some new and polarizing doctrine. And they seem less and less inclined to sacrifice themselves on the chance of a Republican presidency.

In the end, then, two contending candidates for a partisan legacy to the Clinton years remained available. But the legacy as it stood was one of superficial change and fundamental continuity. This is, it must be emphasized, not at all a judgment on personal success, for Bill Clinton or, indeed, for Newt Gingrich. Both were hugely successful on personal grounds, and their individual triumphs did have larger partisan implications. Nevertheless, neither was able to overcome the essence of a continuing political order, especially its programmatic focus and its social coalitions, by dint of simple personal desire. History left open the possibility that one or the other would still appear to have been the key initial signpost of a shift in that essence. Partisan events during the period of their rise to power—each of them—did not yet suggest that this was likely.

2

Campaigning Is Not Governing: Bill Clinton's Rhetorical Presidency

GEORGE C. EDWARDS III

James David Barber has identified three political roles that all presidents must perform: rhetoric, personal relations, and homework. The habitual way of performing these roles is what he terms presidential *style*.[1] The relative emphases in a president's style reflect not only the president's strengths but also his perceptions about the requirements of effective leadership.

The Clinton presidency is the ultimate example of the rhetorical presidency—a presidency based on a perpetual campaign to obtain the public's support[2] and fed by public opinion polls, focus groups, and public relations memos. No president ever invested more in measuring, and attempting to mold, public opinion. The White House even polled voters on where it was best for the First Family to vacation. This is an administration that spent $18 million on ads in 1995—a nonelection year![3] And this is an administration that repeatedly interpreted its setbacks, whether in elections or on health care reform, in terms of its failure to communicate[4] rather than in terms of the quality of its initiatives or the strategy for governing. Reflecting his orientation in the White House, Bill Clinton declared that "the role of the President of the United States is message."[5]

To understand the first six years of the Clinton presidency, we must explore the president's leadership style and ask whether it was effective for advancing his views. The focus on governing to accomplish goals requires us to answer two central questions about the Clinton administration. First, did the president accurately identify the possibilities in his environment for accomplishing his goals and, more specifically, the potential of his governing style? Second, was the president's strategy of emphasizing rhetoric an effective one for accomplishing his goals? These questions tap the essential aspects of the leadership challenges faced by all presidents, independent of their ideologies.

Implicit in the first question is an appreciation for the importance of the context in which the president operates. It makes little sense to fault presidents for not passing a great deal of legislation if their parties had only a modest number of seats in Congress, for example. Similarly, it is much easier to win support for bold initiatives when budgetary resources are available (as in the mid-1960s) than when they are scarce (as in the 1990s).

The first question is also premised on the view that presidents will not be able to change their environments very much. I have discussed this at length elsewhere.[6] To summarize the argument, there is little evidence that presidents can restructure the political landscape to pave the way for change. Although not prisoners of their environment, they are likely to be highly constrained by it.

A critical aspect of presidential leadership, then, is understanding the constraints and possibilities in the environment so as to exploit them most effectively. Once having evaluated the environment, an effective president must fashion a strategy to work within it to accomplish his goals.

In this chapter, I explore Bill Clinton's relations with the public. Because the first two years and the following four years were so different, I discuss them separately.

1993–94: Understanding His Strategic Position

At the core of successful political leadership in America is the ability to understand the political system in general and one's strategic position in it at any point in time so as to assess accurately the potential for policy change. A critical aspect of understanding the political environment is understanding the potential of various sources of influence.

In his first two years in office, President Clinton accentuated a problem inherent in our separation of powers system by overreaching—overestimating the extent of change that a president elected with a minority of the vote could make.[7] Any president elected with only 43 percent of vote should not expect to pass far-reaching social legislation without involving the other party, especially when the public is dubious and well-organized interest groups are fervently opposed. So, a partisan, unitarian approach was unlikely to succeed; yet this is exactly the strategy the president adopted. For example, the "us against them" approach to policymaking encouraged the president to develop his health care plan in Democrats-only secrecy and to pursue a left-in coalition-building strategy instead of a center-out one. Failure was inevitable.

Moreover, the greater the breadth and complexity of the policy change a president proposes, the more opposition it is likely to engender. In an era when a few opponents can effectively tie up bills, the odds are clearly against the White House. Yet when it came to health care reform, the president proposed perhaps the most sweeping, complex prescriptions to control the conduct of state governments, employers, drug manufacturers, doctors, hospitals, and individuals in American history.

A third important element in President Clinton's political environment was the lack of resources for policy initiatives. When resources are scarce, those proposing expensive new programs have to regulate the private sector to get things done, which inevitably unleashes a backlash. So the costs of action are more expensive politically.

In health care, the complex and coercive mechanisms created to require employers to pay for health insurance and to control costs were designed to avoid government responsibility for paying—but it should have come as no surprise that those who bear greater costs, face higher risks, or have their discretion constrained are likely to oppose change.

In the end, the president was not able to cut taxes for the middle class or substantially increase spending on education, job training, public works, and health care. Nor was he able to obtain welfare reform on his terms. He could not devise strategies for moving in the context in which he found himself, partly because he misread his political environment.

Many of his most notable successes, including the North American Free Trade Agreement (NAFTA), family leave, and motor voter registration had substantial support in Congress before he arrived in Washington. In the case of NAFTA, he was able to rely on Republican support for George Bush's policy initiative. He understood that he needed to engage in a bipartisan strategy that had the additional advantage of entailing no direct budgetary implications. In the latter two cases, the bills had passed before (and been vetoed by Bush) and little leadership was required.

1993–94: Fashioning a Strategy

To evaluate the success of the Clinton governing style of the rhetorical presidency, we can ask whether the president was able to

1. set the country's policy agenda,

2. set the terms of debate over the issues on the agenda, and/or

3. increase public support for himself or his proposals.

Setting the Agenda

An important element of a president's legislative strategy is to set the agenda of Congress. In the rhetorical presidency, this means setting the agenda of the public first. An important component of agenda setting is establishing priorities among legislative proposals. If the president is not able to focus attention on his priority programs, they may become lost in the complex and overloaded political environment. Setting priorities is also important because the White House can lobby effectively for only a few bills at a time. Moreover, the president's political capital is inevitably limited, and it is sensible to focus it on the issues he cares about most.

Setting the agenda requires first limiting it and then keeping a focus on priority items. From its very first week in office, the Clinton administration did a poor job at both. The president promised to have legislation ready for improving the economy at the very beginning of his term and to propose a comprehensive health care package within his first 100 days in office. Neither program was ready on time, creating a vacuum that was filled with controversies over issues of lower priority, such as gays in the military, the bungled nominations of Zöe Baird and Kimba Wood for attorney general, and public funding for abortion. These issues left an impression of ineptitude and alienated many in the public whose support the president needed for his priority legislation.

The defining issue of the Clinton presidency was to have been health care reform. The administration set and then badly overshot its deadline for delivery of a reform plan, first arousing and then dissipating public interest. It was more than eight months after taking office before the president made a national address on health care reform, his highest priority legislation. Even then, the pace of rhetoric was out of sync with the pace of lawmaking. The president's speech had the effect of peaking attention in a legislative battle two months prior to the introduction of the bill.

In the meantime, there were important distractions from the president's bill. Eighteen American soldiers were killed on a peacekeeping mission in Somalia, and the U.S.S. *Harlan County*, carrying U.S. troops as part of a United Nations plan to restore democracy in Haiti, was forced to turn around and leave in the face of pro-military gunmen. In addition, the president had to devote his full attention and all the White House's resources to obtaining passage of NAFTA, which was central to his foreign policy priority of increasing international trade.

Yet part of the problem was also the president himself. Clinton and his advisers understood the virtue of a clear, simple agenda, and the president knew that his defining issues had been overwhelmed as he had engaged in issue proliferation. He was not able to contain himself, however. He rarely focused on any bill for more than a few days at a time.

President Clinton has an undisciplined personal style, tremendous energy, a desire to please many sides, a mind stuffed with policy ideas, and a party of interest groups clamoring for policy. He came into office with a large agenda, and Democrats had a laundry list of initiatives that had been blocked by George Bush, ranging from family and medical leave to motor voter registration and health care reform.

He and his fellow partisans believe in activist government and are predisposed toward doing "good" and against husbanding leadership resources. But no good deed goes unpunished. The president's major proposals certainly obtained space on the congressional agenda in the first two years. But the more the White House tried to do, the more difficult it was to focus the country's attention on priority issues. And it was equally difficult for Clinton to receive credit for his achievements when there were so many issues that lay ahead.

Structuring Choice

Presidents not only want the country and Congress to be focused on their priority issues; they also want the debate to be on their terms. Framing issues in ways that favor the president's programs may set the terms of the debate on his proposals and thus the premises on which the public evaluates them and on which members of Congress vote on them.

One of the most serious limitations of the Clinton administration in its first two years was its lack of rhetorical definition. The administration's failure to effectively structure choice for the public and for Congress was not the result of an administration that was unaware either of the importance of projecting a strong, clear vision of its policies or of its failure to do so. Nevertheless, the administration did not clearly define what it was about. The failure to do so left the Clinton administration vulnerable to the vicissitudes of events and to the definitions of its opponents.

The White House allowed the Republicans to define the president's fiscal stimulus program in terms of pork barrel. On his FY 1994 budget, the president's political consultants complained that the Republicans had succeeded in focusing public debate on tax increases rather than economic growth or deficit reduction.

Regarding health care reform, the White House was unable to keep the public's attention focused on the inadequacies of the health care system and the broad goals of reform, partially due to the bill's complexity and partially due to competing plans in Congress and myriad health care industry voices with a deluge of direct mail, radio spots, and advertising, picking out pieces of the plan to oppose. Instead of revolving around a central theme, then, public debate focused on the Clinton plan's pitfalls.

During the first two years of the Clinton administration, Republicans dominated the symbols of political discourse and set the terms of the debate over policy. In 1994 congressional elections, the Republicans framed the vote choice in national terms, making taxes, social discipline, big government, and the Clinton presidency the dominant issues. They tied congressional Democrats to Clinton, a discredited government, and a deplorable status quo. They set the terms of the debate—and won.

Obtaining Public Support

Ultimately, presidents need public support for themselves and their programs. A basic problem for Bill Clinton was his overestimation of the extent to which the public was susceptible to his appeals for support. When the president's first major economic proposal, the fiscal stimulus plan, was introduced, it ran into strong Republican opposition. During the April 1993 congressional recess, Clinton stepped up his rhetoric on his bill, counting on a groundswell of public opinion to pressure moderate Republicans into ending the filibuster on the bill. (Republicans, meanwhile, kept up a steady flow of sound bites linking the president's package with wasteful spending and Clinton's proposed tax increase.) The groundswell never materialized, and the Republicans found little support for any new spending in their home states. Instead, they found their constituents railing against new taxes and spending. The bill never came to a vote in the Senate.[8]

The president's next major legislative battle was over the budget. On 3 August 1993, he spoke on national television on behalf of his budget proposal, and Senate Republican leader Robert Dole spoke against the plan. A CNN overnight poll following the president's speech found that support for his budget plan dropped.[9] Several million calls were made to Congress in response to Clinton and Dole, with the callers overwhelmingly opposed to the president's plan.[10]

When the crucial rule regarding debate on the 1994 crime bill was voted down in the House, the president immediately went public. Speaking to police officers with flags in the background, he blamed special interests (the National Rifle Association) and Republicans for a "procedural trick," but his appeal did not catch fire. Meanwhile, Republicans were talking about pork-barrel spending, tapping public resentment. Clinton's public push yielded only the votes of three members of the Congressional Black Caucus. So he had to go to moderate Republicans and cut private deals.

Most painful of all to President Clinton was his inability to sustain the support of the public for health care reform, despite substantial efforts. Nevertheless, the White House held out against compromise with the Republicans and conservative Democrats, hoping for a groundswell of public support for reform. But it never came.[11] Indeed, by mid-August 1994, only 39 percent of the public favored the Democratic health care reform proposals while 48 percent opposed them.[12] Clinton's tendency to carry the campaign mode to governance by demonizing opponents such as the medical profession and the drug and insurance industries only activated Republican counterattacks and negative advertisements only exacerbated his problem.

Despite energetic efforts, then, the White House was not able to produce groundswells of support for the economic stimulus plan, nor for the budget deal, the crime bill, or health care reform, and it only did a little better on NAFTA. The president's own approval levels averaged less than 50 percent for each of his first two years in office. In 1994 an association with Clinton decreased votes for Democratic candidates for Congress, and the election was widely seen as a repudiation of the president. It is difficult to conclude that the president had a successful governance style.

Governing and Campaigning

Evaluating strategic position and fashioning a strategy appropriate for governing in it can be a difficult and complex task. Moreover, the political environments of some presidents are more difficult to assess than the environments of other presidents. In addition, some administrations lend themselves to agenda setting and structuring choice better than do others. It is especially difficult to develop a clear focus and convey a consistent theme when the president has a large, diverse agenda—as Bill Clinton has, and when the president's views are a complex blend of populism and traditional values—as Clinton's are. This has made it difficult to establish a central organizing theme for the Clinton presidency. Nevertheless, the Clinton White House has also suffered from self-inflicted wounds.

In 1992 Clinton campaigned as a populist, economically liberal (eager for public investments to stimulate the economy) and socially conservative, and as a "New Democrat" who was cautious in domestic policy. But he governed in the first two years as an economic conservative, a social liberal, and an activist in domestic policy. As his pollster, Stan Greenberg, put it, "The mandate he ran on was not necessarily the one he executed. He ran as a cultural conservative and an economic populist. He was the first Democrat to talk about welfare reform and the death penalty." But "the cultural conservative side of Bill Clinton disappeared in the first two years."[13]

Instead, gays in the military, gun control, and abortion came to represent the administration in the minds of many in the public. His major accomplishments, and the ones where he made the crucial difference, were economically conservative policies, including deficit reduction and two free-trade agreements. As Clinton himself declared sarcastically to aides, "We're Eisenhower Republicans here, and we are fighting with Reagan Republicans. We stand for lower deficits and free trade and the bond market. Isn't that great?"[14] To confuse matters further, he also had an ambitious activist domestic agenda in his first two years, signaling that he was more a left-leaning than a centrist New Democrat.

It is not surprising, then, that the president found it difficult to fashion and implement a governing strategy appropriate to his goals and circumstances. His governing style undercut his campaign style. He undermined his supportive coalition and thus his ability to govern or even to receive credit for his accomplishments.

1995–98: Understanding His Strategic Position

The dramatic Republican congressional victory in the 1994 elections forced Bill Clinton to reevaluate his strategic position. The election was a repudiation of his leadership. It was clear that his program was dead. He would not be able to build coalitions or succeed in advocating new, controversial policies in the new political environment. Yet by freeing him from the possibility, and thus the responsibility, for enacting policies, the election also provided the president a new opportunity to define his presidency.

For several months following November 1994, the White House was in the doldrums as it strove to come to terms with the new political environment. Fortunately for the Clinton administration, the opposition eased its analytical burden. The new Republican majorities overplayed their hand and refused to budge on their proposals to reverse the course of public policy, leading to government shutdowns and public perception of the culpability of the Republican Congress. Clinton (and Dick Morris) recognized and exploited the opportunity the Republicans gave him. The president could characterize them as "radicals" and present himself as a "reasonable" alternative in opposition to change.

At the same time, Clinton read his new strategic position as providing for a scaled-down presidency. In this model the president employs executive orders to promote his policy views and the veto to defend moderation. As the president said, "One of the things I have learned in the last two years is that the president can do an awful lot of things by executive action."[15] He views government as a conciliator and catalyst of private actions. This more modest conception of the presidency disappointed Democrats desiring a more activist executive, but Clinton now saw the potential of the presidency in a new light. For example, having lost the opportunity to define the argument in 1994, Clinton did not even reintroduce his welfare bill in 1995. He could not find the funds to pay for his version, his name had become a liability, and he had more flexibility to negotiate if he did not have his own plan to defend. This was a far cry from health care reform in 1993, but it reflected the environment in which the president was operating.

1995–98: Fashioning a Strategy

Understanding his new strategic position, Clinton's primary goal became to block the Republicans' most ambitious plans to reshape government. To accomplish this goal, he fashioned a new strategy, switching from offense to defense. By opposing the Republican majority in Congress, he was able to unify his party, which was scared of staying in the minority. His defensive strategy met with substantial success; divided government matters.[16] It is ironic that following twelve years of conservative Republican presidents, the Clinton presidency's greatest success was in the realm of opposition to change. Nevertheless, Bill Clinton was more successful in defending the status quo against cuts in Medicare, Medicaid, environmental protection, and education spending than he had been in advocating policy change. In other words, he was much more effective as an obstacle to change than he was as an agent for it.

The biggest payoff for the president was reelection. The 1994 congressional elections set the terms of the debate over public policy in America so that the election of 1996 was about the excesses of the GOP as much as it was about high taxes, big government, social decay, and intrusive public authority. This, along with a classic backdrop of peace and prosperity, enabled Clinton to win easily a second term.

Obtaining Public Support

Another benefit of the Clinton public relations effort has been an increase in the president's approval rating. After three years of averaging below 50-percent job approval, he moved into the low 50s in 1996, averaged 58-percent approval in 1997, and soared to 63 percent in 1998. The 1998 figure is all the more remarkable because it was achieved in the face of a wide range of charges and revelations concerning his personal behavior, both before and after entering the White House. The most notable of these revelations was his affair with White House intern Monica Lewinsky. Perhaps even more striking was the president's standing in the polls at the very time that majorities of Americans believed that he was not peculiarly trustworthy and had engaged in behavior of which they disapproved.

The public's low evaluation of the president as a person was nothing new. A mid-1994 Gallup poll found that 39 percent thought he was honest and trustworthy (56 percent did not).[17] A Wirthlin poll taken at about the same time found that only 31 percent of the public responded that Clinton's moral values mirrored their own.[18] What is new is the lack of weight people seem to give the president's integrity in their overall evaluations of his performance in office. As late as mid-1994, when asked to choose between a president who set a good moral example for the country and one with whose political views it generally agreed, the public chose the former by 59 percent to 32 percent.[19] By 1998, things had obviously changed.

We know that when we ask people whether they like a particular president, they typically respond that they do. When we ask the same people whether they approve of the president's performance *as* president, they often respond that they do not. In other words, people frequently like the person but not the performance. Americans are quite accustomed to compartmentalizing their evaluations of the president.[20] In Bill Clinton's case, we see compartmentalization—but in reverse. Many seem to like the president's performance, but they do not have high regard for him as a person.

At any given time there are many issues, both policy and personal, on which the president might be evaluated. The salience of these issues is subject to change. For example, in the spring of 1991, George Bush was near 90 percent in the approval polls, because he was being evaluated for his performance as commander in chief during the Gulf War. The next year he was soundly defeated for reelection because the public was now evaluating him on his performance in handling the economy.

Bill Clinton has served in office at a time when there have been no great divisive issues dominating public discourse. He has presided over peace and prosperity and has been evaluated on the basis of these consensual issues. He had a lucky break in January 1998, when he was scheduled to deliver his State of the Union message the week after the Monica Lewinsky story broke. While ignoring the latter, he spoke to a huge audience and reminded people why they had elected him president. He was able to emphasize job performance, making it salient in the public's evaluations of him. He switched the debate on his presidency from character to leadership and performance. Moreover, his nationally televised unqualified denial of a sexual relationship with Lewinsky seemed to defuse the issue.

The scandal heated up again in the fall, as Independent Counsel Kenneth Starr issued a report to Congress accusing the president of eleven counts of impeachable offenses, including perjury, obstruction of justice, witness tampering, and abuse of power. The president's detractors used the report as a basis for charging that he had broken the law, failed in his primary constitutional duty to take care that the laws be faithfully executed, betrayed the public's trust, and dishonored the nation's highest office. As a result, they argued, the president should be impeached and removed from office. They also argued that other public officials would be removed from office for having an affair with a young intern. Why, they ask, should the president be held to lower standards?

These charges placed the president in peril, but not for long. First, the president apologized to the nation—sort of. Then he engaged in a round of expressions of remorse before a variety of audiences. At the same time, the White House accused Starr of engaging in an intrusive investigation motivated by a political vendetta against the president. The basic White House defense was that the president made a mistake in his private behavior, apologized for it, and was ready to move on to continue to do the people's business of governing the nation. Impeachment, the president's defenders said, was grossly disproportionate to the president's offense.

The president asked the public to evaluate not his character but rather that of his critics and those who report on them. By portraying himself as the victim of an intrusive and irresponsible press and an undisciplined special prosecutor, the president benefited from a backlash of public sympathy. Once again his opponents seemed to have overplayed their hand.

Costs to the Defensive Strategy

There are costs to the defensive strategy, however. Structuring the choice for voters and seeking public support as a more moderate version of the Republicans was apparently quite good for campaigning, and it lifted the president in the public opinion polls. Yet, campaigning, posturing, and pronouncing, although it may have been Clinton's strength, is not governance—certainly not in the usual sense of precipitating great national debates on important questions of public policy or of driving legislation through Congress.

Although the president benefited from standing in counterpoint to the Republicans, he was forced to embrace some of their more appealing imagery in his rhetoric. He changed his rhetoric from programs and dollars to inspiration and values. He defused a host of promising Republican cultural and values issues with his symbolic stands to attract anxious parents: V-chips in television sets, school uniforms, teenage curfews, restrictions on teenage smoking, limits on Internet pornography, school competency tests, Hollywood ratings system, and increased educational programming.

But Clinton did more than simply expropriate the language of values from Republicans. He also co-opted many of their issues. As a result, he had much of his agenda determined by the opposition party. He declared the era of big government to be over and signed the Republican welfare reform bill. Most important, the Republicans forced the president to deal with the budget on their terms. The issue became, first, not whether to balance the budget but when and how—and, later, just how. After submitting a budget in early 1995 that envisioned $200 billion deficits for years to come, a few months later he embraced the Republican orthodoxy of a balanced budget. Shortly thereafter he agreed to Newt Gingrich's timetable of balancing it within seven years.

Moreover, the president was unable to rally the people to support his own initiatives. The two most notable Democratic successes in the 104th Congress, health insurance portability and the increase in the minimum wage, were congressional, not White House, initiatives. The overhaul of the IRS and the massive public works bill in 1998 were led by Republicans.

In 1997–98, the president vocally supported a bill that would tax and regulate cigarettes and would reach a settlement with tobacco companies on their liability for smoking-related health problems. The president wished to portray the bill in terms of discouraging smoking, especially among teenagers, but his opponents spent millions of dollars on television ads portraying the bill as an example of big government and taxation of the working class (whose members are more likely to be smokers). In the end, the opponents prevailed in structuring the choice, and the bill died without a vote on passage. With it also died the president's plan to finance health care for uninsured children, school construction, and other social welfare initiatives.

Most of the president's other priorities met similar fates. Congress would not enact a patients' bill of rights, campaign finance reform legislation, or fast-track authority. In addition, the president desired to precipitate national debates on affirmative action and financing Social Security. Neither occurred. Aspirations are not enough for governing. Once again, the president was hindered by a full agenda, a lack of focus, competition from opponents for the public's attention and setting the terms of debate on issues, and the lack of a sustained effort on behalf of priority measures.

Aside from the essential battle for public support over impeachment, the only public relations battle over policy that the White House won was in the last days of the 105th Congress. Here the Republicans, fearful of repeat of the government shutdown in 1995–96, gave the president a billion dollars for additional teachers. But the administration's successful efforts to place a positive spin on the results of the budget negotiations cannot hide the fact that President Clinton could not look back on 1997–98 and claim a legacy of major legislative achievements.

Governing and Campaigning II

In the second half of his first term, Bill Clinton better understood his strategic position and rediscovered his roots as a Democratic centrist, supporting a balanced budget but fending off extreme cuts and emphasizing social conservatism and family values. By then, however, the president's strategic position was greatly weakened by the Republican victories in the congressional elections. In addition, because Clinton's new campaign style reflected a reactive agenda, it undermined his ability to govern. Although he could gain public support in opposition to the Republicans, he was not able to obtain public support for his own policy initiatives.

The Limits of the Rhetorical Presidency

The belief in the importance of rhetoric is not surprising for presidents elected in the age of mass communications or for White House political advisers who employed public relations techniques adeptly during a successful presidential campaign. Yet there are important differences between campaigning and governing, and the president must adjust if he is to succeed.

The transition is rarely smooth. As Charles O. Jones put it, "After heading a temporary, highly convergent, and concentrated organization" in a presidential campaign, the winner moves into the White House and becomes the "central figure in a permanent, divergent, and dispersed structure."[21] As we have seen, communication becomes more difficult as the president loses control of his agenda and has to convince people not that he is superior to his opponent(s)—a relatively simple comparative judgment—but that his calls for specific change deserve support. At the same time, his opponents need only to cast doubt on the president's proposals to kill them.

In such an environment, it is important for the White House to have a clear understanding of the potential of governing through the rhetorical presidency. To start, there are very real limits to what public support can do for the president. The impact of public approval or disapproval on the support the president receives in Congress occurs at the margins of the effort to build coalitions behind proposed policies. No matter how low presidential standing dips, the president still receives support from a substantial number of senators and representatives. Similarly, no matter how high approval levels climb, a significant portion of the Congress will still oppose certain presidential policies. Members of Congress are unlikely to vote against the clear interests of their constituencies or the firm tenets of their ideology out of deference to a widely supported chief executive. Public approval gives the president leverage, not control.[22]

Yet despite the history of failures and frustrations of the emphasis on rhetoric, the Clinton White House continued to assign strategic primacy to communications. In a discussion of his problems in his first year in office, the president declared that he needed to do a better job of communicating: "There have been times when I've been surprised by my inability to shape the agenda on a daily basis or to shape the message that's going out to the folks. . . . It's always frustrating to feel that you're misunderstood. . . . And you can't quite get through."[23] A year later the president sounded the same theme as the solution to his political problems: "What I've got to do is to spend more time communicating with the American people about what we've done and where we're going."[24] Four years later things had not changed. The president's legislative program was largely dead, and the White House was embattled, fighting charges that the president had committed impeachable offenses. Once again, the White House employed the rhetoric of campaigning in the hopes of surviving to govern for two more years. The question remains whether the president can successfully employ his leadership style to leave his mark on public policy.

3

Demotion? Has Clinton Turned the Bully Pulpit into a Lectern?

COLIN CAMPBELL

This chapter offers a prognosis of Bill Clinton's legacy, focusing on the crucial dimension of political leadership. Until its official expiry date in January 2001, the Clinton administration, barring mortal fate-tempting scandal, probably will continue with its beguiling mixture of rope-hugging tenacity and pugnacious recovery.

From the outset, the administration encountered considerable difficulty in defining, articulating, and staying on its message. In the wake of the 1994 midterm elections, it found itself waging hand-to-hand combat with a Republican Congress, while often appearing to fritter away the prerogatives of the presidency in the politics of least common denominators. Arguably, the administration's difficulties in sustaining its course unfolded independently of its susceptibility to scandal—although the more "mature" rendering of the Clinton legacy certainly must take that dimension into consideration.

The Problem

There are pulpits and then there are lecterns. If you visit the National Cathedral in Washington, D.C., you will see a massive structure in the right-hand side of the

48

sanctuary. It looks very much like the type of edifice from which medieval monarchs addressed their troops before departing on a crusade. That is a pulpit. And, we can assume that when Theodore Roosevelt characterized the presidency as the "bully pulpit," that is what he had in mind. In our current age, however, even spiritual leaders seek the common touch. Many, if not most, priests and ministers rarely climb into their majestic perches, preferring, instead, to preach to their flocks from modest lecterns only slightly raised above the floor of the sanctuary.

Bill Clinton at first fancied himself a Franklin Delano Roosevelt. More than simply providing moral exhortations pointing the country in the right direction, Clinton aspired to lead from the front on a comprehensive revamping of governance. This approach proved too grandiose. By the 1994 midterm elections, Clinton had begun to covet a role more akin to Theodore Roosevelt's power of communication and his resultant ability to employ moral suasion on the issues that really counted. Of course, events surrounding the Lewinsky case then so undermined this president as to erode the moral ground from which he could offer his suasion. Nonetheless, we should strive to focus on the question of whether, independent of the Lewinsky affair, the Clinton years have ushered in a period in which, in his agenda-setting role, the president has stepped out of the pulpit and into the lectern.

Much of the conventional literature on coordination in the executive branch and the role of the White House since World War II has centered on the president's ability to devise a coherent, compelling agenda and deliver on it. The agenda-setting function seemed to rest with the president because of his unique placement within the system. Presidents vary greatly in their perception of the big picture and in their propensity and capacity for leadership and risk taking.[1] Still, we have looked to them to take the lead in agenda setting. George Bush's failure to anticipate and address some of the domestic issues that began bedeviling the country at the beginning of the 1990s exposed him to disquiet on both the right and the left and certainly contributed to his failure to renew his mandate.[2] But the Clinton administration has taken us beyond this simple failure of "vision." First, Clinton's run at agenda setting proved singularly disillusioning by 1994. Then, the onset of Republican control of the House and the Senate ushered in an era of uncertainty over which branch of government should prevail in agenda setting.[3] Inevitably, this shifted the criteria by which to assess coordination in the executive branch and the operation of the White House away from definition, articulation, and delivery of the president's agenda.[4] The current problematic situation tends to rivet most of our attention on whether the president can direct the agenda at all, except of course in matters that many deem peripheral.

Frustrated with deadlock between Republican presidents and Democratic Congresses, Americans elected Bill Clinton president in 1992. Ostensibly, this would provide greater unity between the executive and legislative branches, but it did not. In the first place, public disenchantment with both the Democratic and Republican Parties had propelled the candidacy of Ross Perot to a level that left Clinton only 43 percent of the vote—far from a clear mandate. With a combination of manifest character flaws and weak leadership, Clinton soon frittered away any promise that unified governance might have held.[5] Public neuralgia about divided government soon turned into neurosis about the governability gap. This increasingly prominent feature of the American political landscape has widened relentlessly in the face of the seeming incapacity of Democrats and Republicans to set aside partisan squabbling long enough to solve the problems uppermost in the minds of the electorate.[6] Even when Clinton has enjoyed reasonably buoyant approval ratings—for instance, throughout the Lewinsky affair—this fault line has been apparent in the very fact that political struggles have become so malignantly adversarial that they virtually proscribe the bipartisanship needed for policy agendas, however modest, to move forward. Newt Gingrich, of course, sought to bridge the governability gap by putting Congress in the driver's seat for setting and delivering the agenda, but this proved a conceit based only on Gingrich's unbridled hubris and his fellow Republicans' gullibility about their leader's arrogation of presidential prerogatives. What Gingrich and his party believed would break the logjam of political impasse ultimately served to exacerbate paralysis and further embitter political discourse.

The Clinton administration faced unique circumstances in coping with the rise of the Republicans—especially the ascendancy of Newt Gingrich. Previously, strong Speakers have enjoyed enhanced political leverage when presidents have failed to provide adequate leadership. They have filled a vacuum. While this condition certainly supplied an element of Gingrich's power, another factor amplified its significance. Never before had a strong Speaker emerged in a period of such uncertainty about the fundamental workability of the American political system. Having witnessed Johnson's departure over Vietnam, the pretension and venality of Nixon, Reagan's detachment (especially in the second term), the huge gap between Bush's foreign and domestic policy performance, and Clinton's grandiose fumbling, the public began to believe that the system had become intractable. Thus, it proved much more susceptible than ever before to the pitch of a "Mr.

Fix-it" who promised to come in and put things right. Gingrich clearly saw himself in this light. And his initial success, especially the stunning 1994 Republican election victory, suggested that the public concurred in this view.[7]

Normally, we speak of divided government with reference to periods in which one party controls the White House and the other one or both houses of Congress. Indeed, we often find shades of divided government when the same party enjoys sway over both the presidency and Congress. In this case, contrasts in the perceived mandates of the president and members of his party in Congress reach the point at which the president finds himself unable to reap the benefits of his party's technical control of the legislative branch. Notwithstanding the frequency with which deadlock between the president and Congress emerges, analysts persist in ascribing a greater potential for agenda setting to the executive branch, especially insofar as they maintain that the Founders specifically sought to embue the executive branch with unity and energy.[8]

Thus, highly regarded observers have typically looked to the president for agenda setting on issues of national interest. The so-called bully pulpit theoretically allows him to provide focused leadership on the matters that Congress considers. John Kingdon, for instance, has argued that "presidents can dominate the congressional agenda" and do so to the point of squarely holding the "preeminent position in agenda setting."[9] Similarly, David R. Mayhew has contended that "many, if well short of all, major enactments are presidential projects," and as such are directly correlated with the agenda, will, and skill that emanates from the White House.[10] Executive dominance in agenda setting has even received nodding recognition in the fact that the agenda for Congress's constitutionally defined power of the purse is nominally set by the president. That is, since 1921, the president has commenced the annual appropriations process by submitting a budget proposal to Congress. This practice followed the 1912 Taft Commission recommendation that the president assume greater responsibility for the coherence of the executive branch's program. To be sure, the fate of these documents over much of the past twenty years became so shaky that commentators frequently proclaim a president's budget proposal "DOA" (dead on arrival) when it reaches Congress.[11]

Breaking with the tradition of deferring to the president, at least nominally, as chief agenda setter, the 104th Congress under Republican leadership clearly set out in 1995 to eclipse the president in this role. Ironically, by electing Bill Clinton to the White House with a Democratic Congress just two years earlier, voters had handed the Democrats the potential for unified governance; to use Clinton Rossiter's term, Clinton wore the "hat" of party leader as the president.[12] The message that voters seemed to be sending then was that they wanted to strengthen the executive's ability to control the agenda and then to bring an end to the legislative gridlock that increasingly had plagued the Bush years. Bush had waged Herculean battles with Congress over annual budgets and issued more vetoes than any previous president.

In the midterm elections of 1994, however, voters strongly repudiated the earlier tilt toward fused government by sweeping the Republicans into control in both houses of Congress. Many pundits at the time viewed this momentous U-turn as a revolt against the Clinton policies of the previous two years. The midterm elections were popularly perceived as a stinging rebuke to President Clinton that, insofar as he was headed on a discernible course, he was going the wrong way.

Newt Gingrich, of course, had orchestrated the Republic victory. First elected to the House of Representatives in 1978, Gingrich had come to Washington with a long-term plan for evoking sustainable change in the way government worked. Inspired by the Goldwater mission to end big-government liberalism,[13] Gingrich began to mobilize a revolution that would grip the mid-1990s in the same way that Reaganism had seized the 1980s. In the fore of Gingrich's mind during his rise, however, was a historical perspective that caused him to posit that "the Congress in the long run can change the country more dramatically than the president." He thus defined one of his overarching political goals as making "the House the coequal of the White House"[14] in setting national priorities, more than hinting at his anticipated thrust to set future policy agendas from the Speaker's chair.

Executing the Agenda Grab

President Clinton's first two years in office lacked notable accomplishments, for his perceived mandate led to a number of missteps and failures. Indeed, Clinton had viewed his ascent to the presidency in romantic terms, presenting himself as an outsider who would "tame" Washington and press initiatives in a host of areas after twelve years of putative neglect under the Reagan and Bush administrations.[15] In fact, Clinton's electoral mandate probably did not extend much beyond reducing the public's angst over the governability gap. As would prove the case with the health care crisis, public preoccupations remained ephemeral. Having sought indications that government was responding to its concerns, the public became skittish at the first hint of a comprehensive, indeed, highly rationalistic, effort to repair the obvious defects in the U.S. health care system. Citizens still wanted less rather than more government presence in their lives, while remaining addicted to boutique government—middle class–directed programs of clear benefit to "me" and "mine."[16] As Clinton would discover in the backlash to his health care reforms, the prevailing view of government remained palliative, attuned to voters' specific circumstances, rather than pro-active, with reference to societal obligations toward the less advantaged.[17] The rationalistic intricacy of the Clinton proposals, which proved inaccessible to all but the most sophisticated analysts, simply exacerbated doubts. Divided government under George Bush had scared people. Washington seemed paralyzed in an era in which politics stymied rather than facilitated the delivery of citizens' expected emoluments. Voters wanted a bottom line from Clinton, but his health care plan left them at best cold and at worse highly suspicious.

Under the circumstances, Clinton quickly found the dynamics of policy leadership much more difficult to master than he had anticipated. Moreover, the internal fragmentation within his administration, which Bob Woodward described broadly as the "economists" versus the "political" staffers, led to vicious infighting featuring battles between some monumental egos. Clinton was thus forced to retreat to a Bush-style "let's deal" presidency, in which he regularly abandoned espoused principles in order to attain results. As one aide lamented, the fact that Clinton was "getting defined by his compromises, not his principles" in his first year resulted in his running the risk of becoming "negotiator-in-chief instead of commander-in-chief."[18]

In policy terms, the wreckage began to pile up. Clinton's first policy battle over gays in the military resulted in a compromise that proved unpopular with the American people, expended a lot of political capital, and turned out to be counterproductive for the very group it sought to assist. Moreover, the way in which the ultimate fix came about suggested that the governability gap was widening rather than narrowing. Likewise, the budget reconciliation of 1993 depleted Clinton's political capital to just about "empty," passing with no Republican support and only lukewarm Democratic support—even requiring the vice-president's vote to break a tie in the Senate. The most ballyhooed failure of the first two years, however, was the first lady's health care plan, which did not even come to either legislative chamber's floor for a vote. In foreign policy, no clear "Clinton doctrine" had emerged even by 1994, and a succession of "William the Waffler" moves in Bosnia, Somalia, Haiti, Europe, and Russia had tended to obscure ultimate progress—as was clearly evident with the eventual invasion of Haiti and its successful outcome.[19]

Amid the seeming disarray, Gingrich was positioning himself to capitalize on rising discontent within the nation. Although subsequent mood shifts would prove him too eager by half, Gingrich interpreted the public's rejection of comprehensive state intervention as a signal that the time was ripe for massive withdrawal of the state from people's lives. In 1993 alone, Gingrich visited twenty-three states, expanding his attack on the liberal welfare state, advocating his vision of a "synergistic overhaul of the welfare state," in which there would be comprehensive, not incremental or patchwork, change. He argued that if Republicans "lead that movement to renew American civilization by replacing the welfare state, that movement will entrust us with the power to enact that replacement."[20] In building his base for the 1994 election, Gingrich sought to reach out to every Republican, and indeed every American, for he anticipated a rendezvous with destiny that required pressing ideas across a broad front.[21] Consequently, Gingrich built a wide base of support by capitalizing on the president's palpable inability to address the governability gap during the first two years of his term. Much as he had done among Republicans during his ascent within the House, Gingrich used sweeping rhetoric to evoke discontent and turn it into a foundation for the appearance of a mandate. Unfortunately, using political malaise as a streetcar for mobilizing voter disapproval of the status quo usually proves quite a bit easier than actually rallying support for a positive agenda. This latter task proved beyond Gingrich's grasp.

Enter the Contract

During the 1994 midterm election campaign, Gingrich deployed the Contract with America as a public platform for the advancement of his cause and, not incidentally, of himself. Gingrich used his high-profile unveiling of the Contract to attract attention to the guiding principles that he viewed as the foundation of American civilization:

1. The common understanding we share about who we are and how we came to be

2. The ethic of individual responsibility

3. The spirit of entrepreneurial free enterprise

4. The spirit of invention and discovery

5. Pragmatism and the concern for craft and excellence[22]

Citing these principles, Gingrich and his allies—principally Dick Armey—styled support of Republican candidates as an endorsement of the Contract and so claimed a decisive mandate to address the nation's core issues, with provisions to pare the federal deficit, attack crime, and overhaul welfare. By addressing these concerns of the American public within the concept of an electoral mandate, Gingrich basically sold the Contract as deliverable, if the voters took the first step by electing a Republican Congress.

Gingrich timed his offensive with the Contract for maximum impact: he capitalized on voter disenchantment with the Democrats to propel Republicans to victory. At its unveiling on 27 September 1994, the Contract received much attention; it was delivered to millions of households as an insert in that week's *TV Guide*. Gingrich himself viewed the Contract as the catalyst for a sweeping electoral mandate, recalling that "the Contract brought our campaign into focus. . . . The sense of unity gave us a campaign that was almost unprecedented for Republicans in this century."[23]

Substantively, the Contract extended beyond mere campaign promises and the party platitudes of earlier Republican leaders. It represented a bold enumeration of legislative measures, which many Republican congressional candidates committed themselves to supporting through their own campaign rhetoric. Even the Republican National Committee advertised in bold relief, evincing the Gingrich style: "A campaign promise is one thing. A signed contract is quite another. If we break this contract, throw us out. We mean it."[24] Gingrich himself explicitly characterized the Contract as an instrument for transforming congressional races into votes on the national policy agenda: "The Contract is working perfectly. It is nationalizing the elections."[25]

Gingrich and many other Republicans, especially newly minted freshmen, saw the Contract as the linchpin of their success. Focused as it was on "ideologically cohesive and substantively focused" party leadership,[26] it stood behind the prime ministerial, if not presidential, airs of Gingrich's assumption of the Speakership. Notwithstanding such conceits, however, analysts suggested that voters had registered anger over Clinton more than they had given Republicans a mandate to deliver on the specifics of their Contract. Indeed, Clinton's chief of staff, Leon Panetta, got it about right on the day after the midterm election when he said: "There's no question the voters are sending the same message they sent two years ago"—namely, they were unhappy with gridlock.[27]

Even scholarly assessments saw a strong anomic component in the Republican victory. For instance, Walter Dean Burnham, who went so far as to read the 1994 election results as marking a realignment toward the political right, made a great deal of Gingrich's success at harnessing the anger of the "Great White Middle" as the true source of his party's triumph.[28] The fact remained, however, that many Republicans believed that the Contract had delivered their majorities in both the House and Senate and marked the end of their party's minority status and posture of accommodating itself to Democratic agendas.[29] The Gingrich zealots, especially the freshmen, truly saw themselves as mandated to tackle all at once everything that ailed America by offering a specific but broadly encompassing legislative agenda on which the party would deliver once it was in the majority.

Exit the Contract

The sight of Clinton licking his wounds after the stunning defeat in the midterm elections and the belief in Gingrich's core group that the Contract had made the difference provided just the conditions for the Speaker to steal center stage as the nation's agenda setter. Gingrich came thundering into power at full speed, armed with his ten-point blueprint of legislative proposals for the first 100 days. He filled key committee posts with allies of his revolution in order to ensure that Contract proposals would reach the House floor. Although he did use the institution of the House in pursuing his ends, Gingrich clearly drew his power from the sense of indebtedness that House Republicans, most decidedly the bloated ranks of freshmen, felt toward him.

After dominating the headlines with popular measures during his first 100 days as Speaker, Gingrich lost his momentum for governing because he allowed protracted debate on controversial issues. In dealing with the acrimonious deficit-reduction issue during the final months of 1995, Gingrich could have taken a lead from Roger Douglas, the New Zealand reformer who spearheaded the neo-liberal revolution in the mid-1980s: "Once you build momentum, don't let it stop rolling . . . the fire of opponents is much less accurate if they have to shoot at a rapidly moving target."[30] Instead, the Speaker became mired in a budget battle—one that weakened his credibility greatly. He was seen as holding out for a $190 billion tax cut while simultaneously cutting numerous social expenditures. As the budget shutdown dragged on, Gingrich fell into what David Broder termed "a familiar trap": while popular measures "went by voters in a blur, public attention focused on the things that stirred up big fights."[31]

While being vigorously attacked in public, Gingrich failed to shore up his support within his own ranks. Indeed, Gingrich's base for House support was ultimately an ineffective means for maintaining control over his allies. Previously, strong Speakers had effected their agendas through astute, even despotic, manipulation of House rules (as had Joseph G. Cannon) or deft nurturing of personal relationships with other members on each side of the House (as did Sam Rayburn). Gingrich chose quite another path. Indeed, he fancied himself a "Supreme Commander"[32]—with no apparent awareness of the inappropriateness of such an archetype for a Speaker. Leaders exalted as "supreme" typically possess unquestioned license to issue orders, but as the 1996 elections approached, many Republicans began to view their putative commander as a major liability. Gingrich began to exert less sway over the political, and thus, the legislative landscape. As his numerous personal shortcomings—pride, self-satisfaction, and an inability to grasp the handle of statesmanship—became increasingly apparent,[33] Gingrich rapidly lost control of the agenda that he had so decisively seized from Clinton. But this did not mean that the standard passed back to the president. Indeed, the administration's lethargic response to the Gingrich challenge after the 1994 congressional elections pretty much preordained a prolonged period of uncertainty over responsibility for agenda setting.[34]

Leadership through Meandering

In the Clinton camp, two motifs of response emerged immediately after the stark reality of the election results sunk in. The first, and most obvious, had the administration mouthing conciliatory words about issues on which Democrats and Republicans agreed—making it appear that the president would lead from the center. Clinton himself highlighted welfare reform, reform of Congress, the line-item veto, and the streamlining of government as areas with strong potential for bipartisan agreement.[35] The second motif represented what the administration ultimately would find to be its key to thwarting an effective challenge to Clinton's reelection prospects in 1996. To an extent perhaps beyond the administration's initial realization, the ball was now in the Republicans' court. As White House Chief of Staff Leon Panetta put it, "There's some good news here, which is that

Republicans now have to assume some responsibility to help govern this country."[36] Ironically, this second response motif required cooperation by the Republicans as well—they would have to walk into a trap set early on by the administration. Through a very clever sleight of hand, Panetta and others would seize any opportunity that presented itself to paint the Republicans as unworthy of the trust they had received from the American people.

And Gingrich, through his hubris and erratic behavior, played right into the administration's hand. Just over a month after the election, a Gingrich outburst provoked an on-target rebuke from Panetta: "The time has come when he has to understand that he has to stop behaving like an out-of-control radio talk show host and begin behaving like the Speaker of the House of Representatives."[37] Privately, an outside adviser to the White House told the *Washington Post* that the Democrats' strategy was to make the GOP look extremist, lacking the temperament to govern: "If they provide the rope, we'll help with the hanging."

Gingrich had misinterpreted the 1994 swing to the Republicans as approbation of him. Yet, polls suggested that the public was going from chary to nearly contemptuous of him personally the longer he served as Speaker. Despite his prime ministerial pretensions, Gingrich had to end his practice of daily press briefings because, as his spokesman argued, they "provided an opportunity for obscure journalists to come in and harangue him on their pet points." Late in 1995, Gingrich told his Republican colleagues that he was going to "bench himself." He had just received exceedingly negative press coverage after fulminating over a perceived slight on Air Force One and linking a grisly murder in Illinois to Democrat-backed social programs.[38]

The first prong of the administration's postelection strategy, moving toward the center, eventually proved much more difficult to execute. Partially this was because of the continued indecisiveness of the president. Although the election results sent a jolt through the administration, the mix of in-house and outside advisers continued to serve up a cacophony of views. Newt Gingrich's conceit was that he had become de facto prime minister; the administration's remained that it held the corner on sheer intellect and would somehow work its way through the complexity. Late in November 1994, a White House aide had Clinton "just beginning to synthesize what happened" and trying "to do some thinking, run it through his brain."[39] At the same time, a briefing by Panetta and Harold Ickes, the deputy chief of staff, left chiefs of staff from departments and agencies "in a worse case of anxiety about whether they know what went on out there."

This situation continued until spring 1995, when Clinton essentially handed the task of defining his strategy over to Dick Morris, a political consultant who since 1988 had avowedly worked only for Republicans, although Clinton had often resorted to Morris while governor of Arkansas. Morris imprinted on Clinton the concept of the "permanent campaign,"[40] which translates into focusing on the few commitments that will contribute to a chief executive's reelection and staying away from those that might well be meritorious but would unsettle voters.

Increasingly under Morris's sway throughout 1995, Clinton became resolutely pragmatic about his agenda. Following a strategy that Morris termed "triangulation," Clinton attempted to place himself equidistant from conservative Republicans and liberal Democrats. An obvious difficulty with such a strategy presented itself immediately, given that the 1994 election had produced a 104th Congress long on extremes and short on moderation.[41] As triangulation took hold, Clinton began to construe the debacle of the first half of his initial term as a clear warning against greater accommodation of the left. Thus, he believed that he would have to make his deals with the right in order to obtain the numbers required to govern from the middle. The notion that ultimately Gingrich would spin out of control and leave an opening for a return to a more ambitious, albeit moderate, agenda soon receded into the background.

From the standpoint of many left-leaning, even moderate, congressional Democrats and White House aides, the Morris tack seemed at its height to have resulted in as much strangulation as triangulation. Clinton's new guru seemed to have triumphed in June 1995, convincing the president that he should punt by offering the Republicans a ten-year balanced budget deal. The Clinton-Morris alliance had run roughshod over the White House aides who had served Clinton through thick and thin during the 1992 campaign and the first half of the administration.[42] Some complained of not finding out about major changes in direction until reading about them in the newspapers. Clinton's own soul seemed to be gasping for breath. When he ordered a thoroughgoing review of affirmative action to counter Republican assaults, he proclaimed, "This is what I believe."[43] In fact, the president's stance on affirmative action evolved from one of the few disciplined decision-making ventures undertaken by the Clinton White House, but the glimmer of hope that Clinton the man might have found how to connect principle and programs soon faded.

Occasionally, chief executives so narrowly focus on their own political survival that they discipline themselves to attend only to their "responsive competence."[44] Some, indeed, pursue such unadulterated responsive competence that they pull away from institutional fetters of any kind—including core attachments to their party. For Clinton, such "survival politics"[45]—as crafted by Dick Morris—involved two steps: the president first distanced himself as much as possible from congressional Democrats, then he placed himself as a bulwark against Republican radicals. We have already remarked that triangulation silenced Bill Clinton's soul. It also meant death by a hundred or so strangulations to any prospect that the president might forge alliances with congressional Democrats that could result in a cogent alternative agenda to that pressed by the Republicans. At the time, many analysts concluded that the president found himself bereft of any other options. When we consider Gingrich's chronic lack of popular approval, however, and the American people's repudiation of radical Republicanism once its excesses became patent in connection with the Lewinsky case, it becomes decidedly more difficult to rule out the possibility that, with deft leadership of his party, Clinton could have brought about the reversal of Republican dominance in 1996 rather than in 1998.

Indeed, frequently during the 104th Congress the first prong of the survival strategy left congressional Democrats feeling abandoned. Early in 1995 some observers saw danger in a broad accommodation of the Republicans in an attempt to save only the essential elements of the social safety net. The foreign affairs columnist Jim Hoagland put the risk especially clearly when he likened Clinton's strategy to what François Mitterrand had done to gain reelection in the 1988 French presidential elections.[46] When the trend lines favor the building-down of government, what appears to the left-center party a tactical retreat may end up a loss of ground that it will never regain: "Victories of the left built on centrist or right-of-center economic strategies are Pyrrhic victories, ultimately canceling out the political space the left would normally occupy in a democracy." Significantly, Ralf Dahrendorf has deployed a similar argument in an open letter to Tony Blair critiquing the supposed "third way" that he and Bill Clinton have pursued: "when you define yourself in others' terms, you allow them to determine your agenda."[47]

By mid-1995 Clinton's conciliatory moves on the budget deficit and cuts to social spending had raised the hackles of congressional Democrats. Many believed that the president's approach was pulling the carpet out from under an effective congressional strategy of scoring points against the Republicans on the social consequences of radical cuts. Some Democratic analysts even began to assert that the president's desire to run on his record and leadership clashed with congressional Democrats' objective of regaining control of Capitol Hill. By fall 1995 Clinton was busy rewriting history—claiming that liberal Democrats had pressured him into raising taxes "too much" and not pushing a more stringent welfare reform bill. By early 1996 Clinton gave his "responsive competence" tack away completely by promoting a disconnect between the fortunes of a party's presidential candidate and of those running for congressional seats. He noted that, indeed, linking the two would be "self-defeating. . . . The American people don't think it's the president's business to tell them what ought to happen in congressional elections."[48]

Through sleight of hand, Clinton had jettisoned members of his own party who, much like the "loyal opposition" in a parliamentary system, believed that their party's future rested with defining areas in which its policies would better serve the people. As David Broder observed, Clinton saw his future not in governing with a Democratic House and Senate but in presenting himself as a restraining influence on the Republican majorities in Congress. The new Clinton strategy made the pitch that tough times required a different type of leadership from the assertive approaches that might emerge when a clear consensus has developed about what the nation should do.[49] In this regard, Clinton could even capitalize on the public perception that he at least was trying to do the right thing. Dick Morris himself styled Clinton as a synthesizer,[50] one who would lead by following the flock as it meandered through the pasture:

> What the president is trying to do is take one from column A and one from column B. It's been described as centrism, as triangulation, but it's not those. It's common ground. It's a synthesis of the common wisdom of this country in the last forty-eight months.

The Lost Congress

Since World War II, only three presidents who initially assumed office through election have received a second term: Dwight Eisenhower, Ronald Reagan, and Bill Clinton. In the case of Reagan, reelection was perceived as a renewal of mandate, which prompted a huge effort before the inauguration of the second term to re-jig the administration's agenda. James A. Baker, Reagan's outgoing chief of staff and incoming Treasury secretary, led a concerted effort to enshrine tax reform as the keystone domestic commitment, while Nancy Reagan, working closely with National Security Adviser Robert C. ("Bud") McFarlane and concerned that her husband's foreign policies would leave a hawkish historic legacy, set the stage for détente with the Soviets that eventually would spell the end of the Cold War.

Bill Clinton's reelection prompted a decidedly more cautious tack. To be sure, the president had gleaned only a 49-percent plurality of votes. While an improvement of 6 percentage points over 1992, this result represented a moral defeat because it fell short of a clear majority, the prospect of which had operated as one motive for Clinton's unwillingness during 1996 to stump for a return of Congress to Democratic control.[51] Further, Republican fortunes in Congress, though mixed—losses in the House and gains in the Senate—seemed hardly to amount to a rap on the knuckles. The administration, however, appeared to be avoiding studiously the appearance of reading its victory—in some respects a formidable accomplishment—as a cue for rejuvenating its agenda.

What ensued instead was a tortuous period in which exactly what the administration would identify as core goals for the 105th Congress became more obscure by the day. Senate Democrats dreamed of taking at least a step toward health care reform—guaranteed coverage for 14 million children struck many as a sensible move. Meanwhile, the president's closest budget advisers pressed the administration to reflect at least some Republican priorities as a down payment on a bipartisan deal. A cabinet retreat set a balanced-budget agreement as the philosopher's stone for the second term. The 1997 State of the Union address offered a litany of modest changes to such areas as health care, taxes, highways, and summer jobs. The administration seemed to be gearing up for a repeat of 1995. Aides cited the constraints imposed by fiscal discipline—within twelve months the great debate would magically shift to how to deal with the surplus—and the lack of control of Congress as justification for the "poll-tested" nature of its agenda. Indeed, White House officials came clean with the fact that Clinton was still meeting weekly with his pollsters and campaign media team. They explained that the administration expected that much of its progress in programmatic terms would rely upon the cooperation of interest groups, state legislators, and school districts rather than Congress and the executive branch. Feeling bereft of a mandate to attempt more, the president sought a budget deal as a stepladder to the bully pulpit from which he could then address more substantive issues, such as raising educational standards and getting businesses to hire welfare recipients.[52]

Meanwhile, the Republicans under a chastened Newt Gingrich struck a programmatic posture that proved a mere shadow of the Contract with America. Gingrich offered mea culpas for being "too brash, too self-confident or too pushy" after the 1994 victory.[53] In early January, then, Gingrich put his caucus into review-the-situation mode—assigning examinations of initiatives on such issues as judicial activism, exports, defense policy, and race to various members of the Republican leadership. The product, which took nearly two months' gestation, emerged under the ponderous title, "Creating a Better America for Ourselves and Our Children."[54] Its hesitancy prompted Gingrich to lament that the "winning" team in the congressional elections had acted as if it had in fact suffered defeat.

Falling between Two Solitudes

With the extremes of their respective parties both amply represented in the new Congress, the Clinton-Gingrich centrist axis began to bow under irreconcilable pressure. Liberal Democrats publicly registered their dismay with Clinton. For instance, Peter Edelman, who had left his assistant secretary post in the Department of Health and Human Services over Clinton's signing the 1996 welfare reforms into law, stridently attacked the president for closing his eyes to the new provisions' consequences for the poor. On the right, Ralph Reed, the Christian Coalition director, derided Gingrich's legislative priorities: "We were elected to govern; we were not elected to ride at the back of the bus."[55] Ironically, the coveted budget deal simply widened the chasm between the two party caucuses—House Majority Leader Richard Armey asserted that he would not abide a budget deal about which he had not been consulted, while Senate Minority Leader Tom Daschle and House Minority Leader Richard Gephardt bemoaned their exclusion from key negotiations. By mid-May the Democratic battle lines tightened, with Gephardt sounding very much like he was attacking a Republican White House.[56] Not to be outdone, by mid-June Armey publicly broke with Gingrich over the deal:

> The basic rule around this town is that if you're not in the room and you don't make the agreement, you're not bound by it. . . . You just have to understand you're not going to get acquiescent, conforming behavior to everything that two or three . . . big shots think they agree to.[57]

Meanwhile, Clinton's hope that the budget deal would provide a stepladder to the bully pulpit proved quixotic. The administration agreed to Republican-driven changes to Medicare and Medicaid as large as any previously enacted, without proper review in hearings and according to a fast-track timetable.[58] In the course of two weeks in fall 1997 Clinton opposed and then embraced the proposal to place the Internal Revenue Service under a mainly citizen oversight board empowered to review and approve the agency's operations, budget requests, and long-term strategic plans. Suddenly, the president was endorsing a diminution of executive-branch power over the IRS, a move that Gene Sperling, his National Economic Council head, characterized as "a serious step backwards" and a "recipe for conflicts of interest." Others viewed it as co-optation of a Republican issues that had received the backing of some key Democrats in any case. But Clinton, through his own rhetoric when he tried to use the bully pulpit, basically undermined his potential case. In an astounding concession for the head of the executive branch, especially one who supposedly had been aggressively pursuing the reinvention of government for nearly five years, Clinton washed his hands of any blame for whatever ailed the IRS. He affirmed that he too had become "genuinely angered" at the agency, which had become "all-powerful, unaccountable, and often downright tone deaf." Interestingly, Clinton employed almost precisely the same language over six months later—long after the reform initiative had been approved but before final passage of enabling legislation—this time using the IRS as a whipping boy in one of his weekly radio talks.[59]

As if determined to knock him off the stepladder, congressional Democrats presented Clinton with a resounding rebuke in November when they refused to support legislation extending fast-track review of trade agreements. Apparently ignoring advice from Republican leaders to begin campaigning for the extension in spring 1997, Clinton had not made a concerted effort in support of the legislation until the fall, at which point his effort summoned up memories of the administration's frantic dealing prior to passage of the North American Free Trade Agreement in 1993. As one House Democrat commented, "I've been promised 16 bridges; now all I need is a river." In any case, the deal making failed to pull the fat out of the fire, and Clinton ultimately asked Congress to postpone indefinitely action on fast track. When pressed, many Democrats did not resist the temptation to put a fine point on why—some noting that the president had received payback for his triangulation strategy of the previous Congress and others taking cover in the fact that even Clintonite "New Democrats" failed to support the measure.[60]

Enter Monica

In January 1998 Clinton's alleged sexual affair with Monica Lewinsky got the year off to about as bad a start as one could imagine. The scandal so seized Washington that it placed a dark cloud over the State of the Union address. The administration had identified a reasonable menu of initiatives that might have finally built a stepladder to the bully pulpit, including tobacco controls, Medicare expansion, campaign-finance reform, further relief for child care expenses, patient protections, and a minimum wage increase.[61] But too often it found the president's efforts to advance this agenda drowned out by the Lewinsky matter.

Managing the scandal naturally became a central absorption of the president, the first lady, and, by extension, the White House itself. To be sure, fears of subpoenas deep into the White House organization put the onus on the president to differentiate between his Lewinsky legal team and the rest of the White House. As a result, most aides dealt day-to-day with the same frustration encountered by other supporters—they had to take the president's denials on face value without probing too deeply. The first inklings that key cabinet figures felt betrayed emerged soon after the allegations, and fears mounted in the White House that the administration lacked a long-term approach for handling the crisis.[62]

Nonetheless, the full consequences of the Lewinsky matter did not begin to bear down on the administration until summer 1998. Indeed, divisions in Republican ranks had taken their toll on the party's image. Budget Committee Chairman John R. Kasich became especially strident in advocating further spending reductions so as to insure tax cuts, while the pressure pushed Gingrich into staking out half of the already accrued budget surplus for tax cuts.[63] Astoundingly, when we consider the ground that would be lost by the Democrats in August and only partially regained in the November elections, commentators in late July had even begun to suggest that the Republicans might lose control of the House. For instance, a *Washington Post*/ABC poll had the public trusting Democrats over Republicans at coping with the main problems faced by the nation by 45 to 38 percent—exactly the margin garnered by the Republicans in response to the same question before their 1994 takeover of Congress.[64]

Still, Clinton had lost momentum even in some issue areas that involved simply a lectern-like approach, let alone a bully pulpit. Many of these incidents fit with his pattern of walking away from issues when they became difficult. In this regard, his U-turn on federal funding of needle-exchange programs—arguably a measure that an apt communicator could easily explain to the public—serves as an example. The administration had embraced the policy as a result of an interagency consultative process led by Health and Human Services Secretary Donna E. Shalala. The very morning that Shalala was slated to announce the program, however, she found that Clinton had gotten cold feet. Most significantly, the strongest opponent of the agreed initiative, National Drug Control Policy Director Barry McCaffrey, had done an end-run around his colleagues by using a conversation with Clinton on a flight back from Chile to plead his case.[65] In a move that seemed to speak volumes about Clinton's seeming paranoia about political risk, the president abandoned the program without even trying to deploy his powers of persuasion. If he shrank from the challenges of selling such a modest program, whose importance in the fight against AIDS is so obvious, when would he fight?

Clinton chose to fight on 17 August, after his testimony to the grand jury looking into the Lewinsky matter. After a grueling day, he returned to the private residence solarium, where Hillary Clinton and the president's lawyer, David E. Kendall, urged him to take a steely tone in an address that evening to the nation.[66] But this belligerent self-defense backfired, and soon analysts were projecting an upwards of twenty-seat swing to the Republicans in the House elections and perhaps a sixty-Republican Senate. Republican indignation then went over the top in September, when the House Judiciary Committee released tapes of Clinton's testimony; but, stunned by the image of the president squirming before what seemed to many an inquisition over sex, public sympathy swung back to the president. The result was that the Republicans lost five seats in the House and gained none in the Senate and, thus, while retaining majorities in both chambers, had suffered what appeared to be a moral defeat.

In any case, the Lewinsky scandal had put the president's agenda on hold by summer 1998. Some aides even went on record about the ground that had been lost. As Christopher Jennings, a White House policy coordinator, put it, many in the administration had developed a sense of "lost opportunities and missed opportunities. . . . We are disappointed in him for contributing to his problems in this area."[67] The reprieve provided by the Republicans' September misstep did allow the administration to rally around a few fairly small tangibles in the final budget deal before the elections. In fact, National Economic Council Director Gene Sperling exclaimed joyously: "There's no question that this week solidified that the president maintains significant force to pass and implement his key priorities."[68] Clinton's main accomplishment in the deal was $1.1 billion for 100,000 new teachers. This and other items in the package, however, came at the cost of zeroing out the $2.4 billion pension fund for District of Columbia police, firefighters, and teachers (the pension requirements would now be met through an annual mandatory appropriation—a dicey proposition for a fiscally vulnerable government). A closer look also revealed that the funds actually available in fiscal year 1999 would provide only 30,000 more teachers and that full funding up to 100,000 over six years would require an additional $11 billion.[69] Nonetheless, their leaders' concessions, which paved the way for Clinton's eleventh-hour triumph, infuriated Republican zealots and disturbed even moderates. The stage was set for Newt Gingrich's demise as leader, an event that his party's disappointing election results only accelerated.[70]

Is Competition over Agenda Setting the Clinton Legacy?

The closer we look at Newt Gingrich's rise and fall, the more it appears to be an anomic phenomenon stemming from the exceptional circumstances of the mid-1990s. The 1994 midterm elections would not have propelled Gingrich to power if the nation simply was coping with a weak president who seemed to have left a power vacuum. Instead, the elections took place during a period of protracted frustration with the seeming incapacity of presidents and Congresses to come to grips with the problems facing the country. Anger mounted among many segments of the middle class over their failure to realize their dreams while the system seemed to coddle minorities—perceptions that exasperated the conditions for anomy. Nineteen ninety-four was a flash in the pan, a temper tantrum. As soon as it passed, Gingrich's continued harangues appeared increasingly out of place.

Sadly, the Clinton camp, as we might expect, remained divided between two possible strategies in response. The first, favored by Leon Panetta, would have let the tantrum run its course while the administration, in alliance with congressional Democrats, awaited a timely moment for reasserting itself. The second, proffered by Dick Morris, would essentially co-opt the Gingrich line in more palatable language, with promises to revisit issues on which Clinton acceded to dominant opinion.

Of course, the president ended up adopting Morris's approach and, as a result, probably accommodated the Contract with America much more than was needed to vanquish Gingrichism. Also, this strategy squandered an entire presidential election campaign (1996) by astutely avoiding discussion of what really ails America. So long as this strategy persisted, the governability gap continued to widen—that is, the deferral of tough but soluble issues proceeded apace. Political discourse became exponentially detached from reality as the Republicans pressed their fanciful Contract and the administration's incantations said much the same thing but soothingly. Although the Contract went away after the 1996 election, the governability gap seemed to widen. For one thing, Clinton, exercising his accustomed caution, chose to fight the last war—recovery from the 1994 setback—rather than striking out as if he had received a fresh mandate. More profoundly, the animus between Republicans and Democrats had metamorphosed into bitter adversarial politics *within* as well as between parties. The cumulative distemper culminated, one hopes, in the out-of-control impeachment proceedings against Bill Clinton.

The paradox of that extravaganza rested in the fact that Clinton probably went much farther than required in accommodating the Republican revolution—especially when clear signs began to emerge that the public was developing a jaundiced view of Gingrich. Much of Clinton's difficulty, apart from his character vulnerabilities, rested with his failure to build a stepladder to the bully pulpit once, arguably, he could reclaim the presidential agenda-setting prerogatives after his 1996 election victory. In an era of budget surpluses, governments must, in the words of one senior Canadian official, relearn the management of choice, which, above all, involves "going beyond simply being a short-order cook" with eye-catching projects.[71] Clinton failed to rise to this challenge, and the Republicans, bereft of a political mandate, took the low road in order to keep the president off message.

At this point, a consideration of Joel Aberbach's observations about the emerging cyclical nature of agenda setting is appropriate, since some commentators might believe that it accounts for the Gingrich revolution. Aberbach posits that a pattern has emerged since the Nixon era in which the legislature and the executive engage in provocative attempts to wrest control of the agenda. Specifically, he states that the past few decades have been marked by "a cycle of intense competition for control of policy and administration that has changed patterns of governance, making governing more conflictual and contributing to public disillusionment with the entire process."[72] The result, in Aberbach's view, is the growing inability of the branches to share functions and to act interdependently.

The Gingrich ascendancy seems to have brought this process to its logical conclusion. But it produced a lot less fruit for the Republicans and the institutional power of Congress than we might have anticipated. Also, the issue of presidential versus congressional domination again appears up for grabs. In his rise to power, Gingrich operated brilliantly both within Congress and in the nation to exploit the governability gap. He traveled the nation stirring discontent and used the Contract with America both to attract a constituency and to serve as a focusing device to turn the 1994 election into one that masterfully stole the agenda from Clinton. The Contract offered an outlet for the high degree of national discontent by seeking to fill the governability gap.

At the end of the day, however, Gingrich took us back to square one. Insofar as the public, frustrated with Clinton and congressional politics as usual, had voted Republican because of that party's Contract and its vociferous leader, the 104th Congress undoubtedly proved a great disappointment. Still, the Gingrich era should put us on notice. The public psyche has become extremely volatile. A continued governability gap combined with especially weak presidential leadership still leaves the way open for anomic surges such as the one that brought Gingrich to power. Bill Clinton's failure at bully-pulpit governance—which itself lowered the bar from the more aggressive and comprehensive agenda the administration had set itself at the outset of its first term—provides further cause for concern. The combination of Clinton's character problems and his inability to step up to the plate when obvious opportunities for moral suasion presented themselves has placed his office in serious jeopardy of becoming no more than a lectern. How much irreversible damage will have accumulated when he leaves office in January 2001? Enough to seriously erode an already endangered institution.

4

The President as Legislative Leader

BARBARA SINCLAIR

What is Bill Clinton's legacy as legislative leader?[1] What strategies did he employ and with what policy results? Did Clinton develop strategies for effective legislative leadership in the treacherous environment of contemporary American politics that future presidents can emulate? Did he make mistakes from which they can learn?

When we consider a president's legacy, one of the first things we think about is his record as a legislative leader. Americans expect their president to serve as the nation's premier legislative leader. This was, however, not always so. Nineteenth-century presidents did not act as legislative leaders nor did Americans expect them to do so.[2] During the twentieth century and especially with the presidency of Franklin Roosevelt, legislative leadership came to be seen as central to the role of president; Americans came to expect their presidents to propose a legislative agenda for Congress and to engineer its enactment into law.[3]

The U.S. governmental system and the party system it has fostered make it difficult for presidents to be effective legislative leaders. The Constitution created a national government of separate branches sharing power and, by doing so, established a relationship of mutual dependence between the president and Congress. In terms of policymaking, the president was in the weaker position.[4] The legislative power is vested in an independently elected Congress; the president cannot even compel Congress to consider—much less pass—his legislative program. The only specifically legislative power the Constitution gives the president is the power to sign or veto legislation.

The weak and decentralized party system this constitutional structure fostered does not bind the president and congressional members of his party together in the way that a strong, centralized party system would. To be sure, even in the American party system, members of a party do tend to share policy preferences and have similar electoral interests. Yet the president and his fellow partisans in the House of Representatives and in the Senate are elected by different sets of voters at different times, and their electoral fortunes are only loosely related. Seldom do members of Congress feel that they owe their election directly to the president or that the president's success is the single most important determinant of their future reelection. The party system does not provide the president with great leverage vis-à-vis his fellow partisans in Congress.

Despite these structural barriers, presidents from Franklin Roosevelt to Richard Nixon commanded considerable resources for legislative leadership. During that period the Office of the President developed into an elaborate organization that provided the president with staff and expertise far beyond anything available to Congress. The spread of radio and then television greatly advantaged the president, who, by virtue of being a single executive and the head of government and lacking a singular competitor from the Congress, is by far the most visible elected official in the United States.[5] Congress was decentralized, lacked strong party leadership, and had severely limited legislative resources, particularly staff and access to independent expertise.

Since the mid-1970s, the context of presidential legislative leadership has changed. The decline in the U.S. economic growth rate ushered in a long period of legislative constraint, in which more and more decisions were perceived as zero-sum: to institute new programs required cutting old ones or raising taxes. This presented enormous problems for policymakers, especially for Democrats, whose notions of good public policy and thus of successful legislative leadership frequently entailed the creation of new programs that cost money. In the 1970s Congress significantly enhanced its legislative capabilities by increasing staff and creating entities such as the Congressional Budget Office to provide it with independent information. In the 1980s, as the parties polarized ideologically, congressional party leadership became stronger, more active, and more adept at media relations.[6] The news media and their role in politics changed, becoming more negative, more adversarial, and more central to the political process. By the 1990s, the development of the twenty-four-hour news cycle, media corporations' desperate pursuit of audiences in the highly competitive environment, and reporters' relentless pursuit of professional advancement had produced a rapid-fire electronic political discourse that multiplied competitors to the president in setting the agenda and framing issues.

These secular changes in political context affect the opportunities for and the character of presidential legislative leadership. Bill Clinton was the first Democrat to serve as president in this new environment. The story of Clinton as legislative leader is largely a story of key political actors—the president, congressional Democrats, and congressional Republicans—attempting to adjust their expectations and strategies to a context that had changed in major ways and that continued to change during the course of the Clinton presidency, most notably with the Republicans winning control of the Congress.

Most political actors have both policy and electoral goals; they want to make good public policy and they want electoral success. Political context determines which strategies are effective at advancing each of these goals and, since they may conflict, at striking a satisfactory balance between them. Just surviving and certainly prospering in a significantly changed political context requires adjusting strategies and often expectations as well.

The Clinton presidency can be divided into three periods, each distinguished by a distinctive political context: the 103d Congress (1993–94), during which the new president enjoyed Democratic majorities in both chambers of Congress; the 104th Congress before the budget debacle—essentially 1995—during which a politically weakened Clinton faced confident new Republican majorities in Congress; the period following the budget debacle—essentially 1996 on—during which the political strength of the president and the congressional Republican majority was more evenly balanced. This essay examines the political context and the strategies the actors developed to advance their goals within each of these periods. Politics and policy in each period are then briefly reviewed; I emphasize those events that best illustrate the impact on the policy process of the longer-term changes in political context, such as the greater media role and heightened partisanship.

Great Expectations: Clinton and the 103d Congress

In 1992 Bill Clinton ran for president as a self-proclaimed "New Democrat," fiscally responsible, tough on crime, sensitive to traditional American values such as personal responsibility, and embracing the new economy but dedicated to using government actively to enable people to succeed within the new economy, through investment in education and job training and access to health care. The New Democrat approach was an attempt to counter the negative image of the Democratic Party as addicted to "tax and spend" policies and culturally out of touch with the average American, an image that many believed responsible for the party's defeat in five of six presidential elections since 1968. Although premised on a less intrusive role for the federal government, Clinton's version of the New Democratic "third way" to government by no means entailed a minimalist program. The program Clinton laid out in his first presidential address to a joint session of Congress included a multifaceted economic plan that included deficit reduction and an immediate stimulus package, health care reform, "ending welfare as we know it," NAFTA, and comprehensive crime legislation as the most prominent items on a big, complex, and ambitious agenda.[7]

Potential problems lurked in this program. For a president who had received only 43 percent of the popular vote and thus was not seen as having a mandate for major policy change, it was very ambitious. Because it was complex and did not fit neatly into established ideological categories, it would be hard to explain to the public and the news media. Although much in the program was broadly supported among Democrats, some issues—free trade and welfare reform, for example—would likely split the party in Congress.

In the wake of their first presidential victory since 1976, however, Democrats were euphoric and expectations ran high. They had high hopes that policy goals long stymied by Republican presidents would now come to fruition. Congressional Democrats were eager to legislate. "The climate feels like when JFK was elected," House Majority Leader Dick Gephardt was reported to have told the big freshmen class. "There's now a real opportunity to have a real impact on the future of the country," a senior congressional Democrat noted.

Clinton, then, had proposed an ambitious policy agenda, most of which required congressional action to implement; congressional Democrats supported much of that agenda, significant parts of which stemmed from their initiatives, and were eager for major legislative accomplishments. The congressional Democratic Party had become more ideologically homogeneous since the Carter presidency and, in the House, had vested considerably greater powers and resources in its leadership. Furthermore, Democrats believed they had to break the gridlock and produce. Almost all believed that, given united control, the public would hold them collectively responsible if they failed. "Bill Clinton's success is our success, his failure is our failure," said Representative Bob Matsui (D-Calif.). "The public wants the elimination of gridlock."[8]

Strategies for a Period of United Control

With both the policy and electoral goals of the president and his congressional party so closely aligned, the best strategy for the president and congressional Democrats entailed cooperation and working together closely. The congressional majority leadership, especially in the House, commands procedural, organizational, and informational resources invaluable for building coalitions. The president has resources—favors and especially the bully pulpit—that make him a valuable ally.

For Republicans, the political context provided few incentives for cooperating with the president. The House Republican Party has become increasingly conservative since the mid-1970s; the 1992 elections brought in a large and almost uniformly far-right Republican freshman class. Although nominally led by Bob Michel, a pragmatist from an earlier era, the House Republicans' real leader was Minority Whip Newt Gingrich, an aggressive far-right conservative who believed that confrontation, not cooperation, was the best strategy for winning a House majority.[9] On most issues, Clinton's policy preferences and those of House Republicans were much too far apart to make cooperation a reasonable strategy for either. Clearly, their electoral goals were in conflict; and Clinton's lack of a mandate meant that few individual Republicans would feel constituency pressure to support the president's proposals.

In the Senate, institutional rules give rank-and-file senators great power. In most cases, any senator can offer an unlimited number of amendments to a piece of legislation on the Senate floor, and those amendments need not even be germane. A senator can hold the Senate floor indefinitely unless cloture is invoked, which requires an extraordinary majority of sixty votes. Extended debate became more and more frequent in the 1970s and 1980s as senators' willingness to use that power increased.[10] Since, in the 103d Congress, Democrats were short of the sixty votes needed to shut off debate, Senate rules gave Republicans considerable leverage—making it likely the necessary votes would seldom come cheap. With the context providing few incentives for cooperation, Republicans, hesitantly at first, settled on a strategy of obstructionism.

Politics and Policy in the 103d Congress

Determining an appropriate strategy is only the first step. Were the political actors able to implement their strategies and with what results? How successful were they in policy and in political terms?

Acutely aware of the rocky relationship between Jimmy Carter, the last Democratic president, and congressional Democrats, both the Clinton administration and congressional Democrats set out to avoid those problems, and, by and large, their relationship during most of the 103d was reasonably good. Many Clinton appointees in the departments as well as in the White House were people congressional Democrats knew and respected. Access to the president himself and to the top levels of the executive branch expanded enormously. Agreement on agenda and approach encouraged committees to work closely with the administration. "It's a whole new world," a senior congressional aide said about relations with the administration in 1993.

Throughout the 103d Congress, the working relationship between Clinton and the Democratic congressional leadership was cooperative and close, if not always smooth. Both Speaker Tom Foley and Senate Majority Leader George Mitchell were convinced that the congressional Democrats' fate was closely linked to the Clinton administration's success. "Nobody's going to have divided government to blame anymore," Foley remarked as the new Congress convened. "We will have the first opportunity we've had in a long time to prove government can work—and people will be watching."[11]

Members' extremely high expectations about both policy and district benefits, as well as the differences in constituency and institutional perspective that members of Congress and the president always display, assured that the relationship between Clinton and congressional Democrats would not be without frictions, however. Members complained that the administration did not consult them often enough or keep them sufficiently informed, that it was too slow on matters of special interest to them, and that the bureaucracy was not as responsive as they would have liked. Some griped that the president was asking for too much too quickly, others that he was not bold enough. As a White House liaison staffer explained:

> One of our problems is that we have to tell people "no" a lot, and a lot of times legitimately. This is both on big legislative initiatives and on things for their district. During the past twelve years they were not getting anything from the administration and they saw that as political. Then after twelve years the dam burst, and they found out that there was not much water there.

Different constituencies and different institutional perspectives sometimes caused problems between the president and the congressional leadership as well. Differing electoral constituencies contributed to conflicting positions on the North American Free Trade Agreement (NAFTA). Trade is an issue that highlights differences among Democrats. Majority Whip David Bonior, from a rust-belt Michigan district, and Majority Leader Richard Gephardt of Missouri opposed NAFTA; Speaker Tom Foley of Washington supported it. Clinton, who had committed himself to a free trade position during the campaign, had to rely on Republican votes for approval of the trade agreement.

Representing the interests of the House Democratic membership, its key constituency, the House leadership disagreed with the president's position on aspects of campaign finance reform legislation.

More frequent than policy disagreements were frictions that arose from different institutional perspectives. Presidents, especially ones with ambitious agendas, want to get many things done and done quickly, while congressional leaders know that the legislative process is naturally slow and pushing it too much can create problems. For example, members cut out of the action in the name of speed will have less stake in the success of legislative proposals, and asking members to take too many tough votes too close together is likely to be counterproductive.

From the congressional leadership's perspective, the White House sometimes did not provide the help with public opinion that it might have. "There is not as good coordination of the message of the week between the White House and the Hill as we would like; there will be times when we could very much use a lot of real emphasis on an issue that is coming to a head, where the White House is off on something else," an aide complained. And sometimes the content of the White House message made the leadership uncomfortable. The administration, the leadership believed, sometimes came very close to Congress-bashing. "There can be a problem when the administration decides to counter the Perot phenomenon as, say, with reinventing government because that inevitably poses Congress as a villain and that can cause ripples," a legislative staff member explained.

By and large, however, the relationship between the Democratic leadership and the White House was good. Clinton showed himself to be a willing and adept one-on-one persuader; he took an energetic part in efforts to mobilize votes. The congressional leaders, for the most part, were loyal and effective field commanders in the battle over the president's program.

The first months of the Clinton administration provide object lessons in how strong partisanship, Senate individualism, and more obtrusive news media have changed politics and the policymaking process and also illustrate the continued importance of structural factors such as electoral arrangements and election outcomes. These early months were a period of considerable policy accomplishment but frequent public relations and Senate-related woes. The former illustrates that united control does make a difference; the impact of the latter show what the limits of that difference are. Family- and medical-leave legislation, a central element of Clinton's agenda and a top priority of congressional Democrats, passed the House on 3 February and the Senate on 4 February; President Clinton signed it on 5 February. The House passed "motor voter" legislation to make registering to vote easier on 4 February and, although Republicans used Senate rules to delay and exact some concessions, the Senate passed it by mid-March. Congress had passed both bills before with strong Democratic support, but President Bush had vetoed them. Congressional committees quickly began work on other legislation that had been stymied previously by opposition from Republican presidents and also on Clinton administration initiatives. None of the president's proposals were declared "dead on arrival."

Some long-sought goals of congressional Democrats were accomplished without legislation. On 22 January President Clinton signed executive orders to lift the "gag rule" prohibiting abortion counseling in federally funded family-planning clinics, eliminate the ban on federal funding of medical research using fetal tissue from elective abortions, and reverse the policy barring U.S. aid to international organizations that perform or promote abortion.[12]

In the media, the early legislative successes were overshadowed by controversies that made better headlines. The dispute over gays in the military demonstrates the limitations of a president's control over the media agenda. The administration never considered the issue of top tier importance and certainly did not want it to be portrayed as its number-one priority. Yet the White House could not deflect the media focus and, consequently, had to devote enormous amounts of time to the issue when so much else needed to be done.

The controversy also highlights the extent to which Senate individualism poses a problem for presidents. Senator Sam Nunn, the highly respected chairman of the Armed Services Committee, opposed Clinton's proposal to lift the ban on gays in the military and took on the newly elected president of his party vocally and publicly; for doing so, he received a great deal of media attention. Although Nunn eventually played a key role in working out a compromise, by then a considerable amount of damage to Clinton's image had been done.

Perhaps most important, the controversy over gays in the military—as well as that over Zöe Baird's nomination as attorney general—illustrates that when members of Congress must choose between supporting a president of their own party and following intense constituency sentiment, constituency usually wins out. In both cases, Capitol Hill was deluged by phone calls and letters, and these messages were predominately and vociferously opposed to the president. Clinton had little choice but to compromise significantly on gays in the military and to withdraw the Baird nomination. Even if he could have won in a showdown, as he might have on Baird, the cost would have been too high. No president can expect the members of his party in Congress to vote repeatedly against strong constituency sentiment, nor, since he has an interest in their reelection, can he lightly ask them to do so.

Another early battle that the Administration lost illustrates an increasingly frequently used strategy, one that the new context encourages and that Clinton's opponents used against him a number of times in the 103d Congress, ultimately with devastating effect. Combining aggressive use of the Senate's nonmajoritarian rules and an adept public relations campaign, Republicans managed to defeat Clinton's stimulus plan, one facet of his economic program. Republicans successfully painted the legislation as consisting of wasteful pork-barrel spending and thus were able to kill it through a filibuster without paying a political price—a success which emboldened them.

Political actors have always attempted to use constituency sentiment to influence members of Congress. With partisan and ideological polarization and the suffusion of the political arena by news media with a negative bias and a voracious appetite for conflict, policy battles are increasingly fought in the public arena through public relations wars.[13] During the Clinton presidency, the trend toward waging policy battles through the media accelerated. The fate of Clinton's most important initiatives—the economic program and health-care reform—as well as the political costs of the battles over them, were strongly affected by such PR wars.

To deal with the deficit, slow growth, and a lack of public investment in key areas, Clinton proposed an economic program consisting of an immediate stimulus to jumpstart the sluggish economy, major long-term investment spending in areas such as education and infrastructure, and deficit reduction through tax increases on the wealthy and spending cuts in less essential programs. Although congressional Democrats supported the broad outlines of the program, they knew it would be tough to pass; spending cuts and tax increases are always opposed by the groups affected. The Republicans' decision to oppose the program all-out and their successful campaign to depict it as consisting primarily of taxes on the middle class increased the difficulty of passing it and the cost to Democrats of doing so.

Working together closely and using all the institutional and political tools available to them, Clinton and the congressional leadership enacted most of the economic program. Republicans had killed the stimulus program, but the rest was passed through the budget process and thus protected from filibusters. The congressional leaders negotiated several crucial changes to garner necessary support at a number of stages in the process. The Democratic whip system, the congressional leaders, and Clinton himself all personally lobbied members to support the package, and other influential groups and individuals were enlisted in the effort. When necessary, Clinton made deals: Dennis DeConcini (D-Ariz.) agreed to switch his vote in return for several policy concessions, including a lessening of the tax bite on Social Security recipients; freshman Senator Russell Feingold (D-Wisc.) cut a deal on bovine growth hormone; and a promise of a commission on entitlements finally induced Senator Bob Kerrey (D-Neb.) to declare his support after he had very publicly criticized the package and indicated he might defect.[14] Although the program had survived by a single vote at several steps in the process, on 10 August 1993 Clinton signed it into law.

Passing the economic program was a major legislative victory for President Clinton and congressional Democrats, one made possible by united control of the legislative and executive branches, the more cohesive and, especially in the House, more strongly led Democratic congressional party, and the budget process, which barred opponents from using the filibuster against the budget bills. This victory, however, was costly. House Democrats were upset about being asked to vote for an unpopular BTU tax, which was then dropped in the Senate. Especially after the 1994 elections, congressional Democrats frequently used the term being "BTUed" to mean being induced to support something politically perilous and then abandoned. Democrats in the House and loyalist Senate Democrats grumbled that the president had made too many concessions to individual senators to get their votes. The basic problem, however, was that members were being asked to support broadly unpopular legislation. When Democrats cast the critical final votes, they did so in a context in which constituent phone calls were preponderantly negative.

The public had strongly supported Clinton's economic plan initially, but maintaining support over the long period required from introduction to enactment is not easy. The complexity of Clinton's program put him at a disadvantage vis-à-vis the simple Republican message of opposition to tax increases. "It was a crucial victory," a perceptive House Democrat said shortly after the economic program's enactment, "but this is not a model for the future." To pass legislation making major policy changes, members need public support. Despite considerable policy agreement with the president and the perception that their fate was, at least in part, tied to his, Democrats in Congress could not be expected to support his programs if their constituents opposed them. The health care reform battle demonstrated that, under such circumstances, they would not provide such support again so soon.

Health care reform was a central issue in Bill Clinton's winning presidential campaign, ranking in priority behind only the economy. Whether to undertake a major effort to overhaul health care early in Clinton's term was, therefore, never in question; but no one involved believed it would be easy. The United States spends about one-seventh of its gross domestic product on health care—reform would not only directly touch everyone; it would be immensely complex and would affect the economic interests of a large number of powerful groups. Attempting a comprehensive reform of the health care system was, thus, a gamble—one that the president and congressional Democrats lost.

For Clinton's health care plan, the battle for public opinion was decisive. Early on, the policy process appeared to be taking a traditional course. Clinton's speech unveiling his plan was a major success, and polls showed the public supported his proposal. Key Republicans, including Senate Minority Leader Bob Dole, indicated they were open to some sort of compromise. Many Republicans, believing that health care reform was probably going to pass, wanted to take part in shaping the legislation and garner some of the credit. But crucial Republicans on the hard right of their party, Senator Phil Gramm (Tex.) and most important, Rep. Newt Gingrich (Ga.), decided to go all out in opposing health care reform, which they believed to be detrimental to their party's electoral and policy goals.[15] Groups with a major financial stake in health care reform had started lobbying against the Clinton plan in Washington and at the grassroots early in 1993. In the fall the Health Insurance Association of America (HIAA), a group of smaller insurance companies that would likely lose out under a Clinton-style plan, launched a television advertising blitz. "Harry and Louise" saturated the airwaves with their scary stories of what the Clinton plan entailed.

The public relations campaign orchestrated by opposition interest groups and Republicans turned public opinion around. Through about $100 million worth of media and grassroots campaigning, opponents persuaded the public that the Clinton plan might well lower the standard of health care available to them, decrease their choice of doctors, and raise their costs. The administration and its congressional and interest-group allies attempted to counter this campaign, but the White House could not devote the single-minded attention to the issue its opponents could; its resources paled in comparison to those of its opponents, and it confronted a much more difficult job: to explain an extremely complex problem in a media environment hostile to complexity and to sell a complicated solution to a public disillusioned about government's ability to solve problems.

The success of the opponents of the Clinton health care plan in the battle for public opinion translated into success in the legislative arena. It was the altered views of their constituents that made it impossible for Democrats to put together majorities for any significant health care bill. Members feared being blamed at election time for their failure to produce, but they feared voting for an unpopular plan even more.

Republicans' early and politically costless victory on the stimulus program, combined with Clinton's unimpressive public approval ratings, convinced Republicans that blocking the president's initiatives carried little risk. To an extent unprecedented in modern American history, the filibuster became a partisan tool during the 103d Congress. Republicans wielded the weapon throughout the Congress but especially at the end, when time pressure makes obstructionism especially effective. The health care battle had absorbed an enormous amount of time and effort, making the end-of-the-session crunch even worse than usual. Republicans decided to deprive President Clinton and congressional Democrats of victories by using the filibuster blatantly and often. Republican filibusters killed campaign finance and lobbying reform bills. Although unsuccessful in the end, Republicans filibustered and tried to prevent passage of a massive crime bill, the California Desert Protection Act, and a comprehensive education bill—even though all had had considerable bipartisan support earlier in the process. Republican threats of obstructionist floor tactics were major contributors to the death of important bills revamping the Superfund program, revising clean drinking water regulations, overhauling outdated telecommunications law, and applying federal labor laws to Congress. In the 103d Congress, 47 percent of major measures encountered some sort of extended debate-related problem discernible from the public record and most of these were partisan.[16] By contrast, in the 101st, President Bush's first Congress, 28 percent of measures encountered some sort of filibuster problem and these were not necessarily partisan in origin.

The combination of the health care debacle and the messy impasse at the end of the Congress had a devastating impact on the Democratic Party's image. Democrats had promised that with control of both Congress and the presidency they would end gridlock and show that government could function in the people's interest. Instead, an already cynical public saw bitter partisan combat and seemingly no policy progress at all. The news media judged the 103d Congress a dismal failure, the worst Congress in fifty years, according to the *Washington Post*. Democrats would pay dearly for their failures in the 1994 elections. Their substantial policy accomplishments went unrecognized and unrewarded; some even proved to be as politically costly as their failures.

One battle proved to have particularly pernicious long-term consequences for the relationship between Clinton and congressional Democrats. Congress and the administration had been working together on a comprehensive anti-crime bill during much of 1994. Initially the legislation had garnered considerable Republican support, but when the conference report returned to the House for final approval, Republican leaders decided on all-out opposition. Democrats hoped and Republicans feared that a successful anti-crime bill would go a long way toward reducing the Republicans' electoral advantage on the issue; many Republicans believed the bill spent too much for prevention and was not harsh enough in its penalties; and the National Rifle Association, an important Republican interest group, opposed the assault-weapons ban the bill contained. With only eleven Republicans voting for it, the procedural motion to bring the conference report to a vote was defeated. Fifty-eight Democrats voted against their leadership and the president; ten were Congressional Black Caucus members who objected to the dropping of a "racial justice" provision in conference; most of the rest were members in whose districts the NRA and the pro-gun sentiment it represents were strong.

To save the bill, the president and the Democratic Party leadership had two courses open to them: drop the assault-weapons ban and pick up most of the pro-gun Democrats or make a deal with moderate Republicans who supported the ban but wanted cuts in crime-prevention programs. The Democratic leadership, always eager to unite their membership, argued for the former course; the top three House Democrats went to the White House and "begged" Clinton to do so, according to leadership aides. The congressional leaders, who had not been enthusiastic about the assault-weapons ban to start with because it split the party, feared it would hurt the reelection bids of some of their members who had voted for the ban and even some who had opposed it. Clinton, who had been unmercifully excoriated for abandoning his principles when the going got tough and even for not having any at all, decided that backing down on the assault-weapons ban would be politically too costly and opted instead to make a deal with moderate Republicans. Once the crime bill got into trouble, the best strategy for Clinton and the best strategy for congressional Democrats no longer coincided, a circumstance that became much more frequent after the Republicans won congressional majorities.

Many congressional Democrats believed that the assault-weapons ban and the spectacle of the crime bill's initial defeat cost them control of the House in the 1994 elections. A number of incumbent losses, that of Speaker Foley himself and that of Judiciary Committee Chairman Jack Brooks among them, were attributed directly to their vote for legislation including the provision. Even worse, according to a number of Democrats, however, was that the highly visible defeat on the floor, when combined with the health-care failure, made the Democrats look hopelessly inept and incapable of governing.

In sum, despite the "New Democratic" rhetoric, Clinton in the 103d sought to emulate the old Democratic model of presidential legislative leadership; he offered a highly ambitious program and he worked closely, though not always in complete harmony, with his congressional party, which controlled both houses of Congress. This strategy yielded policy accomplishments that were considerable in absolute terms but meager in terms of expectations and that were, furthermore, overshadowed by the massive political failure of the Democrats' losing control of Congress in the 1994 elections. For Republicans, a strategy of obstructionism that combined aggressive use of the Senate's nonmajoritarian rules with adept PR offensives paid off in policy and even more handsomely in electoral terms.

The 103d Congress made clear the media's central role in politics and the consequent imperative for political actors to make PR strategies central to their policy battle plans. Since significant policy change requires public support, the task of enacting policy change can be made far more difficult if such support can be undermined through a PR campaign. Given the tools available to a Senate minority, a strategy of obstructionism is easy for a partisan minority to execute successfully and, in an environment of pervasive public and media cynicism about government and politics, usually entails little political cost. Making a policy initiative both salient and widely popular would raise the costs of policy opposition and thus prove an effective counter, but this, in turn also requires a successful PR campaign.

Congressional Dominance: The New Republican Majority in 1995

In the 1994 elections, Republicans won control of the Senate and, astonishingly and for the first time in forty years, of the House as well. The new House majority included—and depended upon—a freshman class of seventy-three, most of whom were strongly ideological conservatives, many with little previous political experience. In an unprecedented move, House Republicans had before the elections drafted a policy agenda dubbed the Contract with America and most GOP candidates, incumbents and challengers, had pledged themselves to bringing all the items on it to a vote within the first 100 days.[17] Although polls showed that most voters were unaware of the Contract, euphoric House Republicans saw themselves as revolutionaries mandated to enact revolutionary policy change. Certainly the news media would judge them by whether they fulfilled their promises.

Newt Gingrich, the House Republicans' leader and new Speaker, was credited with the win by most Republicans and the media. The Contract with America had been Gingrich's idea, and he orchestrated its realization. He had also recruited many of the new members and had helped them with fund raising and campaign advice. The election results, thus, gave Gingrich enormous prestige and also provided him with a membership that was both unusually ideologically homogeneous and determined to enact major policy change.

Strategies of Revolution and Resistance

House Republicans believed that, given the circumstances, a congressional majority party dominance model was feasible, and they attempted to follow that strategy in the 104th Congress until electoral fears forced them to change. First with the Contract and then with their set of proposals to balance the budget, House Republicans did indeed set the agenda in 1995. Through a combination of strong party leadership and a committed and disciplined membership, Republicans brought the entire Contract to the House floor within the first 100 days as promised and passed all but the term limits constitutional amendment requiring a two-thirds majority. They drafted and passed, both on an almost entirely partisan basis, an ambitious balanced-budget plan that included big tax cuts, large cuts in domestic spending, and the revamping of major entitlement programs such as Medicare.

In the face of this juggernaut, the White House decided to lie low. Commentators questioned the president's relevance, but the White House knew that there was little the administration could do in the House in the early months. It concentrated instead on the Senate, where the Democratic minority had much more powerful tools at its disposal. To influence policy at all, the president and congressional Democrats knew they had to adopt the erstwhile Republican strategy of obstructionism. To that end, the House Democrats, operating in a majority-rule chamber, could not contribute much initially, but the Senate filibuster and the presidential veto provided Democrats with significant resources.

Both Democrats and Republicans knew that, in the struggle ahead, the public's reaction—and thus the PR war to shape public opinion—would be key. The House Republican leaders certainly knew that the Senate and the White House constituted potential veto points. Gingrich and his followers believed that they could rouse public opinion and put so much pressure on the Senate and the president that they would have to choose between going along with the House Republican agenda or committing political suicide. For their part, Democrats in the White House and in Congress knew they had to discredit the Republicans' policy proposals. Believing those proposals were indeed disastrous for the country and still smarting from the Republican campaign against them and their policy proposals in the previous Congress, few Democrats had much compunction about attacking the Republicans. How far to pursue those attacks and what sort of legislative action should follow sometimes divided the president and congressional Democrats, however; congressional Democrats' minority status meant that the best strategy for the president and their best electoral strategy were not necessarily the same.

Politics and Policy of a Failed Revolution

The Contract items that had flown through the House ran into all sorts of roadblocks in the Senate. Not only Democrats but moderate Republicans as well objected to many of the more extreme measures, and no public groundswell demanding action emerged. By the end of 1995 only five of twenty-one Contract items—and those mostly noncontroversial ones—had become law. Meanwhile, Democrats pursued their media strategy of painting the Republicans as extremists and the Republicans' budget as cutting Medicare to fund a tax cut for the rich. By summer, liberal interest groups had rebounded from the shock of the Republican victory and picked up their activity; environmental groups especially worked effectively to alert their members to Republican legislative proposals.

Republicans managed to get through both chambers a massive reconciliation bill that cut taxes and that would balance the budget in seven years by drastically reducing domestic spending and restructuring a number of the biggest federal entitlement programs, including Medicare. Because budget bills are protected by law from the filibuster, Democrats were unable to stop the legislation in the Senate. Clinton, however, threatened to veto the bill because it cut too much from education, the environment, Medicare, and Medicaid.

Using a traditional congressional strategy, Republicans had attached provisions to appropriations bills that they knew Clinton would veto if the bills came to him as free-standing legislation. Clinton objected to funding cuts and to the extraneous provisions, and he threatened vetoes. Appropriations bills fund the government; if they do not become law by the beginning of the fiscal year, much of the government shuts down. Clinton vetoed the reconciliation bill and several appropriations bills and threatened to veto others.

Republicans were convinced that Clinton would cave in under pressure from the public. When negotiations between them and the White House failed to produce an agreement they considered satisfactory, they several times let appropriations lapse and shut down the government, in one case for twenty-two days over Christmas. Not only did Clinton hold fast, but the public reaction was the opposite of what House Republicans had expected; the public blamed the Republicans, not the president, and Clinton's job-approval ratings went up.[18] The Republicans had, after all, been threatening since early 1995 to shut down the government if they did not get their way, while Clinton had made several compromise budget proposals.

When in early 1996 Republicans voted to reopen the government without having gotten Clinton to agree to a budget deal on their terms, they tacitly admitted that their strategy had been a failure. They had not succeeded in raising the groundswell of public pressure that would force the Senate and the president to go along with their agenda. Consequently, more than a year after their great electoral triumph, House Republicans had enacted hardly any of their major bills, and their electoral prospects looked questionable.

Dealing without Cooperating: Clinton and Congress after the Budget Debacle

The Republicans, then, had neither policy accomplishments nor popularity to show for all their efforts. Democrats had successfully painted them as both "extreme" and "do nothing." Polls showed they were in real danger of losing their House majority. Clinton, in contrast, was in a much stronger position than he had been a year before. Far from being "irrelevant," he had emerged from the confrontation with his reputation as a skillful politician and his popularity with the public much enhanced. Clinton, however, also lacked legislative accomplishments to take into his reelection campaign. His victories had been almost exclusively negative ones; he had prevented Republicans from making policy changes he opposed. He and his campaign adviser, Dick Morris, believed that voters still expected the president to act as legislative leader and to have policy achievements to point to.[19]

Clinton's renewed political strength and the Republicans' fraying sense of mandate put agenda control into question. Clinton, who had dominated the agenda in the 103d Congress but had been totally eclipsed in 1995, now had a renewed opportunity to influence the agenda to his policy and electoral benefit. However, the uncertain mood of the electorate, as well as Republicans' continued control over the congressional schedule, made taking advantage of the opportunity a difficult and delicate enterprise.

Strategies of Combat and Compromise

With Clinton and congressional Republicans needing legislative accomplishments to take into the 1996 elections, compromise seemed to be the best—in fact, the only—strategy for both. Clinton possessed the veto and had shown himself a skillful veto bargainer; on most issues, he could count on Senate Democrats working with him and using their procedural resources toward a goal they shared. On the other hand, Republicans, by virtue of their majority status, controlled great procedural resources, especially in the House. Neither could overwhelm the other.

Yet formidable obstacles to compromise stood in the way. The policy differences between Republicans and Clinton were vast, assuring that the necessary compromises would be acutely painful for one or both. Their agendas and priorities were by and large very different. There were not a lot of policy areas where there existed a change to the status quo that both Clinton and the Republicans preferred. The relationship between Clinton and the House Republicans was marred by a deep distrust; in particular, many House Republicans believed that Clinton had won the budget fight through trickery and by lying to their leaders and to the public. The most ideologically committed Republicans, including a considerable proportion of the large freshman class, continued to resist a strategy of compromise until the summer of 1996. Furthermore, some of them advocated bringing up issues, such as repeal of the assault-weapons ban, on which combat was assured. For their part, congressional Democrats, especially the large liberal contingent in the House, opposed a compromise strategy for both policy and electoral reasons. Their success in portraying Republicans as extremists and as legislatively inept promised to pay off handsomely in the elections, giving Democrats a good chance to take back the House. They objected to any strategy that would blunt their most effective message.

The strictly limited coincidence of interests between Clinton and congressional Republicans, the absence of a great imbalance in political strength between them, and the need of both to keep their parties from splintering dictated a combination strategy of PR combat and selective compromise for both. The policy distance and the lack of trust gave each strong incentives to attempt to change the balance of political strength through PR efforts so that, if and when they did sit down to deal, the issue would be one that advantaged them and was framed in a way favorable to their position. The effectiveness of Republicans' procedural resources or of Clinton's veto could be significantly enhanced or diminished by a successful PR campaign.

Politics and Policy in 1996 and Beyond

In implementing the strategy, the trick for Clinton was to balance the combat and compromise modes in a way that allowed him to rack up legislative achievements, first to take into the 1996 elections and then to burnish his legacy, without, however, compromising so much that he alienated congressional Democrats. Even when his party is in the minority, a president is still dependent on its support. If he must rely largely on the other party, the policy result will almost always be farther from his preferred position because he is dealing from weakness; he needs his party to sustain his veto and thereby maintain his bargaining strength; and, to achieve reelection, he cannot alienate the party's core constituencies that members of Congress represent.

A popular interpretation of the Democrats' 1994 election disaster argued that the 103d Congress's liberal thrust was at fault. Clinton had run as a moderate New Democrat, the argument went; but, once in office he had moved left. Dick Morris was known to contend that Clinton had allowed himself to get too close to the liberal congressional Democratic establishment in his first two years and that, to win reelection in 1996, Clinton needed to "triangulate," to position himself in the center of the ideological spectrum and distance himself from his congressional party.[20]

Clinton did respond to the 1994 elections by moving towards the center, especially in terms of the issues he emphasized. Both his desire to respond to the message sent by the voters and his desire for legislative achievements dictated that response. To stay relevant, political actors must adjust to the political context in which they operate. A president seen as irrelevant is unlikely to win reelection or significantly affect policy. Still, Clinton's policy and electoral goals kept him far closer to other Democrats than to the Republican Party, which had moved sharply right in the 1990s.[21]

Clinton's reelection program was clearly a response to the change in political context. He proposed no grand initiatives but rather a list of more modest items. Still using the New Deal/Great Society model as its standard, the press derided Clinton's proposals as a micro agenda. Clinton, however, had decided that the political context made the old model untenable. He had, after all, tried it in the 103d Congress with limited policy success and disastrous electoral consequences. The 1996 Clinton strategy was to propose initiatives to address issues people care about but to keep them small so that opponents could not portray them as scary big government programs and so that voters would believe they might actually be doable.

Clinton aimed to stake out positions that allowed him to deal from strength. The strength of political actors' positions determines the costs of compromise or of continued combat. In April 1996, again in the fall of 1996, and in the fall of 1998 as well, Clinton and the congressional Republicans came to agreement on spending bills. In all three cases, Clinton was in a strong position, in the first instance because Republicans were desperate to get the budget impasse behind them, in the second and third, because Republicans were even more desperate to avoid another government shutdown shortly before elections. Consequently, Clinton was able to work closely with congressional Democrats, to involve them centrally in the negotiations, and to forge deals that most congressional Democrats found satisfactory.

The reversal of political fortunes after the budget debacle emboldened Democrats, who began a campaign to raise the minimum wage. In his 1996 State of the Union address, Clinton had advocated raising the minimum wage, but, although the proposal was popular with the American public, it was anathema to the conservative Republicans who led and made up the bulk of the Republican majorities in the House and Senate. The proposal was expected to go nowhere. Through an adept combination of a media strategy and the use of the procedural devices available to the minority in the Senate, Democrats made the issue a highly salient one. Senate Democrats offered the minimum-wage increase as an amendment to every bill considered on the Senate floor, compelling the Republican Senate leadership to keep legislation off the floor; and the Senate ground to a halt. Congressional Democrats, the White House, and organized labor all worked to keep the issue in the news. Public approval of a minimum-wage increase went to 85 percent. Eventually political pressure forced Republicans to deal, and by then they did so from a position of weakness.

By the summer of 1996, news stories branding the 104th Congress the least productive in history and polls showing that Republicans might lose the House produced a Republican shift in strategy. The "our way or no way" strategy, which House Republicans had moved away from tentatively and haltingly after the budget debacle, was now largely abandoned. As the election approached, Clinton also became increasingly willing to deal. Compromises were reached on minimum-wage legislation, modest health care reform, a safe drinking water measure, and a rewrite of the pesticide law. Although Republicans had had to compromise more in policy terms, in some of these cases, congressional Democrats, especially House liberals, would have preferred holding out for still greater concessions or having the issue to take to the electorate. However, when Clinton agreed, they had little choice but to go along.

The legislation that put the greatest strain on relations between the president and liberal Democrats was welfare reform. In this case, Republicans held the PR high ground and Democrats had to make the greater concessions. During the 1992 campaign Clinton had promised to "end welfare as we know it." The protracted fight over health care reform had pushed welfare reform to the back burner in the 103d Congress; in the 104th, however, a very different form of welfare reform, one that many Democrats disliked intensely, was at the center of the Republicans' agenda. Clinton vetoed two Republican welfare reform bills, arguing that they were too hard on children and did not provide enough help to recipients in making the transition to work. In the summer of 1996, Republicans, eager for a big accomplishment, stripped alterations in the Medicaid and food stamps programs unacceptable to Clinton from the welfare overhaul bill and softened some other provisions. Many congressional Democrats, as well as Democratic activists outside Congress, argued strenuously that the bill was still terrible public policy and that Clinton should veto it again. Mindful of the message sent by the 1994 elections, his own unfulfilled promise, and the polls, however, Clinton signed. In the view of many liberal Democrats, he thus sacrificed the party's principles for his reelection. Congressional Republicans, for their part, had deprived their presidential candidate of his best issue, thus reducing his chances of election to further their own.

The 1996 election results sent a murky message at best. Clinton was handily reelected; Republicans retained their majorities in both chambers, but their House margin was reduced to a razor-thin one. Politicians and commentators believed that the American public wanted more bipartisan cooperation and less partisan combat; but the elections certainly had not provided much guidance about policy substance. Americans seemed a good deal clearer about what they did not want—the Republicans' Medicare and education cuts, Clinton's health care plan—than about what they did want.

Given no clear signal by the public and with no major change in relative political resources, Clinton and congressional Republicans continued many of the same strategies they had pursued since the budget debacle: deal when you must—when there is a real prospect of getting legislation you want or when necessary to avoid political damage; and use PR and procedural strategies to shape the agenda and the political context to your advantage so that, when you deal, you are dealing from the strongest possible position. Given continued major differences in policy preferences and conflicting electoral goals, the two parties' efforts to shape the agenda and the context entailed sustained and often intense partisan combat.

Clinton, now concerned about his legacy, was determined to get a balanced budget agreement with the Republicans in 1997. The Republicans' narrow margins and internal frictions made their leaders eager for a deal as well. Perceiving the Republicans to be in a weak strategic position, congressional Democrats urged the president to go slow and hold out for further concessions. But, in late spring, when a surprisingly strong economy made possible a deal Clinton found satisfactory, he went ahead.

The 1997 budget agreement was the high point of cooperation between the president and the congressional Republicans in the 105th Congress and probably that congress's most visible policy achievement. Even so, many of the more ideological members of both parties were unhappy with the policy decisions the budget deal contained. Liberal Democratic and conservative Republican members of Congress largely did their grumbling in private, acutely aware of the political damage a high-profile intraparty fight would cause. Conservatives outside Congress, however, scathingly attacked the deal as "timid," "minimalist," and caving in to Clinton. Given rank-and-file dissatisfaction as well as the magnitude of the gap in policy preferences between the administration and the Republicans, actually turning the plan into legislation proved to be a difficult and often acrimonious process. Certainly the entire experience did not build trust or establish a smooth working relationship between Clinton and congressional Republicans.

With no trust to destroy, both parties continued to mount PR offensives in order to gain political advantage. Republicans succeeded brilliantly with their attack on the Internal Revenue Service. Perceiving that they had lost the battle before the legislative process had gotten very far, Clinton and congressional Democrats settled for a few concessions and supported the Republicans' bill. Republicans were much less successful with their multiple investigations of the Clinton administration. Their many congressional hearings never aroused much public interest. Even the impeachment hearings did not lower the president's approval ratings. Senate Republicans harassed the administration on appointments, delaying and, in many cases, refusing to confirm especially (but not only) judicial nominees. Democratic efforts to arouse public opinion and apply public pressure to at least force votes on nominees were sporadically successful, but, the repetitive nature of the problem and the powers the Senate gives individuals greatly advantaged Republicans. With the help of a few key Republican allies, Democrats got tobacco legislation and campaign finance reform into the media and onto the congressional floor, though they did not succeeded in enacting legislation.

In late 1997 and early 1998, Clinton and congressional Democrats worked together to draft a common agenda. Though their relations had hit a low point with the defeat by Democrats of fast-track trade-agreement legislation in the House at the end of the 1997 session, both, recognizing their mutual dependence, worked hard to repair the breech. The agenda, announced in the president's State of the Union address and at a joint press conference, included saving Social Security before cutting taxes, reducing average class size and modernizing schools, establishing a patients' bill of rights, enabling people aged sixty-two to sixty-five to buy into Medicare, and raising the minimum wage. In part because congressional Democrats' expectations had finally decreased in response to the change in the balance of political power, the agenda pleased all segments of the party.

Republicans proved largely unwilling to deal. They disliked the Democratic agenda and did not see it as the basis for bargaining. They confronted severe internal strains of their own. With the 1997 budget deal having provided them with a big achievement to tout in the elections, Republican leaders decided on a "do little and make no mistakes" strategy. Pressure from important constituency groups and polls showing their core voters disaffected led Republicans to alter their strategy in the spring of 1998. They began to talk about a huge tax cut and staged votes on a variety of cultural issues that the social conservatives cared about—abortion, homosexuality, affirmative action. This change in Republican strategy made bipartisan compromise even less likely. Democrats' PR campaigns succeeded in raising a number of issues on their agenda to public prominence and even forced some congressional action but in most cases fell short of successfully pressuring Republicans to deal. On Capitol Hill and in the media, 1998 was about the Monica Lewinsky scandal and impeachment, not about policymaking.

The Republicans' poor showing in the 1998 elections precipitated a leadership upheaval in the House, but it did not really change the strategic situation much. Republicans still controlled both chambers, albeit their House control was by the slimmest of margins. Republicans' pursuit of impeachment in the face of those election results demonstrated that the party ideologues had not been persuaded to adopt a more pragmatic and compromising stance. Democrats, so close to taking back the House and with a shot at taking a Senate majority in 2000 as well, continued to have little electoral interest in making Congress look good. Within a strategic situation such as this, forcing action through the orchestration of public pressure is often the only viable strategy, though one with a modest probability of success.

Evaluating Clinton as Legislative Leader

How successful was Clinton's strategy in terms of its twin aims of maintaining good relations with his congressional party and producing legislative achievements? If the past is a guide, future presidents are often likely to confront highly partisan Congresses controlled by the opposition party. They will certainly have to operate in the new media environment. What does the Clinton presidency teach us about the prospects for legislative leadership in this environment?

Divided control does not relieve a president of dependence on his party in Congress, but it does make the relationship a much more difficult one. The relationship between Clinton and congressional Democrats was best when Clinton was dealing least with the Republicans—when the combat mode dominated the compromise mode. Passing legislation requires votes from the majority party and getting them often requires that the president deal with the opposition party leadership. Whenever Clinton has bargained directly with Republicans, congressional Democrats have feared being marginalized in the decision-making process. Getting a deal has frequently required Clinton to make compromises that liberal Democrats especially believed produced ineffective, and even bad, public policy, and their dislike of the resulting policy increased their disgruntlement with the process. Contributing to the strain was the structural problem of at least partially conflicting interests: for Democrats to win back Congress, they needed to show the Republican Congress a failure. For Clinton to gain reelection in 1996 and to establish a positive legacy, he needed legislative successes. Even beyond any ideological differences between Clinton and congressional Democrats, Clinton had a greater incentive to compromise and take half a loaf than congressional Democrats did. Thus relations were best when Republicans were least inclined to deal.

Attempts to evaluate Clinton's strategy in terms of legislative achievements confront the measuring-stick problem: what standard do we use? The 103d Congress passed family-leave legislation, national service, important education legislation, a big crime bill, NAFTA, and the landmark budget bill. Even after Democrats lost Congress, Clinton and congressional Democrats had some clear legislative triumphs over Republicans: the minimum-wage increase and, to a lesser extent, the Kennedy-Kassebaum bill were forced on Republicans by Democrats' PR victories. On the pesticide and drinking water bills in the 104th Congress and the higher-education reauthorization in the 105th, Clinton and Democrats obtained very favorable compromises, again because they held the PR high ground. Some big nonpartisan bills became law, as they do in every Congress—telecommunications reform in the 104th, the highway bill in the 105th.[22] Although highly dependent on the fast-growing economy, the 1997 budget deal that balanced the federal budget will be remembered as a significant accomplishment.

Clinton's legislative record is neither a New Deal/Great Society class record nor is it a negligible one. The more illuminating question to ask is whether Clinton did as well as the political context in which he operated allowed. Given the constraints of that political environment—conservative Republican majorities in both chambers of Congress, news media more interested in scandals than in policy choices—Clinton probably did about as well as was possible. In fact, Clinton's repeated besting of Republicans in the legislative and political struggle, his doing better than he "should" given the distribution of resources, contributed greatly to the Republican anger that fueled the impeachment drive.

Does that mean Clinton devised a strategy for successful legislative leadership in this difficult environment? If by successful legislative leadership we mean firm agenda control and the sustained translation of the president's program into law, the answer has to be "no." The combination of aggressive veto bargaining, extensive employment of the Senate minority's powers, and frequent and skillful

PR offensives allows a president facing a hostile congressional majority to influence policy outcomes and usually to keep his opponents from making policy changes he strongly opposes; really successful PR efforts may make possible sporadic, significant, positive policy victories. Sustained presidential policy success is, however, an unrealistic expectation. One must remember that even in much more favorable political contexts, presidential legislative leadership is far from easy, and success according to the definition used here is not routine. When the ideological distance between the parties is as great as it is in the 1990s, a president facing a Congress controlled by the opposition party operates in a highly constraining situation, and strategies, no matter how clever or cleverly implemented, cannot overcome the structural impediments and make possible sustained legislative leadership success.

5

Judicial Legacies: The Clinton Presidency and the Courts

DAVID M. O'BRIEN

The judicial legacies of President William Jefferson ("Bill") Clinton are both ironic and paradoxical. Ironically, Clinton, a graduate of Yale Law School and a former professor of constitutional law, failed to give judicial appointments very high priority. By contrast, Ronald Reagan, a former actor and nonlawyer, left a continuing legacy in the federal courts. The Reagan administration, together with that of its successor, George Bush, had a major impact because federal judgeships were viewed as instruments of presidential power.[1] Hence, one of the most rigorous judicial selection processes ever was put into place, in order, as Attorney General Edwin Meese III observed, "to institutionalize the Reagan revolution so it can't be set aside no matter what happens in future presidential elections."[2] In comparison, and despite twelve years of Republican judicial appointments, Clinton deemed the judiciary's institutional integrity and achievement of diversity on the bench more important than ideology or his administration's social policy goals.

During both of his terms in the Oval Office, Clinton repeatedly stressed that he aimed "to select individuals with outstanding capabilities and a broad array of professional experience and individuals who reflect the incredible diversity of our nation."[3] Whereas Reagan viewed federal judgeships as instruments of and opportunities to wield presidential power, Clinton often avoided or abandoned

96

sharply ideological and controversial nominees. As with other contentious policy positions that he initially aimed to stake out, such as those on gays in the military and national health care reform, Clinton did little to defend controversial judicial nominees. Indeed, in failing to do so, he also compromised hard-won prerogatives and privileges of the presidency. As a result, Clinton's approach to judicial appointments ultimately diminished the presidency. Clinton's judicial legacy, at best, is one of appointing highly qualified judges who brought diversity to the federal bench. At its worst, Clinton's legacy is a weakened and diminished presidency.

The story of Clinton's judicial legacies is the product of a series of stages in an embattled presidency, during which presidential prerogatives were compromised and bargained—or taken away. The turning points in his presidency, as discussed in the following sections, are: (1) the president's setting the stage and establishing patterns in his first two years in office; (2) the 1994 midterm election and the administration's consequent problems in confronting a divided government, especially a Republican-controlled Senate; (3) the Republican attack on federal judgeships during the 1996 presidential election year and Clinton's failure to marshal a response; and (4) the new, unprecedented challenges from conservative Republicans and Independent Counsel Kenneth Starr during Clinton's second term that led to the second impeachment of a president in U.S. history and forced even more concessions from a presidency that never arose from disarray.

The First Two Years: Dealing with Disarray and Setting the Stage

In his first two years as president, Clinton failed to convey a clear and convincing political vision as a "New Democrat" or to move quickly to secure a strong staff to carry out that vision. Nowhere was Clinton's failure to fill crucial positions more evident than in his dealings with the Department of Justice (DoJ). Opportunities to forge new legal policy in his first two years were forfeited and lost irretrievably. Mistakes and mismanagement were only part of the story, however, though they reveal much about the importance of a president's first two years in office and how they constrain later opportunities.[4] By the end of Clinton's second year, the administration had nevertheless amassed a commendable record of judicial appointees. Clinton's lower court judges were mostly highly competent and brought diversity to the federal bench; he also named two noncontroversial centrist justices to the Supreme Court.

After his inauguration in January 1993, Clinton's problems with the Justice Department arose almost immediately over the filling of the top position of attorney general. His first two nominees were forced to withdraw from consideration. Clinton's final nominee, and the first female attorney general, Janet Reno, was not sworn into office until mid-March. To Clinton's credit, he did not name a close personal friend or campaign manager as attorney general as have other recent presidents. Reno and Clinton, however, never developed a close working relationship, and tensions between them grew after Reno recommended the appointment of an independent counsel to investigate Clinton's involvement with the Whitewater land deal.

During Clinton's first year or so, controversies over personnel appointments, particularly in filling the lead position in the DoJ's Civil Rights Division,[5] along with turnovers in key positions, dogged the Justice Department. Associate Attorney General Webster L. Hubbell, the third highest ranking official in the department, was forced to resign in March 1994. He followed closely the departures of Deputy Attorney General Philip B. Heymann and White House Counsel Bernard W. Nussbaum. Nevertheless, after their departures, matters improved—first, with the temporary appointment of Lloyd Cutler, a seasoned and respected Washington attorney, and then with his replacement by former appellate Judge Abner Mikva as White House counsel.

By the end of Clinton's second year, the Justice Department was expediting the nomination of federal judges. The legacy of the first year-and-a-half was largely one of controversy, confusion, and lost opportunities. Lost opportunities, and the prospect of fighting rear-guard actions due to the Republicans' takeover of the Senate after the 1994 midterm elections, reflected more than just difficulties in staffing and personnel turnover. They registered the president's own priorities, and Clinton simply did not give the DoJ high priority on his domestic agenda. Preoccupation with health care reform and the president's overall vacillations on issues remained at the root of the problems in filling judgeships and pushing legal policy in new directions.

Bringing Diversity to the Lower Federal Courts

Clinton inherited a record number of vacancies (109) on the federal bench when he came into office. The large number of openings was the result of two factors. First, Congress had created eighty-five new federal judgeships in 1990 in order to handle the flood of criminal and civil cases coming into the federal courts in the late 1980s as a result of the war on drugs and crime. Second, Bush failed to fill very many of those vacancies in his last year in office, in part because of growing opposition from right-wing interest groups and senators. Still, Clinton was slow to move on judicial nominations during his first year. As indicated in table 5.1 there were more judicial vacancies at the end than at the start of Clinton's first year in the Oval Office.

Table 5.1. Filling Judicial Vacancies in the First Year

	Clinton	Bush	Reagan	Carter
Number of federal judges	837	757	660	509
Vacancies upon coming into office	109	40	35	n/a
First year nominations	33	23	44	34
First year confirmations	28	15	41	31
Vacancies remaining at end of year	113	62	33	n/a

Staffing problems and changes in the process of judicial selection led to Clinton's failure to fill more judgeships during his first year. More than eight months of Clinton's first year had passed before the Senate approved Eleanor Dean Acheson to head the DoJ's Office of Policy Development, which handles the screening of potential judicial nominees. The process of selecting judicial nominees also changed in some rather surprising ways. During the Reagan-Bush era, potential judicial candidates were subjected to a rigorous screening process, which entailed a larger bureaucratic operation within the Justice Department, along with greater White House supervision.[6] In addition, both of those administrations followed Democratic President Jimmy Carter's administration in curbing the practice of "senatorial courtesy" by refusing to defer to recommendations of home state senators for district court judgeships.

By contrast, Clinton's administration initially downplayed the DoJ's role and, later, after shifting primary responsibility back to the department's Office of Legal Policy Development, downsized the judicial selection operation. Until the Senate's confirmation of Acheson as head of the Office of Legal Policy Develop-

ment, the selection of lower court judges was a White House operation. Moreover, the administration relied on District of Columbia lawyers to vet potential
nominees, that is, to investigate their records and reputations. Not since the administration of John F. Kennedy had a White House relied so heavily on private
attorneys in such a way. After Acheson assumed responsibility for screening potential judicial nominees, the use of vetters was discontinued. Instead, department
attorneys reviewed candidates' questionnaires and then, in Acheson's estimate,
made from forty to sixty telephone calls to judges and lawyers in the jurisdiction
in which the candidate would sit on the federal bench.[7] After receiving evaluations from the American Bar Association (ABA), the DoJ eliminated some potential candidates and decided on which ones to go forward.

Another major change in the judicial selection process was the Clinton administration's decision to actively seek only *one* nominee for each district court
vacancy from either the home state senator or the ranking state Democrat. That
constituted a return to pre–Carter administration deference to senatorial courtesy.
Notably, the Carter, Reagan, and Bush administrations had curbed senatorial patronage and asserted greater presidential power and control over the selection of
lower court nominees by demanding that senators provide at least three names
for each vacancy. Furthermore, even the preferences of home state senators in the
Republican Party were not always respected during the Reagan and Bush administrations, if their candidates were deemed too liberal on issues such as abortion
or the rights of the accused. The Clinton administration's return to deferring to
senatorial patronage constituted the first of many retreats from past administrations' assertions of presidential power. It registered the low priority that Clinton's
presidency gave to judicial appointments and the greater weight given to avoiding
confirmation battles in the Senate over federal judgeships.

By the end of Clinton's second year, the DoJ had nonetheless amassed a
rather impressive record of appointing highly qualified judges who brought
greater diversity to the federal bench.[8] Indeed, in his second year in office Clinton
appointed more than 100 judges, passing the record set in 1979. Altogether in his
initial two years, Clinton named a total of 129 federal judges, whereas Bush appointed only 187 in four years. Sixty-five percent of Clinton's appointees, furthermore, were rated by the ABA as "well qualified," the ABA's highest ranking,
whereas 59 percent of Bush's, 55 percent of Reagan's, and 56 percent of Carter's
judicial appointees were so rated.[9]

Additionally, 58 percent of Clinton's judges were women and minorities.
Put into historical perspective, Clinton appointed more nontraditional federal

judges than any preceding president. Nearly one-fourth of Clinton's judges were African Americans, 9 percent were Hispanic, and 31 percent were women. In the words of political scientist Sheldon Goldman, who has monitored judicial appointments to the lower federal courts for over thirty years: "This will undoubtedly be the benchmark against which all future administrations will be judged. This tremendous push toward ethnic and gender diversity could break all historic records."[10]

In short, Clinton largely fulfilled his twin campaign promises to seek high-caliber appointees and to bring greater diversity to the judiciary. Only one nominee, African-American prosecutor Alexander Williams, was rated unqualified by the ABA. Yet, he was unanimously recommended by the Senate Judiciary Committee and unanimously confirmed by the Senate.

The quest for a more representative federal judiciary basically replaced ideology in Clinton's judicial selection process. During the Reagan-Bush era, judicial philosophy and candidates' stands on controversial issues such as abortion became litmus tests for nomination.[11] Some liberal interest groups expected the Clinton administration to sharply reverse course and impose its own litmus tests for judicial nominees. Instead, the administration charted a centrist course, searching for nontraditional judicial nominees and deferring to Democratic senators' recommendations for district court judges, even when they went against the president's stand on the right to choose abortion.

Justice Department officials running the judicial selection process denied having a liberal litmus test. "We don't have litmus tests or judicial-philosophy tests," insisted Acheson, adding, "but I do think we've put people on the bench who are interested in people and their problems, in being rigorously fair minded, in making the court an open and accessible place."[12] In the words of former White House deputy counsel Joel Klein: "We don't see courts as a vehicle for social change. It's enough to put people of demonstrated quality on the bench. We've done this across gender, race, and national origin lines. And that is a legacy that the president is proud of."[13] That position was repeated throughout Clinton's administration, though it grew increasingly defensive in the face of growing criticism from liberal groups of the administration's compromises with Republicans over judicial nominees.

Inevitably, neither liberal nor conservative interest groups were pleased with the administration's strategy for judicial selection or some of its judicial nominees. "It's clear that the Reagan and Bush Administrations steered the judiciary in an anti-choice direction," observed Kate Michelman, president of the National

Abortion Rights Action League (NARAL), "and I think its important that the Clinton Administration make a significant effort to correct this."[14] NARAL and other liberal groups were thus disappointed when Clinton named two judges who had spoken against abortion rights. Nan Aron, the executive director of the Alliance for Justice, an umbrella organization that monitors judicial appointments for a coalition of liberal "public interest" groups, agreed. In her words, "We have to be true to our beliefs and principles. If the administration nominates candidates who lack a sensitivity and commitment to constitutional principles, we will work hard to make our voice heard."[15]

Liberal groups, such as the Alliance for Justice and the People for the American Way, pressured the administration into delaying, if not ultimately abandoning, some potential judicial nominees. The Alliance for Justice successfully fought the administration's nomination of Missouri appellate court Judge Gary Gaertner to a federal district court, for instance. Judge Gaertner was a longtime friend of Representative Richard Gephardt, whose role in the Democrats' House leadership made his support essential for the president to achieve his legislative agenda. The Alliance for Justice, having prepared a seven-page "background memorandum" on Judge Gaertner accusing him of insensitivity to the rights of criminal defendants, women, and homosexuals, lobbied hard and successfully against his nomination.[16]

Liberal groups were not always successful, though, in defeating nominees they deemed too conservative. William Downes, for one, was nominated and confirmed for a seat on the federal district court in Wyoming despite strong opposition from liberal women's interest groups. Downes was criticized for reportedly calling abortion-rights activists "bra-burners." He had among other things, led a fight at the New York State Democratic convention in 1988 against a plank endorsing women's abortion rights. Downes, though, was a friend and former law partner of Democratic Governor Michael J. Sullivan, an opponent of abortion and the state's senior Democrat. With no Democratic senator from Wyoming, the White House deferred to Sullivan's recommendation of Downes, and he was confirmed by the Senate.

At the same time, conservative interest groups and Republican senators geared up to fight any liberal judicial nominee from the outset of Clinton's administration. Organizations such as the Free Congress Foundation, which monitors judicial appointments, and the Washington Legal Foundation planned aggressive attacks. In the words of the Free Congress Foundation's Thomas Jipping: "I think there are many liberal judicial activists in Clinton's judicial appointees, and they have been rubber-stamped by the Senate."[17] That was hardly the case. In fact, the Free Congress Foundation and ranking Republican Senators Orrin Hatch (Utah) and Strom Thurmond (S.C.) targeted only two nominees, Judges Rosemary Barkett and H. Lee Sarokin, for defeat in Clinton's first two years. Both were, nevertheless, confirmed.

Although conservative Republicans' two principal attacks on Clinton's judicial nominees failed, they were able to delay the confirmation of others who appeared too liberal and thus established a practice that would become a pattern. That is what happened when the Clinton administration followed through on two judicial candidates, both Mexican-Americans, recommended by California's Democratic Senator Barbara Boxer. Both would have become the first Mexican-Americans to serve on the federal district court in Los Angeles. But, only one, Richard A. Paez, was confirmed by the Senate. The other, Samuel Paz, became ensnared in a controversy and was forced to withdraw from consideration after the 1994 midterm elections. Both Paez and Paz described themselves as liberal but they were otherwise quite different. Paez, a Mormon and former "public interest" lawyer for the Western Center on Law and Poverty and the Legal Aid Foundation of Los Angeles, had served for thirteen years as a municipal court judge. In contrast, Paz was affiliated with the American Civil Liberties Union and had specialized in suits over police brutality and misconduct. Paz was also an outspoken advocate of affirmative action and had publicly defended the 1992 Los Angeles riots as a protest against political and economic inequality. Paz's legal practice and outspoken political views made him an easy target for Republicans, who stalled his confirmation in the 103d Congress and doomed chances for his confirmation afterwards.

The Clinton administration's anticipation of Republican opposition to nominees who could be portrayed as too liberal and its deference to Democratic senators' recommendations for home state judgeships resulted in the appointment of mostly moderate to conservative lower court judges. Clinton's lower court appointments, thus, on balance, disappointed some liberal groups. "Reagan and Bush really changed the philosophy of the courts, and not for the better," was the view of Ninth Circuit U.S. Court of Appeals Judge Stephen Reinhardt, a Carter appointee. Judge Reinhardt concluded:

> Clinton had the opportunity to do the same, and he blew it. There seems to be this sense that the administration doesn't want to do anything to offend Hatch or Simpson. You can't conceive of Bush or Reagan thinking, "let's not do anything that could offend Kennedy." Those of us who have waited for

three decades for a Democrat to be appointing liberal judges, particularly to the Supreme Court, have been deeply disappointed.[18]

But Acheson and others dismissed such criticism.[19]

Avoiding Controversy: Two Moderate, Noncontroversial Justices

After more than a quarter of a century during which four Republican presidents made ten consecutive appointments to the Supreme Court, Clinton had the opportunity to fill two vacancies during his first two years in office.[20] The first came midway in the Court's 1992–93 term, when Justice Byron White announced he would retire at the end of the term.[21]

In announcing his decision to retire almost four months in advance Justice White gave Clinton not only a chance to fill his seat, but also ample time to select his successor. Still, more than three months passed before Clinton finally settled on Judge Ruth Bader Ginsburg as his nominee to become the 107th justice of the Supreme Court. Clinton had wanted a politician, a "consensus builder,"[22] who might pull the Court in more liberal directions on some issues but he also wanted to avoid any major controversy over Senate confirmation.

In the week before announcing his nominee, Clinton vacillated between elevating his secretary of the Department of the Interior, Bruce Babbitt—an old friend and former Arizona governor—or naming one of two appellate court judges, Ginsburg and Stephen G. Breyer. Environmentalists wanted Babbitt to stay at Interior, and he faced strong opposition from the senior minority member on the Senate Judiciary Committee, Senator Orrin Hatch. Both Ginsburg and Breyer had the support of Hatch and Senator Edward Kennedy (D-Mass.), and both had won seats on the federal bench as Carter judges in 1980.

Judge Breyer had served as chief counsel to the Senate Judiciary Committee when it was chaired by Senator Kennedy in the late 1970s. Senators Kennedy and Hatch were instrumental in pushing Breyer's and Ginsburg's nominations through in 1980, when, as the presidential election approached, Republicans threatened to block all further Carter judicial appointees. Hatch knew and liked Breyer for his work as chief counsel. Ginsburg met Hatch at the request of H. Ross Perot, who had been asked to arrange the meeting by his tax attorney and Ginsburg's husband, Martin. Ginsburg impressed Hatch then, and later, with thirteen years of service on the Court of Appeals for the District of Columbia Circuit, during which time she served with future justices Antonin Scalia and Clarence Thomas, as well as defeated Reagan Supreme Court nominees Robert Bork and Douglas Ginsburg (who is no relation to the justice). In 1993 Hatch, though favoring Breyer, remained supportive of Ginsburg.

The day after meeting Judge Breyer at a widely publicized luncheon amid speculation that he would get the nod, Clinton met with Judge Ginsburg. He was touched by the charm and strength of the sixty-year-old Jewish grandmother, jurist, and leader of the women's movement in law in the 1970s. Subsequently, when announcing her selection, Clinton praised Ginsburg as "the Thurgood Marshall of the women's movement."

Born in Brooklyn, Ginsburg attended Cornell University where she met her future husband. Both Ginsburgs went on to Harvard Law School, but after her husband's graduation and acceptance of a position in a New York city law firm, Ginsburg finished her third year at Columbia Law School, where she tied for first place in the class. Following graduation, Ginsburg worked as a law clerk for two years. In 1961 she could not find a New York law firm that would hire her, because she was a woman. After two more years working as a research assistant, Ginsburg was hired by Rutgers University School of Law, where she taught until 1972, when she became the first woman law professor at Columbia Law School.

Because no Jewish justice had sat on the high bench for almost a quarter of a century (since Justice Abe Fortas resigned in 1969), Jewish groups welcomed Ginsburg's nomination, while also rejecting the mythology of a "Jewish seat." Ginsburg had been at the forefront of the women's movement in law in the 1970s. Besides teaching at Rutgers and Columbia law schools, in the 1970s Ginsburg also served as the director of the American Civil Liberties Union's Women's Rights Project, arguing six (and winning five) important gender-based discrimination cases before the Supreme Court.

With little opposition from Republican senators, Ginsburg's nomination sailed through the Senate Judiciary Committee by an 18–0 vote. The full Senate confirmed her on a vote of 96–3, with only Republican Senators Jesse Helms of North Carolina, Robert C. Smith of New Hampshire, and Don Nickles of Oklahoma, voting against. On the bench, there was no sign of Justice Ginsburg experiencing the so-called "freshman effect" as she undertook her share of the Court's opinion writing.[23] She quickly aligned herself with the Court's "left of center" justices: David H. Souter, John Paul Stevens, and, after his appointment, Stephen Breyer.

On 6 April 1994, Justice Harry Blackmun announced he would retire at the end of the Court's term. The eighty-five-year-old justice had served on the Court for almost a quarter of a century. He had been appointed in 1970 by Republican

President Richard Nixon as a "law and order jurist" but quickly asserted his own independence and eventually voted most often with the Court's last liberals, Justices William J. Brennan Jr. and Thurgood Marshall.

Justice Blackmun and Clinton had become friends over the years, attending annual gatherings of the Renaissance Club in Hilton Head, South Carolina. In announcing that he would retire at the end of the term, Justice Blackmun like Justice White, gave the president ample time to choose a successor. Clinton took less time in selecting his second nominee to the Court—taking only thirty-seven days in contrast to the eighty-seven days that passed before he announced his first appointee. But he once again appeared to vacillate, before finally settling on Judge Breyer, whom he had passed over a year earlier.

Clinton had said he wanted a nominee who was an experienced "politician" with a "big heart." Once again, though, some prime candidates withdrew from consideration. Notably, Senate Majority Leader George Mitchell said he had to stay in the Senate to lead the fight for the president's ill-fated health care reform proposal. Clinton also again decided against elevating his secretary of the Interior, claiming that he "could not bear to lose him from the Cabinet." In fact, Bruce Babbitt was the most liberal of Clinton's top three final candidates and would have confronted bitter opposition in the Senate.

In the end, Clinton went against his progressive instincts and, again, aimed to avoid political controversy by naming a centrist jurist who enjoyed bipartisan support in the Senate. The fifty-six-year-old Judge Breyer, who, like Ginsburg, was Jewish, was trained as an undergraduate at Stanford and Oxford Universities. He later received his law degree from Harvard Law School, where he subsequently taught administrative law for more than a decade. After graduating from law school, he served as a law clerk to Justice Arthur J. Goldberg, one of the most liberal justices on the Warren Court. Unlike that liberal justice, however, Breyer proved to be a moderate pragmatist and legal technician during his thirteen years on the federal appellate bench. His academic writings, moreover, primarily concerned issues of administrative law and regulatory policy.[24] And for that very reason the president's advisers correctly anticipated relatively low-key confirmation hearings. The Judiciary Committee unanimously approved him and the full Senate confirmed Breyer by a vote of 87–9 as the 108th justice.

In making his appointments to the Supreme Court, Clinton hesitated and sought advance assurances from Senate leaders that his nominees would not spark confirmation controversies. Both times, Clinton appeared torn between his progressive instincts and rhetoric, on the one hand, and his desire to avoid confirmation battles, on the other.

The 1994 Midterm Elections and
a Republican-Controlled Senate

Clinton's appointments to the lower federal courts in his first two years were basically centrist and symbolic, bringing cosmetic changes to the federal bench. They did not (and his subsequent judicial appointees would not) significantly change the direction of the federal judiciary. The prospects for a greater imprint were, then, further undercut as a consequence of the 1994 midterm elections. With the Republicans winning a Senate majority, the chair of the Senate Judiciary was turned over to Senator Hatch. As a result, Clinton faced making more concessions, compromises, and ultimately naming more moderate-to-conservative judges in order to assure their confirmation or at least avoid courting controversy. The latter course was something that Clinton had no taste for and Republicans knew it. Hence, Clinton's team immediately abandoned some judicial nominees, such as Samuel Paz, who were portrayed as too liberal, too controversial, and certain to face defeat in the Senate. And after months of further delay, the administration was also forced to abandon others nominated for the federal bench, such as Peter Edelman, who had served as counsel to the Department of Health and Human Services, Judith McConnell, and Charles Becton.[25]

Facing the Republican-controlled Senate and Senator Hatch as chair of the Senate Judiciary Committee, the administration confronted an uphill battle, and, thus, it adopted an even more nonpartisan approach to judicial selection. For his part, Senator Hatch began sending judicial nominees a follow-up questionnaire examining their views on "judicial activism" and ideological positions; but even so, he came under increasing pressure from newly elected Republican senators to delay and, if possible, block confirmation of Clinton's judicial nominees. With a view to the 1996 presidential election year, Republicans in the Senate and conservative interest groups aimed to deny Clinton as many judgeships as possible in order to maintain the conservative influence in the judiciary achieved during the Reagan-Bush era.

As a result, in 1995 the Senate confirmed just 53 judicial nominees for a total of 182 judges in Clinton's first three years. Clinton's judges, thus, constituted only 21.7 percent of the federal bench, while Reagan and Bush judges continued to dominate, constituting 56.8 percent of the bench and majorities on all but one of the thirteen federal appellate courts—the Second Circuit was split evenly between Reagan-Bush appointees and those named by Carter and Clinton.[26]

The high costs of Clinton's giving federal judgeships low priority when followed by the Republican takeover of the Senate were apparent in the last years of his first term. First, Clinton's appointees did not fundamentally change the direction of the federal judiciary. Indeed, political scientists Ronald Stidham, Robert A. Carp, and Donald R. Songer found that Carter's appointees were more liberal than Clinton's and that the latter's more moderate judges voted about the same as those appointed by Republican President Gerald Ford, whereas Reagan and Bush judges were much more conservative.[27] Second, the Republican-controlled Senate not only forced Clinton to reconsider nominating and even to abandon some judicial nominees, but it also slowed down the confirmation process. Consequently, and third, the federal judiciary faced a growing problem of judicial vacancies and increasing caseload.[28] Finally, although Clinton brought diversity to the federal bench, the pace slowed in 1995 as most of his nontraditional appointees were named in his first two years. Only 15.1 percent of his appointees were people of color in 1995, whereas in 1993 and 1994 they constituted 25 and 36.5 percent, respectively.

The 1996 Presidential Election Year

If Clinton's judicial appointment process was stalled by the Republican Senate in 1995, it was virtually shut down in 1996. In that year the Senate did not confirm one appellate court nominee and confirmed only seventeen district court judges. By comparison, the last year of Bush's presidency, the Democratic-controlled Senate confirmed sixty-six judges, more than during any previous year of his administration. So, too, the Senate confirmed forty-one of Reagan's judicial nominees in his last year in the Oval Office.

From the outset of the 1996 presidential election year, Republicans sought to deny Clinton judicial appointments and denounced his nominees for "liberal judicial activism." The tenor was set when, in response to the president's 1996 State of the Union speech, Senator Robert Dole (R-Kans.) decried the appointment of "liberal judges." Conservative commentators quickly picked up on that theme.[29] Dole and other Republican presidential candidates reiterated it as a campaign theme, which had worked successfully for Richard Nixon in 1968. Thus, former Nixon speechwriter and 1996 presidential candidate Patrick Buchanan repeatedly warned of a "judicial dictatorship" and attacked the Supreme Court for protecting "criminals, atheists, homosexuals, flag burners, illegal aliens—including terrorists—convicts, and pornographers."[30]

As the election year wore on, Republicans, especially candidates for the presidential nomination, turned up the heat on Clinton's nominees and appointees. The battle, then, intensified after Senate Majority Leader Dole resigned in order to make a full-court press for the presidency in the November election. Consequently, Senator Trent Lott (R-Miss.) became the Republican majority leader, and he had even less interest in seeing the Senate confirm Clinton's judicial nominees. In addition, Dole raised the rhetorical level of attacks on Clinton's judges and on the federal judiciary itself. In his desperate effort to win the presidency and in spite of the voting record of Clinton's judges, Dole claimed that "if President Clinton has four more years and appoints just one more justice to the Supreme Court, we could have the most liberal court since the Warren Court of the 1960s."[31] Although such white-hot rhetoric proved unsuccessful in the election, two Clinton judicial appointees who were targeted in Republican attacks did resign from the bench, decrying the harsh criticism and attacks on judicial independence.[32]

Remarkably, in the face of such heated campaign rhetoric and the Senate's stalling tactics in considering judicial nominees, Clinton not only withdrew support from more judicial nominees but failed to mount a counteroffensive in order to move the judicial appointment process along. Instead, his administration became even slower in selecting and nominating lower court judges, again indicating the low priority given to federal judgeships and underscoring the president's aversion to doing battle with the Senate.[33] As a result the federal judiciary confronted a growing number of judicial vacancies and an increasing backlog of cases.

Although destined for reelection, in his first term Clinton succeeded in appointing only 26 percent (168 out of 645) of the federal district court judges and just 16 percent (28 out of 167) of the federal appellate court judges.[34] His reelection, moreover, did little either to rebuff Republican obstructionism or to give liberals great cause for celebration. To the contrary, Republicans geared up to delay further and defeat confirmation of his judicial nominees, while liberals increasingly lamented the lost opportunities of Clinton's presidency. In the words of legal historian William E. Leuchtenburg, Clinton failed to take "advantage of his tenure as president to offset the decidedly ideological appointments that Reagan and Bush made in the 1980s."[35]

New and Continuing Challenges in Clinton's Second Term

Sworn in to a second term under the lingering clouds of Paula Jones's lawsuit for alleged sexual harassment and Kenneth Starr's continuing investigation of the

Whitewater financial deal, Clinton confronted a resentful and vindictive Senate. The Republican majority was determined not merely to maintain gridlock but to escalate attacks on Clinton's judicial nominees and the federal judiciary.

Shortly before Clinton's second inauguration, Senator Hatch threw down the gauntlet on confirming federal judges, signaling what was to come by promising to get even tougher and to slow down further the Senate Judiciary Committee's hearings on judicial nominees.[36] In fact, Senator Hatch found himself under increasing pressure from conservative interest groups and ultra-right-wing Republican senators to thwart confirmation of Clinton's judicial nominees. Gary Bauer of the Family Research Council, Thomas Jipping of the Free Congress Foundation, the Heritage Foundation, and the Federalist Society each vowed to redouble their efforts to minimize Clinton's impact on the federal judiciary and to curb "judicial activism."[37] In January 1997, former Reagan attorney general Edwin Meese highlighted conservatives' long-standing opposition to the ABA's involvement in the judicial selection process by urging that the ABA be completely cut out of the process.[38] In response, Senator Hatch announced that the Senate Judiciary Committee would no longer consider the ABA's evaluations of judicial nominees, which the ABA had provided since 1947 and which the White House promised to continue to solicit nonetheless.[39] That, however, was only the opening salvo in the battle shaping up over federal judgeships in Clinton's second term.

The Republican attack was concerted and widespread. In the House of Representatives, for example, Majority Whip Tom DeLay (R-Tex.) advocated impeaching federal judges for their decisions, claiming that "the judges need to be intimidated."[40] Senator John Ashcroft (R-Mo.) held three hearings on the subject of "judicial activism." Senator Charles Grassley (R-Iowa) held hearings on proposals to cut back on the jurisdiction of federal courts, as well as on whether appellate court vacancies needed to be filled, thereby attempting to establish that the federal courts were not overworked.

In addition to threatening to target specific judicial nominees, Senate Republicans successfully delayed holding hearings and having confirmation votes on many others. The extent of the gridlock is evident in the number of judges appointed and the number of days between a judicial vacancy, nomination, and confirmation, as shown in table 5.2.[41]

Although the Clinton administration bore some responsibility for the large number of vacancies because of its own initial delays in making judicial selections and advancing nominations, the Senate's intimidation and obstructionism was

Table 5.2. Gridlock in the Judicial Appointment Process

Year	Average Number of Judges Appointed	Number of Days from Vacancy to Nomination	Number of Days from Nomination to Confirmation	Total Number of Days to Fill a Vacancy
1979–96	54	386	78	464
1997	36	428	198	617

unprecedented in his second term. Having failed to assert presidential leadership on judicial appointments in his first term, Clinton found that the institutional circumstances of divided government left him few options other than to adopt minimalist strategies of nominating largely noncontroversial judicial nominees and bargaining over, even trading, judgeships with Republican senators.

The slowdown in the Senate was achieved by several means. For one thing, Senator Hatch simply refused to hold many Judiciary Committee hearings (there were only nine in 1997) and subjected several nominees to a second round of hearings. Yet, even Senator Hatch's tactics did not go far enough for his more conservative colleagues. Breaking with past practice, Majority Leader Trent Lott agreed to permit individual senators to further delay the confirmation process by placing a "secret hold" on nominees in order to deny them hearings before the Judiciary Committee and a Senate vote on confirmation.

When the Senate Judiciary Committee did hold hearings, Senators Hatch, Ashcroft, Grassley, and Jefferson Sessions (R-Ala.) vigorously questioned nominees about their political and judicial views, as well as frequently demanding that they submit additional materials, before proceeding with their confirmations. They defended their diversionary tactics on the grounds that federal courts had usurped the powers of other branches of government and had engaged in "liberal judicial activism." Disregarding the fact that a majority of the Supreme Court and the federal judiciary had been appointed by Reagan and Bush, Senator Ashcroft reasoned: "Over the last half century, the federal courts have usurped from school boards the power to determine what a child can learn, and removed from the legislatures the ability to establish equality under the law. The courts have made liars of Hamilton and Madison, confirming our forefathers' worst fears—for what the Framers intended to be the weakest branch of government has become the most powerful."[42]

Although Clinton began his second term promising to name nominees for the more than eighty vacancies on the federal bench at the time, he was slow to do so and never mounted a countercampaign to the Republican offensive. Notably, during 1997 he gave only one public speech, a radio address, in support of his judicial nominees and in response to Republican attacks.[43]

The low priority given to federal judgeships and the president's growing weakness was underscored by deals struck by the administration with Republicans in the Senate. In early 1997 Senators Jon Kyl (R-Ariz.) and Slade Gorton (R-Wash.) proposed changes in the judicial selection and confirmation process that would have permitted Republican senators to select nominees for half of the judicial vacancies and required the White House to obtain advance approval of appellate court nominees from Republican senators in the federal circuit in which the nominee would sit. Likewise, Senator Phil Gramm (R-Tex.) aimed to give Republican senators a special veto over appellate court nominees by proposing that the Republican majority on the Judiciary Committee be required to vote against a nominee if two-thirds of the Republican senators from a particular judicial circuit objected to the nominee.

These proposals, to be sure, were as much a challenge to the authority of Senator Hatch as chair of the Judiciary Committee as to President Clinton. Hard-line conservative Republican senators were angry with Senator Hatch because he had held hearings on and supported some of Clinton's judicial nominees over their objections.[44] Ultimately, Senator Hatch and the Republican Caucus defeated these proposals.

But, the defeat of those proposals in the Senate did not stop the White House, under growing pressure and assault, from agreeing to deals with Republican senators that gave them more veto power over, and even the opportunity to pick some, judicial nominees. Senator Arlen Specter (R-Penn.), for one, exacted from the White House the promise that for every three Democratic judicial nominees named to district courts in Pennsylvania, a Republican judicial nominee would be nominated.[45] And in 1997, in deference to Senator Specter, Clinton nominated to the district court in eastern Pennsylvania, Bruce Kauffman, who had previously won election to the Pennsylvania state supreme court as a Republican. Even such concessions by Clinton still did not break the logjam or expedite the Senate's confirmation of judicial nominees.

Clinton began 1997 with eighty-four vacancies on the federal bench and ended the year with eighty-seven openings—roughly 10 percent of all federal judgeships remained vacant for well over a year. The Senate confirmed just thirty-six judicial nominees, with the Senate holding hearings on only forty-seven of the seventy-nine nominees proposed by the White House. While that brought Clinton's total judicial appointments to 240 (or 27.9 percent of the judiciary), it was the lowest level of Senate confirmation of judicial nominees in twenty years (at just 45.6 percent).

Furthermore, the Senate confirmed a significantly lower percentage of women and minorities than in Clinton's first term; their hearings and confirmations were also more often delayed than those of white male nominees. More than 80 percent of Clinton's 1997 successful judicial appointees were white males. Of the thirty-six judges confirmed, only six were white females, four were African-American males, and one was an Asian-American male. Although the administration had lost some ground in its quest to bring diversity to the federal bench, two-thirds of the thirty-six were rated by the ABA as "well qualified" and the rest were rated "qualified."

The persistent problem of judicial vacancies continued to grow and eventually drew the attention of Chief Justice William H. Rehnquist in his *1997 Year-End Report on the Federal Judiciary.* The increasing number of judicial vacancies, along with the lengthy delays in filling them and the rising caseloads of the federal judiciary, warned Rehnquist, posed "the most immediate problem we face in the federal judiciary." That problem, he added, could not persist "without eroding the quality of justice that traditionally has been associated with the federal judiciary."[46] Yet, even that harsh assessment from the titular head of the federal judiciary and a leading conservative jurist was quickly rebuffed by the leadership in the Senate, who remained bent on denying Clinton as many judgeships as possible in his second term. Ironically, in light of their ideological agreement with Chief Justice Rehnquist, Senators Hatch and Lott immediately took issue with his assessment and disputed his claim that the federal judiciary was facing a crisis.[47]

Clinton, for his part, responded to the chief justice's concerns by promising to take the offensive in filling judicial vacancies.[48] Given Clinton's previous unwillingness to take on confirmation battles for his judicial nominees, his concessions to Republican senators, the established pattern of obstructionism in the Senate, and the Republican majority's determination to deny him as many federal judgeships as possible, the prospect of Clinton's mounting such a presidential offensive was already dubious. Whatever the chances of that, it was quickly and permanently doomed by the revelation in January 1998 of Clinton's sexual affair with a twenty-two-year-old White House intern, Monica S. Lewinsky, and, the subsequent expansion of Starr's Whitewater investigation into that matter.

Even before he became ensnarled on a daily basis with Starr's investigation, Clinton was forced to withdraw nominees and driven to trading judgeships with Republican senators. In April 1998, for instance, he withdrew the nomination for a district court judgeship of Frederica Massiah-Jackson, a female African-American state court judge. Nominated over a year earlier, Judge Massiah-Jackson had since been targeted and denounced by Republican senators as "soft on crime" and labeled a "liberal judicial activist." On the day before the Senate was to vote on her confirmation, which was virtually certain to be defeated, the president withdrew her nomination.[49]

Clinton also struck more deals with Republican senators, agreeing to nominate their candidates for the federal bench. For example, he agreed to nominate the Washington state supreme court Chief Justice Barbara Durham for a seat on the Court of Appeals for the Ninth Circuit in exchange for Senator Gorton's support for his nomination of William Fletcher for that court. Fletcher, a sixty-two year-old constitutional law professor at the University of California, Berkeley's Boalt Hall School of Law, and a close friend of the president, had been nominated three years earlier, in April 1995. But his nomination had been targeted by Republicans, mired in controversy, and stalled in the Senate, which repeatedly declined to vote on his confirmation. Finally, after the administration's deal with Gorton, Fletcher was confirmed in October 1998.

In striking deals with Senate Republicans and nominating Durham, among other Republican-backed judicial nominees, however, Clinton turned against his liberal constituency. The Alliance for Justice immediately issued a twelve-page report criticizing Chief Justice Durham's record as too conservative on a wide range of issues from the homeless, the rights of the accused, and the death penalty, to sexual discrimination. "The deal is really a Faustian bargain for the Clinton administration," observed the Alliance for Justice: "Chief Justice Durham's record suggests that the primary impetus for her nomination to the Ninth Circuit is political convenience. . . . By granting a senator from the opposing party the opportunity to hand-pick nominees to the Court of Appeals, President Clinton would relinquish his constitutional prerogative to select federal judges, and his most lasting legacy."[50]

As a consequence of withdrawing judicial nominees who proved controversial, striking deals with Senate Republicans, and agreeing to the nomination of more conservative nominees, Clinton was, nevertheless, able to win confirmation of sixty-five nominees in 1998, more than in the previous two years combined, but still leaving fifty judicial vacancies unfilled. In doing so, Clinton alienated liberal supporters by agreeing to name more conservative nominees in order to fill the pending judicial vacancies. This at least allowed him to remain faithful to what had become his sole objective and claim to achievement in judicial recruitment, namely, bringing diversity to the federal bench, even at the cost of appointing judges who opposed his administration's social policy positions. On that score, Clinton achieved more in 1998 than in 1997 but slightly less than in his first term. Of the sixty-five judges confirmed in 1998, thirty-three (50 percent) were white males and twenty-one (32.3 percent) were female. Of the 1998 judicial appointees, eight males and three females were African-Americans, six (three males and three females) Hispanic, and one an Arab-American.

In what remains of his presidency, Clinton can do little other than to make more concessions, withdraw nominees who become too controversial, and strike even more deals with Republican senators in order to secure the Senate's confirmation of judicial nominees. Given the low priority that Clinton gave to federal judgeships from the outset of his presidency, his past dealings with the obstructionism of the Republican majority in the Senate, continued delays and concession after concession appear inevitable. These problems of a weakened presidency escalated in September 1998, when Independent Counsel Starr referred to the House of Representatives his 445-page report detailing eleven grounds for impeachment, including Clinton's lying under oath both in his deposition in the Paula Jones case and before Starr's grand jury, obstructing justice by trying to cover up his affair with Lewinsky, and trying to influence the testimony of his secretary, Betty Currie.

Subsequently, Clinton became the second president to be impeached; in 1868 President Andrew Johnson was impeached but escaped conviction and removal from office by a single vote in the Senate. On 11 and 12 December 1998, the Judiciary Committee of the House of Representatives passed four articles of impeachment. A week later, the full House approved two of those articles: one impeached Clinton for committing perjury and giving misleading testimony to Starr's grand jury investigation of the Jones case and Clinton's relationship with Lewinsky; the other impeached Clinton for obstruction of justice in attempting to cover up evidence related to the Jones lawsuit. Although the Senate failed to convict and remove him from office, Clinton, already seriously diminished, was destined to make more compromises and to bargain away federal judgeships and much else, confronting continuing calls for the president's resignation or removal from office.

Legacies: Clinton, the Presidency, and the Courts

Clinton's judicial legacies reflect his larger presidential legacy: an impeached president and a demystified, weaker presidency. Initially, Clinton underachieved on judicial appointments by trying to overachieve on other matters, and then he found himself increasingly constrained by the institutional circumstances of divided government, the independent counsel's ongoing investigation, and intense Republican opposition. Ironically, this constitutional law scholar turned politician who never was able to escape his past in office failed to give federal judgeships high priority or to view them as instruments of presidential power. Constantly moving from one crisis to another, he failed to achieve an overarching political vision. His administration's goals in judicial recruitment were limited from the outset, and they then became increasingly constrained. Nonetheless, Clinton appointed two Supreme Court justices and a large number of lower court judges (as indicated in table 5.3) who were highly qualified and who increased the representation of women and minorities on the federal bench. Still, he abandoned a large number of judicial nominees, avoided confirmation battles, and, particularly in his second term, was forced to compromise presidential prerogatives in judicial selection by trading judgeships with Republican senators and appointing judges opposed to his political positions. In these and other ways, Clinton weakened the presidency.

Table 5.3. Comparison of Presidents' Judicial Appointments

	Nixon	Ford	Carter	Reagan	Bush	Clinton
Supreme Court	4	1	0	4	2	2
Circuit Court	45	12	56	78	37	49
District Court	182	52	202	290	148	246
Special Courts[a]	7	1	3	10	0	4
Total	238	66	261	382	187	301

Source: Alliance for Justice.

Note: As of 1 January 1999; excludes two Clinton judges who resigned and two elevated from district to circuit courts.

a. Includes the Court of International Trade.

Some scholars and commentators will conclude that Clinton merely damaged himself, not the institution of the presidency. Clinton's judicial legacies not only lie in his failure to assert presidential power in judicial selection but are a part of his presidency's larger legacy—the legacy of an impeached president. Even though he was not convicted, Clinton's presidential and judicial legacies are those of a weakened presidency whose prerogatives were sacrificed not only with respect to judicial selection but also with respect to judicial precedents affecting the conduct of future presidencies.

Ironically, in 1993 Clinton signed the reauthorization of the independent counsel law, although many scholars, politicians, and jurists considered it an unconstitutional intrusion on presidential powers.[51] Then, embattled with Kenneth Starr, Clinton became the first sitting president in 200 years to face a subpoena from a prosecutor, and subsequently the first president to testify before a grand jury and to have his secret videotaped grand jury testimony aired on international television.

During his court battles, Clinton established precedents limiting the institutional prerogatives of the presidency. The Court of Appeals for the Eighth Circuit held that White House lawyers' communications with the first lady were not protected by a government attorney-client privilege. The U.S. District Court for the District of Columbia rejected assertions of executive privilege that would have prevented two senior White House aides from being forced to testify about the president. The Court of Appeals for the District of Columbia ruled that Secret Service agents working in the White House can be compelled to give testimony to a federal grand jury. That court also rejected the application of the common law attorney-client privilege to protect the president's communications with lawyers in the Office of the White House Counsel. And the Supreme Court held, in *Clinton* v. *Jones*,[52] that a sitting president does not enjoy immunity from civil suits while in the Oval Office. Instead of bargaining, compromising, and reaching settlements on these matters, Clinton waged unsuccessful court battles that ultimately diminished the presidency.

All of these aspects of the presidency were once ambiguous and thus gave past presidents leverage, which they exploited. These matters are no longer ambiguous; they are now clear. Whether some of these prerogatives of the presidency are restored to some future president will depend on Congress, not the president. Whereas impeachment records for history Clinton's personal disgrace and the vengeance of Republican retribution, these legacies will haunt future presidencies.

6

A Reinvented Government, or the Same Old Government?

JOEL D. ABERBACH

The Clinton administration has worked hard to make its mark on the executive branch. From its efforts to make the higher reaches of the federal government "look like America," to its well-publicized campaign to reinvent government, the federal executive has been a focal point of Bill Clinton's administration. Few, other than public administration scholars, would ordinarily look to such arcane areas as personnel administration or government management in discussing an administration's accomplishments, but these have been major areas of activity and emphasis during the Clinton presidency. Together with Clinton's use of many of the techniques of the "administrative presidency" to control policy, they are a part of the Clinton presidential legacy that scholars will discuss and analyze for years to come.

While this chapter focuses on the administrative side of Clinton's presidency, administration and politics are inextricably linked, especially at the highest levels of government. The Clinton administration's interest in government personnel and management is connected to its political goals and needs. Diversity, something President Clinton is clearly committed to, is also a way for a Democratic president to shore up the party's (and his own) political base among women and minorities. In addition, it helps legitimate implementation of a more conservative "New Democrat" agenda, something Clinton has also endorsed (if not always acted on consistently) from the beginning of his quest for the presidency.

Indeed, the diverse personnel of the Clinton administration are prominent among the people who are to be at the helm of a government "reinvented" along New Democrat lines for the post-big-government era. Reinvention, which has already pared down the personnel on the direct government payroll, is meant to make government more efficient by making it "work better and cost less" while cutting it back to providing what is "basic." Finally, the administration's use of devices to govern without Congress (the administrative presidency strategy) provides it with mechanisms to get its way in a complex political environment made more difficult by divided government.

After a bumpy start, Clinton's efforts in the areas of personnel and administration have been politically successful. Many of his party's core constituencies are gratified by his personnel policies. And the emphasis on efficiency and cutting red tape while preserving government's most popular services and benefits—covered, at least so far, under the administration's evolving definition of basic—is comfortable for the middle-class general electorate that has felt little pain from the early phases of reinvention. But, as I argue here, it is still much too early to assess the long-term success of the reinvention initiative. It is ambitious, complex, and filled with inconsistencies and possible pitfalls, but that is hardly surprising for a package of government reforms designed and implemented in a changing and often contentious political environment.

This chapter covers Clinton's approach to selecting top personnel for the federal government, with an emphasis on diversity. It examines the difficulties he has faced in getting appointments through the Senate and the devices he has employed, particularly "acting" appointments, to circumvent these difficulties. It then turns to a brief discussion of the Clinton administration's use of the various administrative levers at its command to control policy, particularly after the Republicans won a majority in Congress in 1994. Next, the chapter analyzes the administration's reinvention initiative, using two agencies as examples to highlight the problems and prospects of reinvention. It closes with a discussion of the political decisions that will determine the ultimate significance of Bill Clinton's administrative legacy.

Appointments

Diversity

One of Bill Clinton's main campaign promises was to produce an administration with a demographic makeup resembling that of the U.S. population. He succeeded to a quite remarkable extent.

At a postelection press conference in December 1996, following the announcement of his second-term cabinet officials, Clinton said of his selections:

> I believe that one of my jobs at this moment in history is to demonstrate by the team I put together that no group of people should be excluded from service to our country and that all people are capable of serving. So I have striven to achieve both excellence and diversity. I'm very proud of the first Cabinet that I appointed. I am very proud of this Cabinet. I am proud that they are diverse, but I would not have appointed a single one of them because of their gender or ethnic background had I not thought that they could succeed.[1]

Rhetoric aside, Clinton has delivered on his promise. Not only has his cabinet been unusually representative of the country at large, at least in demographic terms, but his appointees to other major executive posts in the federal government have been similarly diverse. An examination of subcabinet-level personnel in Clinton's first term indicated that about 25 percent of his appointees were members of various groups often described as underrepresented minorities (African Americans, 14 percent of appointees; Hispanic Americans, 6 percent; Asian Americans, 3 percent; Native Americans, 1 percent).[2]

The Clinton appointments approach has been labeled EGG for its emphasis on ethnicity, gender, and geography. The gender component allows us to compare the Clinton administration and its predecessors. A study by Janet Martin of all Senate-confirmed, full-time presidential appointees to the departments, agencies, and regulatory commissions of the federal government from 1961 to 1994 (excepting ambassadors, U.S. attorneys, and U.S. marshals) is quite revealing. Her data (based on an updating of a study done by the National Academy of Public Administration) indicate that of the eight administrations from Kennedy to Clinton, each, except for the Nixon and Reagan administrations, had more female appointees than its predecessor. In this regard, the Clinton administration is part of a general trend toward diversity in presidential appointments. The data also show, however, that the Clinton administration significantly exceeded the record of its predecessors by a significant amount.

A little over 30 percent of Clinton appointees to top positions were female. This contrasts to about 2 percent in the Kennedy administration, 5 percent in the Johnson administration, and 15 percent in the Carter administration, all of the Democratic administrations in the study. It also is almost half again as much as the previous high of 21 percent female appointees in the Bush administration.[3]

Of recent administrations, the contrast between the Clinton and Reagan administrations is particularly stark. Using Congressional Research Service reports as a source, I coded the sex of all presidential appointees requiring Senate confirmation to positions in the fourteen executive departments in 1981, 1993, and 1997.[4] Sex was determined by name, with supplementary sources used in cases where names were not clear guides to the sex of the individual. Of the 222 appointments made by President Reagan in 1981, 9.5 percent were female. President Clinton's appointees, in contrast, were 31.3 percent female in 1993 (76 of 243 appointees) and 28.9 percent female in 1997 (31 of 128). In short, women appointees, while by no means equal in proportion to the share of women in the U.S. population, were present in historically high proportions in the Clinton administration. And while Clinton did not initiate the trend toward more female personnel in high federal government positions, he doubled the record of his most recent Democratic predecessor (Carter) and was well ahead of the Republican whom he succeeded (George Bush).

A fair summary would be that while Clinton's record on diversity compared with that of past presidents is partly magnified by the packaging (using catchy phrases like having an administration that "looks like America"), it also represents significant accomplishment of his stated goal.

Not surprisingly, Clinton's overt and quite successful quest for minority and women appointees stirred some controversy. That opponents of aggressive forms of affirmative action might be dismayed by the Clinton efforts is easily understood. More interesting is that groups purporting to represent the beneficiaries of EGG also expressed discontent when the number or level of appointees did not match their high expectations.

For example, at the start of Clinton's second term, Rep. Robert Menendez (D-N.J.) used Clinton's own words to complain: "We find ourselves with an administration that is looking less and less like America instead of more and more like America." And Rep. Xavier Becerra (D-Calif.), the chair of the congressional Hispanic Caucus, said: "Either there's a belief that there's not enough qualified Latinos, or they're ignoring us."[5] The White House personnel director, Bob J. Nash, himself an African American, defended the administration, indicating that appointments of minorities and other previously underrepresented groups can take longer to bring to fruition than other appointments because of the longer search time necessary to find qualified candidates.

As in the personnel searches carried out in the first Clinton administration, there were also problems of balance in selecting second-term appointees because of the White House's desire to have appointees from a wide variety of groups. Many times, this created confusion and delays in the process. Burt Solomon quoted an official in a cabinet agency who indicated that an intricate dance often took place after a cabinet member suggested an appointee. The official cited an example in which a white woman was suggested for a job in the agency. The White House then responded by asking the department to "look at a Hispanic male, a lesbian, and a black woman [whose] resumes look good." As the official somewhat dryly noted about a process fraught with political symbolism and conflict: "These are political appointees. There are politics involved."[6]

The emphasis on politics is well placed. While representatives of many of the groups the administration favored with appointments may have complained in an effort to prod the administration to do even more for them, they nevertheless stood firmly behind Clinton when he faced impeachment during his second term. An objective observer would have to conclude that Clinton's diversity policies were not only effective statistically—his administration was extraordinarily diverse by contemporary standards, that is, if one's focus on diversity emphasizes race, gender, and sexual preference—they were also effective politically. The leaders (and constituencies) of the groups Clinton favored stood behind him when he needed them most.

Problems and Controversies

Diversity does not necessarily imply controversy. Clinton's cabinet and subcabinet appointees have, for the most part, been politically moderate, and therefore not the sorts of people one would expect to stimulate great disagreement.[7] The Clinton administration, however, has clearly had a difficult time with the appointments process. The pace of appointments has been slower than that of other recent administrations, and it has taken longer to get appointees confirmed. The latter is certainly one factor leading to the controversy the administration has had with Congress about its extensive use of acting appointments to executive posts.

On the simple matter of appointments confirmed by the Senate, available data indicate how much trouble the Clinton administration has had. For example, although the number of appointees requiring Senate confirmation has grown over time, during his first year in office Clinton had 499 appointees confirmed compared with 662 for Reagan in his first year and 637 for Carter in his first year.[8] In addition, a recent study by Rogelio Garcia comparing the first years of the Reagan and Clinton administrations shows that it took Clinton longer to submit nominations and it took the Senate longer to confirm the nominations it received.[9]

Table 6.1. Average Number of Days to Nominate and Confirm Executive Department Appointees, First Years (1981 and 1993) of Reagan and Clinton Administrations

	Reagan	*Clinton*	*Clinton Difference*
Time to administration's submission of nominations	112	133	+21
Time from submission to Senate confirmation of nominations[a]	30	44	+11
Total time	142	174	+32

Source: Rogelio Garcia, "CRS Report for Congress, Filling Policy Positions in Executive Departments: Average Time Required through Confirmation, 1981 and 1993" (Washington, D.C.: Congressional Research Service, 28 July 1998), 98-641 Gov.

Note: Days when Congress was adjourned not included in the calculations.

a. The small number of cases where nominations were withdrawn were included. Here the date of withdrawal was counted as the final day of the process.

As table 6.1 indicates, on average it took the Reagan administration 112 days to submit a nomination in 1981, and the Senate took an average of 30 days to confirm each nomination. That was hardly a rapid pace, but it looks positively swift compared to comparable figures for the Clinton administration in 1993. Clinton averaged 133 days before submitting a nomination and it took, on average, 44 days for each Clinton nomination to be confirmed. In short, Clinton took 21 more days to submit nominations and the Senate took an average of 11 more days to confirm nominees than during the Reagan administration.

Garcia's explanations for the differences between the two administrations are quite reasonable. Both, he notes in looking for factors that they had in common, had Senates controlled by their own parties in their first years in office (both also had predecessors from the other party). Both also "faced a similar appointments process"—similar investigation and clearance processes, committee questionnaires and other forms, and committee hearing procedures.[10] Therefore, he concludes, the differences in time to submit nominations may have been a function of the Clinton administration's effort to achieve greater diversity and of the larger number of positions to be filled (at least 62 more) by the time Clinton took office. Garcia is less certain about why it took the Senate longer to act, but he speculates that the larger number of nominees may have been a factor.

It is likely that some additional factors were at work. First, Reagan's transition was highly organized, with lists of potential nominees at the ready. Clinton's was more chaotic, and the desire for "balanced tickets" in each agency compounded the difficulties in finding nominees and putting them forward. Second, the Republicans took over the Senate in the same year Reagan was elected. Many Senators felt they owed their election to him. In addition, the new majority and their staff were just finding their footing in 1981, a factor that may have made them more amenable to acting with dispatch on their president's nominations. Clinton, on the other hand, faced an established standing majority of his own party in the Senate, and he was not considered a major factor in their electoral fortunes.

There were some controversies over Clinton's first (1993) set of nominees—particularly notable were the difficulties he had in securing an attorney general and the Lani Guinier controversy[11]—but the results of the November 1994 elections promised to make the administration's situation more problematic than it had been before. Republicans took over control of both houses of Congress in an election that shook American politics to its foundations. The Republican congressional majority, confident that it represented a new wave of deep conservatism sweeping the country, was in no mood to make life easy for the president or his administration.

Much research still needs to be done on the consequences of the complex political and administrative problems the Clinton administration faced after the 1994 midterm elections, but the already difficult appointments process clearly became even more difficult. A study of time to fill appointments made during the first session of the 105th Congress, for example, found that it now took an average of 73.3 days for a nomination to be confirmed, up from the 44 days reported in table 6.1.[12] The Clinton administration was now knee-deep in controversy over its use of acting appointments and other devices it used to circumvent problems in getting the Senate to confirm its choices for top administrative posts.

One of the most effective, and controversial, devices for placing one's choices in top administrative positions is the "acting" appointment. According to a 1998 Congressional Research Service report on acting appointments in the executive departments:

> As of the end of February 1998, approximately sixty-four acting officials were serving in presidential appointee positions requiring Senate confirmation in

fourteen executive departments. The sixty-four officials occupied 20 percent of the 320 positions requiring Senate confirmation in the departments. The Vacancies Act, which is the exclusive statutory authority for the designation of acting positions to such positions, limits to 120 days, except in certain circumstances, the time an acting official may remain in a position. At least forty-three of the acting officials were apparently serving beyond the 120-day limit imposed by the act. Approximately thirty-four acting officials had been serving for over six months, with ten of them serving for over one year.

The Department of Justice claims that the Vacancies Act and its restrictions are not applicable to the executive departments. Justice asserts that the act is superseded by certain provisions in the enabling statutes of the departments that authorize their heads to designate acting officials to the vacant positions.[13]

As noted, the extensive use of acting appointments has been a source of significant controversy. There are at least two causes for this. The first stems from a long-standing dispute between the branches about the use of acting appointments. In this, Clinton stands in a long line of contemporary presidents who have aggressively used administrative strategies to advance their policy goals and improve their strategic positions in the ongoing conflict between Congress and the president that is inherent in the American system of separated institutions sharing powers.[14] Acting appointments under this strategy are a means to avoid Senate confirmation, rather than a stop-gap measure to fill a position for a brief period. The second cause of controversy derives from the fact that Clinton's extensive use of acting appointments follows an attempt in 1988 by a Democratic Congress to correct the problem through amendments to the 1868 Vacancies Act. In part, as a result of these amendments, some Democratic senators have spoken out against the administration's use of this device.

Clinton, to repeat, is not the first president to use acting appointments to circumvent Senate approval for appointees. They were, in fact, also a favorite tool of both Presidents Reagan and Bush.[15] Moreover,

at least since 1973 [in the Nixon administration], DOJ [the Department of Justice] has taken the position that any Executive department or agency whose authorizing legislation vests all powers and functions of the agency in its head and allows the head to delegate such powers and functions to subordinates in her discretion, does not have to comply with the [Vacancies] Act, which limits the time during which advice and consent positions may be filled by temporary designees before a nomination is forwarded to the Senate.[16]

An example of the use of an acting appointment—and one that has been particularly controversial—is the selection of Bill Lann Lee as acting assistant attorney general for civil rights. Lee had been a lawyer for the NAACP Legal Defense and Education Fund prior to his government service, and controversy about him focused on the politically contentious issues of racial quotas, preferences, and timetables.[17] President Clinton nominated Lee for the civil rights job in July 1997. Lee's nomination did not make it through the Judiciary Committee, however, and therefore it was never considered by the full Senate. Attorney General Janet Reno "nevertheless designated Lee as acting chief of the division" on 15 December 1997, and President Clinton "again formally nominated Lee to the post" on 29 January 1998.[18] According to press reports, Lee "contends that failing to win Senate confirmation and serving in an acting capacity has not interfered with his ability to run the [Civil Rights] division. He concedes, however, that if he had been confirmed, 'I'd feel a little better.'"[19] However Lee might feel, under the Justice Department interpretation of the law, he can certainly remain acting director beyond the 120-day limit that the Vacancies Act established

Congressional Republicans (now in the majority) are not the only ones disturbed by presidential use of acting appointments, because the issue is one of interbranch relations (and therefore power), as well as a struggle over who will fill positions ostensibly requiring Senate confirmation. Aside from the ever-vigilant Senator Robert Byrd (D-W.Va.)—well known as a defender of the Senate's institutional prerogatives—Senator John Glenn (D-Ohio), who was chair of the committee that participated in amending the Vacancies Act in 1988, also spoke out strongly on the need to revisit the issue. (The 1988 amendments to the 1868 Vacancies Act increased the time that an acting official may serve from 30 days to 120 days.) Glenn remarked: "We saw this problem building up through the Reagan and Bush administrations, and we thought we had corrected it." Since, however, the Justice Department persisted in its view, he suggested that Congress clarify the situation once again so that administrations "cannot interpret the law in any way except to preserve the advice and consent role of the Senate . . . [which] right now . . . is being bypassed."[20]

There are several proposals before Congress to assure that the Vacancies Act supersedes other statutes, but Glenn and others also acknowledge that Congress shares much of the blame for the problem. As the confirmation process has become increasingly politicized, it takes longer and longer to get people through. In Glenn's words: "Congress shares some of the blame here because it has become so partisan that people are being held up in the process for something that they had nothing to do with."[21]

The contentiousness of the appointments process started well before the Clinton administration and will almost surely continue after it if the government remains divided and the parties stay as polarized as they have become. Clinton's use of acting appointments has given this mechanism for promoting presidential interests particular prominence, but the underlying problem was not created by the Clinton White House, nor can it be solved by the White House alone. When the president and the Senate disagree on who ought to fill executive positions, they can either compromise or fight. Creative administrations will figure out ways to undermine the intent of almost any statute Congress passes to increase its leverage in the appointments process.

In sum, aside from the Clinton administration's extraordinary success in making the top level of the federal executive look "more like America" than that any of its predecessors, Clinton's legacy in the appointments area will probably not be particularly notable. Clinton appointed some very able people and some who were less able, some who were controversial and some who were not. From the limited evidence available, most of his appointees were pragmatists. But he was unable to get appointments made and confirmed expeditiously, and he was unable to solve the problem (indeed, quite the opposite, especially after the 1994 Republican election triumph) of increasing tension between the White House and Congress over executive appointments.

Governing Alone

Executive Orders and Regulations

The executive order is an invaluable tool a president can use to influence policy. As Robert Durant notes, executive orders are

> extremely easy to wield unilaterally. Indeed, as long as [presidents] can demonstrate that they have the statutory or constitutional authority to support their actions, any E.O.s they issue carry the force of law. What is more, since the late 1970s, presidents increasingly have relied less on statutory authority and more on their inherent constitutional powers when justifying executive orders that they issue.[22]

President Clinton has been an active issuer of executive orders. Early in his administration he did the expected and reversed two Bush administration executive orders opposed by organized labor. He then issued some additional orders on controversial topics such as sustainable development and entitlement cuts.[23] According to Durant, Clinton issued 27 executive orders in the first year of his administration when Democrats controlled the Congress and 102 in the first ten months of 1998, the period leading up to the midterm elections and, of course, a time when Republicans controlled Congress.[24]

Indeed, press stories in 1998 emphasized Clinton's plans to use executive orders to bypass Congress. Elizabeth Shogren, for example, noted in July 1998:

> President Clinton plans a blitz of executive orders during the next few weeks, part of a White House strategy to make progress on Clinton's domestic agenda with or without congressional help. . . . Clinton's proposals are intended to make gradual progress on largely popular social reforms until Republicans in Congress start to cooperate—or lose power after the November elections.[25]

Shogren cited examples ranging from plans to announce a new federal regulation on warning labels for juices to efforts to add to the Medicaid rolls.

Another story, with the expressive title "The Presidential Pen Is Still Mighty," emphasized that "Mr. Clinton is continually stretching his executive and regulatory authority to put his stamp on policy. He has issued a blizzard of executive orders, regulations, proclamations, and other decrees to achieve his goals, with or without the blessings of Congress." The story tellingly cited a recent Clinton order adding significant new protections for Medicare beneficiaries. This instance concerned rules that "not only carry out a 1997 law, but go beyond it, adding many of the safeguards proposed by a Presidential advisory commission—for women, for people with serious illnesses, and for patients who cannot speak English."[26]

Clinton's advisers are open about their use of these devices. Gene B. Sperling, director of the National Economic Council, said: "In '93 and '94, we were very legislatively minded. After we lost Congress, we were just playing defense and fighting for our lives. But by the end of '95, we were learning how to explore the full range of presidential power." And Rahm I. Emanuel, a senior Clinton adviser, observed about administrative action: "Sometimes we use it in reaction to legislative delay or setbacks. Sometimes we do it to lead by example and force the legislative hand. Obviously, you'd rather pass legislation that can do X, but you're willing to make whatever progress you can on an agenda item."[27]

Conservative and libertarian critics are angered by these actions.[28] Jeremy C. Taylor of the Cato Institute, for example, noted indignantly that "this president distinguishes himself by the aggressiveness with which he has expanded his authority without explicit Congressional approval."[29] But Louis Fisher, a much-esteemed Congressional Research Service expert on the subject, is probably closer to the mark when he says: "Clinton is doing what a lot of presidents do in a second term when the legislature doesn't look too inviting. Nixon did the same thing. There's nothing new in this pattern."[30]

Regardless of whether the Clinton administration has surpassed its predecessors in the use of tactics such as executive orders and regulation writing to get its way in policy struggles with Congress, Clinton is clearly within the tradition of recent presidents who have used the administrative presidency strategy to achieve their goals.[31] Particularly after the Republicans took control of Congress in 1995, the Clinton administration worked assiduously to use the administrative levers at its command to get its way on policy. In this, it follows in the footsteps of recent assertive, policy-oriented administrations that had disputes with Congresses controlled all or in part by the opposite party—the Nixon and Reagan administrations are especially identified with aggressive use of this strategy.[32] There are differences in policy goals, of course, and the Clinton administration has refined the techniques of its predecessors, but it does not appear to be a major innovator in this regard. Clinton's legacy is a contemporary demonstration, if one was needed, that employing an administrative presidency strategy is not a matter of a president's party affiliation. When there is divided government (especially when the president is an activist), Democratic presidents, like their Republican counterparts, are tempted to use and refine many of the devices often identified with the Nixon and Reagan administrations.

Line-Item Veto

One area where President Clinton might be said to have been an innovator, even if not the major force behind the change, has been in the area of the line-item veto (technically, enhanced rescission authority). Here, ironically, Clinton was the beneficiary of one part of the 1994 election campaign, in which an element of the Republicans' Contract with America was a promise to institute this power that presidents and congressional Republicans have long sought. Clinton was able to use the line-item veto (established by statute in 1996), making him the first president in U.S. history to have and employ this authority; the Supreme Court, however, invalidated it in 1998.[33]

The 1996 Line Item Veto Act allowed the president to reduce the budget deficit—line-item vetoes were only permitted when the budget was in deficit—by canceling specific items (lines) of spending or specific tax breaks. The Supreme Court ruled against it on grounds that the line-item veto was incompatible with provisions of Article I of the Constitution (the "presentment clause"). Pulling out all the stops, the Court quoted a statement by George Washington, when chair of the Constitutional Convention, that the president must "approve all the parts of a Bill, or reject it in toto."[34]

Clinton used the line-item veto eighty-two times before it was invalidated, canceling provisions for funds for New York City hospitals and a tax break for Idaho potato farmers, which were the focal points for the Supreme Court case. How successful the veto actually was in saving money is not clear, but it was the source of a spirited debate about both its constitutionality and its effectiveness. Some argued that the line-item veto would tip the balance of power between the president and Congress. As Guy Gugliotta and Eric Pianin noted in an article on congressional reaction to President Clinton's use of the veto: "Both Republicans and Democrats worry presidents may use the veto to extract promises of support on unrelated legislation, exact revenge against political enemies or to make policy, leaning on individual legislators where they are most vulnerable—tending to their home town affairs."[35] But others, while acknowledging the added political leverage the veto gave the president, were less certain about the extent of the leverage. For example, Robert Reischauer, a Brookings Institution scholar and former director of the Congressional Budget Office, described the veto as "a two-edged sword. The more influence the president tries to exert, the more backlash he will see."[36] He argued that the line-item veto would lead to more negotiations with the president on spending items, but that since presidents want spending too—and often lots of it, as in Clinton's wooing of California prior to the 1996 election—the negotiations would not be as one-sided as many opponents of the veto feared.[37]

One thing we know for sure is that the line-item veto, when it was used, sometimes inspired statements of outrage from affected members of Congress. For example, after Clinton vetoed 38 projects from a military construction appropriations bill, the chair of the Senate Appropriations Committee (Ted Stevens, R-Alaska) stated angrily: "We're dealing with a raw abuse of political power by a president who doesn't have to run again."[38]

The line-item veto was not in place long enough to allow a definitive resolution of the debate about its effects. The money savings were relatively small (estimated at less than 1 percent of the total federal budget[39]), and the political effects of the veto not yet fully clear at the time the Supreme Court invalidated it. But its short life will be the source of much debate among scholars of executive-legislative relations. In that limited way, the Line Item Veto Act of 1996 will be a part of Clinton's administrative legacy.

Reinventing Government

Issues

The Clinton administration's efforts to "reinvent" the government will long be remembered and studied by experts on administration. Even if the reinvention campaign is ultimately unsuccessful, it is significant enough so that it will be a focal point, probably even the main emphasis, of any assessment of the administration's place in governmental history.

Reinvention has been one of Vice-President Al Gore's major responsibilities. In line with a worldwide management reform trend and consonant with the political agenda of centrist New Democrats—while Governor of Arkansas, Clinton had been head of the Democratic Leadership Council, the organization of the New Democrats—Gore launched the administration's reinvention effort in 1993.[40] Reinvention aims, in the words of the first report of what was then called the National Performance Review (NPR), "to make the government work *better* and cost *less*" (emphasis in the original).[41] These are goals most can agree on. Neither is easy to achieve. Accomplishing both simultaneously would be a legacy any administration could point to with pride.

The reinvention effort has gone through several phases.[42] Phase I focused on the "works better, costs less" formulation. It emphasized cutting red tape (to enable agencies to focus on results and not rules), putting agency "customers" first, empowering government employees to get results (giving more authority to frontline employees), and cutting back to basics. Phase II, developed in response to the Republican victory in the 1994 congressional elections, put its focus on what government ought to do. "Works better" clearly slipped behind "costs less" as a focus. The question was more what government ought to do and less how it could do what it does better. Phase III changed the name of the effort from "National Performance Review" to the "National Partnership for Reinventing Government." The notion was "to signal a reinvention of reinvention."[43]

In Donald Kettl's words, Phase III had

> five new strategies: work to transform 'high-impact agencies' [such as the Internal Revenue Service] into more productive government operations; use outcome strategies to transform federal management; build partnerships and develop strategies to prevent problems; give employees more freedom to do their jobs while holding them accountable for achieving outcomes; and develop one-stop information and service.

These strategies were directed toward broader goals such as building a "safe and healthy America," a "strong economy," and "safe communities."[44]

Tomes will be written about the National Performance Review and the National Partnership for Reinventing Government. They are already a major topic of recent literature on public administration.[45] Critiques focus on the problems that accompany attempts to cut red tape (rules exist to ensure citizen access and rights), to put customers first (who are the customers and how do we deal with the interest of the citizenry as opposed to program beneficiaries?), to empower government employees to get results (how long will this last after there is a significant scandal?), and to eliminate government programs and services we do not need (this involves significant political decisions based on values and is not at its core a management decision). As noted earlier, NPR II's focus on cutting programs reinforced the "costs less," cutback-to-basics element of reinvention and served to counter the agenda of the new Republican majority in Congress. But it did this at the cost of deemphasizing the "works better" side of the reinvention effort and diminishing enthusiasm for it among government employees.[46] And Phase III compounded reinvention's problems by putting a spotlight on broad policy goals such as "safe communities" that even the best-run federal government programs cannot guarantee because results in these areas are driven by complex forces only partially under government control.

The strategies promoted by NPR are, to understate the problem, not always consistent. For example, some emphasize control from the bottom, putting the focus on consumer preferences and demands driving service and results. Programs and managers are then rated by customer satisfaction with products and services. Other NPR management approaches stress control from the top, with managers and programs rated by whether they achieve specified goals. Kettl calls these the "let managers manage" and the "make managers manage" approaches, and argues that they often "drive in opposite directions."[47]

I will not dwell further on NPR's problems and inconsistencies. It is almost certainly too much to ask of a complex package of government reforms, especially reforms designed and implemented in a highly political and contentious environment, that they be consistent or coherent. Changing management systems and, especially, cutting government programs affect many interests in society. They are thus inherently political and only secondarily dry questions of management approach or objective discoveries of which government activities are "basic" and which are superfluous. Deciding what government should do is a fundamental function of the political system. NPR often envelops many of these basic political decisions in a haze of management rhetoric, but the ultimate success or failure of the reinvention effort will rest on answering the political questions.

Examples

No set of examples is definitive, and those in a short chapter cannot do justice to the problems and prospects of NPR. My purpose here is simply to illustrate some of the problems faced by those who would reinvent the government.

The National Aeronautics and Space Administration (NASA) is one of the "high impact agencies" targeted by the National Partnership for Reinventing Government.[48] "NPR will work in partnership with these agencies to help them transform themselves entirely to focus on customers and getting results that matter to Americans. This process builds on agencies' strategic and annual performance plans . . . as well as ongoing quality improvement efforts."[49] NASA was a natural agency for NPR to pick because NASA's director, Daniel Goldin, is renowned for reciting as his goal for the agency words that should be dear to the hearts of reinventers—"faster, better, cheaper"[50]—and for his commitment to reinvention.

NASA, under Goldin's tenure, has done many things favored by the reinvention effort. Goldin's budget has gone down, but he has still insisted on quality performance, made innovations in his management of the agency, and attempted to raise money for it in a variety of entrepreneurial ways. Still, NASA has had numerous problems. The space station, for example, was reported to be $3.6 billion over budget in early 1998.[51] This was due to a combination of factors, including some beyond NASA's control, such as problems stemming from Russian participation in the program. Other difficulties, however, were due to contractor problems with firms such as Boeing. The latter are attributed in part to a poorly negotiated contract, a problem one would not expect from an agency so committed to reinvented management.

Critics of the agency's management, and implicitly of the management strategies advocated by reinvention, have been quite vocal. An article in the *New York Times*, for example, entitled "NASA Learns That Faster and Cheaper Isn't Always So," reported NASA's shifting its focus from large satellites to smaller, less expensive craft "that exemplify its new 'faster, better, cheaper' philosophy of doing business." The article's author then asks:

> But what if faster, better, cheaper proves to be none of the above? What if the process of narrower program requirements, speedier, incentive-based contracts, more contractor responsibility and less Government supervision or oversight fails to pay off? Then the Government and the taxpayers could end up with Lewis and Clark [a failed low-cost, advanced technology space satellite program focused on in the story].[52]

The article, as one might imagine from the passage cited, goes on to document a series of management problems that stem from efforts to manage programs in the manner (although not with the results) that NPR advocates. My point here is not that NPR is necessarily advocating something that is bound to fail, but that it will take great skill to manage programs in the more flexible and less rule-bound style endorsed by NPR, and that success is far from guaranteed.

Other problems with reinvention are exemplified by recent efforts to transform the Internal Revenue Service (IRS)—like NASA, one of NPR's high impact agencies. As the nation's tax collector, the IRS is the least popular federal agency (although a strong majority of taxpayers who actually have direct contact with it rate its services favorably).[53] The IRS has had management problems, is a tempting target for politicians, and was also cited by Kettl in his 1998 report on NPR as demonstrating "reinventing government's problems in identifying and preventing management disasters."[54]

IRS has had serious problems in managing and transforming its out-of-date computer systems. In the mid-1980s the IRS decided to overhaul its aging, once state-of-the art computers. It spent 10 years and $3.4 billion and did not achieve what it had promised. The reason, according to Arthur A. Gross, the agency's head of computer services, was that the IRS lacked "the critical mass of intellectual capital" to redo its computer system without outside help.[55]

Clearly, the IRS has been unsuccessful in the computer area in managing both governmental and nongovernmental contractors. A new IRS commissioner,

Charles O. Rossotti, a man with great experience in this area as chair and co-founder of a successful private-sector information technology company (American Management Systems, Inc.), was appointed by the Clinton administration in 1997 to run the agency. And in late 1998 the IRS signed a contract with a firm called Computer Sciences Corporation to modernize its computer systems. The contract is worth up to $7.5 billion over its lifetime, more than double what the IRS has spent on previous modernization efforts.[56] How well the firm succeeds in updating the systems will provide a major test of the effectiveness of turning to the private sector for help in a highly sensitive area such as taxation, where efficiency and great discretion in handling information are called for.

While the IRS has been heavily criticized for its problems in managing its computer systems, it has truly been lambasted for its treatment of taxpayers. Congressional hearings and actions in 1997 and 1998 put a spotlight on this problem. Following sensational revelations of IRS abuses (and building on the work of the bipartisan National Commission on Restructuring the IRS), Congress overwhelmingly passed and President Clinton signed legislation to reform the agency. Among its many provisions, the legislation established new rights for taxpayers (shifting the burden of proof in many cases from the taxpayer to IRS), set up a nine-member IRS oversight board, and gave the IRS more flexibility in hiring managers from the private sector to help in solving problems like those it has had with its computer systems.[57]

Although the legislation ultimately gained almost unanimous approval and was embraced by President Clinton, it was not without its critics. Some criticisms came from the Treasury and focused on questions of control over IRS. These were dealt with by weakening the authority of the oversight board in the final legislation. But more fundamental issues were basically ignored. Critics argued that shifting the burden of proof in tax cases to IRS would actually lead to more record-keeping requirements for taxpayers and benefit only a small number of individuals, mainly those in the upper-income brackets and tax cheats. As Donald C. Alexander, who was IRS commissioner under Presidents Nixon and Ford, said: "The changes will make it more difficult and expensive to enforce the tax laws against people who don't pay. And unless Congress provides more funds for enforcement, which it won't, then these changes will help some people get away with not paying." And Lee Sheppard, a writer for a publication specializing in tax policy, was quoted to the effect that the bill "should be called the mobsters and drug dealers tax relief act" because of the way it would hamper enforcement and collection efforts.[58]

When one looks carefully at the abuses highlighted in the congressional hearings, in fact, much of the blame for the legitimate problems that were uncovered goes back to Congress itself. For example, the IRS was shown to be targeting low-income taxpayers, in part because they are easy targets who do not have legal help, but also because "Republicans have helped to encourage that policy by harping for years on 'tax cheats' who take advantage of the Earned Income Tax Credit for low earners. Such open-and-shut cases also reduce an agent's hours per caseload, increasing efficiency—and that's a congressional mandate too."[59] The IRS was also chastised for using collection quotas to evaluate employees in violation of the 1988 Taxpayer Bill of Rights, although Congress had also been pressuring the IRS to increase tax collections and "in the 1980s and early '90s repeatedly voted to increase penalties and toughen IRS compliance efforts, thereby garnering additional billions of dollars for the Treasury."[60]

And probably the biggest cause of IRS's problems with taxpayers is the tax code itself, a code written and rewritten over the years by Congress and amended in 1997 with language creating 284 new sections and amending another 824.[61] As William Gale of the Brookings Institution noted about the likely after-effects of the 1997 legislation:

> One of the great ironies of all this is that one direction the debate goes is that now Congress will focus its attention on the IRS and claim that they're doing a poor job administering the tax system and neglect to mention the fact that the tax system is a holy mess precisely because of the laws that Congress has passed. The IRS is by no means a perfect agency, but having to administer the tax system, they're starting with one hand tied behind their back.[62]

In short, IRS has numerous problems, some of which are clearly the result of poor management. NPR-type reforms may well help to alleviate some of these problems. But the IRS also suffers from the need to administer the complex tax code written by politicians intent on helping favored interests and giving breaks to a variety of constituents, while at the same time ensuring that the government collects enough in taxes. There is a tension here that management reform cannot be expected to address. Forms can be simplified, service can be improved, and computer systems can be updated, but in the end taxpayers will find the complexities brought on by a complex tax code frustrating, and, of course, they are not likely under any circumstances to take much pleasure in paying taxes.

The IRS, in concert with the NPR, has unveiled a new mission statement. "One of the most far-reaching proposals would change how IRS workers are evaluated—to reward them for good customer service instead of by the number of cases processed, which can lead to abuse of taxpayers."[63] The idea is to rate employees on the basis of customer service and business results. There is an inherent tension between these two criteria. A tax policy expert at Coopers and Lybrand stated the problem clearly and concisely: "There is a constant tension between effective tax administration and the perception the public has of an overbearing tax authority. That tension has existed since the dawn of time."[64] The test will come in a less prosperous period when the government needs to increase its revenues. The odds are that the business results factor in evaluating employees will be reemphasized at that point, with Congress pushing the IRS again to stress revenue collection.

Assessing the Administrative Legacy

The jury is still out on Bill Clinton's administrative accomplishments, and it probably will be for some time.

There can be no doubt about Clinton's success in choosing political appointees who look more like the general population than the top administrators selected by any of his predecessors. While his cabinet and subcabinet appointees have not been extraordinary in any other way, they seem to have been at least as able as those selected by the average administration. Future administrations will likely be widely criticized if they fail to follow Clinton's lead in publicly seeking out women and minorities for appointment to high administrative posts.

Clinton's use of acting appointments and other mechanisms to circumvent the traditional process of Senate confirmation may help spur efforts to expedite both the clearance process and the work of Senate committees in processing nominations. While not a high-probability event, that would be all to the good, and a useful consequence of the controversy over the extensive use of acting appointments by the administration. Even expedited clearance procedures and a liberalization of the rules on disclosure, however, are not likely to solve the problem fully in situations of divided government where there is little consensus on policy.

The Clinton administration's use of devices such as executive orders to govern without Congress is neither unique nor particularly egregious by contemporary standards. Nixon developed the administrative presidency strategy, and Reagan improved upon it and applied it effectively. The Bush and Clinton administrations, more moderate in their use of power and in their goals, have also employed the strategy, but in more subtle and refined ways. Clinton now stands in a developing tradition of presidents who govern alone when they wish to make a point quickly or cannot get Congress to go along with them. It's not the most exalted of legacies, but it does show clearly that activist Republican presidents are not the only ones who find the administrative presidency strategy attractive.

Besides diversity, Clinton's major administrative legacy is likely to come from the reinventing government initiative. Whether it succeeds or fails, it will be studied carefully for years to come by students of administration and probably as well by those who administer government.

It is still too early to assess the impact of reinvention. As indicated earlier, many parts of it are controversial. The test will come when problems such as those outlined below arise. It is not clear, for example, how effective and long-lasting internal government deregulation will prove to be. Some scandal will inevitably be blamed on loosening the government's rules for procurement of goods and services or on expedited hiring practices. Congress will then be tempted to remedy the problem by insisting on tighter standards and controls over the behavior of frontline administrators or on stricter hiring practices. At some point there will be a lively discussion about what it means to "put customers first," particularly when the customers are unpopular groups such as welfare recipients or regulated interests such as broadcasters or drug manufacturers. In fact, the question of who the customer actually is will come up when one gets beyond agencies serving the general public, such as the postal service.

Phase III of reinvention puts an emphasis on results. Controversy will likely arise, however, over what results should be achieved—the Government Performance and Results Act leaves it to the agencies to propose goals, a clear formula for conflict between the agencies and the White House, and particularly between the executive and legislative branches of government.[65] And it is unclear how administrators will be held accountable if Congress does not appropriate the funds agencies expect and need to achieve their goals. In addition, the general goals established under Phase III are not well linked to what government actually does, so the system may seem a failure even if objective observers regard it as a relative success.

Perhaps the most difficult part of reinvention is in the politics of government cutbacks. Few would object to a government that works better and costs less, but many may object when cutbacks affect them. One of President Clinton's most famous declarations is that "the era of big government is over." That has a nice ring in the contemporary political environment, and the statement is clearly related to the goal under reinvention of cutting back to basics. However, determining what is basic and what is not is fundamentally a political, not an administrative decision. NASA may or may not be able to manage effectively under the new system—the first results, as we have seen, are mixed at best—and the IRS may prove more popular under its new regime—though it is likely to come under fire if collections decrease. But in the end political leaders must themselves decide, and then get the public to accept, what it is the public sector is to do. No amount of management reform can substitute for this decision. Clinton will face this hard fact if he pursues fundamental and long-lasting solutions to the problems of Social Security and Medicare.

When the fundamental decisions about what the government is to do are made, we will know better whether Clinton's legacy is a truly reinvented government or something more akin to the same old government with some interesting and often controversial administrative changes. The latter would certainly be important, and for good reason public administration scholars would continue to write about it for years to come. In that respect, it would be a major part of the Clinton legacy. But candor forces me to admit that it would not likely find a place in the first line of any overall assessment of the Clinton administration.

7

Clinton and Organized Interests: Splitting Friends, Unifying Enemies

MARK A. PETERSON

Although nowhere mentioned in the Constitution, organized interests are as much a core feature of American politics and governance as the presidency, Congress, and courts. Some observers have even dubbed them the fourth branch of government. To any president they represent both a challenge to and an opportunity for the exercise of leadership. Interest groups expose presidents to the threat of mobilized opposition to their agendas. They can exacerbate the difficulty of governing in a system embodying abundant veto points created by constitutionally "separate institutions sharing powers," in Richard Neustadt's classic characterization, as well as a bicameral legislature and sovereign states. At the same time, precisely because successful leadership in the United States is predicated upon the continuous building of supporting coalitions in a number of institutional venues, organized interests can serve as beneficial allies of presidents. Working in concert with the White House, their ties to other elected officials and capacity to mobilize constituencies can be used to forge winning alliances that bridge the institutional divides of American government. As either adversaries or collaborators of the president, interest groups cannot be ignored, nor can their relationship with the presidency be viewed in isolation from other elements of presidential coalition-building strategies.

By the time Bill Clinton took the oath of office, these verities of the modern presidency were well understood by both his Republican and his Democratic predecessors. They had put into place a number of practices and formal organizational arrangements in the Executive Office of the President to design and orchestrate interest group strategies. Contemporary politics and his own policy ambitions would compel Clinton to build on these traditions, albeit with his own distinctive touches. The coalition-building tasks he faced when inaugurated in January 1993, and those that arose later during his term in office, have been as challenging as any that other modern presidents have encountered. He began his tenure as only the fourth chief executive in the twentieth century to assume the presidency without the benefit of a popular majority (and like Woodrow Wilson, in two elections never gained one). He has endured most of his administration as the first Democrat since Harry Truman to experience divided government. In an era defined until recently by the legacy of divisive federal budget deficits and the perceived social disruptions of economic globalization, and lacking the Cold War opportunity to unify people by playing to the threat of the Soviet Union as an adversarial superpower, no overarching consensus existed on which Clinton could build a reliable base of support among the public or even among his fellow Democrats in Congress. In addition, casting Clinton as the exemplar of the baby-boom generation in both age and behavioral excesses, the highly mobilized self-proclaimed defenders of traditional values targeted the president for vilification and ultimately impeachment, resulting in the first Senate trial of a president in over a century.[1]

Policy success for Clinton, indeed ultimately his survival as president under the weight of impeachment, therefore demanded astute coalition building. Seeking to enlist directly the favor of the people or his party's members in Congress would not be sufficient, although focused efforts to secure those ends would be crucial as well. Like his predecessors, he would have to turn to a strategy—or variegated strategies—for garnering the assistance of organized interests in pursuit of his political and policy objectives under changing circumstances. The task for us here is not only evaluating the effectiveness of the president's strategies, but also determining whether he brought to this enterprise any new approaches or techniques, or engineered rearrangements of organizational influence, that would have lasting impact on the office or his successors.

To provide the basis for judging the nature and import of President Bill Clinton's relationships with the interest group community and their lasting consequence, if any, for the presidency, I begin by providing analytical background on the context, means, and purposes of White House group relations as they pertain to the Clinton years. I describe the broadly transformed social and political world that Clinton has confronted and how it has posed both new risks and openings for group coalition building compared to those of previous presidents. Next I consider the process by which formal linkages to organized interests became a standard feature of White House operations in the postwar period and a fully developed instrument available for Clinton to amend and exploit for his purposes on this new political terrain. I then present a generic typology of interest group liaison initiated by the White House that identifies the ways in which different types of presidential objectives and political conditions trigger quite varied group strategies. An activist president wishing to pursue a major and contentious legislative agenda, for example, turns to politically compatible and influential groups as participants in a "governing party" coalition. Chief executives with less divisive programmatic initiatives can approach diverse organized interests to help nurture policy consensus. The mechanisms of interest group liaison can also be used by presidents for more symbolic or representational purposes, either to reach out to marginalized interests counted among their electoral constituencies or to secure support from a wide array of mainstream groups in order to protect or recapture the political authority of an administration under siege.

When one looks at Clinton's actual engagement with the group system, as expected one observes a president and White House using the established institutional resources of the Executive Office to pursue a number of interest group strategies, both simultaneously for divergent purposes and sequentially as the political ground shifts dramatically under the president's feet. These activities, however, have been at best only modestly successful in fulfilling the president's objectives. For the most significant programmatic initiative of the administration, health care reform, an elaborately orchestrated coalition-building strategy not only failed to forestall legislative defeat but may have contributed to it. More significantly, in no small measure due to the health care reform fiasco, the legacy Bill Clinton hoped to craft from his approach to interest group relations is far more limited and considerably less favorable than he anticipated. The president sought to divine a New Democratic "middle way" set of policies designed to avoid the traditional cleavages associated with various social policies. They would merge the commitment of public-sector involvement in problem solving with the use of private-sector instruments such as market competition. Traditional liberal allies within Democratic constituencies would be joined in support of these initiatives by business and other interests more typically associated with the Republican ranks. The result would be federal programs that reinforced the ties of the primarily middle-class electorate to progressive (Democratic) government and a concomitant enduring rearrangement of group alliances that expanded the Democratic Party's constituency base—bringing together labor and management, environmentalists and manufacturers, patients and health care providers, police and community activists—while whittling down the Republican base to extremists on the right.

No such legacy emerges from the Clinton presidency. Instead, the complicated nature of the political setting, complexity of the issues on the government's agenda, inherent contradictions in the New Democrat group strategy, and simple blunders by the administration in the end worked far more effectively to unite the president's opposition than either to fortify the natural Democratic organizational base or to make it more inclusive. Indeed, the contradictions and failures of his group strategies in the first two years of Clinton's administration—pushing the North American Free Trade Agreement (NAFTA) in opposition to organized labor while simultaneously striving to enact health care reform predicated on labor's support, attempting to enact an amalgamated health care initiative whose success depended on the avid and active support of unions and consumer groups but that only brought out the passions of its conservative opponents, and opening his first term with a commitment to protect gays in the military that cascaded into a policy of "don't ask, don't tell" that pleased no one and generated the ire of everyone—left the administration without either a set of popular programmatic achievements to carry into the 1994 congressional elections or a secure group base that would facilitate challenges to the new Republican majorities in both houses of Congress. The president had his successes after the 1994 electoral debacle, such as blocking some of the most contentious Republican efforts to recast Medicare, Medicaid, and education programs, as well as continuing to advance a new profile of crime legislation, but his reelection in 1996 and high level of popular approval late in the administration have had more to do with the health of the economy and the overplaying by the Republicans of the scandal and impeachment card than any orchestrated programmatic agenda and associated interest group strategy. President Clinton will leave office having demonstrated the full operational potential of the modern interest group liaison apparatus in the White House, but without having produced any lasting measurable broad-based impact on the organization of interests or presidential relations with the interest group community.

The Changing Structure of Social Organization

By most accounts President Franklin Delano Roosevelt initiated what we now refer to as the modern presidency. By the time Bill Clinton became president, however, much had changed about the requirements of presidential leadership and the environment in which it is practiced. When FDR served in the White House, political party organization was still instrumental in choosing nominees for office and state party leaders played a significant role in formulating successful campaigns. The president spoke to the public in occasional "fireside chats" via the new medium of radio, but public opinion polling had not become routine; transportation technology limited the reach, frequency, and timeliness of the chief executive's travels throughout the country; and the dominating image and words of the president on television remained years in the future.[2] Although voluntary associations are as old as the republic, and group mobilization flourished in the late nineteenth and early twentieth centuries, often nurtured by democratic institutions and government itself,[3] the nation's capital was not awash in organized interests, advocacy centers, and lobbying firms. The primary groups of concern to the president were those included among his electoral constituencies, and there were few effective challengers to business interests other than the emerging and now federally protected labor movement. Politically marginal groups, such as African Americans, were given only the most subtle access to policymaking and the presidential establishment.[4]

The half-century between Roosevelt's death and Clinton's ascension to office witnessed a profound transformation of the structure of social organization in the United States, with important implications for the relationship between interest groups and the contemporary presidency. The public became vastly more educated and thus more primed for direct and targeted communications from particular interests rather than just the mass mobilization of political parties, trade unions, or occasional broad-based movements such as the temperance movement. In 1952 just 15 percent of the electorate had any college-level education, and only six in ten had ventured beyond elementary school. By 1988 almost everyone enjoyed more than a grammar school education and more than 40 percent had attended college.[5] Technological progress also altered the means of public communication and group organization. At first the rapid spread of television ownership in the 1950s and 1960s picking up broadcasts over a limited number of channels offered the president particular political advantage—no one else could command or dominate the medium as thoroughly as the White House. Computer-assisted polling, advanced telecommunications, satellite transmission, the shift toward cable television, and jet airplanes all accelerated unmediated interchange between the electorate and the president, but also between the public—more specifically specialized publics—and allies as well as adversaries among groups and within Congress. The improvement of computer, telephone, direct-mail, and television technologies greatly enhanced the capacity of organizational entrepreneurs to identify and communicate with more easily identified potential supporters and members, no matter how narrow the niche of interests.

At the same time, the civil rights movement gained momentum in the 1950s and led not only to the massive expansion of political participation by African Americans, but also furnished the training ground and paradigm for successful social action, subsequently exploited first on the left by the women's, consumer, environmental, and gay rights social movements, and later by the Christian right and its compatriots, all of which spawned new sets of enduring formal organizations to represent these interests both in the streets and in the established corridors of power. The broad patterns of social change in the 1960s and 1970s also overwhelmed the traditional political party organizations, shifting the nomination process for the presidency and for congressional offices from state and local party leaders to a primary system based more than before on personal campaigns, utilization of the new technologies of communication with the electorate, and movement politics. In FDR's time, the congressional parties were tied closely to the party apparatus in each state, leading to important divisions in the Democratic ranks between southern conservatives, often in alliance with Republicans, and more liberal northerners. The social and demographic changes reflected in the new group system resulted in altered parties in Congress by the 1980s. With conservative southern districts and states electing more Republicans and fewer Democrats, congressional Republicans became more uniformly right-of-center and Democrats became more consistently left-of-center, yielding a far more polarized House and Senate along party lines.[6]

The transformation of the interest group system has been especially noteworthy. In terms of raw numbers, the scope of organized interests grew dramatically by every available measure. The number of voluntary organizations listed in the *Encyclopedia of Associations* jumped fourfold from 5,843 in 1959 to 23,298 in 1995. Forty percent of the organizations included in the 1981 edition of *Washington Representatives*, entities with a formal presence in the nation's capital, reported founding dates since 1960; a quarter arrived on the scene during the decade of the 1970s. These numbers do not even fully incorporate the massive proliferation in nonmembership advocacy outfits, legal action centers, think tanks, corporate public affairs offices, and for-hire lobbying and law firms often representing numerous clients.[7]

More important, the overall character of the interest group community has changed. The growth in the system has not been a matter of more of the same.

Emerging from the social movements of the 1960s and 1970s were myriad new "citizen groups," leaning to the political left, that challenged existing interests, especially those representing the for-profit and business sectors. They disrupted old policy monopolies in various policy areas and achieved a more secure organizational footing than similar groups in the past because of entrepreneurial leadership and the help of wealthy benefactors, foundations, government agencies, and other "patrons of political action."[8] While the number of voluntary associations representing the profit and nonprofit sectors grew by around 60 percent between 1960 and 1995, and unions remained fairly stable, the number of citizen groups such as the National Organization for Women, Citizen Action, Friends of the Earth, and the National Council of La Raza jumped 180 percent.[9] The complexion of the interest group system shifted again, as the emergence of increasing numbers of organizations derived from liberal social movements stimulated a response on the right, leading to the formation of conservative think tanks (the Heritage Foundation), legal action centers (the Washington Legal Foundation), advocacy entities (the Family Research Council), and the mobilization of grassroots conservatives (best illustrated by the Christian Coalition).[10]

Strategic approaches for influencing policy and politics blurred. Where once the liberal citizen groups and their social movement forbears concentrated on "outside" strategies, including grassroots mobilization at the community level, while commercial and other traditional interests relied on "inside," more quiet lobbying of government officials, by the 1990s conservatives had their own pro-Christian, antigovernment, antitaxation broad-based movements and business interests were using new consulting firms (and new technologies) to launch what appeared to be grassroots responses favoring their policy agendas (often called Astroturf mobilization to capture its stimulated, largely targeted, and less authentic quality). Additionally, environmental, women's, consumer, and even gay rights organizations had become "establishment" enough to have direct access to the president and Congress.[11] Amid this ferment on both the left and right, however, came declines in "peak associations" that could speak for significant segments of the polity and that were sources of traditional broad-based organizational strength in support of liberal and conservative issues. For example, organized labor, the backbone of the drive for much liberal social policy and a mainstay of Democratic electoral coalitions, saw union membership drop from nearly 30 percent of the workforce in the 1950s to less than half that at the dawn of the 1990s (and fall from a third of self-identified Democrats in 1960 to just 11 percent). Barely one out of ten employees working for private business belonged to a union. The figures were even lower in the South. To many members of Congress, the AFL-CIO was "just one more PAC," or political action committee, among hundreds. On the other side, the American Medical Association (AMA), long the voice of medicine (as well as unfettered free enterprise), with almost all practicing physicians as members and few organizational challengers, could claim just over 40 percent of doctors as members in the early 1990s and struggled with myriad organizational competitors.[12]

Bill Clinton thus became president facing a particularly uncertain social and political environment. Because of technological advances and demographic changes, he would have perhaps greater capacity to communicate with the public en masse and through specific messages than did any of his predecessors, but so would organizational interests antagonistic to him and his programmatic agenda. Both would be attempting to entice a relatively disaffected middle class, concerned about its economic situation and the state of the social order but skeptical about what government could accomplish, and also less tied to party and other aggregating institutions. Clinton came to Washington with Democratic majorities in both houses of Congress, and they were probably less ideologically divided within their caucuses than at anytime in recent memory. The majorities were not large enough, however, to grant the party's leadership command of a legislature, especially the Senate, that widely disperses institutional resources among its members, including Democrats skeptical of the president's initiatives. Moreover, however much party unity had grown among congressional Democrats during the 1980s and 1990s, it was not a unity predicated on Clinton's New Democratic approach or his strength at the ballot box. The Republican opposition was at least as ideologically cohesive and ready to exploit the system's numerous potential veto points to thwart Clinton.[13] The 1994 elections, which brought cohesive, conservative Republican majorities to the House and Senate, profoundly aggravated the coalition-building situation for the president.

Working with (as well as working against) interest groups to piece together support among the public and in Congress played a large role in the administration's political and policy strategies. The rise of citizen groups supportive of a Democratic agenda (and the decline of some older order interests such as the AMA) could bring new organizational resources to the coalition-building enterprise. But there would be challenges as well as opportunities. Trade unions remained the most significant single set of organizational assets, but their reach within the electorate and influence with members of Congress had been greatly diminished. The new citizen organizations, often, as Theda Skocpol has noted, "staff-led, mailing list associations" with their checkbook memberships, could not conduct face-to-face grassroots mobilization as did labor in the past. They also tended to hold presidents to higher standards of policy purity. President Jimmy Carter complained that "when you don't measure up 100 percent with those so-called liberal groups, they demand a gallon of blood. There's no compromise with them."[14] Many representatives of these groups, such as Ralph Nader of Public Citizen, offered similar warnings, if implicitly, when Clinton's presidency began. In addition, there were new organizational opportunities for those likely to challenge Clinton's policy visions. Business interests had learned to mimic the grassroots mobilizing techniques of the left and could potentially join forces with the energized social movements on the right.[15]

Presidents and the Group System

Although the challenges and opportunities confronting him might have been novel, Bill Clinton did not have to invent from whole cloth how to integrate an interest group approach into his larger political and policy designs. FDR's world was different from Clinton's, but it was not devoid of attention to interests. Subsequent presidents continued to introduce thematic and organizational adaptations. To enhance their sway in the realm of politics and many domains of policy, chief executives, especially in the modern era, have employed three general strategies: intimidating the opposition, promoting and winning friends, and mobilizing allies to achieve specific political or policy objectives.[16]

Ronald Reagan pursued the most aggressive strategy of any modern president for enfeebling the organized interests perceived to be working at purposes contrary to those of the administration. Believing that government itself through grants and contracts provided much of the financial wherewithal of liberal groups lobbying for more government services at higher cost to the taxpayer, Reagan initiated a campaign to "defund the left" by stripping these organizations of their federal subsidies. The attack turned out to be poorly aimed, however—the president's most vociferous citizen-group adversaries relied relatively little on revenues from government, obtaining the bulk of their support from foundations, wealthy individuals, unions, and other sources. Instead, largely nonpartisan and far less political nonprofit organizations representing everything from city officials to service providers received substantial funding from the federal government, and the cutbacks tended to alienate and politicize them.[17]

Although by the time President Clinton was sworn into office, the political right had become highly mobilized and would prove to be an unending reservoir of aggression against the president on through impeachment proceedings, the Clinton administration never initiated a counterassault beyond rhetorical retorts. No explicit effort was made to undermine these groups organizationally; there was, of course, no spigot of federal funds to shut off. Instead, by advancing an unusual policy agenda for a Democrat that included "ending welfare as we know it," focusing on crime and punishment, promoting school discipline, and promising a balanced budget, the administration hoped to reduce the popular appeal and political influence of conservative interests and their Republican allies by appropriating important elements of their policy agenda. This strategy mirrored Ronald Reagan's use of tax-cutting and family-oriented social policy initiatives to break the traditional economic hold of the Democratic Party on urban ethnic groups, white southerners, and the middle class.[18] Indeed, it was the new Republican majorities in Congress, starting in 1995, not the president, that tried to intimidate opposition forces. These Republicans exploited proposed changes in federal expenditures and tax law, as well as IRS code enforcement, and silenced groups that were avidly working to derail the Republicans' plans for Medicare and Medicaid, education programs, and environmental policy and that in other respects were allied with Clinton.[19]

All presidents in one way or another engage in activities that promote and win friends, including those in the interest group community. That objective is most easily fulfilled in personnel decisions, most notably by the use of patronage, over which presidents had considerable control until the introduction of the civil service in the late nineteenth century.[20] Today the pattern continues, less in terms of numbers than of symbolic bearing. Candidate Clinton promised to appoint to the cabinet and senior agency positions several hundred individuals who "look like America"—and, one might add, more like the constituencies of the Democratic Party—than had any of his predecessors. Frustrated with "bean counters" among the advocacy groups, who challenged Clinton to do more, the president nonetheless did nominate and secure appointments for greater numbers of women and minorities.[21] Fulfillment of this commitment, along with other policy decisions, no doubt helped ensure the acquiescence of women's groups such as the National Organization for Women and more fervent succor from African-American groups when Clinton needed to defend himself against impeachment charges stemming from his extramarital relationship with a young White House intern.

During his administration, however, Clinton has not taken the next step to actively reshape the organization of interests to his advantage, as had John Kennedy, Lyndon Johnson, and Ronald Reagan. Much of the women's movement, for example, organizationally sprang forth from actions taken by the

Kennedy White House. Johnson's Great Society programs, such as the War on Poverty, included provisions that required the maximum feasible participation in program implementation of the populations receiving social services. Many of these initiatives failed to fulfill their explicit policy objectives, but they nonetheless helped to develop new leaders and organizations that would ensure the presence of additional institutional allies of liberal programs in the future. Reagan, naturally, sought the reverse. His administration assisted in bringing to the fore more effectively mobilized Evangelical Protestants, joined with Catholics, to combat abortion, and melded business and the professional class to serve economic interests, all intending to "reconstitute society" and recast who is represented and how alliances are formed within the interest group community.[22] Presidential and congressional electoral politics were remade as a result of these efforts. Other than seeking to promote temporary new alliances among organized interests on some issues, typically unsuccessfully, Clinton leaves no legacy of having similarly altered the group system through executive engagement.

The signature feature of the modern presidency in relations with interest groups has been the increasingly institutionalized process of mobilizing organizational allies to use their representational and lobbying resources in support of presidentially defined political and policy goals. The stature and relevance of such ties is best indicated by the establishment of the Office of Public Liaison (OPL) at the outset of Gerald Ford's administration and its continuation in every White House since. After the creation of the Executive Office of the President (EOP) in 1939, some of FDR's assistants were designated informally to maintain ongoing communications with blacks, Jews, farmers, and other constituencies participating in the president's electoral coalition. The Johnson and Nixon White House staffs expanded on that representational function to include more explicit efforts to win the active backing of groups of various kinds. But the OPL formalized both of these functions and provided staff specifically intended to fulfill the associated responsibilities to "communicate, articulate, and support the president's programs, policies, and priorities in order to mobilize support for them."[23] To be sure, the general task of "interest group liaison" remains the province of staff members scattered throughout the units within the EOP, and in some administrations is often done more effectively by people outside the Office of Public Liaison, but the ongoing presence of the OPL underscores the significance of instrumental links to interest groups for all contemporary chief executives.[24] Bill Clinton has been no exception. As we will see, the interest group mobilizing strategy was both front-and-center for his administration and a reflection of its political troubles.

Presidents have a number of diverse needs and objectives, with different implications for how relationships with various kinds of groups are to be pursued. We can bring some conceptual order to interest group liaison approaches, and thus Clinton's particular tactics, by identifying four types and the goals and incentives that are likely to produce each one. Two primary characteristics are distinguished among White House approaches to coalition formation using organized interests. First, there is the purpose of the engagement with groups—whether it is intended to marshal support for the president's programmatic initiatives, such as legislation proposed to Congress, or whether it serves to promote the president's role as an elected representative, such as improving and maintaining an incumbent's political standing with various constituencies. Second, there is the breadth of interactions with the interest group community—whether they are inclusive, extending broadly across an ideological or partisan spectrum of groups, or whether they are exclusive, focused on a more narrow, politically homogeneous subset of interests.

As shown in figure 7.1(p. 152), combining these two dimensions yields a four-fold typology of interest group liaison by the White House. In the first type, *liaison as legitimization*, presidents seek ties to organizations well beyond their electoral coalitions to improve or consolidate the appropriateness of their roles as national leader and head of state, which may be under threat. President Ford, for example, approved the establishment of the OPL as a way to develop group ties to help surmount his difficult position as an appointed vice-president subsequently brought to the highest office by the resignation of his predecessor. Unusual adverse political circumstances and a desire to win public approval for his new role as chief executive dictated the kind of group strategy President Ford would pursue.

Liaison as outreach also advances the representational function of the presidency, but in response to quite different circumstances and for quite different purposes. In this instance, presidents are secure in their own political standing but use interest group liaison to reach out to a select set of groups that traditionally have had limited access to the core centers of policymaking but that have demonstrated support for the president and could be important elements of the reelection coalition. FDR, Kennedy, and Johnson opened White House doors to African Americans; Johnson to consumer representatives, women, and environmentalists; Carter to women and gays; and Reagan to the Christian right.

The third approach is *liaison as governing party*, in which the collection of targeted groups is also limited but the goal is to stimulate advocacy and use of group resources to help forge assertive coalitions outside government to influence the emergence of successful ones inside government that favor the president's policy positions. The president wants to pass a piece of legislation, for example, and the task is to bring under a governing-party umbrella the collection of organized interests, constituencies, and members of Congress who can secure enactment of the bill. This approach to group relations became a centerpiece of Carter's White House when the president, articulating a full policy agenda, suffered early legislative defeats and strove to improve his effectiveness with Congress in subsequent sessions. It was also instrumental to Reagan's successful effort to enact major tax and budget cuts in his first year, pulling together an active alliance of organizations that shared the administration's policy convictions and had the financial and staff resources, as well as lobbying experience, necessary to ensure congressional attention.

The final form of liaison, *consensus building*, differs only in the expectation that enough agreement can be generated across diverse interests that it is worth extensive and more inclusive communications directed at organized interests with the intention of promoting a consensus coalition in favor of the president's preferred policy action. For example, when promoting civil rights and overcoming the problems of the poor were popular in the 1960s, and a growing economy produced an increasing flow of revenues for the government without raising taxes, Lyndon Johnson wanted to unite as many groups as possible, such as bringing together community activists, civil rights groups, service providers, and the construction industry to support public housing.[25]

		Breadth of Group Interactions	
		Inclusive	Exclusive
Purpose of Group Interactions	Representational	Liaison as legitimization	Liaison as outreach
	Programmatic	Liaison as consensus building	Liaison as governing party

Figure 7.1. Typology of White House Liaison with Interest Groups

Which approach to interest group liaison presidents attempt, therefore, depends on what presidents want to achieve (are they activists intent on reordering federal policy or are they defenders of the status quo?); the prevailing conditions specific to individual presidents (are they well supported by the public and does their party have considerable influence in Congress, or is their own political standing precarious?); and the attributes of the issues under consideration (are there deep partisan or ideological divisions within Congress and the electorate, or is it possible to achieve a consensus?). In addition, these characteristics are likely to vary both across issues and over time within a single administration, so all presidents are likely to engage in all four approaches, but to varying degrees. All of these considerations became readily apparent during the Clinton years.

Clinton's Problematic Group Mobilization Strategies

As suggested earlier, no matter what he hoped to accomplish, Bill Clinton was going to need beneficial and efficacious relationships with organized interests, but how would he orchestrate them and what would be the lasting impact of his efforts? Previous practice and institutional development in the White House presented him and his staff with the instruments necessary for a mature set of interest group liaison strategies. His choices about exactly how to utilize them, though, would be predicated on his objectives as president and his perceptions of how those matched with the prevailing political conditions and nature of the issues he wished to highlight.

As the 1992 campaign made clear, he would begin his administration with an activist policy agenda, proposing in relatively short order to increase revenues while restoring greater progressivity in tax rates; to introduce major new federal investments, albeit with some cuts in other areas and an eye toward balancing the federal budget after years of enormous deficits; to revamp entirely the financing and organization of the U.S. health care system, constituting one-seventh of the economy; to "end welfare as we know it"; to strengthen environmental protections; to employ federal programs to enhance education from kindergarten through college; to guarantee the protections of family and medical leave; to develop new approaches to crime policy; and many other controversial initiatives needing congressional enactment.[26] These legislative plans were supplemented with commitments to bring increasing numbers of women and minorities into senior positions in the executive branch of government and to formally open the military to participation by gays and lesbians, both of which objectives required congressional deference.

Such an assertive agenda would seem to call for an interest group strategy that emphasized liaison as governing party. The White House was certainly prepared to bring supportive groups into the fold. Where Jimmy Carter, the last activist Democratic president before Clinton, at first believed that interest groups could be largely ignored in presidential policymaking, President Clinton had no such illusions. He immediately upgraded the Office of Public Liaison in both relative organizational stature and role compared with its place late in the administration of George Bush. Because Bush was a decidedly nonactivist president in domestic policymaking, the White House had recast OPL as a subunit within the Office of Communications, reducing the number of staff members and typically failing to name directors with any real entrée to the centers of power in the EOP, a distinct contrast from the heady early years of the Reagan administration, with its sweeping program of tax cuts, budget reductions, deregulation, devolution of programs to the states and local government, and privatization.[27] Under Clinton, OPL was once again an independent unit, grew to a stable staff of around twenty individuals, and was directed the entire first term by Alexis Herman, a well-regarded senior White House official who later became secretary of labor.[28] An administration that came to office nurtured during the 1992 campaign on the effectiveness of its "war room" strategy was primed to include interest group liaison among its political armaments.

Clinton, however, sought to advance this dense and contentious programmatic agenda as a New Democrat, mixing nostrums about personal responsibility with a helping hand extended from a sympathetic government, the virtues of the market and competition among private institutions with the demand for a layer of personal and social security for people in the middle class or those striving to get there, who "worked hard and played by the rules."[29] As Stephen Skowronek argues, Clinton's "third way," not unlike the approaches of previous presidents ranging from Woodrow Wilson to Richard Nixon and Andrew Johnson to Dwight Eisenhower, was an "unabashedly mongrel politics, an aggressive critique of prevailing political categories, and a bold celebration of new mixtures"—and note that Clinton, like two others on this list, experienced impeachment proceedings.[30] Old cleavages that in the past forestalled comprehensive reform of health care and the welfare system, or that pitted economic development against cleansing the environment, or that treated crime as solely a matter of either social responsibility or individual punishment, were to be closed by divining new alliances among previously disparate interests and constituencies.

This outcome was intended to be the enduring organizational legacy of Clinton's presidency, to be achieved using a variation of interest group liaisons as consensus building, extending beyond the conventional constituency base of his party. But there were structural reasons to have little optimism about the viability of such a strategy, inherently constructed on contradictions. "The policy corner that Clinton's 'New Democrats' trapped themselves into," Bert Rockman notes, "was to create proposals of monumental complexity . . . regulating the private sector into doing what they would like it to do."[31] The decaying Democratic New Deal coalition may have been wearing thin and looking ragged, but there was as yet no natural, comprehensive organizational footing for mobilizing a New Democratic alliance among interest groups—and none would materialize. The increasing partisan polarization on Capitol Hill in the 1980s and early 1990s, running against the impulse for "new mixtures," did not make the attempt any easier, as was made clear by the administration's embarrassment with health care reform, as well as the failed effort to find a workable compromise on gays in the military and other early initiatives.

Not long into Clinton's presidency, two political shocks only served to complicate the president's situation even more. First, the 1994 Republican takeover of Congress, producing the first combined House and Senate Republican majorities since President Dwight Eisenhower's initial term, completely transfigured the political environment, putting an abrupt end to visions of an activist presidency and forcing a defensive posture. Guided primarily by the new Speaker of the House, Newt Gingrich (R-Ga.), the strikingly conservative Congress launched an activist—Gingrich called it "revolutionary"—program threatening the core Democratic accomplishments of the past half century. The White House and its allies were left with the task of formulating a veto strategy. Liaison as governing party or consensus building suddenly had to give way to liaison as opposition party. Second, the persistent investigative focus on perceived scandals within the administration, reaching maximum force with the House impeachment and Senate trial of Clinton over claims that he had lied under oath about his relationship with White House intern Monica Lewinsky and engaged in obstruction of justice, directly endangered the authority of his presidency. To the extent that there was an interest group strategy on this front, liaison as legitimization took center stage, but the president's defense involved more of a campaign for public opinion through media coverage than an effort to influence Congress through organizational activity. What we see from these remarkable shifts in the political terrain during Clinton's administration is both an inability to settle into a single, effective pattern of interest group interactions and a changing array of approaches to interest group liaison taken by the White House, but with few obvious successes.

Three exemplary cases illustrate the predominant characteristics of the relationship between the Clinton presidency and the interest group system: the debate over Clinton's Health Security Act, representing a failure in both group strategy and policy, and of such consequence that it set the stage for all that followed, including the withering of a comprehensive group strategy; the passage of NAFTA, an instance of policy success, but one that required a group strategy both harmful to other initiatives and indicative of the organizational dilemmas confronting New Democrats; and the administration's continuing commitment to a new order of crime policy, which has yielded both legislative success and the elements of a productive group strategy. Last, I consider as a whole the period of time following the advent of Republican majorities in Congress, during which White House interest group liaison has been of relatively little explicit importance.

Health Care Reform

Enactment of the president's proposed Health Security Act, which would have extended the guarantee of private health insurance coverage to all Americans below the age of sixty-five by expanding upon and reorganizing the existing employer-based insurance system, was to be the cornerstone on which Clinton would build a successful administration—"the Social Security Act of this generation . . . that would establish the identity of the Democratic Party."[32] It was the boldest of initiatives on an activist's agenda, pursued in a political context of both opportunity and unpredictably. In this setting the president chose to seek a New Democratic policy path that turned out to be ripe with internal contradictions that stood in the way of the White House developing a productive interest group liaison strategy, which, in turn, contributed to the program's legislative failure, in concert with myriad other factors beyond the scope of this chapter.[33] It is the most important interest group story of the Clinton administration, with the longest-lasting consequences.

Unabated inflation in medical costs, a rising tide of uninsured individuals, and growing doubts among the middle class about its health care security in the midst of recession propelled the issue of health care reform back onto the political and policy agenda in the early 1990s. Like Harry Truman, Richard Nixon, and Jimmy Carter before him, Bill Clinton proposed a comprehensive solution to the ills of the health care system. Unlike them, he would be launching his initiative in a world of interest group politics that had changed in profound ways. For the first time, the American Medical Association no longer had the power or inclination to be an obstacle to reform, and physician specialty societies both developed their own independent presence in Washington and often, as in the case of the American College of Surgeons, supported major federal intervention.

After years of frustration and failure at stemming the costs of health insurance coverage for their workers, many large employers endorsed the idea of large-scale government efforts to reform the system. The insurance industry was in political disarray. The Health Insurance Association of America, the trade association of commercial carriers, now represented firms writing only one in three private health insurance policies as a result of the acrimonious departure of the "Big Five" insurers and the small carriers to form their own diametrically opposed organizations. At the same time, the emergence of new citizen organizations had brought greater organizational diversity, stability, and resources to the pro-reform alliance, including Citizen Action, Families USA, Public Citizen, and the American Association of Retired Persons (AARP), among others. On the other hand, labor unions had lost strength both in numbers and in the fortitude of their past positions on reform by becoming more closely aligned with business interests wrapped up in employer-based insurance and support of federal provisions, such as ERISA—the Employee Retirement Income Security Act—that preempted state regulation of self-insured plans (which predominated among large employers).[34] In addition, small business—typically opposed to any federal market interventions—was maturing into a greater force in Washington politics, and conservatives had become more mobilized at the grassroots since the last failed effort at health care reform in the 1970s. With the burgeoning of health care expenditures and employment, the financial and institutional stakes involved were also reaching proportions that made it increasingly difficult to challenge prevailing health care arrangements.[35] A successful effort at coalition building would have to exploit the shifts in the group system that favored reform and stymie those that threatened it.

In formulating a health care reform plan, Clinton had three conventional options. First, he could choose to inaugurate a bipartisan process that brought together representatives of both parties to hash out an acceptable compromise plan. This kind of inside bargaining strategy would seem to comport with the need to secure enough Republican support to overcome filibuster threats in the Senate and would require a less developed plan for interest group liaison. The previous two bipartisan efforts to identify a viable health care reform plan, however, had foundered in Congress. Nor was such an approach likely to yield legislation of the scope Clinton desired to contain costs, control federal health care spending, and ensure universal coverage, as well as to win credit for himself and fellow Democrats.

Second, the president could adopt as his own a reform plan that fit with the preferences of the median legislator, the representative and senator in each chamber (in the realm of moderate Democrats and Republicans) who represented the pivot point for a winning majority. Again, the approach would emphasize inside bargaining between the White House and select members of Congress. These reform plans, though, either incremental in nature or subscribing to initiatives that would institute versions of managed competition among private insurers without the requirement of universal coverage, would fail to relieve pressures on the federal deficit (so would not fare well when evaluated by the Congressional Budget Office), make little if any progress in expanding insurance coverage, and could possibly increase the cost of insurance for the currently covered middle class.

Third, the administration could attempt a different kind of bipartisan approach, one that Charles Jones calls "copartisan."[36] Each party develops its own proposal in "parallel," often quite different from one another, but then engages in a process of competition, negotiation, and concession that ultimately produces a compromise program that attracts bipartisan support for final passage. The president might have begun with the kinds of proposals that had won considerable support within the Democratic caucus of each chamber: either "pay-or-play" plans, which mandate that employers provide insurance coverage to employees or pay for their inclusion in a public insurance program, or versions of "single payer," which set up a system of publicly-financed insurance. To ensure maximum leverage in the course of legislative deliberations over such options, the White House would naturally turn to interest group liaison as governing party. A coalition of like-minded and committed organized interests, comfortable with these policy approaches and with experience and resources relevant to influencing members of Congress, could be assembled under the direction of the administration. The natural allies for this project would include most trade unions, the new array of liberal consumer and other citizen groups, and perhaps some renegades from the business and health care provider communities.

President Clinton, for the most part, rejected each of these strategies and instead chose, in the course of the presidential campaign, a fourth that embodied New Democratic inclinations. Described by Jacob Hacker as a "liberal synthesis," the plan of "managed competition under a budget" was intended to attract support on the left by ensuring universal coverage and providing a regulatory check on cost increases, while garnering the acceptance of the right by relying primarily on private institutions, including insurers, as well as market competition as the first line of attack on underlying cost pressures.[37] The great divide in a near century in health care reform debates would be bridged by weaving these themes together into a single initiative. The interest group strategy was intended to mesh with both the new opportunities created in the changing group dynamics within the health care reform domain and this effort at substantive synthesis, if not quite full consensus (the administration never expected to pick up the endorsement of hardline conservatives).

According to internal White House memoranda, the strategy had "three essential components." A base of "natural allies" would be nurtured among senior citizen associations (which had "the grassroots ability to counterweight small business groups"), consumer groups (which "have more credibility [with the public] than any other group on the health issue"), as well as unions, liberal provider organizations, religious associations, and a variety of organizations representing women, children, and minorities. These groups were committed to universal coverage and typically supported single-payer plans. The second component was devised to "win significant enough business support, from both large and small businesses, to reassure conservative Democrats and moderate Republicans" in Congress. Finally, the intention would be to "keep the health industry divided, sector from sector and within sectors, . . . [working] to keep . . . doctors, hospitals, insurers, and pharmaceuticals . . . shooting at each other, and . . . mak[ing] sure some players in each sector are with us." As was written to Hillary Rodham Clinton by Mike Lux, head of public liaison for the health care reform plan, "we have to have *all* of these groups to win . . . . The trick in passing health care reform has always been in part to *figure out a package that can draw some business and provider support, while exciting the people who should be our base.*"[38]

The trick misfired on both counts. Although the U.S. Chamber of Commerce and American Medical Association initially announced acceptance of a main feature of the Clinton plan—employer mandates—both ultimately withdrew that support when challenged by the opponents to health care reform. The administration could never land the endorsement of the Business Roundtable or the National Association of Manufacturers, despite the benefits large employers would derived from specific provisions in the Health Security Act. Representatives of other groups felt that they were being taken for a ride; each being promised something different—and contradictory, in their view—by Ira Magaziner, the president's adviser who worked with Hillary Rodham Clinton on the development of the Health Security Act. Perhaps even more discouraging, the complicated nature of the plan—a complexity resulting directly from the effort to use private institutions and mechanisms to achieve equitable universal coverage and cost control—left the administration's natural allies bewildered while it fueled the opposition's own coalition-building initiatives and public campaign against reform. Groups the administration had counted on to stimulate public support were "having to devote enormous amounts of resources to educate their activists, let alone their members. . . . Until they get ahead of the curve on this process, grassroots pressures on our side will be relatively sparse."[39]

In the meantime, the No Name Coalition fighting the Health Security Act had formed, resource-rich and with the full panoply of grassroots mobilizing and inside lobbying potential of the National Federation of Independent Business (the most effective association representing small businesses), the Health Insurance Association of America (and its famous "Harry and Louise" television campaign), Independent Insurance Agents of America, the National Restaurant Association, as well as the Christian Coalition and its grassroots allies. Its members used the complex language of the reform plan to label it "government-run health care." Mike Lux's greatest concern had been fulfilled: "we may end up with a reform package that excites no one except our opposition."[40] In addition, the prospects for a bridge-building coalition led by the administration were further dimmed by the partisan alignment on health care reform and the tensions embedded in the president's ultimate political objectives. Clinton wanted to use enactment of health care reform as a prime means for creating and solidifying a long-term Democratic majority in Congress and control of the White House (including his own reelection). Conservative Republicans, led by Newt Gingrich, understood the threat to their party's interests and orchestrated a comprehensive campaign, joining congressional Republicans with the No Name Coalition, to defeat the president's proposal, or any substitute for it.[41]

Many factors converged to keep the House and Senate from even bringing the Health Security Act to either chamber's floor. But the White House was not able to devise an interest group strategy that would have facilitated the emergence of a better result. It needed the enthusiastic engagement and unified support of prime Democratic target groups—those that shared the commitment to universal coverage and had the wherewithal to make a difference with the public and directly with Congress. Only a quarter of these organizations, however, formally endorsed the Health Security Act, another quarter informally favored its passage, and half expressed mixed reactions, agreeing with some of the plan's features and opposing others.

In contrast, the opposition, prime Republican target groups, had no difficulty identifying their position and acting on it. Sixty-nine percent of them were hostile to the president's efforts, nearly six in ten actively so.[42] The administration's struggle over health care reform failed to assemble and sustain an interest group coalition that would be a viable force undergirding New Democratic approaches, but it did stimulate the formation of a tightly knit, highly effective, and enduring coalition of adversarial interests, linking major business organizations and the Christian right even more closely with the Republican Party. The No Name Coalition in varying forms appeared time and again during the rest of the administration, favoring GOP plans for major tax cuts and restructuring Medicare in the 104th Congress and working to defeat the Patients' Bill of Rights response to managed care in the 105th Congress—although now out in the open and with clear names, such as Coalition for America's Future and the Healthcare Leadership Council.[43] Moreover, the prominence of the health care reform debate and the inauspicious demise of Clinton's most important policy initiative contributed to the Democrats' stunning setback in the 1994 congressional elections. The new Republican majorities put the president out of the business of leading the nation's policy agenda and thus made far more problematic the programmatic objectives of interest group liaison by the White House.

NAFTA

When he became president, Bill Clinton could not avoid having to decide about whether or not to endorse and push for congressional acceptance of the North American Free Trade Agreement negotiated with Canada and Mexico by the outgoing Bush administration. Although candidate Clinton had railed against features of NAFTA, once in office he pledged to strengthen environmental and labor protections associated with the treaty and to support, as had all modern presidents, the objectives of free trade that the agreement would promote. The timing required for Congress to consider the agreement, however, could not have been worse—the fall of 1993. It demanded the president to shift his attention from health care to NAFTA, especially because the agreement seemed destined to go down to defeat in the House unless salvaged by a major lobbying effort by the administration (it would pass easily in the Senate). That granted more time for the No Name Coalition to mount its campaign against health care reform.

More important, administration efforts to influence congressional responses to presidential initiatives cannot be viewed in isolation from one another. The president's endorsement of NAFTA put him seriously at odds with core interests he needed to do battle in favor of health care reform, as well as much of the Democratic leadership of the House. Failing to obtain passage of the implementing legislation would expose Clinton's limited influence with Congress right before the great legislative debate on health security. On the other hand, winning the legislative fight, "an extraordinary victory" that Clinton achieved on a 234–

200 vote in the House, would weaken the unity, as well as help deplete the resource base, of some groups that he needed to be among his closest allies on health care reform. Policy success on NAFTA, facilitated by a group coalition of odd bedfellows, contributed to diminishing the effectiveness of the interest group liaison strategy for health care reform.[44]

Labor unions, environmental groups, and some manufacturing businesses were adamantly opposed to the agreement. As Representative Dennis E. Eckart (D-Ohio) put it, "Politically, NAFTA is not a winner for the president. On the left, the labor folks and environmentalists are all upset and they are core constituencies for the Democratic Party." Organized labor threatened to use all of its available resources, including funds committed to health care reform, to defeat the bill in the House and to "punish" representatives who voted for the accord.[45] To secure passage of the NAFTA-enabling legislation, Clinton assembled a quite different coalition, one that perhaps hewed closer to New Democratic themes, mixing far less reliance on constituencies of the old Democratic Party with strong support from business interests and Republicans. Indeed, "many of Clinton's most vocal opponents became, for the solitary purpose of passing NAFTA, his hardest-working allies," such as then Minority Whip Newt Gingrich. In classic interest group liaison fashion, administration officials met weekly with a number of business representatives to map out the legislative campaign. The president had "demonstrated his capacity to move beyond the traditional Democratic Party coalition that helped elect him."[46]

But this was no enduring New Democratic coalition. Prior to NAFTA not a single Republican in the House or Senate had voted for the president's 1993 budget and economic program. After NAFTA, they quickly fell away from health care reform and other administration proposals. Labor's abilities to influence the health care reform debate were weakened by NAFTA, but there was no compensatory mobilization of business interests, most of whom left the president's side after the trade accord had been approved by Congress. The legislative triumph with NAFTA was sweet reward for Clinton, as had been the down-to-the-last vote success on the economic program, but it did not mitigate, and probably aggravated, his coalition-building challenges on other programmatic initiatives throughout his administration, especially health care reform.

Crime Control

Early in his first term and continuing through his administration Bill Clinton pursued other policy issues with a New Democratic approach, including what became one of his signature policy successes, crime control legislation. The contrast with health care reform, albeit entailing a much grander policy initiative, is quite striking, especially since "politically . . . crime and health care share much. Both have long been mired in clashes of ideology, partisanship, and the self-interest of powerful lobbies; both have stirred up fear and frustration."[47] As the 103d Congress came to a close, it also appeared that the president's anti-crime initiative would succumb, along with health care reform, to deep partisan divisions and a successful effort to block the legislation by Republicans. But after losing on a 225–210 procedural vote barring floor consideration of the bill in the House, the administration waged a "tenacious battle that transformed devastating defeat" into "a spectacular 235–195 comeback victory," joined by forty-six Republicans, and despite the concerted efforts of the National Rifle Association.[48] One may debate whether enactment of the president's Violent Crime Control and Law Enforcement Act of 1994, and subsequent legislation and administrative policy, has contributed to the nation's declining crime rate, but this initial legislative triumph reaped political rewards. Public opinion surveys conducted by a GOP pollster, for example, showed a rise from around 50 percent to 70 percent in the public's favorable rating of Democrats on crime from the time the bill was passed in 1994 to a comparable poll three years later.[49]

Unlike the case with health care reform, the New Democratic approach to crime, in both the substance of policy and the interest group strategy used to develop a winning coalition, proved efficacious. As with the Health Security Act, the administration tried to bridge previous ideological and partisan schisms by formulating a policy design—"punishment, prevention, and policing"—that offered attractive features to potential supporters across the spectrum of opinion.[50] For the right there was an emphasis on holding criminals responsible for their actions, imposing harsher sentences, expansion of federal death-penalty offenses, and generally elevating the penalties for committing a crime. The left would be enticed by the assault-weapons ban as part of the overall legislative package, increased attention to violence against women, and significant additional investments in programs designed to prevent crime by engaging young people in midnight basketball and other activities that would keep them off the streets. For everyone, there was the vision of 100,000 more police officers and promotion of community policing. Although conservatives and most congressional Republicans objected to what they termed the "pork barrel" features of the bill, a bipartisan coalition could be formed among groups and among members of Congress. Indeed, conservatives worried that passage of the crime bill signaled Clinton's capacity to capture the political center on an ongoing basis. As Rich Lowry lamented in the *National Review*, "If Clinton can recreate the crime bill's bipartisanship on other issues—and Republican negotiator Michael Castle (Del.) says Clinton confided to him that he'd like to 'institutionalize' such bipartisan bartering—he'll have found a formula to revitalize his presidency and deflate the opposition."[51]

Clinton did not discover the means to exploit such an approach consistently across different policy issues, especially after the Republicans took control of Congress. In contrast to the NAFTA experience, however, the newly crafted interest group base for crime policy had considerable endurance. Striving to take crime legislation out of the traditional congressional election cycle by using four-to-six-year time frames, and emphasizing relatively flexible funding of state and local initiatives, the administration was able to pull together a supportive coalition of organized interests rooted in state and local institutions but with a presence in the nation's capital. White House efforts to influence members of Congress from key House districts by bringing in state and local law enforcement officials, clergy, judges, antidrug groups, and diverse community-based groups ultimately generated a list of thousands of people in a multitude of House constituencies. Combined with police unions and associations representing police chiefs, groups that promote gun control, and mayors active on the national scene, the administration maintained a diverse and engaged alliance of interests.[52]

After the 1994 Earthquake

The results of the 1994 congressional elections reintroduced divided government in Washington following the short hiatus of the 103d Congress (1993-94). The 1996 elections maintained it, leaving the nation with elected officials at the national and state levels of governments almost perfectly balanced between the two parties. Divided government alone need not be a source of inescapable partisan conflict or policy stalemate. David Mayhew, for example, found the U.S. government to be as legislatively active under divided government as it is when the executive and legislative branches are unified under the banner of a single party.[53] Although it could be more difficult under these conditions, a president could pursue a programmatic agenda and stimulate support for it using either interest group liaison as governing party or as consensus building, depending on the nature of the issues involved. Bill Clinton, however, faced a decidedly conservative and hostile congressional majority, certain it was elected in specific rejection of the president by the public and determined to prosecute a distinctly partisan agenda of its own. An array of business and conservative interests energetically endorsed its policy agenda (and were often invited by the Republican leadership to participate directly in the drafting of legislative language). Many in this camp, such as the Family Research Council, Christian Coalition, and Washington Legal Foundation, also contributed vigorously to the overt challenges to the legitimacy of Clinton's presidency.[54]

In this setting, the president's first worry was to regain his institutional standing. In the weeks following the 1994 election, Clinton even felt obliged to state publicly that he remained a relevant player in Washington policymaking.[55] To the extent that the White House had an overt interest group liaison strategy, and none is readily apparent from media coverage or scholarly investigation, it was one that emphasized representational objectives, especially legitimization— reaching out to a variety of interests to reaffirm the president's authority. Once the scandal over the president's relationship with White House intern Monica Lewinsky broke, setting into motion the series of legal and political events that culminated in the Senate's failure to convict Clinton, the use of interest groups to promote the president's political and constitutional legitimacy became even more crucial. Clinton was aided in this endeavor by women's groups, for example, because of his programmatic deeds—enacting family and medical leave, holding the line in protection of abortion rights, and so forth—and the long-standing use of the Office of Public Liaison to bring women's interests into the White House. Going beyond the practice of past presidents who had an OPL staff member serving as the liaison to women's groups, the Clinton OPL in 1995 established a project on Women's Initiatives (later renamed Women's Initiatives and Outreach) with its own director and deputy director.[56]

Despite the unusual circumstances of the Clinton era, this altered role for interest group liaison later in an administration was actually not far from typical. Following Reagan's legislative successes on the massive National Economic Recovery program during the first Congress of his administration, the White House had less of a policy agenda to project, and interest group relations drifted from liaison as governing party to such things as outreach to conservative organizations.[57] Interest group liaison activities also disappeared from view, as occurred again during Clinton's administration after the 1994 midterm elections. A search of newspaper reports, accounts in the specialized media, and articles by academics furnished no meaningful assessment or even description of White House–interest group relations following the 1994 election.

That is not to say that major legislative and policy battles did not occur during the subsequent four years of the Clinton administration. In many respects they dominated the 104th Congress (1995–96), but with the president and Democrats on the defensive. At best there were moments of interest group liaison as *opposition* party, when Clinton finally joined the ranks of congressional Democrats and various liberal interest groups fighting to block Republican efforts to restrict dramatically future funding for Medicare and Medicaid, restructuring the former from a defined benefit to a defined contribution program and devolving the latter into a block grant to states; to close cabinet departments; to cut back on education funding; to limit environmental regulation; and the like. The president vetoed the budget plans enacted by the Republican Congress that included these provisions and won the public opinion battle over the subsequent partial shutdown of government.[58] But one would be hard-pressed to claim or find evidence that the White House took the lead on these campaigns. Liberal organized interests and the Democratic leadership in Congress led the assault. And when the president ultimately signed the Republican-designed overhaul of welfare—the Personal Responsibility and Work Opportunity Reconciliation Act of 1996, which replaced the Aid to Families with Dependent Children entitlement program with block grants to the states, including Temporary Assistance for Needy Families—many groups that had been an important part of the administration's organizational base were in earnest opposition. For example, Marian Wright Edelman, president of the Children's Defense Fund (for which Hillary Rodham Clinton had been a board member), claimed that President Clinton's acceptance of the legislation "makes a mockery of his pledge not to hurt children. It will leave a moral blot on his presidency."[59]

Failure of the Centrist Strategy

There are two ways in which presidents can establish meaningful legacies in their relations with the interest group system. One is to use the resources and offices of the federal government to transform the community of organized interests, influencing which constituencies are represented and the degree to which they are effectively mobilized for political action. Presidential administrations have long played an instrumental role in group formation, from William Taft's encouraging the formation of the Chamber of Commerce of the United States, to John Kennedy's providing the opportunity for initiating the National Organization for Women, to Lyndon Johnson's stimulating groups representing African Americans and the poor, to Ronald Reagan's facilitating the mobilization of Evangelical Christians.[60] Some have also sought openly to challenge their organizational adversaries, as Reagan did when he tried to "defund the left." Bill Clinton's legacy in this respect is quite unusual. As revealed in the cases of health care reform, NAFTA, and gay participation in the military, he seemed most effective at transforming the group system by invigorating and unifying groups that stood in opposition to his presidency. His unsuccessful campaign for comprehensive health care reform combined with the extraordinarily visceral reaction he engendered among conservative grassroots organizations and their leaders helped to nurture long-lasting coalitions of business associations, advocacy centers and think tanks, and the Christian Right. Those coalitions in turn became effective proponents of the agendas put forth by the Republican congressional majorities that entered office in 1995.

The other type of potential legacy is to build new alignments among organizations allied with the president. FDR's New Deal coalition, which affected the course of federal policy for decades, is a prime example. Relying on New Democratic policy formulations, Bill Clinton sought to create a comparable and enduring coalition of the center that encompassed liberal interests traditionally tied to Democratic administrations with business representatives, provider groups, and others open to using limited government action to direct private institutions to fulfill public purposes.

For the most part it proved to be an unworkable formula for interest group coalition building. It could never excite the unions and citizen groups who are the most natural allies of a Democratic administration nor secure enduring commitments from other interests, such as large employers, whose availability as a coalition partner depended on the issue being addressed. The policies designed to attract these diverse coalitions, such as the Health Security Act, also contained too many internal contradictions to permit a lasting marriage of interests. Ironically, the failure of what Clinton perceived to be a middle course on health care reform contributed primarily to the defeat of moderate Democrats in the 1994 election, which both assisted the Republican victory that year and aggravated partisanship and ideological divisions in Congress.[61]

The one area where the president has left a positive legacy is in support of crime-control policy. But it has depended on local and state-level organization and involves a coalition of interests—law enforcement, judges, community anti-drug groups, and the like—that is not readily transferable to other issues. The history of previous presidents who pursued such "third way" politics, argues

Stephen Skowronek, would not have provided much encouragement to Clinton's efforts.[62] The reality is that the political center lacks the consistency, passion, and organizational foundation upon which coalitions depend. Consider the parallel story of electoral dynamics. When the Democratic base was not effectively mobilized in the 1994 congressional elections but Republican constituencies were, the Democrats lost control of Congress and suffered a defeat of historic proportions. When that base was far more energized in the 1998 elections, expected Republican gains vanished and for only the second time this century in midterm elections the president's party in the House picked up seats. The polarization of American politics over the past two decades, reflected in the behavior of the congressional parties and the interest group system, only exacerbates the challenge of organizing for centrist ventures.

8

Race, Gender, and the Clinton Presidency

VIRGINIA SAPIRO AND DAVID T. CANON

Thank you, my friends, for years of friendship.

— President Bill Clinton speaking to the Congressional Black Caucus, 19 September 1998

As the old saying goes, "When you are down on your luck, you find out who your real friends are." In his tumultuous second term, President Clinton learned that among his best friends are African Americans and women. This support was first evident in his initial election to the presidency in 1992, when an overwhelming majority of blacks and a substantial plurality of women voted for Clinton over George Bush and Ross Perot,[1] and was maintained through the 1994, 1996, and 1998 elections. Some of the strongest images of this unshakable support among blacks and women occurred in 1998 during the turbulence surrounding the Lewinsky affair. Consider the dramatic night of the 1998 State of the Union message, when allegations of the Lewinsky affair had just exploded in Washington, leaving many congressional Democrats scrambling for cover and unwilling to offer their public support to the president. In stark contrast, many members of the Congressional Black Caucus, in their eagerness to show their support, arrived several hours before the speech so they could grab the seats on the aisle and shake the president's hand as he walked toward the podium.[2] Similarly, 1998 was punctuated with images of top-level women politicians and women's movement leaders

169

pointedly demonstrating their support for Clinton, despite constant and voluble charges of hypocrisy launched by conservatives and, indeed, critics across the political spectrum.

This enthusiastic support suggests the obvious questions: What was their motivation? What did they gain in return? These questions focus attention on the permeation of the Clinton presidency with gender and race politics. As we show, a portrait of the Clinton presidency that does not highlight racial and gender politics is incomplete, to say the least. But the task of this chapter is the more difficult one of identifying the gender and racial politics aspects of the *legacy* of the Clinton presidency, rather than simply describing how they influenced his tenure.

In the next section we argue that the Clinton presidency follows a period of substantial change in the nature of gender and racial politics in the United States, and that a Democratic president of his era and generation would have been unlikely to ignore the major implications of those changes. But did Clinton leave his own lasting mark on this era of politics? Will gender and racial politics in the United States, and especially the role of women and minorities in electoral, appointive, and policy politics be any different because of Clinton's presidency? Or was he merely caught in a tide that would have produced similar outcomes without him?

We attempt to answer these questions by examining the historical context of racial and gender politics, women and minorities' electoral and public support for Clinton, his appointments and inner circle, and his policy legacy and issue stands and actions. This thematic organization reveals the dynamics of the racial and gender politics of the Clinton administration and suggests their larger implications for American politics at the threshold of the new century. Before Clinton came to office, African Americans, Hispanics, and women had become potentially important building blocks of support for a Democratic president; he, in turn, focused substantial attention on the distinctive needs of these groups, and they, then, responded with their support.[3] These historically under represented groups have emerged from the political periphery to help shape the last presidency of the twentieth century. It is unlikely that any president in the future—certainly any Democratic one—will be able to ignore minorities and women.

Setup for Success: The Historical Context of Racial and Gender Politics

For Americans born and raised in the last half of the twentieth century, it is not news to say that African Americans and women vote disproportionately Democratic. This was not always the case, and to understand current race and gender politics, one must understand the dynamic of race- and gender-based partisanship by examining the partisan change that occurred historically.

Law and discrimination severely limited African Americans' electoral participation until the 1960s. From the Civil War until the 1930s, they primarily supported the Republican Party, the "party of Lincoln," in opposition to the Democrats, the party of southern segregationists. In many black families, supporting a Democrat was considered political treason. As recently as 1932, three-fourths of blacks still voted for the Republican presidential candidate over the Democrat, FDR.[4] Blacks began to move to the Democratic Party during the Roosevelt administration, when New Deal programs gave unprecedented assistance to black as well as white people to pull them out of the depths of the Great Depression and began to address race discrimination.[5] Black support for the Democrats continued to build through the next several decades as the northern Democratic Party, and its leaders, such as Harry S Truman and John F. Kennedy, proved consistently more antisegregationist than the Republican (or the southern Democratic) Party. The final blow to black Republicanism came in the 1960s, when a Democratic president, Lyndon Johnson, and a Democratic Congress pushed through the crucial 1964 Civil Rights Act and 1965 Voting Rights Act over Republican opposition.[6]

The campaign strategies and presidencies of Richard Nixon (especially his "southern strategy" of attracting white voters through thinly veiled racial appeals) and Ronald Reagan reinforced the racial divide in partisan patterns of voting. Consequently, more than 90 percent of black voters supported Democratic presidential candidates, even in the losing campaigns of 1980, 1984, and 1988. (For race differences in voting patterns, see figure 8.1, p. 172.) Meanwhile, as racially exclusive policies faded, African Americans had not only become more Democratic, but also more politically active, prominent, and influential at all levels of politics, especially because of the substantial decrease in both legal and informal discrimination against African Americans in the political arena.

The gender basis of political affiliations and participation also underwent important shifts. Gender differences in partisanship were never as large as race differences; in fact, men and women, as groups, have usually voted similarly. But where differences appeared, for example, in the 1950s, women tended to be a bit more Republican than men. This began to change in the 1960s, especially as the parties diverged more markedly in their levels of defense hawkishness, their stands on social welfare, and their levels of support for civil rights and antidis-

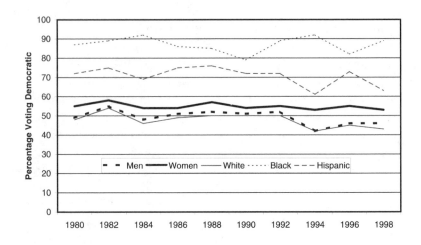

Figure 8.1. Democratic Vote in Congressional Races, by Race and Gender

crimination policies. The parties became divided on many policies relating to specifically to women and gender questions, from antidiscrimination policies to
abortion to policies related to violence against women. Because of the disproportionate prevalence of poverty among women, social-welfare politics should be included among these gender-related issues; women's movement organizations have
long defined poverty and social-welfare policy in general as especially relevant to
women.

The actual policy and social changes were so great in the 1970s that they
became a key focus of the conservative backlash that gained force within Ronald
Reagan's campaign for the presidency in 1980. As a result of this combination of
policies, the 1980 presidential and congressional elections produced the first no-
ticeable "gender gap," in which men voted disproportionately Republican and
women disproportionately Democratic. Although the *degree* of gender difference
in the vote has varied in subsequent elections, there has been a strong tendency
for men to vote more Republican than women. For gender differences in congressional voting, see figure 8.1.

Research shows that the emergence of gender differences in any given election depends on the specific context and the degree to which it happens to be
laden with the kinds of cues that stimulate political gender differences.[7] These

cues vary from election to election. Despite some moderation in Democratic stands—encouraged in large part by the Democratic Leadership Council, of which Bill Clinton was an early leading member—the parties have remained distinctly different on a combination of issues that encourages gender differentiation in the vote.[8]

Even though gender differences in the *vote* do not emerge in every election to an equal degree, since the late 1970s men's and women's basic *partisan allegiances* have become different.

By the beginning of the 1990s, an important fact of political life was that in the general erosion of the New Deal Democratic coalition at the mass level, young white men, white ethnic men, and southern men had left the Democratic Party in disproportionate numbers, while women and African Americans were more resistant to the anti–welfare state, anti–affirmative action, and conservative "family values" messages of the Republicans. Black and female voters, therefore, offered a needed well of support for the Democratic Party, but important differences between these two groups as collectivities have different implications for strategies necessary for drawing from that well. Let us look at them briefly, then see how Clinton acted on these implications.

Women comprise a majority of the population (especially among the elderly), are geographically evenly distributed across the nation, support Democratic candidates only somewhat more than Republicans (although the gender difference depends on the context), and, since 1980, have voted at rates that are higher than or equal to those of men. African Americans comprise 12 percent of the population, are concentrated in specific geographic regions (especially the South and urban areas), overwhelmingly support Democrats, but have relatively low voting rates (in recent elections, an average of 8 percentage points less than white voters).

Consequently, the incentive to appeal specifically to women voters or to minority groups depends on the specific political context and office, and the most appropriate strategy for doing so must be different. The key for Democrats in gender politics is to stimulate women's disproportionate support for them without simultaneously draining men's Democratic support. The key for the Democratic Party's race politics is to mobilize its base of support among black citizens and get them to the polls without, at the same time, alienating white voters whose security within the Democratic ranks may be more fragile. This is a difficult balancing act. A Democratic candidate can easily become caught between African-American leaders, who have complained for years that Democratic candidates take their votes for granted (in some cases hinting at a willingness to use abstention as a weapon of rebuke), and Republican opponents, who have sometimes capitalized on white fears of the Democratic Party's courting of black votes, as the infamous "Willie Horton" commercial run by the 1988 Bush campaign demonstrated.

Thus, as Bill Clinton was formulating his campaign for the presidency, one key element that would affect his potential for success would be how his campaign played into the structure of gender and race politics. As it happened, Clinton was of just the right generation and position to understand and use these features of contemporary politics with respect to race and gender politics and was in a unique position, as he moved from the governor's mansion to the White House, to take advantage of them.

Much has been made of the fact that Clinton was the first U.S. president to be born in the post–World War II era, going through his formative years in the 1950s and 1960s, then crafting his political style in the 1970s and 1980s. This is especially important in his relationship to gender and race politics. From 1946, the year of Bill Clinton's birth, to the period when he launched his bid for the presidency, the United States was transformed from a race-segregated nation in which blacks could rarely participate in electoral politics to a country in which there was equal protection under the law and a much greater role for blacks in the electoral process. The exciting civil rights movement that took place in Clinton's youth evolved into a more mature policy area, but remained central both to American politics generally and to the development of Clinton's political identity.

In that same period, women's roles and affiliations in politics, as well as social and economic life, also changed substantially. In 1946 only 28 percent of women were in the workforce, only eleven women served in the House of Representatives, and none were in the Senate or the cabinet. In contrast, by 1992 a majority of women—even mothers of small children—were in the workforce. The proportion of women in public office had risen somewhat (although they held only 6 percent of the congressional seats and 18 percent of statewide elective offices). The women's movement had been reborn, and even if most women never labeled themselves "feminists," the majority of women persistently believed that increasing gender equality in the family, education, economic life, and politics was a desirable goal, and that there was need for a women's movement to help achieve it.[9]

Clinton's personal circumstances offered him strong links to the black community, he has spent his adult life surrounded by professional, politically active, feminist women (including his wife), and he is a politician with an inclination always to have one eye on the public opinion polls and focus group results. Neither Clinton's success in 1992, nor the outcomes of the subsequent three elections, can be understood without examining the importance of women and minorities in the Democratic Party.

Parties, Public Opinion, and Electoral Support

We now turn to the center of our argument: the relationship of race and gender to Clinton's electoral and public opinion coalition. We examine each election of the Clinton era in turn to track the gender and race politics of public support for the president and his response to those social groups.

1992: The First Election of Bill Clinton

Gender politics was highlighted early and vociferously in 1992. It was the widely declared "Year of the Woman,"[10] a term coined during the 1992 campaign, in reference primarily to congressional election campaigns. Women were encouraged to run in unprecedented numbers at all levels of government. This infusion of women candidates trumpeting their gender and bringing attention to "women's issues," combined with the predominant influence of the Christian Coalition on the Republican platform. Many of the events of the Republican convention focused on gender issues in the presidential race. Women increased their numbers in the House (from twenty-eight to forty-eight) and in the Senate (from two to six). The gains were due to the unprecedented number of female candidates rather than to a higher success rate among women in the 1992 elections.

The gender gap in the presidential vote was small (about 5 percentage points difference), partly because of the confounding effects of the Perot candidacy, which took a disproportionate number of young male votes from George Bush. But especially where women were on the ballot for major offices, thus "cueing up" gender in the campaigns, Bill Clinton benefited strongly from women's votes.[11] When the dust cleared, Bill Clinton and the Democrats had another lesson in the importance of paying attention to women's political organizations—especially feminist organizations. The PACs and related organizations contributed substantial amounts to political campaigns in 1992; indeed, EMILY's List bundled more money and shipped it off to campaigns than any other political contributor in the nation, outstripping the traditional big guns such as doctors and realtors.[12]

In contrast to the attention received by women, more contradictory tendencies emerged with respect to racial minorities in 1992. On one hand, blacks increased their membership in the House from twenty-six to thirty-nine and Latinos from eleven to seventeen, because of the creation of fifteen new U.S. House districts that were specifically drawn to help elect African Americans and ten districts that were drawn to provide opportunities to elect new Latino members.[13] Thus, the 1992 congressional elections could have been characterized as the "Year of the Minority," but the presidential campaign was an entirely different matter. Running as a "New Democrat," Bill Clinton actively sought to distance himself from this traditional base of the Democratic Party while emphasizing that he was not beholden to the "special interests." He favored the death penalty, "ending welfare as we know it," and supporting people who "work hard and play by the rules," moves that could be seen as attempts to separate himself from the African-American community and win back some of the white voters who had been voting Republican.

In a defining campaign moment, Clinton used his address before Jesse Jackson's Rainbow Coalition in June to attack Sister Souljah, a black rap star who, in speaking to the organization the day before, had said, "If black people kill black people every day, why not have a week and kill white people?"[14] The rebuke was also aimed at Jesse Jackson, who moments earlier had mentioned with some pride the presence of Sister Souljah at the Rainbow Coalition meeting. Until the "Sister Souljah speech," Clinton was running third behind President Bush and Ross Perot. Political columnist Clarence Page wrote that the Sister Souljah event was the "most important moment in the 1992 presidential race."[15]

Black leaders were angry, but Clinton knew that voting for Bush was a less attractive alternative for most blacks than voting for him. Charles Rangel, a prominent black House member from New York, remarked, "The damn strategy is working." He compared (with some prescience!) Clinton's treatment of black voters to a man who tells his mistress, "Meet me in the hotel room; I don't want to be seen with you in the lobby."[16]

However, Clinton's campaign strategy did not completely turn its back on the black community. He did, after all, make his Sister Souljah remarks at a Rainbow Coalition meeting, suggesting a second, perhaps simultaneous interpretation—an effort to attract *middle-class* black voters. (It is crucial to remember that although African Americans are overwhelmingly Democratic, they by no means constitute a politically homogeneous community.) Moreover, even while Clinton publicly distanced himself from Jesse Jackson, he was strengthening his base of support among moderate black leaders such as John Lewis (D-Ga.), Mike Espy (D-Miss.), and William Jefferson (D-La.) in the U.S. House, Baltimore mayor Kurt Schmoke, and Atlanta mayor Maynard Jackson. And, he continued to advocate a range of issue stands that found favor in the black community, as did his promise to make government more representative.

The strategy was a resounding success. In the primary elections Clinton received 70 percent of the black vote;[17] roughly 20 percent of Clinton's votes in the primary came from black voters. In the general election, Clinton received 89 percent of the black two-party vote (82 percent overall) and Hispanics gave Clinton 71 percent of the two-party vote (62 percent overall).[18]

While black voters helped deliver the presidency to Clinton, some evidence supports the "strategic abstention" argument outlined earlier. While black turnout was marginally higher in 1992 than in 1988 (up 2.5 percent), black voters declined as a proportion of the electorate (from 10.5 percent in 1988 to 8 percent in 1992) because white turnout was up 4.5 percent in 1992.[19] Without Jesse Jackson running in the primaries, black registration dropped a bit in 1992,[20] and Clinton's strategic distancing probably alienated some black voters who stayed home on election day.

The 1994 Midterms: The Republican Landslide—among White Men

Unlike presidential elections, no single campaign brings parties together or focuses voters' attention during midterm elections. The 1994 elections, however, were different: the midterm backlash against the president's party, encouraged by a national campaign, was so strong that the Democrats lost both houses of Congress for the first time in forty years. In the previous congressional election year, 1990, people had voted for Democratic over Republican candidates by a 52–48 margin; in 1994 they voted for Republicans over Democrats by a 53–47 margin.[21] The backlash occurred primarily among white men and, to a lesser degree, among Hispanic men and women.[22]

The 1994 midterms were noteworthy for two reasons. First, a gender gap, in some races impressively large, again emerged across the country. Second, blacks supported Democrats at their typically high levels, but relatively low black turnout hurt Democratic candidates nationwide.

As the *Chicago Tribune* reported, "If women voters had prevailed in the midterm elections, the Senate would have remained in Democratic hands and several governors' seats would have gone to Democrats instead of Republicans."[23] But how can we account for the gendered nature of the electoral response? The "angry white male" was the main rhetorical device that journalists and pundits seized upon as the apparent inverse of the 1992 "Year of the Woman." The angry white male was said to feel left out and left behind, especially by the president's emphasis on such issues as gays in the military; affirmative action, which might help blacks and women; the North American Free Trade Agreement (NAFTA), which was widely seen as hurting the bulk of traditional blue-collar working men; his large number of controversial appointments, especially of women and minorities; his failure on the health care plan, spearheaded by the dreaded Hillary Rodham Clinton; and his inability to follow through on promises to cut taxes and "end welfare as we know it."

If many white men saw these policies and felt left out, presumably women, minorities, and the other named vulnerable groups saw the same policies and felt, at least to some degree, that the administration had kept them in mind. That is certainly what their votes suggest. But, although strong black turnout was pivotal in helping Democrats win a few key races, such as Chuck Robb's victory over Oliver North in the most hotly contested Senate race of the year, relatively low turnout limited black voters' influence overall.

1996: Clinton's Reelection

The 1996 presidential election was similar to the 1992 election in many ways. Clinton's themes did not change dramatically. He intensified efforts to court women's votes in particular, partly through the White House Office for Women's Initiatives and Outreach, established in June 1995. This office, designed to "amplify the president's pro-woman, pro-family agenda," held roundtables called "At the Table" events, reflecting the idiom long used to indicate inclusion and exclusion from the centers of power.[24]

The potential power of the women's vote emerged early in the 1996 electoral season. First, the game of budgetary chicken Congress and the president played late in 1995 magnified the gender gap. In a poll taken at the beginning of January 1996, 38 percent of men and 50 percent of women blamed the Republicans in Congress for the recent government shutdown.[25] A gender difference emerged in the presidential horse-race polls, and before long women's support for Bill Clinton over Bob Dole became so large—as much as 30 percentage points difference among women—that Republican strategists were calling the phenomenon a gender *canyon* rather than a gender gap.[26]

From early summer on, the Dole forces looked increasingly desperate in their attempts to gain some female support. The Republican convention highlighted women speakers; Dole's campaign strategists attempted to moderate the harsh tones the party had been taking, especially with respect to abortion, and to emphasize any support for safety-net policies they had. Nevertheless, Republican campaign experts knew they had a fundamental problem: their base of support was primarily male, and their appeal was weak among women on both policy and tone grounds. As Linda DiVall, a key Republican pollster, said as the Republican convention began,

> One clear explanation for it is that women tend to see a greater role for more activist government than men do. . . . Men are mad at the taxes they pay; they want government out of their lives. Women are not necessarily looking for big government and more intrusive government, but they do appreciate certain things that government does well, . . . so one of the goals of this Republican convention . . . is to . . . change the face and the perception of the Republican Party.

She added, "You're going to see, *I want to say, a new Republican Party, but that's not the case at all,* but you'll see Republicans showcased who demonstrate the values [discussed above], have a sense of enthusiasm and compassion . . ." (emphasis added).[27] This was one of the first indications that the Republican Party was going to make moves toward repairing its relationship with women.

The effort did not work, as polls and the final vote showed. Even during the Republican convention, 55 percent of people polled by CBS thought that Democrats would do better at dealing with "the needs and problems of women," compared with 24 percent who thought the Republicans would do better; 42 percent thought the Republicans would do better at dealing with "the needs and problems of men" compared with 33 percent who thought this of Democrats.[28]

Meanwhile, the Clinton campaign carefully and consciously built part of its electoral strategy on its potential strength among women. Clinton campaigners rarely failed to mention that Dole's party was Newt Gingrich's party, a leader who had 19 percentage points more unfavorable than favorable ratings among men, but 38 percentage points more unfavorable than favorable ratings among women. Clinton operatives found that the key to women's support was a series of policies such as support for workplace and education equality policies, increasing the minimum wage and Earned Income Tax Credit, parental leave, enforcing child support, protection against violence against women and children, increasing funds for women's health care (especially breast cancer research), and other policies offering specific help to women.[29]

Both the Clinton campaign and some Republican strategists understood that the key to women's support was their disproportionate presence among the poor and the elderly, among those who had the direct, day-to-day responsibility for caring for their dependent children and elderly parents, among those who needed help balancing the demands of caring for their families and supporting them financially, and among those who were employed by the public sector. The current leadership of the congressional Republicans scared them, and they were less likely than men to believe that the country would be better off if the government could be trimmed by cutting the economic safety net for those most at risk. Ironically, for many women's movement leaders, as for black leaders, Clinton's chief policy liability was that he had signed the welfare reform bill, which promised to "end welfare as we know it"—a move that protected his right flank.

The strategy of emphasizing women's issues paid off. Bill Clinton did not win the 1996 election among men; he won it among women. More specifically, he won a landslide victory among unmarried women (62–28 percent), he had a strong lead among unmarried men (49–35 percent), won among married women (48–43 percent), and lost among married men (40–48 percent).[30]

The racial politics of the 1996 campaign mirrored the gender politics much more closely than the more arms-length approach of 1992. Clinton was aware of the need to mobilize black voters, but he also knew that the dynamic of "structural dependence" was still working in his favor (that is, blacks were unlikely to vote for the less attractive Republican alternative). Nevertheless, Clinton knew that many black leaders were outraged that he had signed the welfare reform legislation and that he would have to mend some fences with black voters. He repeatedly pointed out that he had vetoed two earlier, and more punitive, versions of the bill; he also promised to fix some of the more extreme aspects of the bill, such as the provision that would have denied assistance to legal immigrants. These efforts moderated some criticism of him.

Welfare reform gave Clinton more leeway with white male voters. So did the very strong economy, and the end to the budget deficit, a feat for which he was happy to take credit. Having established his credibility as a New (i.e., moderate) Democrat, he could turn to the difficult task of solidifying his base. This type of balancing act is the stuff of coalition politics, and Bill Clinton was a master at keeping people happy. Clinton used three issues to reach out to black voters:

speaking out against the burning of black churches in the South, affirmative action, and the ban on assault weapons.

In the year preceding the election, more than 100 black churches in the South were burned. While some critics pointed out that most of these fires were not racially motivated, the rash of fires reawakened the searing images of the KKK fire-bombing black churches during the civil rights movement, providing fertile ground for symbolic race politics. Bob Dole was one of the first in Congress to advocate a concerted national effort to find and punish those responsible, and Clinton convened a White House meeting of southern governors, promised aggressive action from the Justice Department, and spent his fiftieth birthday helping to rebuild a burnt Tennessee church. He frequently expressed his outrage against the church burnings when campaigning across the country.

Speaking out against church burnings is a relatively easy position to take politically, and one with potent symbolic appeal, but Clinton also staked out potentially more divisive positions on racial issues. Affirmative action is one of the clear "wedge issues" that divides black and white voters. Depending on the wording of the specific poll, about two-thirds of blacks favor affirmative action, compared with less than a quarter of whites. Clinton supported affirmative action, preferring to "mend it, not end it," while Dole opposed what he called "quotas and preferential treatment," the label he always attached to affirmative action. Beyond the differences between the candidates and their parties on race issues, Dole never seemed comfortable discussing the question of race, while Clinton seemed to treat it almost as home turf, sometimes sounding like a participant in a diversity training workshop.[31]

The ban on assault weapons was another issue that was strongly favored by blacks (and women) and by Clinton and opposed by Dole. African Americans are disproportionately victimized by crime, especially gang-based use of assault weapons. Clinton chose an address to the National Association for the Advancement of Colored People (NAACP) to state his commitment to veto any attempt to override the gun ban. Dole, invited to speak on the same subject, declined to attend, claiming a scheduling conflict. Ultimately, he accused NAACP head Kweisi Mfume of trying to "set me up" and confessed a preference for audiences he can "relate to."[32] Black leaders were outraged; the editorial commentary was scathing:

> One wonders what Dole was expecting from an NAACP audience—a fusillade of rotting tomatoes? Sure, they might have been cool, even skeptical. But they would have listened, given him a chance to make the case that the big,

Republican tent is the place for blacks to be. Instead, he spurned them, and that forces a question: Do you really want us under your tent, Bob? I mean, c'mon. This is courtship? If I'd gone courting like the GOP, I'd still be a bachelor.[33]

Dole tried to compensate for the blunder. In a meeting with the National Association of Black Journalists, Dole apologized for "not knowing" about the NAACP convention. "I deeply believe that the Republican Party will never be whole until it earns the broad support of African Americans and others by speaking to their hopes," he said.[34] By then it was too little, too late; 84 percent of blacks voted for Clinton and only 12 percent for Dole. Hispanics went for Clinton by a 72–21 percent margin.

Clinton explicitly appealed to black voters to turn out to vote. Black churches cooperated in crucial ways in this effort. Henry J. Lyons, the president of the association of black Baptist churches, appeared with Clinton at the black Baptist convention, saying, "Two years ago, we let something happen that never should have happened. We had the numbers on the books, but we did not go to the polls. We cannot let it happen again."[35] Other black ministers concurred and joined in.[36] Black voters responded to the call and helped deliver a second term to President Clinton, composing 10 percent of the electorate.

The 1998 Midterm Surprise and Scandal

Women's support for the president remained relatively high, compared with that from men, and blacks' support for Clinton was unshakable throughout the second term. The greatest test came through the long, grinding months of the increasingly explicit revelations of the Clinton/Lewinsky scandal throughout 1998. Much of the press and most pundits expected Clinton's support to weaken disproportionately among women, especially among feminists, who had long made sexual harassment a key issue. They were wrong, and many continued to be baffled as the evidence poured in showing that women and men at the mass level tended to react roughly the same way, but where there were differences, men were harsher in their judgment of Clinton and reacted more negatively in their support scores than women did.

For example, in a Gallup survey conducted in the middle of August 1998, when President Clinton had already made his speech to the public admitting to his "inappropriate relationship" with Lewinsky and was about to testify to the grand jury about his relationship with Lewinsky, 59 percent of men and 63 percent of women approved of the job Clinton was doing as president. A CBS poll taken at about the same time put black approval at 94 percent. Roughly the same proportion of men (68 percent) and women (70 percent) thought that whatever Clinton and Lewinsky had done was a private, not a public, matter. Men, but especially women, were less supportive of the president in his private behavior—52 percent of men and 45 percent of women respected Clinton as a person.

Why did women seem, if anything, less harsh on Clinton *as president* than men were? Many reasons were offered, but they seem to boil down to three things. First, the public and interest group leaders alike responded to the scandal in a partisan manner, and women are more Democratic than men, thus more supportive of a Democratic president. Second, and closely related, gender differences in issue priorities—women's coinciding more with the Clinton agenda—bolstered women's views of Clinton as *president,* if not as a person. Third, polls showed that even though the public did not like Clinton's actions, they believed the process that *revealed* his actions and judged them was highly partisan and its investigations excessive. Congress seemed to be paying attention to little else (the budget bill, for example, was delayed until it was pushed through in a harried rush at the very last moment), and the public became about as negative toward the Republican Congress with respect to how it was doing its job, as it was with regard to Clinton, the man. The lack of support for Congress was especially great among women.[37]

Black support for Clinton was evident for many of the same reasons, especially partisanship and suspicion about the motivations of the Republican Congress and Kenneth Starr. A September 1998 CBS poll asked, "Whom do you blame more for the current scandal situation, Clinton or his political enemies?" Blacks were more likely to blame his enemies (55–27 percent), while white were more likely to place blame on Clinton (59–32 percent).[38] Many black leaders and commentators have speculated that blacks are more likely to support Clinton than whites because of the shared sense among blacks of what it means to be singled out for harsh treatment. As Rep. Charles Rangel (D-N.Y.) said, "The more they beat up on him, the stronger his support will be among the African-American community. African Americans know what persecution is."[39] Rep. John Lewis (D-Ga.) explained that his constituents did not want to see Clinton resign or have him impeached: "They just want us to leave him alone because there's this deep feeling in the black community that this president has been there for us."[40]

Turnout among blacks and women and the gender and racial gaps in the 1998 midterm elections helped deliver historic results for the Democrats. For only the second time since the Civil War, the president's party actually gained ground in the House (picking up five seats) and held even in the Senate. Although the gender gap was not quite as great as it had been in 1994 (11 points in 1994 versus 6 points in 1998; see figure 8.1, p. 172), it was still there and made the crucial difference in high-profile races, such as those in New York and North Carolina where Republicans lost key seats, and in California, where an extremely vulnerable Democrat kept hers.

The front-page headline in the *New York Times* following the stunning 1998 results said, "Democrats in Political Debt for Black Turnout in South."[41] Black voters supported Democratic congressional candidates at their typical 89–11 percent rate, and they comprised 10 percent of the electorate. In some key states, such as South Carolina, Georgia, and Alabama, black turnout was extremely high. Clinton and the Democratic Party actively wooed black voters with massive direct-mail efforts, an appearance by Clinton on BET, and many visits to black churches by Clinton. The Georgia Democratic Party exploited the Republicans' effort to bring up the Lewinsky scandal in a $30 million ad campaign (which was widely viewed as an ill-advised move) with a mailing sent to black voters with a picture of Newt Gingrich and Kenneth Starr saying, "They couldn't win at the ballot box, so now they want to overturn your choice. Send them a message."[42] And they did.

David Gergen summarized the 1998 midterm:

> Along both coasts, the key swing voters have become women, blacks, and one of the fastest-growing minorities in the country, Hispanics. National Democrats understand their political power and have effectively appealed to them, while national Republicans have not. Too many women and minorities now see the GOP as a haven for macho white males.[43]

Especially in 1998, traditional Democratic constituent groups such as the unions were crucial. But it was also important that the Clinton campaigns and administration successfully worked to exploit (and even institutionalize) the race and gender divergence in partisanship and party support that had begun long before the Clinton years. Much as the Republican Party had successfully detected and then built recruitment and mobilization strategies around issue- and demographic-based trends in the South or among some white ethnics in recent decades, Clinton's forces did so with respect to women and minorities. The policy agenda he promoted, the policy directions, and, perhaps more important, the symbolic politics embedded in his appointments, and the manner in which he dealt with progressive women's interest groups and civil rights and with black interest groups each flowed from and contributed to continued institutionalization of women and minorities as a necessary pieces of a successful Democratic strategy.

Movement and Interest Group Leaders

The leaders of women's and minorities' groups played crucial roles in influencing Clinton's presidency and, most likely, his legacy. We argue that a two-step process of communication occurred that has been familiar to students of public opinion at least since V.O. Key's classic writings on the subject. This classic formulation of "opinion leaders" who help shape the opinions of the less attentive public describes, at least in part, the relationship between Clinton and women's and minorities' interest groups and leaders. Clinton's message often was directed at group leaders who would respond favorably and then convey their support for Clinton to their members. Many of the moves he made that were aimed at gaining women's and African Americans' support went undetected by much of the mass public, and he and his aides must have known it. (Who knew, for example, what a large new program in breast-cancer research, detection, and intervention the administration launched? How many people were aware of the administration's ultimate support for an African woman seeking asylum in the United States for fear of having to face genital mutilation if she returned to Togo?) But these efforts would certainly attract the attention not just of interest group and social movement leaders per se but of opinion leaders in the black community and among women who, in turn, provided a bulwark of strong support at critical moments. (Both interest group leaders and important segments of the opinion leading attentive public would have been aware of both of the stories just cited.)

Thus, we hypothesize, this two-step process had both direct and indirect effects on Clinton's presidency. Direct effects are rooted in specific support actions taken by various groups, such as the financial support provided by women's PACs, or the get-out-the-vote efforts sponsored by black groups, or the public displays of support offered to the president by interest group leaders and leading black and female politicians. Indirect effects refer to the ability of group leaders to drum up support for Clinton among their members, and to the tendency for opinion leaders, more generally, to influence a wider segment of members of their community or social group. We have seen evidence of these direct effects in the results of polls and elections, discussed earlier.

Evidence of the indirect effects is more difficult to detect, and some would argue that the connections between the leaders and the larger mass public are tenuous. Indeed, some critics argue that the leadership of women's and minorities' groups is "out of step" with their constituents. Feminist group leaders tend to be much more homogeneously Democratic, liberal, pro-choice, and pro–gay rights than women in the mass public are. Black members of Congress differ in key respects, for example, on school choice, abortion, and gay rights, from African Americans in general. Nevertheless, while groups such as the Leadership Conference on Civil Rights and the NAACP are generally more liberal than their members, there are few differences between them and the rank and file on issues that comprise their core agenda: affirmative action, opposition to discrimination, policies to aid the inner city, and government support for education and economic development. Likewise, women seem to have responded well to the agenda that women's group leaders have urged on the Democratic Party in general, and Clinton in particular. It is symbolically important that women leaders—not just avowedly *feminist* leaders, but a large number of women leaders from many walks of life—have expressed support for the policies that Clinton has supported, with the possible exception of the welfare reform law.

Group leaders have also influenced Clinton's success and his legacy through congressional leaders. In the Democratic Party, members of Congress have always been important leaders of the women's movement and black groups. Bella Abzug, Barbara Jordan, Patricia Schroeder, Adam Clayton Powell, Ron Dellums, John Lewis, and Charles Rangel are among the most visible women and black leaders of the past generation. Female and black members of Congress were among the most supportive of Clinton's policies.

In contrast, not only Republican strategists such as Linda DiVall, but even some members of the Republican congressional delegation have argued that the Republican Party has an image problem that cedes too much minority and female support. In the 1998 postelection leadership shuffle, when Jennifer Dunn announced her unsuccessful challenge to Dick Armey for the majority leadership of the House, she said, "We must broaden the base of the party by crafting a message that reaches out to everybody from every background." This represents an explicit strategy by Dunn to "focus energy on helping the Republicans improve their standing among female voters."[44] In that same shuffle, the only black Republican in the House, Rep. J.C. Watts Jr. (Okla.), won the position of chair of the House Republican Conference, a move that was widely seen as an additional attempt to broaden the Republican base.

African-American and women's group leaders, then, were highly visible components of the coalition of support Clinton pieced together out of the political fabric that was being woven together by the two parties throughout his career, and certainly before he became president. Thus, late in 1998, many observers who perhaps had not been paying close attention were shocked to see black, women, and gay interest group and movement leaders being demonstrative about their opposition to what they considered partisan campaigns against the president and their opposition to impeachment. In a joint press release issued in late September 1998, fourteen leaders or former leaders of major women's organizations charged that the process of developing and issuing the Starr Report was partisan and "a failure of fairness and has violated the fundamental value of due process," part of a "relentless campaign . . . to hound President Clinton out of office." It is symbolically important that the parties to this press release were not just associated with umbrella feminist groups such as the National Organization for Women, the Feminist Majority, the National Women's Political Caucus, and the National Council of Women's Organizations. In an obvious strategy to press the point about the "rainbow" of opposition to the moves against Clinton, the list included leaders of the National Council of Negro Women, the United Farm Workers, Black Women United for Action, the Black Leadership Forum, and the National Asian Pacific Legal Consortium.[45]

The bottom line for these leaders had to do with recognition of progress in policy and representation, as they saw it, and the possibility of backsliding if the less sympathetic Republican congressional majority was to have its way with policy. To understand the strength of these views, it is necessary to look at the tangible signs these opinion leaders assessed in their perception of Bill Clinton and his opposition in relation to their own interests: appointments and public policy.

Appointments and the Inner Circle

Candidate Clinton promised a government that "looks like America." By this, of course, he meant no complicated theories of representation; rather, he was promising social groups that heretofore felt underrepresented in a *descriptive representation* sense—that is, not enough people "looked like them"—that the face of government would literally change. Historically, no major social group was as unrepresented in this sense as women, who have always constituted a majority of the citizenry but only a handful of those in government outside of clerical and nonmanagerial positions. But African Americans and other racial minorities were also dramatically underrepresented in government when Clinton took office. In the end, his cabinet, subcabinet, and judicial appointments achieved the greatest gender and racial balance of any in U.S. history.

Judicial appointments are important objects of attention for any underrepresented group seeking increased presence. The courts have arguably played a more central role in advancing the agenda of progressive women's interest groups over the past three decades than have legislatures, and they have certainly been crucial for racial minorities. Thus, these interest groups eagerly anticipated a Democrat in office who might increase the proportion of women and minorities in judgeships. Clinton did make a difference, and quickly. Less than 2 percent of the U.S. District Court appointments made by LBJ, Nixon, and Ford were women; 14 percent of Carter's appointments, and 9 percent and 7 percent, respectively, of Reagan's first- and second-term District Court appointments were women. George Bush expanded that number significantly, to 20 percent, and in Clinton's first term he raised the figure again to 31 percent (62 of 202 positions).[46] Twenty-eight percent of his appointments to the federal bench were minorities.[47]

Even more noticed, of course, was the 1993 Supreme Court appointment of Ruth Bader Ginsburg, a former Columbia University law professor whom President Carter had successfully nominated to the United States Court of Appeals for the District of Columbia Circuit in 1980. Ginsburg was well known in the feminist movement; she was one of the most prominent of the early law professors who published scholarly books and articles on women's rights and contemporary legal issues such as the Equal Rights Amendment. Despite her explicit feminism, however, Ginsburg's confirmation sailed through the Senate.

Clinton also changed the gender and racial composition of executive appointments substantially. Some of his appointments were extremely controversial and notable for the ways in which they raised conflicts over gender-related policies and what some people call "political correctness." Even before he took office, conservative critics accused him of using gender and race as criteria for appointments, while some feminist leaders expressed frustration at what they saw as slower progress in appointing women than they had hoped. Clinton lashed back in public against the "bean counters," who, in effect, wanted him to use quotas. Patricia Ireland, president of NOW, compared his reaction to the Sister Souljah incident: "I don't know whether this was designed to lower expectations or to separate himself somehow from being pushed around by women. The fact is it just makes us that much more determined that we will have to keep the pressure on."[48]

By the middle of his second term, President Clinton had successfully nominated five women and ten minorities to cabinet positions, including nontraditional positions, such as secretary of state and attorney general, and had appointed unprecedented numbers of women at "cabinet level" and on the White House staff. In the autumn of 1998, the White House reported that 41 percent of presidential appointees were women, including 29 percent of the positions requiring Senate confirmation.[49] Fourteen percent of Clinton's first-year presidential appointments were African American (compared with 12 percent of the population), 6 percent were Hispanic (compared with 9.5 percent of the population), and the percentages of Asian Americans and Native Americans appointed were identical to their proportion in the population.[50] Clinton also appointed the first (self-acknowledged) lesbian and gay people to senior-level positions in the administration. Just before the 1998 midterm elections, the Republican Senate rejected Clinton's nomination of an openly gay man as U.S. envoy to Luxembourg. Clinton's administration certainly looked more "like us" than any other had previously.

A small but notable number of these appointments stirred up controversies relating specifically to women's roles, gender, sexuality, and racial politics. The saga of choosing an attorney general is one of the signal cases; in Clinton's attempt to make the cabinet "look like America," one woman after another appeared in the parade of potential and actual nominees for the office, until the press and critics commented that it seemed that the main qualification for this office was being a woman.[51] Ironically, after two nominees failed because of controversies over the conditions under which they had hired domestic help (Zöe Baird and Kimba Wood), Clinton found a single, childless woman (Janet Reno), who would not fall victim to a "Nannygate" issue.

Clinton's nomination of Lani Guinier, an African-American civil rights lawyer and law professor, for the position of assistant attorney general for civil rights also became emblematic to Clinton's critics of his determination to make "politically correct" appointments governed by his close relationship with "special interest groups." There were not any illegal aliens in her past, but Guinier's academic writings proved to be her undoing. In various law review articles Guinier had expressed doubts about the ability of our political system to represent the interests of blacks. Instead she called for a system of "proportionate interest representation" that would involve procedures such as veto power over certain legislation for minorities and different electoral institutions, such as cumulative voting.[52] When a firestorm of protest erupted, Clinton hesitated, but then withdrew her nomination, saying that he was not familiar with some of her more controversial ideas when he made the nomination. This displeased civil rights activists who argued that her ideas were misrepresented and that at the very least, she should have been granted a hearing. Some critics attributed Guinier's problems to her race and gender rather than to her controversial ideas. As occurred a number of times, Clinton's attempts to balance his commitments to both representation of women and minorities and the political moderation necessary for protecting the Democratic base caught him in a political windshear.

It happened again in the story of the rise and fall of Dr. Joycelyn Elders as surgeon general. Elders, the African-American former head of the Arkansas Department of Health, was well known for her bluntness and firmness in support of sex education and abortion. Clinton himself symbolically linked her to the history of race relations and politically inflammatory women; he was reported to have said of her, "Now I know how Abraham Lincoln felt when he met Harriet Beecher Stowe. He said, 'This is the little lady who started the great war.'"[53] Elders was a thorn in the side of conservative, fundamentalist, and Catholic groups—quite an accomplishment for a rather low-level appointee. Clinton was finally forced to ask for her resignation in the political conflagration that followed Elder's response to a question about her views on masturbation: "I think that is something that is a part of human sexuality and it's a part of something that perhaps should be taught. But we've not even taught our children the very basics. And I feel that we have tried ignorance for a very long time and it's time we try education."[54]

Racial politics also figured prominently in other Clinton appointments. His choice of a chief for the Equal Employment Opportunity Commission (EEOC) was delayed for more than a year while Clinton searched for a Latino to fill the spot. Critics pointed out that the result—leaving a Reagan/Bush administration holdover to run this important department—may have been too high a price to pay for diversity. One article asked, "Is the symbolism of naming a Latino to the job more important than the impact of leaving leaderless the agency charged with enforcing laws prohibiting hiring discrimination on the basis of race, sex, age, or physical disability?"[55]

Bill Lann Lee's appointment to the position that initially would have been Guinier's was also controversial. Many people saw the nomination of the first Asian American appointed to this important civil rights post as overdue recognition of the increasingly multiracial composition of the United States, although some traditional black organizations, such as the NAACP, saw it as a possibly unfortunate movement away from recognizing the black-white divide as the central racial cleavage in American society. Many of these same issues would be revisited in the debates over Clinton's "Race Initiative," which we discuss later.

By far the most important and continually controversial relevant personnel issue, however, was the White House role of Hillary Rodham Clinton. Much has been written about the changing roles of the "first lady" in modern American history, and certainly a lot on Clinton herself.[56] Not since Eleanor Roosevelt had there been such heated argument over a first lady; like Hillary Clinton, Eleanor Roosevelt was both despised and revered (by different groups of people, of course) for both personal and political reasons, some relating specifically to her gender and race and to the gender and race politics of the presidency.[57]

Hillary Clinton became a center of attention during the first campaign, as her political-activist and feminist credentials became a source of appeal on the left and of ridicule and attack on the right. Not just her views and political and professional background, but her name and her hairstyle became newsworthy. In the transition period it became clear that the president's wife would be given unprecedented roles in the new White House. She was included in the inner circle of advisers and quietly given the supervisory role on domestic policy, excluding economic policy, but including especially the Department of Health and Human Services (to be headed by her colleague from the Children's Defense Fund, Donna Shalala) and related issues, and she oversaw the ill-fated appointment process for attorney general. Internal debates ensued over whether she should have a formal title (she did not), but for the first time in history, the first lady gained an office in the powerful West Wing of the White House.[58]

The saga of Hillary Rodham Clinton in the Clinton presidency is far too long to list even the main events. But the choice of the first lady to run the health care policy development process in the first term, the manner in which that process was organized (or not, as was perhaps closer to the case), her own suspect business dealings, her particular emphasis on women's issues, President Clinton's constant use of her at home and abroad as the chief administration spokeswoman on "women's issues," the unabashed admiration of the feminist community for her, and ultimately, her defense of the president during the events leading up to his impeachment made her an easy target for Clinton's detractors. She became one symbol of the Clinton administration that served as a focus of attention for the various controversies that swirled around the White House, but amazingly, in the midst of the Lewinsky scandal, she emerged as one of the most effective Democratic campaigners in the 1998 congressional elections.[59] She also served as a catalyst for debates of perhaps more lasting import.

But beyond the clearly partisan, political reactions, the powers and centrality of Hillary Rodham Clinton (and Clinton's close friend, Vernon Jordan, who had no official title after the transition was over but who worked closely with him) underscored a continuing debate in the modern presidency: What should be the shape and composition of the president's *real* inner circle, given the size and complexity of government machinery. Certainly most presidents in memory have had some close associates who were not elected or formally appointed government officials but who, by dint of the president's personal trust in them, actually held considerable power. And certainly other presidents had included family members and good friends in formal positions. But Hillary Clinton was clearly brought more formally into the process of governing and policymaking than any president's wife had been before. The only close family member of any sort with more power—Attorney General Robert Kennedy—at least had to go through a Senate confirmation process. In an age when husbands and wives, at least in the professional classes, are increasingly likely to share professional interests, this is not likely to be the last administration in which the spouse's role becomes an issue.

The overall social and political complexion of Clinton's appointments, and the specific controversies that erupted over them, sent very strong messages about his administration's goals but also embroiled him in controversies that had wider implications for the way the government is staffed. From the point of view of women's groups, feminists, and racial minorities, Clinton was effecting historic changes in the presence of underrepresented groups in the top ranks of government. As *both* liberal and conservative groups saw it, Clinton was not just increasing the numbers of women and minorities, but doing so in a manner that specifically enhanced a liberal, feminist, and race-conscious agenda. For women, minorities, and those on the left, these appointments seemed almost literally to provide a long-sought seat at the table; for the right, they represented the worst of "political correctness" and the politicization of administration. Above all, these controversies underscore the difficult political balancing act that must be performed by a Democratic leader of this era.

Values, Issues, and Policies: Symbolic and Tangible Representational Links

While there are many parallels between the support women and minorities give the president, the diversity of presidential appointments, and the two-step communication flow between women's and minorities' interest groups and their rank and file, an interesting disjuncture occurs when it comes to policy concerns. The connection that many blacks feel with President Clinton is deeply personal, while his policy record on racial issues is somewhat mixed. On the other hand, Clinton's personal behavior contradicts principles for which women's groups have been fighting for a generation, but his policy advocacy and record are generally consistent with agendas laid out by feminist organizations with two major exceptions: his signature on the welfare reform bill (1994) and on the "Defense of Marriage Act" (1996), which defines marriage as a "legal union between one man and one woman as husband and wife." (Many feminist and women's movement organizations are in alliance with the gay movement and organizations on most policy issues.)

The personal connection that many African Americans feel with President Clinton is clearly rooted in symbolic politics. Toni Morrison, the Nobel Prize–winning author, developed this point in her well-publicized comment that, "White skin notwithstanding, this is our first black president. Blacker than any actual black person who could ever be elected in our children's lifetime. After all, Clinton displays almost every trope of blackness: single-parent household, born poor, working-class, saxophone playing, McDonald's-and-junk-food-loving boy from Arkansas."[60]

While critics from the left and right howled in protest,[61] Clinton has undoubtedly connected with African Americans as no other president had. In addition to the life-connections noted by Morrison and others, many symbolic gestures and policy stands attracted black leaders to his side beyond the mere fact that, as a Democrat, he was likely to be more on their side of issues than the partisan alternatives. Clinton (and his wife, with him and separately) made trips to Africa, and there he made a point of apologizing for slavery, just as he had apologized to the victims of the Tuskegee syphilis experiment. (These apologies were met with derision from conservatives.) He drew attention to racial issues through the "national conversation on race," made record numbers of minority appointments, and firmly supported affirmative action despite how politically vulnerable that stand made him. From the White House website to numerous speeches, especially during the 1998 campaigns, Clinton repeatedly emphasized his support for policies such as the expansion of the Earned Income Tax Credit, which benefits the working poor; raising the minimum wage; increasing funding for civil rights enforcement and programs to help the disadvantaged in health and education; and the often dramatic improvement in employment and education of African Americans. (Of course, the strong economy helped him here as it did in other ways.) No doubt, most black leaders are aware of the full litany, although they are also aware of the welfare reform bill, the dumping of Lani Guinier, and other similar events.

In the end, however, as pointed as Clinton would like to claim many of these policies were, he probably drew the best connection through the symbolic politics of many of his issue stands, his relationships in the black community, and the diversity of his appointments. But to say that much of his impact was likely in "symbolic politics" is not to say his legacy will be minor. The partisan alternative, witnessed during the Bush and Reagan years, was to dismiss most of the issue stands on African-American organizations' agendas as "special interest pleading" by those who refuse to take care of themselves independently, as overreliance on a bloated public sector, or as demands for special privileges. In contrast, Clinton's use of the "bully pulpit" of the presidency, especially through such efforts as the Race Initiative, keeps these questions on the table for discussion. Nor was the Race Initiative merely symbolic politics; the breadth of the panel's undertaking was impressive. About 590 colleges and universities participated in the "Campus Week of Dialogue," 40 states participated in "Statewide Days of Dialogue," more than 18,000 people in 113 cities participated in more than 1,400 "One America Conversations," the advisory board met with 291 different organizations and 62 American Indian Tribal Governments, and the advisory board organized 15 televised town-hall meetings. While the panel did not have authority to actually implement any changes, it did suggest a range of policy proposals for future action.[62]

The Clinton policy record on women is regarded by most women's interest group and social movement leaders as far better than that of any president who went before. The White House maintained special channels relating to women's policy issues, including the White House Office for Women's Initiatives and Outreach and the President's Interagency Council on Women. The Office of the First Lady also focused considerable attention on women's issues, both domestically and in other countries.

Women's groups did not forget that the first act pushed and signed into law by the new president in 1993 was the Family and Medical Leave Act, a much weaker form of parental leave than is available in most other OECD (Organization for Economic Cooperation and Development) countries, but nevertheless, one that took the United States off the very small list of countries lacking a parental-leave policy. Given the relative poverty of women, most of the policies aimed at assisting the poorest Americans also give particular assistance to women. Clinton supported legislation that toughened enforcement of child-support collections. Non-payment of court-ordered child support by fathers has long been one of the major factors contributing to the poverty of single mothers. At the same time, the restrictions posed by the welfare reform law have particularly severe effects on women. Clinton often pointed out that he had vetoed welfare reform laws that he regarded as more punitive and initiated efforts later to relax some of the harsher provisions.

Despite the failure of the comprehensive health care reform plan, an issue women regard as very important, a number of specific policies aimed at women and children's health have been important for women and have received a lot of support within the women's policy community: expanding health care for uninsured children, increasing funding for breast-cancer research and improving access to mammography, requiring hospitals to allow at least forty-eight-hour stays in hospitals following mastectomies, and developing a program for combating osteoporosis. Key portions of the "patients' bill of rights" that Clinton pushed (and that was buried by the Republican House shortly before the 1998 election) were the requirements that insurers cover at least forty-eight hours of hospitalization following childbirth and at least seventy-two hours following a cesarean delivery and that women have access to obstetricians during a pregnancy.

Perhaps the best-known policies endorsed by Clinton that found great favor among women's group leaders related to violence in general, but especially violence against women and children. Women are consistently more in favor of gun control than men, and Clinton's Brady Law and its extension, which prohibits anyone with a domestic violence conviction from owning a firearm, were greeted very favorably. Clinton appeared to take violence against women more seriously than did any of his predecessors, resulting in his signing the Violence against Women Act and increasing funding for domestic violence shelters. For much of the women's movement, Clinton's pro-choice abortion stands were also crucial, including his opposition to further limitations on abortion rights and eliminating the "gag rule," first implemented under President Reagan, that had forbidden family-planning clinics with any public funding from dispensing information that might help a woman obtain an abortion, and his endorsement of the Freedom of Access to Clinic Entrances Act, creating a buffer zone around clinics in which abortions are performed.

The Clinton administration took strong stands against gender discrimination, the EEOC became more active than it had been under recent administrations (as in its sexual harassment suit against Mitsubishi), and the Justice Department was active on these fronts as well (as in the injunction against Virginia Military Institute for excluding women). Clinton vigorously supported continuation of affirmative action and, except for the Defense of Marriage Act, pushed for policies to eliminate discrimination on the basis of sexual preference, and he endorsed legislation and administrative rulings that would curb harassment of and violence against people on the basis of their sexual preference. Hillary Clinton's frequent trips abroad, especially to the developing nations, always included attention specifically to women's poverty, housing, and health care needs. The policy stands of the president were crucial for solidifying the partisan gender gap that had been long developing. As far as these leaders were concerned, they got not just symbolic politics, but real policy change.

Gender and Race Coalitions in Contemporary Politics

I'd like to know that your love
Is love I can be sure of
So tell me now, and I won't ask again
Will you still love me tomorrow?

> — Gerry Goffin and Carole King, "Will You Still Love Me Tomorrow," Number 1 hit song for The Shirelles in 1961, when Bill Clinton was fifteen years old

Bill Clinton's skills as a political operative are clearly illustrated by his relations with key social groups that have come to be identified with the political left including, most notably, African Americans and women, but also certain other racial groups and gays. The strategies Clinton, as campaigner and Democratic leader, used with respect to these groups must be understood as part of the continuing process both political parties use to secure coalitions that will allow them to obtain and protect their offices, and perhaps govern. The New Deal coalition has long been under threat, partly because of the effects of race politics that began to peel away southern white voters in the 1960s and put them in the Republican camp. A wide range of policies, many having to do with race and gender issues, also eroded support among the working class, union supporters, and white ethnics. Likewise, they tended to weaken support among men in general in the late 1970s and 1980s, as the Republican leadership offered an explanation for the bad economic times that rested on the twin ideas of too many government programs (therefore not enough money left in the private family household budget)

and too much preferential treatment for women and blacks, leaving more meritorious white men in the lurch.

Many Democrats, therefore, realized they had to moderate the leftward image they had acquired, especially since the McGovern campaign of 1972, while
Republicans played increasingly to their newfound strengths, swinging further
rightward. The result was that African Americans, Hispanics, women, and gays
became increasingly available as key elements of the potential Democratic coalition. Bill Clinton's policy views and political instincts put him in a position from
which he could manage a delicate balancing act. There is no doubt that the balance did not always work. And ironically, given that Clinton early gained a reputation for wanting everyone to like him, this particular strategy was bound to
make most people unhappy some of the time, even if, in the end, he maintained
almost unbelievable public support in the aggregate.

Some Democrats were worried from the beginning that, as a leader in the
Democratic Leadership Council, he would moderate the party too much. Simultaneously, he was criticized from the right as a tool of the leftist "special interests." In the end, he *was* able to offer some of the more moderate constituencies
from the traditional Democratic coalition what they needed to come back to the
party, as reflected in his consistent support for capital punishment and his willingness to sign the welfare reform bill. He also offered not just token policies to the
more progressive wing of the party, but policies and appointments—practices that
they found, if not everything they wished, a good bit further down the road than
the opposition was offering. Clinton's strategic efforts were aided in no small
measure by two other conditions: first, the economic strength that became apparent after the 1994 election (and allowed him to take credit for balancing the un-
balanceable budget) and, second, the continued Republican strategy of relatively
unmoderated conservatism. Thus blue-collar and union voters, who might not
have forgiven Clinton for NAFTA (on top of all their other disagreements), still,
in the end, found Republican attacks on the safety net worrisome.

Clinton has sometimes been accused of being a wholly political animal,
with no strong commitments other than keeping himself in office and his public
support strong. It is clear that while African-American and women's interest
group and movement leaders have not always been satisfied by Clinton's actions
in policies and appointments, they have indeed felt that he brought them "to the
table," and that there have been tangible results. A reading of the White House
website under Clinton is remarkable in revealing a persistent, consistent pattern
of raising issues key to the agendas of these groups, and in terms and frameworks

more consistent with those groups' views than they had long come to expect even from leading (white, male) Democrats.[63]

We may also suggest another test. If the particular outreach to women and racial minorities was merely a matter of convenience, the final congressional election of the Clinton presidency should surely signal an abatement of those efforts. He did not, in fact, miss a step. On the day after the 1998 election, Clinton wrote a memorandum to the director of the Office of Personnel Management charging that office to develop a guidebook for federal officials who had suffered domestic violence and, additionally, he ordered that from then on a victim of domestic violence would be able to get a new Social Security number merely by providing written affirmation from a third party that she had suffered abuse. This changed the old regulation that a victim would have to prove that her Social Security number had actually been the cause of further abuse. Two days later Clinton appeared at an elaborate signing ceremony for a law designating Little Rock Central High School, the scene of one of the major desegregation battles of the 1950s, a national historic site. In his relatively lengthy remarks on the occasion, Clinton said that Little Rock Central was as hallowed a site as Gettysburg and Independence Hall. He took the opportunity to comment on the elections earlier that week, commending the importance of the high turnout of African Americans and also noting, in light of the events in the history of the civil rights movement that they were commemorating, that an African American had been elected attorney general of Georgia and that African-American members of Congress had been reelected in what were now majority white districts in the South.

There may be specific policy legacies resulting from Clinton's concerted pro-feminist stands, but many of the specific policies he put in force can be reversed, just as he reversed some of the tendencies of previous administrations. Certainly, future administrations can slow the progress of appointments, perhaps making the administration look a little "less like America." There are certainly likely to be serious long-term negative consequences to women's groups from the Lewinsky affair, given the muddying of the waters over what constitutes sexual harassment and given feminists' determination to "stand by their man." But the effects on women's and African-American groups of having had a supporter in the White House will not soon fade even if Bill Clinton was, in so many ways, disgraced.

These pro-feminist policies and many of the policies the black community supports are easier to accomplish when the economy is strong, and Clinton has been able to capitalize on that. It would be difficult for the Democratic Party to beat a massive retreat. But the most lasting effects could, ironically, be on the Republican Party. We are arguing that Bill Clinton was a master at understanding the political opportunities open to a moderate Democrat to crystallize a base of support crucial for a winning strategy. But the real lesson he taught may be to the Republicans who are already showing that they are unlikely to stand idly by—at least if they can neutralize the far-right flank—and watch the Democrats soak up the votes and support of African Americans and women.

9

Clinton's Domestic Policy: The Lessons of a "New Democrat"

PAUL J. QUIRK AND WILLIAM CUNION

The record of President Bill Clinton in domestic policy provides an opportunity to consider an important question for future presidents: What happens when a politically moderate, or *centrist* president attempts to lead a deeply divided, or *polarized* Congress? Can such a president set and hold a moderate course for domestic policy? Or will his or her agenda fall victim to simultaneous attack from the left and the right? If a moderate agenda is possible, what kinds of policies will it consist of? Will they be mere compromises, or can they somehow rise above ideological conflict to serve the nation's broadest interests?

The dynamics of electoral competition in our era suggest that presidents are increasingly likely to face these questions. On the one hand, the national electorate prefers a moderate Democrat or a moderate Republican over a more extreme candidate of either party in general elections for the presidency. On the other hand, state and House-district electorates increasingly are sending either liberal Democrats or conservative Republicans to represent them in Congress. As a result of these trends, presidents may increasingly find themselves almost alone—in conflict with most members of both congressional parties—in the middle of the political spectrum.

Clinton's case tells us a good deal about what such presidents can accomplish in domestic policy, and what they cannot. Judging from his experience, they

200

can certainly win public support (contributing, in Clinton's case, to his ability to ride out the Monica Lewinsky scandal). They can also produce significant policy change. Nevertheless, the accomplishments of such presidents are likely to fall short of those Clinton promised in campaigning for president as a centrist "New Democrat." Rather than rising above divisive ideological conflict, as he promised, such presidents may sink beneath ideology to an unprincipled deference either to public opinion or to the most active and powerful groups on an issue. In this chapter, we consider the general prospects for centrist presidential leadership and then review the evidence of Clinton's record, with special attention to four major and representative areas of domestic policy: the budget and the economy, health care, welfare reform, and the environment.

Varieties of Centrist Leadership

A centrist approach can produce highly effective campaign rhetoric. At least in the current state of party politics, however, it is more problematic as a strategy for governing. We consider the two uses of centrist positions in turn.

Centrist Leadership as Campaign Strategy: Clinton in 1992

For more than three decades leading up to the 1992 election, Democrats had seemed virtually incapable of winning the White House. Despite controlling Congress and having a nominal advantage in party identification among citizens, Democrats had broken the apparent Republican lock on the presidency only once—Jimmy Carter's 1976 victory in the aftermath of Watergate—in the six elections from 1968 to 1988. A leading explanation held that the Democrats habitually nominated candidates who were too liberal to win a general election. In 1992, however, Clinton broke this pattern.

Clinton sought to appeal to Democratic loyalists, swing voters, and even Republicans by campaigning as a New Democrat. He rejected, in particular, the image of a "tax-and-spend liberal," in effect endorsing the standard Republican critique of *Old* Democrats. Instead, Clinton sought to stake out the political center, and to redefine it as something other than halfway between the two parties: "The change we must make isn't liberal or conservative. It's both, and it's different."[1] His 200-page book of promises, *Putting People First*, sometimes reads like a Republican treatise—"we must reward work, demand responsibility, and end welfare as we know it"[2]; sometimes like a handbook for liberal Democrats—"health care should be a right, not a privilege"[3]; and sometimes like a new way of thinking, rising above old conflicts—"we need to adopt an aggressive market-based national strategy to cut pollution . . . shatter the false choice between environmental protection and economic growth."[4] He advocated a strong defense, restraint in social policy, and fiscal discipline. As one journalist wrote, Clinton proposed a "more efficient activism," one that would tame runaway government while maintaining the ideals of the New Deal and the Great Society.[5]

Taking advantage of Republican President George Bush's economic troubles, Clinton assured the voters he could "feel your pain"—presumably an Old Democrat's empathy. And he offered a program to boost the economy without sacrificing important social programs. He proposed to stimulate economic growth through investment in areas such as education, job training, and research, and to shift the tax burden toward wealthier citizens. Middle-class Americans would receive a tax cut. At the same time, Clinton promised to make major steps toward balancing the budget. And he assured voters that in contrast with Bush's ineffectual efforts, his moderate economic package would actually work.

The New-Democrat posture certainly worked as a campaign strategy. In particular, it helped win back many voters—especially middle-class whites and working-class Reagan Democrats—who had jumped ship from the Democratic Party in the early 1980s.[6] And although Ross Perot's strong third-party candidacy helped keep Clinton well short of an absolute majority of the popular vote, at 43 percent he defeated Bush comfortably, by about 7 percent of the two-party vote.

Centrist Leadership as Governing Strategy: Varieties and Circumstances

Clinton's campaign claimed, in effect, that a New Democrat can be all things to all people. In reality, however, centrist policymaking rarely can approach such broad appeal. To see why, we consider three different ways a president can stake out a centrist position.

First, a centrist president can simply take a middle-of-the-road position on each issue in dispute between liberals and conservatives, from abortion to enterprise zones. Such a mechanical approach, however, has little to recommend it and rarely occurs. On some issues, such as abortion or capital punishment, there is no plausible middle position. A consistent middle-of-the road position will generally prove inferior to a more discriminating strategy of some kind. In any case, this *split-the-difference* centrist approach is precisely what Clinton claimed his New Democrat strategy was *not*: a mere compromise.

Second, a centrist president can try to find policies or combinations of policies that reconcile the goals of both liberals and conservatives, or genuinely serve their common interests, more effectively than issue-by-issue compromise. This *principled* or *integrative* centrist approach is what Clinton intended to suggest when he promised a program that would presumably be neither liberal nor conservative, but "both" and "different." Certain policies arguably have such integrative properties: Economists claim, for example, that market-oriented environmental controls (such as pollution taxes) can reduce pollution more effectively, yet at lower cost, than conventional regulatory methods.[7] They also argue that lower budget deficits will produce greater wealth in the long run. Some social-policy analysts suggest that giving the dependent poor generous assistance, while also demanding serious effort on their part, is the only way to overcome dependency.[8] In a broad sense there is an integrative effect, enhanced achievement of common interests, with any policy that takes reality into account more fully than the alternative: doing what actually has desired effects.

Although a principled centrist approach is attractive in the abstract, it is likely to pose difficulties in practice. Unfortunately, it often requires promoting policies that lack effective political constituencies—usually because many citizens do not understand them or have difficulty accepting the means to achieve them. Thus, for example, very few citizens understand the economic rationale for taxing pollution, instead of simply prohibiting it.[9] Many will reject an increase in taxes or a reduction in benefits to lower the budget deficit. And what comes easily to people is either to be generous toward the dependent poor or to go hard on them—but not to do both by tying benefits to supervision and responsibility. In other cases, going beyond a mere compromise of liberal and conservative positions depends on new ideas—finding more effective solutions than policymakers and analysts have found previously. Regrettably, a president cannot count on such discoveries. Thus although the general idea of a principled, triangulating, both-liberal-and-conservative program is appealing, the specific policies of such a program will often be hard to sell, if indeed they even exist.

Third, a centrist can capture the middle the easy way: by adopting whatever position—liberal, conservative, or in-between—has the most voter or interest-group support on each issue. Conservative positions generally have stronger support, for example, on taxes, crime, and welfare; liberal ones have more support on Social Security, Medicare, tuition assistance, and the environment. (Other issues, such as gun control and affirmative action, have comparable support on both sides.) So an *opportunistic centrist* strategy simply switches back-and-forth between liberal and conservative positions as political opportunity beckons. This strategy requires a president to keep his distance from his political party and its constituencies, thus entailing some political risks, especially the loss of an enthusiastic political base.[10] Nevertheless, it has obvious political benefits. In many cases, an opportunistic centrist will do just the opposite of what a principled centrist must do: adopt the policies that are easiest for uninformed swing voters to understand and accept. Unfortunately, responding too readily to an uninformed, and often distorted, public opinion may have adverse consequences for governing.[11]

A president's ability to use the various centrist strategies depends on the prospects for assembling supporting coalitions in Congress, and thus on the state of the political parties. One factor is unified or divided party control of government: If the president's party also controls Congress, he will encounter greater pressure to adhere to an ideological party line; but if the rival party controls Congress, he will need its support, and can more readily promote centrist policies. A second factor is the ideological polarization of the congressional parties: If polarization is severe—so that congressional Democrats are mainly strong liberals, and Republicans strong conservatives—the president will have trouble finding support for centrist policies; but if there are numerous moderates—often, in particular, conservative Democrats and liberal Republicans—they will provide a natural base for such policies.

A final factor is the disposition of the parties to cooperate: If the two parties are in fighting mode, bent on discrediting each other in every way possible, they will not support centrist measures; if one party believes it has the upper hand in the national political debate, it will not risk losing momentum by compromising with the opposition; but if political leaders are willing to set aside partisan conflicts to some degree, they will more readily support centrist measures. This acquiescence may occur on a policy issue of extraordinary importance to the nation. It may also happen when partisan conflict is so destructive that it produces a backlash and a demand for more cooperation from the public.

The strength of congressional moderates and the disposition toward bipartisan cooperation are especially important for a principled or integrative centrist approach. Because such policies are often hard to sell, each party is tempted to oppose them for partisan advantage. The more intense the partisan conflict, the stronger that temptation, and the less opportunity for integrative policies.

The Stages of Clinton's Domestic Presidency

What political conditions did Clinton face? What strategies did he pursue? At different stages of his presidency, Clinton encountered a wide range of conditions, and adopted correspondingly varied strategies. Broadly speaking, he started out vacillating between conventional partisan and principled centrist strategies but eventually gravitated toward a largely opportunistic form of centrism. More precisely, there have been four distinct periods of Clinton's domestic presidency.

Defining an Agenda, 1993–94

The first period, from Clinton's inauguration as president in January 1993 to the midterm elections in November 1994, was shaped by unified Democratic control of the presidency and Congress, severe partisan conflict in Congress, and high ambition and confidence on the part of the Clinton administration. Clinton's agenda consisted in roughly equal parts of liberal social reform—the Great Society revisited—and principled centrist leadership. Substantively, this agenda led to both major accomplishments and major failures. Politically, the result was an unqualified defeat in the midterm elections.

Despite his New Democrat strategy's effectiveness in the 1992 campaign, Clinton's aspirations for a principled centrist agenda encountered political obstacles from the outset of his presidency. The congressional election had continued a long-term trend of making moderates scarce.[12] Most Democrats in Congress were Old Democrats, more liberal than the president. And in 1992 women, Latinos, and African Americans were elected to Congress in record numbers, moving the ideological balance among Democrats further left. Complicating his problems with the party, Clinton had virtually no coattails in the congressional election. Democrats gained no seats in the Senate, and lost nine in the House. Clinton ran ahead of a victorious Democratic candidate in only five congressional districts; other Democrats had little reason to side with him on the basis of his standing with their constituents.[13]

Congressional Republicans attributed Bush's defeat largely to the weak economy and to Clinton's borrowing of Republican themes, and they were unimpressed by Clinton's 43 percent of the popular vote. The ballots were still being counted on election night when Senate Minority Leader Bob Dole of Kansas promised to represent the majority of Americans who had rejected Clinton's candidacy and forecasted, "It's not going to be all a bed of roses for Governor Clinton."[14] In fact, Republicans demonstrated remarkable unity in opposing the president. In its year-end analysis, *Congressional Quarterly* pronounced the first year of the 103d Congress the most partisan session since it began keeping the statistics in 1954.[15]

Whether by conscious calculation or through inadvertence, Clinton responded with an incongruous mix of New Democrat principled centrism—keeping his campaign commitment to balanced deficit reduction—and Old Democrat tax-and-spend liberalism. His 1993 economic package was an experiment in principled centrism. The package included a five-year plan to reduce the deficit by over $700 billion—with more than half of the reduction resulting from spending cuts (the conservative element), and the rest from tax increases mainly affecting upper-income groups (the liberal one). He stuck with that formula even though no Republican in either chamber stepped forward to share the burden of voting for it. To pass his package, Clinton leaned hard on congressional Democrats, especially liberals, who were asked to impose the unpleasant medicine of program cuts on their own constituencies to underwrite the president's credibility. The adoption of Clinton's 1993 economic package was therefore a case of balanced deficit reduction in which one party bore all of the political costs. Although enjoying help from Republicans' traditional support of free trade, Clinton took on a similar burden of principled centrist leadership in promoting the North American Free Trade Agreement (NAFTA) despite strong opposition from labor unions.

In most other matters, Clinton followed the path of least resistance and looked for support in Congress where he could find it, that is, mainly among liberal Democrats. Although some moderate Democrats, such as Oklahoma Senator David Boren, pressed Clinton to seek bipartisan support, Vice-President Al Gore urged him to keep his distance from the Republicans and that view was reinforced by a liberal and inexperienced White House staff.[16] Clinton spent most of his first two years in office riding along with the Democratic congressional majority. He won several legislative victories by promoting liberal bills that President Bush had vetoed, such as the Family and Medical Leave Act, motor voter registration, and a gun-control measure, the "Brady Bill." With support coming overwhelmingly from Democrats, Clinton, in 1993, had a success rate of 86 percent on votes in Congress, one of the highest figures for a president's first year in the past half-century.[17]

In some cases Clinton's liberal positions went too far for Congress. He attempted, unsuccessfully, to make good on a campaign promise to remove the ban against homosexuals in the military. After criticism of his plan by military leaders led to a wave of public opposition, Congress forced him to back off. Most important, Clinton assigned two leading administration liberals, Ira Magaziner and First Lady Hillary Rodham Clinton, to head up the formulation of his proposal for health care reform. The 1994 proposal, discussed more fully later in this chapter, insisted on expensive, high-quality coverage; bypassed private insurance companies; promoted managed care over traditional fee-for-service medicine; and created a substantial new government bureaucracy, so-called health alliances, to help control health care costs. Despite initial public support, the proposal was perceived with some justice as a throwback to traditional big-government liberalism. And it fell victim to Republican opposition, an insurance-industry publicity campaign, and rising public doubts.[18] Ultimately, even many Democrats refused to support it.

By the November 1994 midterm elections, Clinton was apparently failing politically. He could claim credit for a major deficit-reduction package but had suffered harsh criticism both for its tax increases and its benefit cuts. He had been widely criticized as reneging on his campaign promise to govern from the center. His promotion of gay rights in the military had enraged social conservatives. And he had suffered an embarrassing defeat on his health care plan, failing to deliver on one of the major promises of his campaign. Added to his problems with policy, Clinton's presidency had been rocked by a series of gaffes, scandals, and disasters—from Whitewater, to Travelgate, to the suicide of Vincent Foster. And his public approval ratings had sunk to 41 percent.[19]

Resisting a Revolution, 1995

The second period of Clinton's domestic presidency lasted only about one year, from the 1994 midterm congressional elections to the belated adoption of a fiscal year 1996 budget in December 1995. It differed from the preceding period because of three significant features: the resumption of divided party control of government (with Republicans controlling Congress instead of the presidency), the erroneous perception by the Republicans that the election was a mandate for a sharp turn to the right in national policy, and Clinton's discovery of an opportunistic centrist strategy to defeat their plans and reclaim the initiative. The result was deadlock in policymaking, but political rebirth for the Clinton presidency.

The Democrats were the majority party in the House from 1955 to 1994—the longest stretch of unbroken party control in either chamber in U.S. history—and in the Senate for the same period except for six years during the Reagan administration. In the 103d Congress (1993–94), Democrats had comfortable majorities of 258–176 in the House (with one independent) and 57–43 in the Senate. But the November 1994 elections turned the tables. Republicans picked up an extraordinary 54 seats in the House, giving them a solid 230–204 majority. With the help of two senators defecting from the Democrats after the election, they took a 54–46 edge in the Senate. Walter Dean Burnham called it the "most consequential off-year election" in a century.[20] Republicans called it a "revolution."

Beyond having majority control, the Republicans, led by Speaker of the House Newt Gingrich (Ga.), had run a coherent, national campaign for Congress. Most Republican House candidates had signed the Contract with America, pledging support for several conservative measures, such as a balanced-budget amendment, welfare reform, and congressional term limits.[21] Although polls showed most voters unaware of the Contract, the Republicans believed the electorate had endorsed it.[22] "This was clearly an historic election which clearly had a mandate," Gingrich said.[23] And he was determined to fulfill it, with or without Clinton's consent. "I am very prepared to cooperate with the Clinton administration. I am not prepared to compromise."[24]

Throughout 1995 congressional Republicans so dominated policymaking that it was in effect the "Gingrich administration." For several months, Clinton was at a loss. His State of the Union address contained few proposals. He was "speaking muffled thoughts in muffled tones," remarked journalist Elizabeth Drew.[25] And his legislative success rate was the lowest *Congressional Quarterly* had ever recorded.[26] To prove that he was still relevant to government, he was reduced to citing the Constitution.[27]

The president's constitutional authority—the veto power—was, in fact, the key to restoring his political role. That the Republicans pushed policies far to the right of any national consensus gave him the opportunity. At first, Clinton was reluctant to provoke confrontation. In February, House Republicans introduced a bill that would have killed the school lunch program, replacing it with a block grant funded at a lower level. Despite the easy target, Clinton was "leery of a full frontal attack on the Congress," according to press secretary Mike McCurry.[28] He exercised his first veto in response to a Republican deficit-reduction bill in mid-May. While bowing to the importance of deficit reduction, he attacked what he claimed were extreme and unwarranted spending cuts: "A bill that cuts education to put pork in is the wrong way to balance the budget."[29]

The veto led to an agreement that preserved many of the Republicans' spending cuts but added $700 million demanded by Clinton for education, job training, childcare, and the environment. Both sides claimed victory. But the confrontation taught Clinton that he could score political points by portraying the Republicans as extremists, while positioning himself—as he had failed to do in the previous Congress—as a moderate.

The climactic battle of the 104th Congress came on the fiscal year 1996 budget. After the disappointing political results of his first-year deficit-reduction effort, Clinton had turned dovish on the deficit.[30] His FY 1996 budget projected $200 billion deficits well into the next century. Refusing to make peace with deficit spending, however, Republicans, in May, offered a plan that provided for a balanced budget by 2002. Virtually every area of government spending was to be reduced (with Social Security a notable exception). The plan eliminated the Department of Commerce, along with more than one hundred federal programs. It converted Medicaid into a block grant, turning over responsibility for health care for the poor to the states. Most controversial, it cut the growth of the politically popular Medicare program by more than $250 billion by 2002. The plan also included $227 billion in tax cuts—although by reducing the Earned Income Tax Credit, it raised taxes for the working poor. A bold, if not radical document, the Gingrich budget afforded Clinton ample opportunity to cut deficits substantially and yet appear more moderate.

For several weeks, nevertheless, the White House ruminated about whether to offer an alternative plan. Finally, in a prime-time television address from the Oval Office, Clinton defined a centrist plan to abolish the deficit. He promised to "cut taxes for the middle class and not the wealthy," to cut welfare but "protect children," and to "balance the budget by controlling health care costs."[31] Warning that cutting deficits too quickly could hurt the economy, he projected a balanced budget in ten years, not the Republicans' seven. Although Clinton's proposal was more moderate than Gingrich's, it still contained major spending cuts, including a $125 billion reduction in Medicare, and provided for $98 billion in middle-class tax cuts. Congressional Democrats were angered by Clinton's willingness to cut programs to pay for tax cuts.[32]

By distinguishing himself from Democrats in Congress, Clinton aggressively implemented the centrist strategy that political adviser Dick Morris, a post-midterm election addition to the White House, now called "triangulation." On the whole, his approach was shaped by political opportunity: in particular, Clinton attacked Republican cuts in the Medicare program. These attacks were highly debatable on the merits. Informed commentators, both liberal and conservative, had long viewed Medicare spending as out of control. But the "Mediscare" rhetoric was effective with the voters, especially the elderly.

During the summer—only months after many commentators had written him off—Clinton's public support began to climb. By October the public trusted Clinton to handle the nation's problems more than the Republican Congress. By November Gingrich's favorable rating had dropped to 25 percent while Clinton's approval had risen to 52 percent, its highest level in eighteen months. A majority of the public thought Republican spending cuts went too far.[33]

In the increasingly friendly climate, Clinton could afford to take a hard line with the Republicans. When the two sides remained deadlocked six weeks into the fiscal year, Clinton vetoed a further extension of temporary spending authority and forced a shutdown of government offices on 13 November. Clinton eventually accepted some of the Republicans' key demands, including balancing the budget in seven years. But he had won the political battle: the public blamed the government shutdown on the Republicans by a margin of 2 to 1.[34] Reflecting on the episode, Republican Senator John McCain of Arizona paid tribute to Clinton's political skill: "He played us like a violin."[35]

From the standpoint of his personal political interests, the traumatic Democratic defeat in the midterm election became in some respects a blessing in disguise for Clinton—encouraging him to keep some distance from his party and its constituencies. "Amid the total rubble of a destroyed Democratic congressional majority," Morris later wrote, "there was no need to compromise with the past."[36] At least, collaborating with Old Democrats alone no longer promised the ability to govern.

Negotiating Agreement, 1996–97

The third distinct period of Clinton's domestic presidency—markedly different from either of the first two—began in January 1996, in the aftermath of the government shutdown, continued through the election year and the entire first year of Clinton's second term, and ended with the eruption of the Monica Lewinsky scandal at the beginning of his sixth year. It was a period of relatively cooperative divided government. The president continued his opportunistic centrist approach. And the Republicans backed away from their aggressive posture of 1995. Both sides tried to appear reasonable. The result was major policy change on several fronts.

In terms of real consequences for the lives of citizens, the government shutdown was a trifling event: offices closed, phones not answered, for a matter of days. Vital functions, such as sending out Social Security checks, continued. But the shutdown made an impression on the public, suggesting a pathological excess of partisan conflict, and led to widespread demands for more cooperation between the branches. Gingrich's determination not to compromise was no longer tenable for the Republicans. Clinton, eager to bolster his record in an election year, was also prepared to be flexible.

The result was a notable amount of significant legislation. During 1996, despite the elections approaching in November, Clinton and the Republicans reached agreement on a radical overhaul of the nation's welfare system. As we see later, the president's endorsement of the Republican reform bill seemed to sacrifice his own principles about welfare in deference to the popular demand for substantial reform.[37] The president and Congress also reached agreements to rewrite telecommunications law (after two decades of failed efforts), set new standards for safe drinking water, guarantee health insurance for workers who lose or leave their jobs, and give the president the line-item veto, among other things. In the end, 1996 was a highly productive one for Congress, especially for a presidential election year with divided government.

Clinton supplemented this legislative record by undertaking a series of minor initiatives designed to generate publicity, appeal broadly to the electorate, and neither cost much money nor require legislation. For example, he advocated that public schools require students to wear uniforms, a matter not previously a federal issue, and urged the television networks to adopt a voluntary rating system. The Clinton organization won admiration among commentators for the cleverness of these initiatives, if not for their significance as public policy.

Along with a continuing strong performance of the economy, Clinton's consistent, flexible, and occasionally creative moderation during 1996 helped to complete his political recovery from the disastrous midterm elections and raise his public approval to impressive levels. By September Clinton was enjoying approval ratings of 60 percent, comparable to those of popular, easily reelected presidents such as Dwight Eisenhower and Ronald Reagan at the same stage.

Clinton cruised to reelection, winning 49 percent of the popular vote to Republican presidential candidate Bob Dole's 41 percent. Dole, who had correctly predicted some of Clinton's first-term difficulties, found that in response to those difficulties Clinton had essentially stolen the Republican agenda—moving far enough to the right on issues such as welfare, crime, and taxes to satisfy most voters. Despite Dole's best efforts to depict Clinton as a liberal, most voters saw him as a moderate.[38] When Dole proposed a 15-percent tax cut in an effort to find a major issue that would work for him, it was widely dismissed as an act of desperation.

Even though the Democrats picked up only nine seats in the House and lost two in the Senate, and even though the Senate became even more sharply polarized (five moderate Republican senators retired and were replaced by conservatives), the election-year openness toward bipartisan cooperation continued beyond the election. Despite protests from militant conservatives, Gingrich, Senate Majority Leader Trent Lott (R-Miss.), and many other Republicans had learned a lesson from the 1995 budget showdown. Gingrich, in contrast to his post election remarks two years earlier, pronounced, "We ought to work with [the president] and give him a chance to lead in the direction he campaigned on, and if he sticks to the things he campaigned on, we should be able to find some common ground."[39] When Clinton unveiled his budget proposal in February, Republican Senator Don Nickles of Oklahoma added, "We don't have any choice but to work together. A repeat of last year is not acceptable to anybody."[40]

Indeed, during 1997 Clinton and the Republicans continued to find opportunities for agreement. Congress passed Clinton's children's health initiative (providing $20 billion in medical insurance for children in poor families) and approved increased funding for education (with most of the increase going toward Republican priorities); Clinton went along with long-standing Republican proposals for a $500-per-child tax credit and a cut in the capital gains tax.[41] Most important (as we describe more fully later in this chapter), Clinton and Republicans agreed on a plan to balance the budget by 2002.

In the relatively cooperative divided government of his fourth and fifth years in office, then, Clinton's opportunistic centrist strategy worked well. Republicans were compelled to deal with him. Clinton bent over backwards to allow them to do so. And he had much to show for it, both politically and in substantive policy change.

The Monica Lewinsky Scandal and Policy Standstill, 1998–99

The period of constructive negotiation ended abruptly in February 1998 with the eruption of the Monica Lewinsky scandal. It led to an explosion of partisan conflict, as Democrats and Republicans fought over the conduct of Independent

Counsel Kenneth Starr's investigation, the House impeachment inquiry, and aspects of the Senate trial. More important, the scandal thoroughly distracted Congress's and the nation's attention from matters of public policy.

In his 1998 State of the Union address, delivered days after the first revelations of his alleged perjury and obstruction of justice in the Paula Jones case, Clinton attempted to forge ahead with his policy agenda. His main theme was expressed in a slogan, "Save Social Security first"—meaning that the impending budget surplus should not be raided for tax cuts or spending increases in other areas until the retirement program had been put on a sound financial footing. Implicitly, it was a call for exploiting the growth of general revenues—and providing increased subsidies for retirees—rather than struggling to balance Social Security benefits with revenues from the payroll tax. He also called for tax credits to help parents pay college tuition. Characteristic of Clinton's post-1994 opportunistic centrism, both notions appealed primarily to middle-class citizens.

Although Clinton's speech was well received, his agenda was dead. Massively preoccupied by the scandal and investigation, the media and Congress largely ignored Clinton's initiatives. Ironically, the Republican leadership's fixation on the scandal led to a September agreement on the fiscal year 1998 budget that favored Clinton's positions and proved an embarrassment to the Republicans. Widely criticized as neglecting the country's business to pursue impeachment, the Republican leadership could not afford to stand firm and risk provoking another confrontation on the budget. So they gave Clinton a deal that outraged the Republican rank-and-file and conservative groups. But for the most part, it appeared that action on major domestic issues would be held up—and Clinton's domestic presidency essentially suspended—until the matter of impeachment was resolved.

Policies and Accomplishments

In the end, the significance of Clinton's centrist strategy and the legacy of his domestic leadership lie in his achievements in policymaking. In the rest of this chapter, we look more closely at several areas of domestic policy—the economy, health care, welfare, and the environment—to assess those achievements. The substantive results of Clinton's brand of centrist leadership have been less imposing than its political successes.

The Economy

It is obvious what is the most positive element of Clinton's legacy: he has presided over one of the most prosperous eras in the nation's history. Nearly every indicator of economic health improved during his tenure in office. From 1993 to 1998, the jobless rate fell by a third, from 7.3 percent to 4.7 percent. The poverty rate dropped—though only from 14.8 percent to 13.7 percent. Inflation was down from 2.9 percent to 1.7 percent. The Dow Jones index of stock prices more than doubled.[42] Personal disposable income was up, and so was new-home construction.[43] A $290 billion annual budget deficit was transformed into a $75 billion surplus. One could, however, easily overstate Clinton's responsibility for this prosperity.

Clinton's policies, especially early in his term, probably contributed to the long-lived economic expansion. As we have seen, his 1993 economic program was the high point of principled centrist policymaking in his administration. Reviewing Clinton's economic decision making early in his term, the *New York Times* observed:

> Time and again, he was forced into hard choices about economic policy. In almost every instance, he took the route favored by Wall Street, business executives and conventional economists, not the ones that ordinary people might have favored and that almost certainly would have been easier to defend politically.[44]

Clinton also refrained from criticizing the Federal Reserve Board and reappointed its respected chairman, Alan Greenspan. As Laura D'Andrea Tyson, a top Clinton economic adviser, explained, "We decided early on that the financial markets could misinterpret criticism of the Fed. And the Fed itself might react in unpredictable ways."[45]

Although his early economic management scored points with Wall Street, it was not the major cause of the expansion. Simply stated, presidents do not control the economy, except marginally.[46] If any institution of government does control it, in this era, it is primarily the politically independent Federal Reserve System—which manages interest rates and the money supply. But even the Fed cannot fully control the business cycle, which in the end is largely determined by its own dynamic as well as by economic events. Like any president's economic results, good or bad, Clinton's success was more than anything a matter of luck.

With respect to the period after the 1994 midterm elections, moreover, Clinton deserves only limited credit even for reducing the budget deficit. Chastened by the poor political reception for his 1993 economic program, he opted out of providing leadership on deficit reduction. Fortunately, from the standpoint of fiscal policy, the Republicans took over the lead. In any case, the sustained growth of the economy and revenues, not tough policy decisions, did most of the work of cutting the deficit. And even so, the president and Congress left long-term financial problems unresolved.

Congressional Republicans put balancing the federal budget by 2002 on the table in early 1997. Clinton agreed with that goal in principle, but the two sides were miles apart on the means of achieving it. Republicans wanted almost $200 billion in tax cuts (starting out, so to speak, by taking a large step backwards); Clinton's plan offered less than half of that.[47] In addition, much tougher decisions were on the agenda. One controversial proposal was to revise the Consumer Price Index (CPI) to reduce estimates of inflation and thus the benefits of programs with automatic cost-of-living adjustments.[48] Another, opposed by all fifty governors, was Clinton's proposal to cap the growth of per capita Medicaid spending.[49]

Before such tough decisions were actually made, however, the Congressional Budget Office (CBO) stepped in and saved the day by announcing that the booming economy would yield $225 billion of unexpected revenue. The CBO projected a fiscal year 2002 deficit of only $105 billion, only a third of what had been predicted two years earlier.[50] Some joked that Clinton and the Republicans would have to strike a deal quickly, before the budget balanced itself.[51] (In fact, it did just that the following year, yielding a $75 billion surplus for fiscal year 1998.) The CPI adjustment and the Medicaid cap were dropped instantly. Defense spending went up, as did welfare spending. And although congressional Democrats complained of being shut out of the negotiations and objected vigorously to some of the provisions, balancing the budget was easy enough that Clinton could tout the final agreement without hinting at any pain:

> It includes the largest increase in college aid since the GI Bill, the largest increase in children's health since the creation of Medicaid over 30 years ago, tax cuts that are the equivalent of a $1,000 raise in take-home pay for the average family with two children, and much more that is good for America.[52]

Commenting on criticism from House Democrats, a White House official acknowledged "an honest disagreement . . . [about] the future of the Democratic Party." The president, he explained, believed that Democrats needed to be viewed as "fiscally responsible."[53]

In any case, the budget agreement did not carry fiscal responsibility to any extreme. It conveniently deferred most of the spending cuts to the final two years of the period covered, and ignored the long-term problems of Social Security and Medicare.[54] Journalists Jack Germond and Jules Witcover quipped that according to actuaries, Medicare now would "go bankrupt in 2008, not 2001."[55]

Health Care

No item of Clinton's 1992 campaign platform was more ambitious than his promise to fix the two major problems of American health care: rising costs and widespread lack of coverage. Spending on health care had increased rapidly for many years, amounting to 13 percent of national income by 1991.[56] The cost of corporate health benefits by 1989 was equal to more than half of profits.[57] More important from the public's perspective, vast numbers of Americans—estimated at 30 to 40 million—had neither private health insurance nor coverage under a government program; and many others had coverage that would end if they quit or lost their jobs. In his 1992 campaign, Clinton promised to abolish this insecurity: "No American will go without health care."[58]

Americans still go without health care. The failure of Clinton's health care reform was partly due to the daunting complexity of the issue. But it also reflected mistakes and deficiencies in Clinton's effort: the drift toward liberal, partisan positions of his first two years; a lack of competence in the process of formulating a policy; and in the end, the promotion of a massively costly, overly bureaucratic, and ill-explained plan. Clinton "destroyed the chances for a very significant and productive reform of the health care system," said Alain C. Enthoven, the Stanford economist who devised the concept of managed competition central to the plan. "He blew an historic opportunity."[59]

In one of his first official acts as president, Clinton named First Lady Hillary Rodham Clinton and business consultant Ira Magaziner to head the White House Task Force on National Health Care Reform, charging them to draft a reform plan within 100 days. They both represented the liberal wing of the Democratic Party, and neither had prior experience in managing policy development in the federal government. According to critics, they also shared an arrogant refusal to compromise.[60] Mrs. Clinton and Magaziner devised an exceptionally awkward advisory process, with more than 500 experts from within and outside government meeting secretly in dozens of subcommittees. Five months after their deadline, they brought forth a 1,300-page bill, which the president sent to Congress as his proposed Health Security Act.

Announced amid fanfare and high expectation, the plan encountered numerous difficulties. It was massively complex—with mandated employer-paid insurance, subsidies for small employers, publicly provided insurance, managed care, price controls, and new federal purchasing cooperatives, among other features; Republicans produced a flow chart of the plan that looked like a "street map of Istanbul."[61] It promised splendid benefits, the equivalent of those provided to employees of a Fortune 500 company, without accounting for the costs. The president largely failed to explain the plan to the public. Political scientist Theda Skocpol notes, "Little was said about employer mandates, finances, and regional health alliances. The American people were never told much about what was *in* the Health Security bill."[62]

Departing from its supposed centrist strategy, the administration refused to work with congressional Republicans. At the outset, some Republicans expressed their willingness to help develop a reform bill. Senator John Danforth, a Republican from Missouri, declared, "We will pass a law next year."[63] But presumably to avoid serious compromise, the White House shut the Republicans out of efforts to devise a politically workable plan.[64] If there had been any hope for ultimate bipartisan support, that decision killed it. Meanwhile, congressional Democrats had diverse views of their own. Some liberals even favored a single-payer plan—modeled after the British and Canadian systems, with the government paying for health care for all citizens.

With the Democrats in disarray, Republicans and the insurance industry went on the offensive to defeat Clinton's proposal. Republicans attacked the plan as "socialized medicine" and the employer mandate as evidence of Clinton's fondness for "big government."[65] The health insurance industry sponsored a series of television advertisements raising the specter that people would lose the ability to choose their doctors. And the attacks worked. By the time Democratic congressional leaders seriously attempted to hammer out a compromise, public opinion had turned against them. By July, 55 percent of Americans disapproved of the Clinton plan.[66] In September, with no agreement in sight, Senate Majority Leader George Mitchell pronounced the Clinton bill dead. After Republicans swept the November congressional elections, any prospect of a renewed push for universal health care in the 104th Congress lacked a pulse as well.

Clinton and the Republican Congresses after 1994 have taken modest, further steps on health care. A bipartisan congressional initiative that was passed in

1996, the Kennedy-Kassebaum bill, made it easier for people who changed jobs to keep their health insurance. A 1998 measure, promoted by Clinton, provided more health care coverage for poor children. To a great extent, attention has shifted to dealing with the problems of quality that arise under managed care—which even without the enactment of Clinton's plan has rapidly become the nation's dominant form of health care, accounting for 85 percent of the insured population.[67] Clinton and the Democrats have made popular proposals to set standards for managed care, for example, by prohibiting "drive-by births" (very brief hospital stays after childbirth), requiring payment for unauthorized emergency-room care, and giving patients a right to appeal denial of services. Republicans have attempted to develop their own managed-care bill, with looser requirements, but no agreement has been reached. In any case, the condition that caused a sense of crisis in the early 1990s has not improved: the number of Americans who have no health coverage has increased to more than 40 million.[68]

Welfare

One of the clearest expressions of Clinton's principled centrist aspirations during the 1992 campaign was his repeated promise to "end welfare as we know it." Addressing widespread public concerns about chronic welfare dependency, he declared that "welfare should be a second chance, not a way of life."[69] Yet he did not advocate simply cutting welfare benefits or severely restricting eligibility. He instead aimed to "empower people with the education, training, and child care they need" to break free from dependency.[70] Clinton did not, however, take the initiative on reforming welfare during his first two years, when he was in his principled centrist phase and Democrats controlled the congressional agenda. He acted in response to Republican initiatives after the Republican takeover, and when he had shifted into a politically oriented, opportunistic centrist mode.

Clinton put welfare reform on hold for most of the 103d Congress largely because he believed that Congress could not deal with both health care reform and welfare reform at the same time. Not only were both issues massively complex and contentious, but they were in the jurisdiction of the same committees. Some challenged Clinton's choice of priorities. The centrist Democratic Leadership Committee pressed him to deal with welfare reform first to avoid losing support from the middle class. Senator Daniel Patrick Moynihan (D-N.Y.), a thoughtful moderate on welfare, remarked, "We don't have a health crisis in this country. We do have a welfare crisis."[71]

But Clinton argued that welfare reform was unworkable until health care reform was in place, and did not make a welfare proposal until June 1994, far too late for Congress to act on it before the November elections. During the succeeding 104th Congress, Republicans controlled the agenda on welfare. They could draft bills to their own specifications, pass them without significant Democratic support, and deposit them on the president's desk. Clinton had to sign them or explain his veto to the public.

The Republicans' Contract with America had declared war on the welfare system, promising to "reduce government dependency, attack illegitimacy, require welfare recipients to work, and cut welfare spending."[72] Accordingly, the Republican Congress in 1995 twice passed bills making monumental changes in welfare policy—providing for strict time limits on benefits and so-called family caps (prohibiting women on welfare from collecting increased benefits as a result of having more children). But Clinton vetoed both bills, calling them extreme and portraying himself as a moderate. Explaining his first veto, he said the Republican bill was "too weak on work and too tough on children."[73] He reinforced his moderate stance by endorsing waivers that permitted several states to opt out of the federal system and experiment with their own welfare-to-work plans.[74]

Notwithstanding this vigorously advertised moderation, repeatedly vetoing welfare reform was politically risky. Clinton's sincerity about changing welfare was increasingly subject to challenge. "When it comes to real welfare reform," said Rep. Bill Paxon (R-N.Y.), "Clinton is the great pretender."[75] When the Republicans passed a third reform bill in July 1996, Clinton faced strong political pressures to go along with it.[76]

From the standpoint of a principled moderate, the Republican bill had serious defects. Abolishing federal Aid to Families with Dependent Children, it provided for lump sums of federal money for income support for each state. States were required to get recipients into jobs within two years and to enforce a lifetime maximum of five years of benefits; they were permitted to set even shorter time limits. Advocates of the bill failed to address obvious problems: What if there are no jobs? What if recipients are incapable of holding jobs, or of earning enough to support their families? And how can the law be tough on adults living on the borderline of poverty without harming their children? In fact, a report by the Department of Health and Human Services (HHS) estimated that the Republican proposals would push more than a million children into poverty.[77]

For such reasons, even some leading conservative commentators, such as Lawrence Mead and James Q. Wilson, had criticized the measure. Joining Clinton on a flight to New York, Senator Moynihan reportedly engaged him in a "screaming fight" over it.[78] But Clinton's political advisers, citing White House public opinion polls, warned of dire consequences in November if Clinton vetoed yet another welfare reform bill.[79] And in an almost apologetic statement, Clinton announced in late July that he would sign it. He admitted that the bill had "serious flaws" and called parts of it simply "wrong." Yet "on balance," he concluded, it was "a real step forward for our country, our values, and for people who are on welfare."[80]

To many liberal and even moderate Democrats, Clinton's decision did not rise above or somehow integrate liberal and conservative values, as his New Democrat rhetoric promised; Clinton had merely betrayed liberals' humanitarian concerns to help ensure his reelection. Several high-level administration officials resigned in protest, and one of them, Peter Edelman, wrote a scathing magazine article entitled "The Worst Thing Bill Clinton Has Done."[81]

In its first two years of operation, welfare reform has had more apparent success than such critics would have predicted.[82] In just over a year the number of people on welfare dropped by almost a third, to 8.4 million.[83] And all thirty-six states reporting data met the law's requirement that 25 percent of welfare recipients hold jobs or be actively preparing for work within two years.[84] But the real test is yet to come: Many of the welfare recipients who are now working do not have earnings that would support a family. Moreover, no recipients have yet reached the five-year limit on benefits. And of course we have not seen how time limits would work during a recession. Moynihan may still be right in predicting that the 1996 welfare reform will be "the most brutal act of social policy since Reconstruction."[85] It certainly risked that outcome.

The Environment

The environment was a secondary issue in the 1992 presidential election. Although vice-presidential candidate Al Gore was a leading Senate environmentalist, Clinton had a moderate environmental record as governor of Arkansas, often favoring economic concerns over environmental quality. According a *New York Times* editorial, he had "courted the Arkansas poultry industry, a world-class polluter of that state's rivers and streams . . . and winked at pollution to attract industry and jobs to a poor state."[86] Only 6 percent of the voters identified the environment as the main issue in deciding their vote, mostly preferring the Democratic ticket.[87]

Clinton's position on the environment in the presidential campaign had two contrasting elements. On the one hand, he vowed to fight pollution very aggressively, making commitments to tough policies in several areas, such as passing a new Clean Water Act, improving enforcement of environmental requirements, allowing citizens to sue federal agencies to compel such enforcement, and increasing investments in renewable energy sources.[88] In effect, he adopted a standard Old Democrat line—to the left of his record in Arkansas—that has worked well for the party in national politics.

On the other hand, he also outlined a New Democrat, centrist position on the environment. He said that the time-worn debate on jobs-versus-environment presents a "false choice," and promised to reconcile regulation and economic efficiency. As we noted earlier, such an agenda would require considerable efforts to explain to the public how more efficient regulation was possible and why it would produce important benefits. In any case, apart from occasional puffery about making his administration "the greenest in history,"[89] Clinton has not treated the environment as a central focus of his presidency.

The combination of an ambivalent strategy and low priority has not led to major legislative accomplishments on environmental policy. Clinton has rarely taken the strong stands promised in his Old Democrat rhetoric. Environmental interest groups thus have charged that Clinton's environmental record has been one of "retreats, defeats, and half measures."[90] Nor has he articulated a set of principled moderate policies or vigorously pushed reforms aimed at improved efficiency in this area. Clinton has achieved significant political successes on the environment, however, by opposing unpopular anti-environmental proposals by the Republicans after their takeover of Congress.

Early in his first term, Clinton created the President's Council on Sustainable Development with the principled centrist mission "to find new ways to combine economic growth and environmental protection."[91] But that mission was neither a prominent nor a successful part of Clinton's domestic agenda. In July 1993 Clinton attempted to settle a decade-old dispute between environmentalists and the timber industry over logging in old-growth forests in the Pacific Northwest. His proposed compromise permitted less logging than the industry sought and less forest protection than environmentalists wanted. It also offered economic assistance for the region, but less than local officials wanted. "So nobody is happy," one analyst observed.[92] In another early initiative, Clinton sought to end the century-old subsidies for logging, mining, and grazing on public lands. But when Democratic lawmakers from western states objected, the White House backed away from the proposal. The Council on Sustainable Development proposed a framework for environmental regulations that was endorsed by both Dow Chemical and the Sierra Club, but legislation to implement it was not introduced.[93]

Clinton attempted to use a largely symbolic measure—elevating the Environmental Protection Agency to cabinet-level status—to help establish his environmentalist credentials. But he again backed off when conservatives insisted on tacking on a burdensome requirement that all regulations pass strict tests of cost-effectiveness.[94] Rather than investing effort and political capital to overcome resistance to his environmental initiatives, Clinton was usually content to fight his main battles elsewhere.

After the 1994 midterm elections, however, Clinton found a substantively compelling and politically viable mission of defending existing environmental controls against incautious Republican attacks. The Republican Congress tried to roll back environmental regulations and cut the budgets of the agencies enforcing them. "This Congress is on the wrong track," Clinton declared.[95] When Republicans attempted to revise the Clean Water Act to eliminate federal jurisdiction over wetlands and ease controls on industrial pollutants, he accused them of colluding with business groups to produce a "Dirty Water Act."[96] Clinton followed up his charges with vetoes and threats of vetoes. And he won the battle for public support.[97] Even at the height of the Republican Revolution, the public strongly preferred Clinton's approach over that of the Republicans on the environment.[98] Substantively, Clinton's major achievement on the environment has been to ward off extreme anti-environmental measures advanced by the Republican Congress.

The Prospects for Centrist Leadership

To assess the long-term significance of Clinton's domestic policy, it is useful to review his record from two perspectives. The first concerns his major decisions, the resulting legislative or other policy outcomes, and their social and economic effects: that is, what he did, and with what results. Largely because he has faced a Republican congressional majority for most of his presidency, he has accomplished less than many citizens seem to think.

In one crucial area, of course, Clinton has had extraordinary success: he has presided over a stable and growing economy, enjoying one of the longest economic expansions in American history. More than anything, this economic performance (like economic conditions during any president's term) has been a matter of luck. But Clinton's policies—especially budget balancing, promotion of free trade, and reductions in taxes and social spending—have contributed to the prosperity. They should continue to yield benefits. Of course, much of the initiative for these policies, especially after 1994, was provided by the Republican Congress.

In other areas, however, Clinton's accomplishments were generally quite limited or of uncertain significance. In health care, Clinton failed to secure a bill providing for universal health coverage, arguably botching an opportunity for a major advance in social policy. In environmental policy, he did not make notable progress in strengthening environmental controls or in improving their efficiency. Clinton reluctantly signed a welfare reform bill whose wisdom he himself seriously questioned. Although the radical measure was certain to reduce welfare rolls, only time would tell whether it would do so mainly by helping poor families become self-supporting or by abandoning them to destitution. Finally, despite cutting entitlement spending to balance the budget, Clinton largely postponed resolving the long-term problems of Medicare and Social Security. Setting aside the ambiguous case of welfare reform, then, there have been very few high-profile achievements in domestic policy. Apart from the healthy economy and balanced budget, Clinton's main domestic accomplishment arguably has been the negative one of blocking the more extreme items on the Republicans' agenda.

The second perspective in assessing Clinton's domestic legacy, more general than the first, concerns his experience as a centrist president attempting to lead a highly polarized, partisan Congress—what his case tells us about future presidents who are likely to face similar circumstances. Judging from Clinton's example, there is both bad news and good news about their prospects.

The bad news is that a president in these circumstances will encounter severe constraints on his policy leadership. In particular, there are apparently limited prospects and few political rewards for promoting the kinds of principled centrist policies that Clinton defined in 1992 as the central feature of a New Democratic agenda: social policies that combine compassion with individual responsibility; regulatory policies that preserve markets and maximize efficiency; economic and budget policies that emphasize investment and jobs; in general, policies that integrate liberal and conservative values.

The difficulties appear under both unified and divided party control. Clinton pushed a balanced and ambitious deficit-reduction package with a Democratic Congress in 1993. Although he succeeding in passing it, he received no support from Republicans and only rebuke from the voters. Stung by the lack of credit, he opted for politically easier routes in future budget struggles. In 1997 Clinton and the Republican Congress reached an agreement to balance the budget by 2002. But the growth of revenues had done most of the work. On other issues, principled centrist proposals were never prominently discussed. Clinton did not attempt significant market-oriented reforms of environmental regulation. And the debate on welfare reform was dominated by the Republicans' hard-right approach.

The good news, at least for the president and his party, is that an *opportunistic* centrist strategy can be highly successful politically. Since the 1994 Democratic election defeat, Clinton has almost made it a principle to respond to the most popular opinions or the most powerful constituencies, whether liberal or conservative, on each issue. Gliding easily along the political spectrum, he has been liberal on Medicare, Social Security, education funding, the environment, and regulating HMOs; conservative on crime, taxes, television ratings, and welfare. He has devotedly served the interests and values of middle-class citizens.

The result has been clear: from the standpoint of maximizing public support, the strategy works. According to a January 1999 Pew Center poll, most Americans favored Democratic positions (that is, primarily Clinton's) over Republican ones on the issues that mattered most to them, including Social Security, education, and the regulation of HMOs.[99] Although Clinton's main strength has been his economic good fortune, his consistently popular centrist positions undoubtedly helped produce the high approval ratings that sustained him politically throughout the potentially devastating Monica Lewinsky scandal.

Indeed, as the impeachment trial in the Senate finally ended with an anti-climactic acquittal in February 1999, Clinton quickly picked up his opportunistic centrist agenda roughly where it had been left at the outbreak of the scandal more than a year earlier. The main new feature was that the budget surplus and continuing economic growth made it possible, if not entirely responsible, to focus exclusively on new benefits and reduced burdens.[100] In his 1999 State of the Union address, delivered in the heat of the trial, Clinton proposed using the budget surplus to solve the long-term financial problems of the Social Security system. He also renewed his effort to regulate the quality of care in HMOs and promised a host of new, mainly middle-class benefits. He showed no particular concern about the need for principled choices among competing demands. Republicans were nevertheless hard-pressed to find a reply. "If you're in a popularity contest with someone who's giving away money," observed a South Carolina Republican official, "it's hard to win."[101]

When Congress got back to work on matters of policy in mid-February, it was apparent that Clinton had the upper hand over the Republicans politically. Republicans criticized Clinton for failing to propose substantial restructuring of the Social Security and Medicare programs—something that both sides concede is necessary in the long run—but Clinton was unlikely to suffer political damage by keeping his distance from the notorious "third rail of American politics." Republicans also sought to promote a 10-percent across-the-board income-tax cut, but found little support among the voters and soon abandoned it. A Clinton proposal to hire 100,000 new teachers for the public schools seemed to have the rhetorical advantage over more fiscally conservative Republican ideas for education. Even if the president and Congress did very little in the 106th Congress, Clinton was more or less assured of looking good while doing it.

From the standpoint of the performance of government, the conclusion that presidents can succeed politically with an opportunistic centrist strategy is not necessarily good news. It suggests that public policy will be highly responsive to uninformed swing voters—the people who are liberal on Social Security and Medicare, conservative on taxes, eager for simplistic solutions on crime and welfare, and happy to postpone dealing with problems. If that is what centrist leadership comes to, the nation may be better off with a president who is a liberal Democrat or a conservative Republican.

10

Engaging the World: First Impressions of the Clinton Foreign Policy Legacy

Emily O. Goldman and Larry Berman

It has become commonplace to criticize the Clinton administration's foreign policy for being indecisive, incoherent, contradictory, confused, lacking vision and purpose. A virtual cottage industry has emerged around this theme.[1] Even when the president has been credited with articulating a clear set of foreign policy goals, he has been criticized for failing to develop the means to achieve them or to rally Congress and the American public on their behalf. A reframing of America's role in the world has always been, and will inevitably be, an evolutionary process. As one scholar points out, "historically, watershed events, such as the end of the Cold War, have produced new or revised visions of America's role or roles in world politics, although rarely has a single vision prevailed quickly."[2] We believe it is important to present a balanced assessment of Clinton's foreign policy accomplishments and shortcomings and to offer a more compelling explanation than has been advanced to date for his foreign policy. Has Bill Clinton left a legacy others can build upon, develop more fully, articulate more clearly, and implement more effectively? Will Bill Clinton's legacy be that of a president who took bold action to stop ethnic cleansing or will he be remembered as the president who committed America to a long-run engagement in the Balkans but was inconsistent on military intervention, having taken a "pass" on the genocide in Rwanda?

In our earlier essay assessing the Clinton foreign policy record at midterm, we posited that "U.S. policy abroad has been cast adrift, buffeted by political calculations with only minimal evidence of coherence and consistency."[3] We cautioned, however, that indeterminacy in the post–Cold War international environment had to be taken fully into account when judging Clinton's midterm foreign policy record. We asserted that strategic uncertainty was a primary cause of foreign policy vacillation and drift. This logic remains in vogue, as Secretary of State Madeleine K. Albright recently observed: "Like a kaleidoscope, the patterns of world affairs shift with each spin of the globe. . . . the challenges we face, compared to those confronted by previous generations, are harder to categorize, more diverse, and quicker to change."[4]

We remain comfortable with our characterization of Clinton's foreign policy as lacking coherence. Here we extend our analysis beyond the president's specific shortcomings to explain why *any* president at this historical juncture would likely have difficulty defining a vision that convinces a skeptical and essentially disinterested American public of the benefits of American engagement abroad. Americans have demonstrated a propensity to withdraw from the world during past times of economic prosperity. Today, this propensity is compounded by the absence of the Soviet "pull-factor," and the United States again faces its "historic dilemma," as John Ruggie characterizes it: "how to secure sustained American political engagement in world affairs to promote a stable international order, and one that [is] favorable to the pursuit of U.S. interests."[5] Other presidents before Clinton, most notably, Theodore Roosevelt and Woodrow Wilson, faced similar challenges and suffered diminished legacies by failing to meet them.

President Clinton's primary interest has not been in the area of foreign policy. Though some aides describe Kosovo as Clinton's "finest hour," he is still likely to be remembered as "perhaps the first in line of domestic presidents who followed the Cold War."[6] Welcoming Milosevic's acceptance of NATO demands in the Rose Garden, Clinton quickly turned to the issues of Medicare and environmental protection.[7] One of the most striking aspects of the Clinton first term was not merely the absence of a foreign policy agenda, but the public's lack of interest in this absence. Four years earlier, in the wake of the Cold War's end and the search for new paradigms, incumbent President George Bush could at least emphasize his foreign policy credentials over those of the challenger, Governor Bill Clinton. This had profound implications because candidate Clinton was forced to take strong stands on the use of force against Saddam Hussein in Iraq, on handling the situation in Bosnia, and in dealing with the Chinese. Readers may recall candidate Clinton criticizing George Bush for appeasing Saddam prior to Iraq's seizure of Kuwait and for coddling dictators in China, while advocating the United States join a multinational coalition to shoot its way into Sarajevo.

By leaving the impression that he was a Democrat willing to use force and do so decisively, the candidate set the stage for limiting his options once he became president. The international context for the 1996 campaign was a nation at peace; "no imminent threat appeared from overseas."[8] As a consequence, international politics was virtually invisible during the campaign, and Bob Dole showed little interest in bringing foreign policy to the forefront. There was even the "extraordinary spectacle," wrote *Congressional Quarterly*'s Carroll J. Doherty, "of presidential debate moderator Jim Lehrer casting about futilely for someone—anyone—to ask the candidates a foreign policy question."[9] Clinton's laser-beam focus on the economy seemed to have succeeded in taking foreign policy off the radar screen as a criterion for evaluating the president or presidential aspirant.

Even in the best of times, presidents who are thinking about their legacy go abroad. Bill Clinton is certainly thinking about a foreign policy legacy. He has made the most trips abroad of any president and logged the most miles, earning the nickname "the Cal Ripken of presidential travelers." White House officials have said that this rate of travel indicates Clinton's intent to improve upon his foreign policy record in his second term. President Clinton also reshuffled his advisers for the second term, placing Sandy Berger at the helm of the National Security Council (NSC), William Cohen at Defense, and Madeleine Albright at State. Most observers agree that the new team has given strategic direction to administration policy that may shape a more positive legacy.

Interestingly, in the campaign for the White House 2000 some GOP hopefuls have sought to rekindle the public's interest in foreign policy and national security issues. In January 1999, prior to NATO intervention in Kosovo, Dan Quayle said, "No presidential candidate should be taken seriously unless he or she understands the importance of foreign policy." Quayle criticized the Clinton administration for frittering away opportunities in China, Cuba, Iraq, North Korea, and Russia. "Major issues are being ignored, standards are lowered. There's a sinking feeling around the world that America has simply lost its will and credibility to lead."[10] Kosovo may have put foreign policy back on the political stage for the moment, but it could easily fade. When fighting ends, public attention usually reverts to domestic affairs and not treaty implementation.

Will there be a foreign policy legacy? Historians are likely to judge the Clinton presidency as one of opportunities wasted because of the president's own reckless personal choices. During the "impeachment winter" of 1999, it appeared to us that future generations would likely recall Monica Lewinsky before the Wye River Memorandum, the Clinton scandals before the Clinton doctrine, Kenneth Starr before Saddam Hussein. This speaks volumes about the overall tragedy of the Clinton years. Yet, as a result of NATO intervention in Kosovo, foreign policy may now provide the best opportunity for shaping a legacy that includes something more than tabloid script.

History shows that the last refuge of our modern presidents in trouble has often been foreign affairs. When Watergate revelations surrounded Richard Nixon, the president received a hero's welcome in Moscow and international acclaim for his China initiatives; when Iran-*contra* revelations came to light and damaged Ronald Reagan's credibility, the president traveled to Moscow and signed the historic arms control agreement with Mikhail Gorbachev. But, no one does better when he is in trouble than this Harry Houdini of American politics, and it comes as no surprise that on 26 February 1999, President Clinton delivered what his aides described as the State of the Union address for foreign policy.

Speaking before the Pacific Council for Globalization, the Commonwealth Club, and the World Affairs Council, the president outlined the five great international challenges that require American engagement abroad. The president referred to the "inexorable logic of globalization" and the essentiality of an active American role in guaranteeing the future. "The promise of our future lies in the world. Therefore we must work hard with the world—to defeat the dangers we face together and to build this hopeful moment together, in a generation of peace, prosperity, and freedom."[11] The president used this speech to focus on the crucial foreign policy issues that he intended to address in the final two years of his presidency as well as the challenges for the twenty-first century.

In this chapter, we begin by looking back at our earlier appraisal of Clinton's foreign policy. We assess the foreign policy record and consider the charge that the first truly post–Cold War president lacks a foreign policy doctrine. We believe the debate on a Clinton doctrine has been misguided because many scholars and pundits are not sure what a foreign policy doctrine is, in much the same way that they argue the president is not sure what *his* foreign policy doctrine is. We argue that the Clinton administration articulated an overarching foreign policy strategy, that spoke to many important issues, though not to all of them. The administration backed away from the substantive dimension of its strategy—enlargement—because it was difficult to sell at home and failed to produce rapid enough results within the administration's four-year time frame. Still, a major problem, as we see it, is less the lack of a strategy than the dearth of foreign policy tools to carry out a post containment strategy, and the difficulty of framing post–Cold War policies in terms that Americans will accept risks to promote.

The administration's use of the diplomatic and economic tools of foreign policy has been far more adept than its use of military force. We surmise that this reflects a pressing need for the foreign policy and national security establishments to reassess the role that force can and should play today, how it can be effectively applied, and how commercial priorities can be better integrated into U.S. foreign and national security policy. We believe the conclusions from such a dialogue would be far different from those reached in the shadow of the Cold War, because the threat has changed, while the tools of foreign policy have not evolved in tandem.

Finally, we cannot overlook the ways domestic political calculations have influenced foreign policy choices, in particular the impact of the 1994, 1996, and 1998 elections on congressional-executive interactions over foreign policy initiatives. We ask in conclusion whether or not there are lessons for future administrations other than to be so fortunate as to have a prosperous domestic economy that tends to create an American public disinterested in the subject of world affairs.

The Past as Prologue

Writing on the subject of Bill Clinton's foreign policy in 1995, which was then midway into his first term, we observed that the president had yet to formulate a strategic vision for the post–Cold War era. He had not provided a convincing declaration of purpose or a conceptual rationale for sustaining American leadership in the world. An overriding set of principles to guide U.S. foreign policy was still in the making. We focused a great deal on the post–Cold War environment and the challenges that it posed to American leadership. With no predictable adversary, no familiar structure of conflict, and few external constraints, the challenge was to build a new foundation from which to articulate a foreign policy. We saw a world full of uncertainty, but also of opportunity. We saw an ambiguous external environment that presented the opportunity for strong and focused executive leadership.

We gave great weight to the congressional elections of 1994 that had just ushered in a Republican majority and to the 104th Congress's mandate to implement the Contract with America. With Republican majority control in both Houses, we hypothesized that Clinton was unlikely to move ahead with bold new initiatives in domestic politics. We were a bit off target. Little did we expect Clinton to outmaneuver that Congress by morphing himself into the moderate alternative to Newt! Nor did we expect Clinton to adopt so many Republican positions on foreign policy; indeed, by the time of his 1999 State of the Union message, Clinton was even endorsing bigger defense budgets, breaking a long cycle of budget reductions for the military.

In 1995 we thought that the president's role as chief diplomat would provide more room than that of chief legislator. But we did not consider the new role adopted by Clinton as the Peacemaker in Chief. We expressed concern about a personal style in foreign policy that had been characterized by a high degree of energy, rhetoric, an appetite for information, and a preoccupation with detail, but that was nevertheless overshadowed by Clinton's own personal indecisiveness and sporadic engagement. To political allies the president was a pragmatist; to critics he waffled and placated. He had yet to demonstrate the leadership skills and level of commitment in foreign policy that he so evidently possessed in the domestic and economic arenas. The first insider's account of foreign policy decision making inside the Clinton presidency was offered by Richard Holbrooke, former assistant secretary of state and architect of the Dayton Peace Accords that ended the war in Bosnia. The story is of an inattentive and disengaged Clinton, forced only by bureaucratic pressures to send 20,000 troops to Bosnia. The president and vice-president rarely attended the "principals" meetings, so nothing much got done.[12] For all the brilliance demonstrated by Clinton in making strategic adjustments in the domestic arena, his foreign policy still looked like "strategic incoherence."[13]

Today, the general assessment is that focused presidential leadership never materialized. Looking back at the foreign policy record of the first truly post–Cold War, post containment president, seven contributing editors and one guest contributor in a special issue of *Foreign Policy* drew devastating portraits of Clinton's foreign policy and potential legacy. The most common theme was that "Clinton is unlikely to be remembered for his foreign policy record."[14] The primary reason was "Clinton's lack of a coherent, long-term strategy or vision." From Tokyo, Yochi Funabashi identified a "notable lack of the vision thing." From France, Jacques Attali saw a Clinton presidency "lacking a long term vision, [so that] his administration seeks to impose its fancied solutions on an ad hoc basis." On Latin America, Jorge Dominguez sardonically observed, "I long for Bush's vision." From Moscow, Yegor Gaidar concluded that "one of the chief distinguishing characteristics of President Clinton's foreign policy has been his unwillingness to make clear choices or to provide a coherent vision." From London, Rupert Pennant-Rea observed that "it is surely fair to be disappointed by Clinton's foreign policy record: relentlessly tactical and never in the cause of strategy." Even in the area of the Middle East, Fawez Gerges concluded, "Clinton appears to conduct foreign policy on an ad hoc basis, often gearing it toward satisfying domestic constituencies." And from Asia, the area with so much potential for a Clinton legacy, "the indirection that has marked Clinton's policy toward the region has only confirmed the initial apprehension of 1992."[15] Yet the ultimate paradox of the Clinton foreign policy record may very well be that William Jefferson Clinton will be remembered for what he described as "a just and necessary war."[16]

The Clinton Record, or . . . Why the Individual Parts Do Not Make a Doctrine

From the president's perspective, his record on issues of peace, freedom, and prosperity has been pretty good. In his 1999 State of the Union address, Clinton attempted to write the first paragraph of his foreign policy legacy. "If we do all these things—pursue peace, fight terrorism, increase our strength, and renew our alliances—then we will begin to meet our generation's historic responsibility to build a stronger twenty-first century America in a freer, more peaceful world." A month later the president elaborated on these points in his San Francisco foreign policy speech: "The United States has the opportunity and, I would argue, the solemn responsibility to shape a more peaceful, prosperous, democratic world in the twenty-first century." The president focused on five central national security challenges for the next century, each of which would require American leadership: (1) building a more peaceful world, (2) bringing Russia and China into the international system as open and stable nations, (3) protecting Americans against threats that know no borders, (4) creating a global trading and financial system that will benefit all Americans, and (5) building a world where freedom remains ascendant.

Whether we choose to call it ad hoc or the vision thing again, Clinton's two-term record to date is still marked by significant achievement that includes restoring momentum to the Middle East peace process and brokering the Wye River Memorandum; leading efforts that produced the Good Friday peace agreement in Northern Ireland; brokering the Dayton Peace Accords—ending four years of bloodshed in Bosnia; leading the way on NATO expansion and Russian integration—helping to ensure a more stable, democratic Europe; securing bipartisan Senate ratification of the Chemical Weapons Convention and the START II Treaty; leading efforts to rid the world of land mines; negotiating 240 separate trade agreements—tearing down trade barriers to U.S. goods, helping to increase exports by nearly 50 percent and creating 1.7 million export-related jobs; "containing" but not ridding the world (yet) of Saddam Hussein through diplomacy, economic sanctions, and military force; deepening security alliances with Japan and South Korea; building a more constructive relationship with China through engagement and frank dialogue on human rights, security, and trade; expanding trade relations and strengthening democracy in Asia and Latin America; building partnerships with Africa; opening markets abroad through NAFTA, GATT, and 270 other free-trade agreements; addressing the global economic crisis by leading international relief efforts and stimulating worldwide growth; containment of financial panic in Mexico in 1995; and leading efforts to establish world financial and trade systems for a twenty-first-century economy that benefits ordinary citizens in all countries.

With a record like this, we need to ask, "Who needs a doctrine?" After all, if George Bush, with his extensive foreign policy background and interest and focus, could not develop one, perhaps the world we live in no longer requires an overarching vision such as containment. "I honestly don't believe we'll see the equivalent of George Kennan's 'X' article outlining a strategy as cohesive as containment," remarked Eliot Cohen.[17] Is it fair to charge, as does Jacques Attali, former special adviser to French President François Mitterrand, that "simply put, the president lacks a long-term vision. Leadership becomes an empty concept when day-to-day actions do not occur within a broader context."[18] It comes as no surprise that Secretary of State Albright thinks that such criticism is unfair. The secretary points out that it is pretty easy to state a vision and even to formulate a framework; the real challenge is in "implementing a framework."[19]

In Search of a Doctrine

Perhaps no sighting other than that of extraterrestrial life has been more debated than the question of a Clinton doctrine. Clinton has been compared to his predecessors unfavorably because he has not clearly articulated such a doctrine. A brief perusal of popular commentary reveals many candidates for what may comprise the Clinton doctrine. One suggestion is "we only intervene when there is a vital national security interest, particularly if a domestic special-interest group supports it and the risk of casualties is low."[20] Another variant is "regionalism," an updated version of the Nixon doctrine, relying on regional organizations to keep the peace worldwide, with the United States directly involved only in Europe and the Caribbean.[21] A third variant is "limited intervention" abroad to respond to events in places such as Bosnia and Rwanda.[22] A fourth perspective characterizes the Clinton doctrine as avoiding war but using American troops in modest numbers to create space for democracy or to keep warring factions from fighting.[23]

In the aftermath of Operation Desert Fox, one critic wove together the characteristics of a Clinton doctrine in the form of an indictment, citing

> the extraordinary importance assigned to avoiding U.S. casualties, thereby advertising America's own point of vulnerability; the hand-wringing preoccupation with collateral damage, signaling the United States has no stomach for war as such and thereby encouraging adversaries to persevere; the reliance on high technology weapons employed at long range, inviting confusion between the technical capability to hit targets and the achievement of operationally meaningful results; vaguely formulated objectives often explained in terms of "sending messages"—allowing for facile claims of "success" and the prompt recall of the forces engaged.[24]

The Clinton doctrine has also been linked to U.S. support for expanding the mission of the International Monetary Fund (IMF).[25] Others contend there simply is no Clinton doctrine.[26]

Part of the reason for the lack of agreement on the existence and tenets of a Clinton doctrine is that the term "doctrine" is used so loosely in the foreign policy context. The Truman doctrine advocated containment of Russian expansionism. The Nixon doctrine called for building up regional allies so they could defend themselves without U.S. troops. The Carter doctrine declared the Persian Gulf a vital interest. The Reagan doctrine called for backing anti-Soviet guerrilla forces. Some have to do with means; others address ends. Graham Evans may be correct when he contends these doctrines are little more than "theological battle cries."[27] But they certainly do not meet his criteria for doctrine: "a body of beliefs, principles, or guidelines which inform policy formulation and conduct" or "a set of dogmatic principles about the meaning and practical consequences of American values and interests in contemporary world politics."[28]

Foreign policy doctrines were never coined prior to the Cold War. The more common definition of doctrine is a set of prescriptions that specify how *tools* should be employed in the service of strategy and that serve as a guide to decision making.[29] The Powell-Weinberger doctrine specifying when and how military force should be used in support of the national interest is a case in point. If we accept this definition, then the question of "to what purpose" those tools should be employed rightly becomes a question of grand strategy (e.g., how a state causes security and prosperity for itself). Grand strategy involves identifying threats and opportunities, establishing priorities, and devising means to promote and defend one's interests.

Since the dawn of the Cold War, we have come to expect that our leaders will articulate a clear strategic vision. This suggests that a more damaging critique of a presidential administration lies in the failure to develop a coherent grand strategy.[30] In our previous essay, we spoke in terms of a "national purpose," which, we argued, "expresses a people's orientation toward the world and understanding of their society's role in it." We argued that what consistency was evident in Clinton's foreign policy could be tied to a domestic national-purpose orientation, which located the chief threats to U.S. interests in the domestic economic and social conditions of the nation. But this domestically based vision provided limited guidance for U.S. actions abroad. We wrote then, "Foreign policy needs external (what we want to achieve abroad) as well as internal (what we want to achieve at home) anchors. Absent the former, the Clinton administration has continuity only from the latter."

Coherent grand strategies seem to take hold generally under one of two conditions—when there is a compelling external threat, such as the Soviet Union represented during the Cold War, or alternatively, when there is a compelling sense of national mission. In the late-nineteenth to early-twentieth centuries, Americans assumed the mantle of progressive imperialism and embarked on the mission of providing order and justice to an anarchic world, in the belief that fulfilling the nation's expansionist destiny would simultaneously improve the condition of the American people.[31]

Today there is no compelling external threat against which a grand strategy can be articulated, and so in 1994, the Clinton administration proposed a strategy of "enlargement and engagement." Enlargement represented a shift away from a threat-oriented strategy to a mission-oriented one. The successor to containment, as Anthony Lake articulated in his often referenced speech at the Johns Hopkins University School of Advanced International Studies (SAIS) on 21 September 1993, would be a strategy that sought to strengthen the community of market democracies, to foster and consolidate new democracies and market economies, to counter aggression and support the liberalization of states hostile to democracy, and to help democracy and free market economies take root in regions of greatest humanitarian concern.[32]

The first prong of democratic enlargement was aimed at Europe and Japan; the second at emerging democracies in the former Soviet Union and Eastern Europe; the third at such "rogue" states as Iraq and North Korea; and the fourth at the large numbers of developing nations facing the challenges of economic development and ethnic conflict among other social, political, and economic ills.[33] Douglas Brinkley points out, however, that the Clinton administration did not commit the United States to promote democracy everywhere, but chiefly where the nation had major strategic and economic interests, implying the kind of discriminate intervention associated with selective engagement.[34]

By 1997 the administration had dropped "enlargement" from its strategy, leaving "engagement" to stand on its own. A confluence of factors led to this reformulation—evidence from Russia and Haiti that enlargement was not working or was taking too long to produce results, and in the case of Russia was actually counterproductive; confusion between democratic enlargement and NATO enlargement in the public debate; a set of academic arguments that democratization was often a conflict-prone process; and the perception that enlargement was too pacifist. Democratic enlargement was difficult, and other foreign policy issues that did not fit neatly under the rubric needed attention.

By 1998 emphasis had shifted to "homeland defense,"[35] by which the administration meant transnational threats such as terrorism, international crime, and drug trafficking; threats to the United States from weapons of mass destruction; and protection of critical infrastructure. The bombing of the World Trade Center and the release of the toxic substance sarin on a Tokyo subway had profoundly affected the president. Abroad, the emphasis shifted to managing the international financial crisis. The 1998 National Security Strategy document expanded a three-paragraph discussion on the global financial crisis to three pages. The administration continued to put a tremendous amount of effort into managing international financial markets. Finally, the administration emphasized its regional focus and articulated a profound restructuring of U.S. foreign policy toward Africa, calling for reliance on private investment to promote development in Africa rather than depending exclusively on humanitarian relief and aid.

The 1998 document *A National Security Strategy for a New Century* articulates three national objectives upon which our security strategy is based—enhancing the nation's security, bolstering its economic prosperity, and promoting democracy abroad.[36] Democratic enlargement has not disappeared, despite claims that it failed as a strategic guidepost for the post–Cold War era,[37] and despite the fact that the administration subsumed it under engagement.

To evaluate the Clinton foreign policy legacy, we must go beyond specific issues and events to Clinton's attempt to chart a strategic course for the post–Cold War world. The attempt to redefine U.S. strategy from threat-based containment to mission-based enlargement demands close scrutiny because it provides perspective on Clinton's successes and failures, on the criticisms leveled at him, and on which critiques are truly warranted. The fate of the strategy of democratic enlargement tells us a great deal about the challenges future presidents are likely to face in the foreign policy arena.

The idea behind enlargement was that the United States should strive to expand the sphere of market-oriented democracies because open, democratic, and free-market societies further the security and economic interests of the United States. Democracies are good for peace (based on the belief that democracies do not easily go to war with one another). Free markets are good for business (based on the belief that more market economies will expand the global market and global economic well being). Free markets are good for peace (based on the assumption that no two countries with a McDonald's will go to war with each other, and that cooperation in "low politics" arenas will lead to cooperation in "high politics" as well).[38] And democracies are good for business (based on the belief that as free states grow in number, the international order will become more prosperous). As Graham Allison noted, "the cornerstone of any Clinton Doctrine will be the creation of a new world order of open markets in a global economy."[39] In his San Francisco speech of February 1999, the president referred twice to the "inexorable logic of globalization."

To the extent that democratic enlargement serves American economic interests, this dovetails with our characterization of Clinton's foreign policy as grounded in a domestic national purpose orientation of enhancing America's economic competitiveness. Enlargement was posited to be closely linked to domestic renewal because of the synergistic relationship between markets and democratization and the positive impact of each on the U.S. economy. The world economy without borders that would result from the growth and spread of free-market economies would demand political openness, stimulating the spread of democracy. The growth in number and strength of democratic states would produce a consumer-oriented middle class that desires peace and wealth through market-based economies. By promoting democratization through markets, U.S. exports would grow and domestic renewal would follow. In this way, U.S. foreign economic policy became U.S. foreign policy. U.S. policy was tied to an ideological sense of Wilsonianism. Yet while Wilson's formula for spreading democracy was to promote national self-determination, Clinton's formula is markets and more markets, which has far greater appeal to Americans interested in growth in the domestic economy than in pursuing an ideological crusade. In many ways, the Clinton approach has deep roots in the Founders' vision of commerce as the essence of democracy, "a source of social cohesion at home, and a means to tie different nations together to help civilize people."[40] At the same time, this economic-centric approach to foreign policy can easily become "an international variant of pork-barrel politics," subject as it is to the whim of every private lobby.[41]

Selling "Enlargement"

It was not easy for President Clinton to sell his strategy of enlargement. His failure to do so has been attributed to his lack of leadership and active engagement in foreign policy, as well as to deficiencies in the strategy itself, chiefly its inability to provide pragmatic policy guidance.[42] To be sure, foreign policy has traditionally been low on Clinton's priority list, so he never did the groundwork to build a domestic consensus on enlargement. This was particularly important because enlargement was out of sync with the national mood and with Congress. Nevertheless, it seems to be inherently easier to mobilize support for threat-oriented strategies than for mission-oriented ones and to make sacrifices on behalf of the former than the latter.

Threats create a situation of compulsion that necessitates action (or at least foreign policy during the Cold War tended to be framed in such terms), while a national mission lacks necessity and demands that the state be proactive, accepting risks when the gains may be uncertain. From a threat-oriented perspective, it is easier to imagine what in fact will be lost if risks are not taken, and so leaders can more easily sell "negative" goals, like those of containment (e.g., what we want to prevent, rather than what we want to achieve). From the vantage point of "prospect theory," containment is a strategy that resides in the domain of losses, while enlargement is a strategy that resides in the domain of gains. It follows that actors will assume greater risks and accept greater costs to defend a strategy of containment than to promote a strategy of enlargement.[43] Enlargement, like any post–Cold War strategy that cannot be defined mainly if not exclusively in terms of negative goals, was bound to be difficult to sell, Clinton's personal shortcomings in the foreign policy arena aside.

A core tenet of prospect theory is that people react differently to the prospect of losses than to the chance of reaping gains. People are risk-acceptant for losses and risk-averse for gains, are more willing to pay a higher price and accept greater risks when faced with the prospect of losses, and are more reluctant to take advantage of opportunities to expand and reap gains at some risk. Losses tend to loom larger than gains, a phenomenon called *loss aversion*. In the United States, the deeply held foreign policy mythology of the domino effect reinforces this tendency. As Robert Jervis explains,

> American decision makers seem to believe that small losses will multiply via the domino effect. Gains are not expected to have such consequences. So a rational statesman would not be willing to run high risks in order to secure a moderate gain but would accept much higher risks to avoid a short-run loss of the same magnitude because it would lead to greater losses over a longer period of time.[44]

Michael Mandelbaum's comparison of the U.S. experience with two Caribbean invasions nicely illustrates how varying risk propensities have affected public support for the use of force, one in the context of containment, the other in the context of enlargement.[45] In two instances, ten years apart, the United States militarily intervened to dislodge an unfriendly government—in Grenada in 1983 and in Haiti in 1993-94. Haiti is larger and more proximate. The United States has a history of intervention in that small nation. And the flood of refugees presented a real economic cost to the United States. Yet as Mandelbaum points out, Grenada was far less controversial. Grenada was part of the Cold War, while Haiti was not. The former could be portrayed as a potential loss—another domino falling to the Soviet Union. Military intervention could be sold to prevent the loss.

Haiti, on the other hand, an intervention to reinstate the first democratically elected president in the country's history—Jean Bertrande Aristide—who had been overthrown by a military junta, was hard to sell as a loss. Everyone recognized that even if military action succeeded in toppling the junta, the task of nation building would be long, arduous, costly, and uncertain. As Mandelbaum points out, "the administration had promised not simply to return Aristide but to restore (or, to put it more accurately, create) democracy and help the country lift itself out of destitution, which required the establishment of a stable political system, the rule of law, and a freely functioning market economy."[46] This would require a substantial American commitment, with no guarantee of success.

Since gains and losses are treated differently, *framing* of the choice problem as a gain or a loss will affect the level of risk people will accept. Accordingly, it made sense to frame the dispatch of American troops to Haiti and Bosnia in terms of minimizing losses (leaving as quickly as possible with as few casualties as possible) rather than in terms of gains (doing "whatever was necessary, for as long as necessary, to keep [or make] peace").[47]

When people assess losses and gains, the reference point used is important. Usually, the reference point is the status quo, and people tend to have a status quo bias. Greater efforts tend to be exerted to preserve the current situation against a threatened loss than to improve one's position by a comparable amount. So sacrificing to maintain democracy should be easier to sell than paying the costs to spread democracy, whether in Bosnia, Somalia, or Haiti. One implication of this status quo bias is that the first prong of the administration's enlargement strategy, aimed at Europe and Japan, was easiest to sell, followed by the second prong, aimed at the former Soviet Union and Eastern Europe. The last two prongs, aimed at promoting internal change in rogue states and developing nations, were inherently more controversial because they called for a greater shift from the current policy. A second implication concerns the administration's policy toward Iraq, dubbed "containment plus opposition," implying some commitment to roll back or overthrow the Iraqi regime. Forced on the administration by Congress, the policy will probably be difficult to sell fully to the public, for while the containment portion suggests maintaining the status quo, the rollback dimension demands changing it.

Enlargement, like Wilsonianism, is a strategy that builds on a belief in inevitable progress. It implies a steadily changing reference point. This has two consequences—people must continually bear costs to preserve each new equilibrium,[48] and the criteria for assessing success are never clear. Richard Haass points out that during the Cold War, "the measure of U.S. policy was how well it limited and, where possible, rolled back the expansion of Soviet and communist influence."[49] Part of the problem with defining a new yardstick of success for a mission-oriented strategy is that the objective—enlargement—by definition, keeps shifting, paving the way for continual criticism. Moreover, the ultimate goal is a long-term one, making it impossible to reach the end state within the four-year time horizon of a presidential administration.

Even if the choices of political leaders are *not* governed by the psychological processes posited by prospect theory, domestic opinion does seem to operate according to its predictions—accepting high risks to avoid even small losses, avoiding risks that promise comparable gains, and punishing leaders who permit losses to occur. Not surprisingly, the Clinton administration lacked popular support for its Haiti policy. This reading of domestic opinion dovetails with post–Cold War arguments that the American public is "pretty prudent" when it comes to the use of military force.[50] Americans are more willing to use force to coerce an adversary engaged in aggressive actions against the United States—to prevent losses— than to engineer internal political change in another country's government—to promote gains.[51]

As one foreign policy scholar puts it, "The United States continues to have national interests, although they can no longer be expressed simply as opposition to the Soviet Union. Perhaps the most important task the Clinton administration faced as it entered office was to state these interests in a way that would guide the foreign policy bureaucracy, inform the international community, and persuade the American public."[52] But as we can see, even allowing for Clinton's lack of attention to building a foreign policy consensus at home, he carried a greater political burden than did his predecessors. Cold War presidents could frame foreign policy in terms of a zero-sum game with the Soviet Union and could sell their policies to a public more willing to take risks to minimize losses. As Mandelbaum argues, during the Cold War, U.S. presidents did not necessarily know *when* to use force, but they knew *why*—to prevent the loss of a country to communism. After all, the "loss of China" hung heavily over the heads of all post–World War II presidents.

Framing foreign policy today in terms of losses is trickier. Preventing the spread of weapons of mass destruction clearly resides in the domain of losses, and the stakes are high. As the *New York Times* editorialized on 26 February 1999, "history will judge the Clinton Administration's foreign policy record partly by its success in helping Russia reduce the nuclear remnants of the Cold War."[53] NATO enlargement can be seen in terms of minimizing losses if couched in terms of ensuring that Eastern Europe is not lost again, as it was after World War II, to an expansionist Russia tempted to extend its strategic frontiers.[54] Promoting democracy and fostering human rights, however, reside in the domain of gains. Not surprisingly, both the administration and the public have been far less willing to support these lofty post–Cold War goals. Public unease over Kosovo revealed itself in the steady drop in Clinton's public approval rating.

As the editors of a recent volume on strategic adjustment wrote when reflecting on previous periods in American history, such as the 1890s, when national leaders similarly sought to alter the nation's approach to the outside world, "these periods [are] marked by great uncertainty over the meaning of international developments for the nation's security and well-being, as well as by protracted and divisive debate over how the nation's interests could be most effectively promoted and secured."[55] Then, as now, the United States faced no external threat. Then, as now, a new vision for America's role in the world had to be sold not only in terms of external mission, but also in terms of internal gains. Then, as now, the United States was in the midst of a profound cultural transformation. Just as American society a century ago was experiencing new class fissures and the "arrival of substantial numbers of linguistically, religiously, and ethnically distinct immigrants from Central and Southern Europe," it is once again significantly more demographically heterogeneous than at the previous foreign policy turning point after World War II.[56] The target domestic audience is more diverse, further exacerbating the challenge of selling a coherent strategic vision.

The Implementation Challenge

"Whatever the specific strategy should be, it must rest on a cold-eyed assessment of the means to carry it out," write Jonathan Clarke and James Clad.[57] They go on to quote Herbert Croly, who in 1909 wrote, "the American habit is to proclaim doctrines and policies without considering either the implications, the machinery necessary to carry them out, or the weight of the resulting responsibilities."[58] Strategy requires more than prioritizing goals. As George Kennan understood, in foreign policy, the "what" cannot be separated from the "how."[59]

If we accept that Clinton did articulate a strategy—although we may disagree with its wisdom—we must consider the record of implementation. The tools of foreign policy in the American arsenal were honed for a strategy of containment; they were not designed for a strategy of enlargement. It should come as no surprise, therefore, that the four key speeches that laid out enlargement "glided over the question of means available to attain the goals."[60] No one is sure how we go about building democracies, or even whether promoting democracy is always compatible with promoting free trade.

In implementing enlargement, the Clinton administration privileged some foreign policy tools over others. One of his legacies most surely will be the elevation of trade and economics as foreign policy instruments, in a contemporary version of "dollar diplomacy." Early on, the administration launched its "Big Emerging Market" or BEM strategy, based on the premise that economic success at home would require deepening engagement in the world's rapidly growing economies—China, India, Indonesia, Brazil, Mexico, Turkey, South Korea, South Africa, Poland, and Argentina.[61] Given that these countries are both regional economic and foreign policy drivers, American interests would be doubly served if a convergence of interests and values with these countries could be achieved. Early hallmarks of the strategy were the passage of NAFTA and renewal of MFN trading status for China.

The strategy, however, was not without its detractors. Challenges to it predate the Asian economic crisis. One problem is conceptual, namely how to integrate commercial concerns with traditional security interests, particularly when competing priorities surface, which they invariably do. In South Asia, for example, proponents of a commercially minded foreign policy strategy emphasize the need to promote foreign trade with, and investment in, India to encourage domestic growth and more stable regional relations. Those with a more traditional power-politics view fear any initiative that might undercut Pakistan. Elevating commercial relations on the foreign policy agenda requires a fundamental rethinking of the tools of foreign policy, particularly since commercial relations have traditionally been viewed either as separate from, or as subordinate to, more traditional national security concerns.

Implementation of Clinton's commercially oriented foreign policy has also been confounded by institutional factors. We are only beginning to develop the necessary infrastructure for utilizing economic instruments effectively. The stature of the Commerce secretary has grown, and Clinton created a National Economic Council (NEC), a cluster of economic agencies coequal collectively to the National Security Council, designed to open up strategy making to a broader array of actors, particularly economic ones. Still, rival foreign policy fiefdoms detract from coherence in foreign policy. The tension emerges starkly in policy toward China. Commerce handles trade and economic issues, human rights are the State Department's bailiwick, exchange-rate policy falls within the purview of Treasury, and the Pentagon takes the lead on missile exports. Nonetheless, Clinton's penchant for weighting the economic perspective more heavily is evident at the highest levels of the policy process. Secretary of the Treasury Robert Rubin was more influential than either Secretary of State Albright or NSC Director Sandy Berger. And, in addition to the individuals required by law to attend all NSC meetings, Clinton makes sure his three key economic advisors—secretary of the Treasury, head of the NEC, and director of the Office of Management and Budget—are always present.[62]

While bureaucratic tensions always exist, they come to the fore more starkly during periods of strategic adjustment when both policy and its institutional foundations are in the process of shifting. As at previous times in the nation's history when the foundations of foreign policy were reexamined, power shifted among existing institutions, the balance of resources among bureaucracies altered, and the locus of strategic decision making changed. The departments of Commerce, Labor, Agriculture, and Interior were privileged before World War II. In the immediate post–World War II years, State and Treasury dominated a government organized around the economic agenda of promoting international trade and investment. As the Cold War heated up, military-security concerns moved to the forefront, the military establishment became transcendent, the intelligence communities mushroomed, and NSC shouldered aside State. Today, the balance of interbureaucratic power in the American state is once again in a period of transition, reflecting a belief that the Cold War bureaucratic balance is ill-suited for foreign policy in the current international environment. Under these conditions, a coherent strategy might exist, while coherent implementation does not.

Finally, the commercially oriented strategy Clinton has consistently promoted requires a long time frame to implement and bear fruit, risking the neglect of more immediate and pressing matters, such as containing backlash states or mitigating humanitarian disasters. The challenge is to make the link between economic integration through more stable and prosperous markets, which supports the strategy of enlargement, and the isolation of backlash states, which is reminiscent of containment. As one Clinton supporter argues, prosperous BEMs should help isolate backlash states, inspire reformist elements, and generate resources to curtail secessionist tendencies; BEM domestic failures can produce humanitarian disasters and major threats to regional and global security.[63] Like the strategy of enlargement in general, the BEM strategy raises the question of the extent to which the distinction between foreign and domestic affairs has disappeared, whether U.S. foreign policy should be geared chiefly to a state's internal development or to its external conduct, and whether privileging the former undermines our ability to influence the latter.

Another legacy of the Clinton foreign policy will be the debate it has raised about the appropriate mode for engaging in the world and what the balance should be between selective engagement and unilateralism on the one hand, and multilaterialism and strengthening international institutions on the other. As we noted earlier, by 1997 the Clinton administration had dropped the term enlargement and began promoting a strategy of engagement. In contrast to enlargement, engagement is a process, not an end state. It begs the question, "engagement for what?" The administration's response has been two-fold. First, there is an emphasis on negotiating, on making a deal. The goal is on developing partnerships, to which the idea of "strategic partnerships" with Russia and China attests. In Russia, U.S. goals to promote democracy and markets were deemed too ethereal. Not only did they fail, but the administration determined they actually made matters worse. The power of the oligarchs increased, government legitimacy fell, and the needs of the Russian people were ignored. Now the emphasis is on food aid and a partnership for cooperative threat reduction to control nuclear weapons.

A second approach to engagement is what Sandy Berger calls the "entangling web strategy of engagement."[64] The goal is to create a network of institutions with a common purpose to strengthen the gains of democracy, roll back enemies, and promote U.S. values. Where possible, the United States will act multilaterally; where necessary, unilaterally. The most important goal is to preserve the U.S. role as a force for stability, because, in Albright's words, the United States is the "indispensable nation."

Clinton came into office strongly committed to multilateralism, in particular with a vision of a United Nations that could keep the peace abroad. The president endorsed creation of a UN standing army and putting U.S. soldiers under UN command. But dreams of assertive multilateralism in the military arena died a quick death on the floor of a Republican-led Congress. More recently, the policy of relying on the United Nations to disarm and contain Saddam Hussein has collapsed.

Nevertheless, as the "entangling web strategy" indicates, strengthening international institutions remains an important dimension of the Clinton legacy. John Ruggie notes that in previous instances when the remaking of the international order was at stake, American leaders reached for the principles of multilateralism.[65] Despite strident opposition to his vision for a multilateral security order, Clinton has sought to promote the role of multilateral institutions in managing the international economic order. To stabilize the international financial system, he has called for strengthening the World Bank and expanding the capabilities of the International Monetary Fund. The IMF is stepping beyond its traditional role of lending money to countries with balance-of-payments problems or short-term liquidity needs, to financing a global bailout. Given strong Republican opposition, Congress again may determine the fate of Clinton's multilateral vision.

A Use of Force Doctrine?

For a president who is often criticized for his lack of military experience, President Clinton has embraced an expanded concept of his power as commander in chief. He has sent troops and taken action in Bosnia, Haiti, Somalia, Iraq, Afghanistan, Sudan, and Kosovo. Major criticisms center on the ways domestic political calculations affect just about everything the administration does. The focus tends to be on short-term considerations, lurching into crises, improvising his way out of them, and minimizing friendly casualties above all.[66]

The administration's inability to use force effectively early on undermined U.S. credibility in important ways and led to a long line of challenges to U.S. resolve in Iraq and the Balkans.[67] Clinton's dogged pursuit of NATO victory in Kosovo and his determination to see the war through to the end have brought peace though not necessarily a durable settlement. More important, the cost to civilians in Yugoslavia during the air campaign, in comparison to zero allied casualties, sends an unsettling message to the rest of the world: the U.S. is willing to fight, but only when it can be sure it will not have to pay the ultimate cost.

Force was the most important tool of foreign policy during the Cold War. A great deal of time and effort was devoted to honing the tool (e.g., building a large, complex, and diverse arsenal of military weapons, and training a highly capable volunteer force to use them), developing theories for how force could be effectively used in a world of nuclear superpowers (e.g., deterrence), creating elaborate international institutions with doctrines for the use of force in the confrontation with the Soviet Union (e.g., NATO), and staffing a large domestic bureaucracy that integrated the pieces together (e.g., the national security establishment). We have yet to devise theories, tools, and effective bureaucracies, at home or abroad, for the use of force in the service of enlargement. Emphasis on precision attack capabilities alone cannot be the answer. We have yet to determine how force can be most effectively employed in the service of this new strategy, short of the argument that global military preeminence is always something good to have.

To the extent that a set of principles pertaining to the use of force has emerged, it includes the following guidelines, which are drawn from official and public statements. The most complete statement of a Clinton doctrine on the use of force can be found in the administration's 1995 and 1996 National Security Strategy documents. When vital interests are at stake, the nation must do whatever is necessary to achieve quick victory with low casualties; when important but not truly vital interests are at stake and when the projected costs and risks of military action are commensurate with those interests, limited military means may be used for limited political objectives. In all cases political leaders should provide military commanders with clear political objectives that can be translated into clear and attainable military missions. Before forces are committed to action, there should be a clear measure for accomplishment as well as an exit strategy. There should also be reasonable assurance of congressional and public support.

The statement that it was appropriate to use military force for vital interests, lesser interests, and for other (i.e., humanitarian) needs, was an important change and significant departure from past policy. Specific guidelines for the use of force were drawn from the Powell-Weinberger doctrine, with modifications from experiences in Somalia, Haiti, and Bosnia. Sandy Berger called the new doctrine of limited violence for limited aims "Powell-plus." The U.S. cannot stay out of all conflict short of total war.[68] According to Charles A. Stevenson, the strength and viability of this doctrine for the use of force

> rests on its utility to most policy makers. It protects the president against hasty, ill-considered actions that force him to choose between admitting a mistake or making a worse one. It protects the military from being sent into operations against their will or contrary to solid planning. Yet it allows a full spectrum of military actions in support of well articulated national goals. These protections are not absolute, but they should be reassuring as we continue our journey through the post–Cold War era.[69]

Still key features of the use of force doctrine, such as exit strategies and low casualties, are difficult to reconcile with Clinton's long-term strategy and with developments on the ground that often cannot be resolved quickly and bloodlessly.

The debate wages on with respect to whether or not President Clinton was correct when he said, "we have a clear national interest in ensuring that Kosovo is where the trouble ends; . . . if we don't stop the conflict now, it clearly will spread. And then we will not be able to stop it, except at far greater cost and risk."[70] The opposition comes from both sides of the political aisle. Former Secretary of State Henry Kissinger argues that the president has yet to provide a statement of strategic purpose or an exit strategy: "The proposed deployment in Kosovo does not deal with any threat to American security as traditionally conceived. . . . We must take care not to treat a humanitarian foreign policy as a magic recipe for the basic problem of establishing priorities in foreign policy. . . . I see no need for U.S. ground forces; leadership should not be interpreted to mean that we must do everything ourselves."[71] Lee Hamilton, former Democratic chairman of the House International Relations Committee and currently director of the Woodrow Wilson Center, adds that "there are greater threats to our national interests than those posed by the problems of the former Yugoslavia. If we don't put the perpetual crisis there into proper perspective, we will be less able to respond to the real threats to our security and national interests."[72] Powell himself recently observed that "the challenge of just using air power is that you leave it in the hands of your adversary to decide when he's been punished enough. So the initiative will remain with President Milosevic."[73]

Even the modified Powell doctrine is incomplete as a guide to the use of force the post–Cold War period. It addresses the question "how do we intervene?" but is vague on the more important prior question "why are we intervening?" and nearly silent short of invoking the national interest on the question of "when and where should we intervene?" Kosovo suggests intervention on behalf of human rights, but there is a danger in overlearning that lesson, just as there was in overlearning the lesson of overwhelming force from the Persian Gulf War. Moreover, the Powell precepts, while important components of a military strategy, do not address the use of the military (American troops or a multilateral force) in noncombat capacities to create conditions for democracy to take hold. The administration has yet to articulate a doctrine for the use of force that could serve a strategy of enlargement.[74] The Kosovo victory could crumble as NATO seeks to implement it on the ground. As one analyst recently explained, the United States, and the West in general, continue to rely on the Cold War model of deterrence, where force was used to "deter the other side from doing bad things outside its borders. Today force is needed to compel the other side to do good things inside its borders. The difference is fundamental. . . . Deterrence is a military task; compellence a police function."[75] The uses of force have changed, and our strategic thinking is sorely lagging behind real-world developments. As a top Bush State Department official put it, Kosovo is "one early precedent, and I think it reflects a kind of groping toward a new set of rules for an entirely new international environment." But it "turned out to be more difficult, much messier than they could have imagined."[76] No doubt this reflects the difficulty of reconciling America's domestic imperative for bloodless wins and its need to maintain coalition unity (which dictate restraint on how force is to be applied) with the brutality of civil wars and genocide (which demand swift resolution).

The Political Context of Clinton and Congress in Foreign Policy

There are several ways to evaluate how a president deals with Congress; we can analyze the president's personal skill, his agenda, and the political environment. During the second term Clinton did not succeed in most respects with Congress, primarily because he had not made the effort to convince voters to elect a Democratic Congress. He was more concerned with "building a bridge to the twenty-first century" than with building a bridge between Congress and the White House. As a result, Clinton had to fight for each vote on an array of tough issues. He lost on some issues that were extremely important to him, personally, most notably on fast-track trade authority.[77]

With respect to his own policy proposals, Clinton's record with the 105th Congress was a failure; but with respect to the political context of preventing the Republicans from achieving their policy goals, the Clinton record was much better. According to *Congressional Quarterly*'s latest success scores, Clinton succeeded on 51 of 152 House and Senate floor actions on which he took a position. For the sixth year of a second term, this rate was lower than those of Eisenhower, Reagan, and Nixon.[78]

With respect to foreign policy and defense, in 1998 Clinton won on 15 of 20 foreign policy and defense votes in the Senate, but was only 4 for 13 in the more partisan House. His biggest victory came on NATO expansion, allowing Hungary, Poland, and the Czech Republic to join the strategic alliance. Equally important were repeated victories for Clinton on the U.S. mission in Bosnia and funding of $18 billion for the International Monetary Fund, an essential step in his plan for staving off an economic downturn. The president's most significant failures were on the Comprehensive Nuclear Test Ban Treaty and on paying off the U.S. debt to the United Nations. The House also voted twice to restrict technology transfers to China, despite strong administration lobbying on the issue.[79]

In his year 2000 budget request, which could impact profoundly the foundation for any legacy, the president proposed a massive $1.77 trillion plan that continued funding for many existing Cold War weapons and contained the biggest military pay raise since 1982. Secretary of Defense William Cohen called the request the "first sustained increase in defense spending since the end of the Cold War." Even though the budget request was $112 billion more than the six-year plan submitted last year, the Republican-controlled Senate and House were critical of the budget request as being much less than had been requested by the Joint Chiefs of Staff. The Democrats also knocked the plan; Senator Tom Harkin said that Clinton seemed to have forgotten that the Cold War was over and the Pentagon did not need "new, expensive toys."[80]

As we look ahead to Clinton's relationship with the 106th Congress, it is difficult to be optimistic with respect to foreign policy goals that will involve extensive cooperation with the partisan chamber that just impeached the president and the Senate, which just wanted to send the House managers packing. The issues are serious ones—involving weapons of mass destruction, the proliferation of weapons technology, trade legislation, international economic demands—that will all require bipartisan action and the possibility of sending troops abroad. Already held over from the 105th Congress are fast-track trade legislation and ratification of the nuclear test–ban treaty. Any Clinton legacy in foreign policy will be dependent on ratification of arms-control treaties, the curtailing of rogue states that continue to build their arsenals, and the success of trade proposals between the United States and the European Union.

As we write, the administration is requesting $1.2 billion as part of the Wye River accord to finance Israel's pull-out from the West Bank; $400 million for the Palestinian authority, and $200-$300 million for Jordan. The foreign affairs budget for FY 2000 reflects the president's hope for his role as "peacemaker." Indeed, in his San Francisco foreign policy speech the president said, "I intend to use the time I have remaining in this office to push for a comprehensive peace in the Middle East, to encourage Israelis and Palestinians to reach a just and final settlement, and to stand by our friends for peace, such as Jordan." An uncertain peace in the Balkans may undermine Clinton's legacy as peacemaker. "From the outset," said Democratic Senator Robert G. Torricelli, of New Jersey, "[the Balkan operation] never had more vision than the next day."[81]

The Pros and Cons of Muddling Through

Just prior to delivering the 1999 State of the Union address, the president received a letter from former senator and 1996 GOP challenger Bob Dole. "In my view," wrote Dole, "history will look favorably on any leader that has the courage to end Milosevic's reign of terror. It is my hope that you will be that leader."[82] Has peace come to Kosovo? Maybe for a year or two but the long term could hold a resumption of hostilities. There is little consensus among elites and scholars on whether the president had a strategic plan for getting in, or for getting out, nor on whether he ever justified engagement in Kosovo on the basis of U.S. security interests. "Kosovo is no more a threat to America than Haiti was to Europe—and we never asked for NATO support there," writes Henry Kissinger.[83]

We cannot possibly predict what the Clinton legacy will be in Kosovo; and the full lessons of the air war will not be known for some time. Senior NATO officials are admitting that allied success depended on the ground presence of the Kosovo Liberation Army. Clinton did back up threats with force this time. But his reliance on airstrikes still poses questions about the linkage between military force and political objectives and has raised the terribly unsettling impression abroad of a nation that can act but only at no cost to the lives of its people. Alliance officials have also scaled back their initial estimates of damage inflicted by the air campaign on Yugoslavia's front-line military capabilities.[84]

President Clinton is likely to be remembered for his commitment to free trade, NATO enlargement, his role as a peace mediator in Ireland and the Middle East. The Asian economic crisis of collapsing currencies and plunging stock markets required an economic bailout by the IMF to Thailand, Indonesia, and South Korea. The crisis provoked a wake-up call in the United States, and in April 1998 Treasury Secretary Rubin outlined an American initiative to avoid economic convulsions in Asia. With the support of Federal Reserve Chairman Alan Greenspan, Rubin outlined new rules that would compel foreign nations to disclose embarrassing financial data that traditionally had gone unreported and would require more international inspections and monitoring of foreign national economies. International financial management is a major Clinton priority, perhaps his first foreign policy priority. It is the international infrastructure needed to ensure domestic economic prosperity. Accordingly, international financial management is high on Clinton's "legacy list," along with the Middle East, Northern Ireland, the Comprehensive Nuclear Test Ban Treaty, START III, commercial development in Africa, and strategic partnerships with China and Russia.[85]

We have argued that articulating a coherent foreign policy vision at this historic moment is fraught with difficulty. This may explain why Barry Posen and Andrew Ross characterize the Clinton administration's grand strategy as "selective (but cooperative) primacy," an uneasy amalgam of selective engagement, cooperative security, and primacy.[86] Enlargement—the administration's only real attempt to chart a long-term post–Cold War strategy—faced significant obstacles in the arena of public opinion, even though it has been tied to goals most Americans can easily identify with, namely domestic renewal and economic growth. It is as if the public is having as difficult a time integrating commercial priorities with traditional national security concerns as is the foreign policy establishment. These problems are compounded by obstacles to effective implementation of Clinton's strategy. Chief among these are the need to institutionalize a new balance among the relevant foreign policy bureaucracies and to develop a more comprehensive paradigm for the application of military force for the post–Cold War era. Absent a strategic guidepost, Clinton's foreign policy has been broad but shallow; many international initiatives underway but few resources and little time devoted to any one because of a lack of priorities. Absent enlargement, all we are left with is engagement, with no sense of why we should engage or how we should engage. The tendency of the administration to juxtapose engagement with isolation is a false one that only succeeds in polarizing the foreign policy debate further.

In conclusion, we observe that foreign and defense policy have never been high on the Clinton agenda. Threats were seen in domestic terms. Short of Congress's skepticism about international activism, there is no foreign policy consensus in the legislative branch. In many respects, the president's priorities reflect the mood of the people and Congress. This begs the question of whether the best strategy is not one that plays domestically and that emerges from the interplay of domestic preferences. After all, perhaps there are too many forces in the international environment weighing against grand visions of foreign policy. Given the unpredictability of the current international environment, is a coherent strategy necessary?

The argument has been made that muddling through may be the best one can hope for and a desirable strategy at that.[87] While it might encourage speculation among allies, it also keeps the bad guys guessing, which is not such a bad thing. Professing an overarching strategy and not following through on executing it could hurt U.S. credibility, while developing a strategy in response to the wrong threat could hinder U.S. adaptability. Too much investment in one strategy might also make it difficult to redirect capabilities against an emerging threat. In a period of uncertainty, flexibility is crucial. So perhaps the United States is better off preserving its minimal national interests while reserving the right to intervene when and where it wants, maintaining above all the flexibility desirable in uncertain times.

Many countries have been struggling to find their bearings since the demise of the communist threat. The United States, however, is different because it is perceived by many around the globe as the most consequential player. So strategic drift by the United States matters more. The Europeans have looked to the United States for direction on policy toward Russia and Bosnia, the Japanese for the reassurance that justifies perpetuating nonnuclear status in the face of a nuclear North Korea, and the Ukrainians for reassurances against the specter of a resurgent Russia. The success of United Nations peacekeeping operations frequently hinges on U.S. logistical support and intelligence capabilities. So a perception abroad that the United States lacks direction, priorities, and, in particular, a sense of when and how to commit military force, risks undermining confidence in America's willingness to act, may diminish U.S. influence on issues difficult to anticipate at present and ultimately tempt others to discount the United States. Strategic drift could prove to be very costly in the long run if the United States is compelled to respond to a situation that festered under benign neglect, like Bosnia or Kosovo, but might have been nipped in the bud earlier on. A strategic approach to international engagement can serve minimal national interests while also positioning the nation better to respond to potential midterm and long-term challenges by projecting greater confidence at home and credibility abroad. Flexibility is not antithetical to coherence; nor does setting priorities preclude adapting and adjusting along the way. Moreover, a foreign policy strategy can help convince a skeptical public that engagement abroad is worthwhile, reassure friends, and deter potential enemies. But, we recognize, it must be sold at home, and this is likely to be difficult.

Clinton's enlargement vision concentrated on promoting internal changes and altering domestic institutions, emphasized long-term objectives that take time to evolve, and focused as much attention on internal affairs of state as the external conduct of the state. Time will tell whether this ambitious agenda will be carried on by his successors, and whether his legacy will extend beyond issue-specific accomplishments to the more far-reaching challenge of laying the ground work for a new post-containment American mission in the world.

11

Clinton in Comparative Perspective

GRAHAM K. WILSON

What will President Clinton's *political* legacy be to the repertoire of leadership styles and strategies in advanced democracies? Note the stress here on the word "political"; this chapter does not aim to examine Clinton's foreign policies or the degree to which he deserves credit for progress toward peace in the Middle East or Northern Ireland. A focus on Clinton's political legacy asks instead whether there are important aspects of his style and strategy that have been, or are likely to be emulated profitably by leaders in other advanced industrialized democracies.

At first glance, it seems obvious that Clinton's saga is of little relevance to other democratic leaders. The Clinton story will strike many as a uniquely American tale. Beginning in a "little town called Hope" as the 1992 campaign materials emphasized (glossing over the fact that the president spent little time there), the story of how the son of an easy-living mother and an alcoholic stepfather rose to be a Rhodes scholar, governor of Arkansas, and, ultimately, president of the United States[1] embodied national ideals of equality of opportunity. Top politicians in other countries such as Britain also often come from humble backgrounds; nonetheless, this familiar "log cabin to White House" story has often been thought to embody the promise of American life. The latter stages of the presidency, as Clinton was forced to reveal intimate details of his sex life as he fought against charges of perjury, obstruction of justice, and abuse of power, also seemed peculiarly American, though as a nightmare, not a dream. As the United

254

States watched its president describe where and how in the White House he received sexual gratification from an intern, Monica Lewinsky, citizens of most other countries watched in horror what was widely regarded as overly intrusive inquiry into the president's private life. "Hell," one dismayed French newspaper remarked "is America."[2]

Yet behind the drama of what may well be the uniquely American drama of Clinton's personal fortunes lay several features of his presidency that were often seen as being of considerable relevance to politicians in other countries.[3] American presidents, of course, always make an impact on other countries, simply by being presidents of the United States. The power, wealth, and cultural dominance of the United States insure that American presidents always have influence far beyond its borders. While Clinton devoted a lower percentage of his speeches to foreign affairs than any president since Ford,[4] he traveled extensively, even in his first term. Ragsdale shows that Clinton averaged thirty-two foreign appearances a year during his first term, the highest figure for any post–World War II president, and a figure that would be exceeded in the second term (see table 11.1, p. 256). As president of the United States, Clinton had seemed a symbol of hope to people in countries that he visited, from Romania[5] to Northern Ireland, South Africa to the Caribbean, although he also played a less gratifying role as the symbol of evil to Islamic fundamentalists from Afghanistan to east Africa.

As the leader of the world's only superpower, a nation that enjoys unprecedented cultural as well as economic and military dominance in the world, an American president is well positioned to reflect changes in the climate of opinion not just nationally but internationally. Kennedy had reflected just such a change of mood in 1960, as his youth and vigor contrasted markedly with elderly, often weary leaders such as Adenauer, Macmillan, and de Gaulle. In his famous inaugural address, Kennedy emphasized that this election marked something more than merely a change of president; it marked the "passing of the torch" of leadership to a new generation. Similarly, Clinton was the first president of the United States from the "baby boom" generation born after World War II, coming to political consciousness during the tumultuous era of the civil rights movement and anti–Vietnam War protests. Among the leaders of major democracies, the only baby boomer to precede Clinton as a chief executive was the unprepossessing John Major of Britain. Major, a compromise candidate for the leadership, did not put his stamp on his own nation, nor even on his own party. Clinton, in contrast, as a charismatic president of the United States, had the possibility to be of far greater symbolic importance.

Table 11.1. Foreign Appearances of Recent Presidents

	Number of Appearances	*Yearly Average*
Eisenhower I	7	2
Eisenhower II	115	29
Kennedy	77	26
Johnson	55	11
Nixon I	108	27
Nixon II	25	14
Ford	63	29
Carter	69	17
Reagan I	82	21
Reagan II	51	13
Bush	113	29
Clinton I	129	32
Clinton II[a]	47	—

Source: Lyn Ragsdale, *Vital Statistics on the Presidency: Washington to Clinton* (Washington D.C.: CQ Press, 1998), 173.

Note: Appearances include formal remarks, toasts to another head of state, airport greetings, remarks to reporters, and remarks to Americans who reside in the host country.

a. 1997 only.

Are there any signs that Clinton followed Kennedy in inspiring the citizens of other democracies? Kennedy's stature—marked by gestures such as the naming of streets after him in almost every major city in France and the erection of a memorial close to the site of the signing of the Magna Carta in Britain—grew abroad as at home after his assassination. Clinton, marred by political defeats and scandal, is unlikely to come close to Kennedy in the affections of foreigners. Nonetheless, it was striking that Clinton could attract large crowds on every continent, and when the Lewinsky scandal broke, he secured more sympathy than criticism outside the United States. A petition in support of Clinton was started in France, and British public opinion was resolutely supportive of the president, even while deploring his deceit of his wife and the nation (see table 11.2).

The argument that Clinton left an important political legacy internationally goes far beyond the apparent popularity of his style overseas or the possibility that he symbolized a generational shift among world political leaders. Clinton, contended his advisers, had shown the center-left how to gain, keep, and use power. One Clinton adviser remarked off the record that "Clinton wrote the

Table 11.2. British Public Opinion on the Lewinsky Scandal (in percentages)

From what you know, do you think that Bill Clinton, the President of the United States, is honest and trustworthy or not?

Yes, he is honest and trustworthy	20
No, he is not honest and trustworthy	74
Don't know / refused	6

In view of his confession in the Monica Lewinsky case, do you think that Bill Clinton is or is not a fit person to be President of the United States?

Yes, he is a fit person	63
No, he is not a fit person	32
Don't know / refused	5

Based on what you know at this point, do you think that Bill Clinton should or should not be impeached and removed from office?

Yes, he should	26
No, he should not	69
Don't know / refused	5

Which do you think is the greater wrong, that he had an inappropriate relationship with Monica Lewinsky or that he misled both his wife and the public with his public comments on the issue?

His inappropriate relationship with Monica Lewinsky	9
The fact that he misled both his wife and the public with his public comments on the issue	84
Don't know / refused	6

Source: Gallup (UK). Fieldwork 19–25 August 1998.

book that the British Labour Party and the German Social Democrats have followed since." Just as Thatcher's victory in 1979 had apparently shown the way for the right to triumph in the United States, Germany, and France, so Clinton and his admirers felt that he had written the book on how the center-left could win and succeed in governing after decades in the wilderness. It is worth recalling that when Clinton was elected in 1992, the British had recently decided to extend the period in office of the Conservatives, who had been in power since 1979, by what turned out to be a further five years. Germany was in the midst of the long reign of Chancellor Helmut Kohl and his center-right coalition. Although France had been ruled by a Socialist president (François Mitterrand) during the 1980s, he presided over a party that had ignominiously abandoned its commitment to socialism in the face of economic catastrophe in the early 1980s.

By the middle of Clinton's second term, however, the political balance had shifted, and in Europe in particular the center-left had restored its fortunes. Often with coaching from Clinton campaign consultants, left-of-center politicians such as Britain's Tony Blair and Germany's Gerhard Schröder had come to power, in both cases encouraging speculation that they were the domestic equivalent of Clinton. Clinton could claim with some plausibility that his victories in 1992 and 1996 did not merely happen to precede this change but contributed to it somewhat. For Clinton appeared to show how to resolve a number of problems that had threatened to keep left-of-center parties from power indefinitely. The lessons he offered concerned positioning, presentation, and governing in an era of constraints.

Positioning

A great deal of attention has been paid to the influence of Dick Morris, the libidinous campaign consultant, on Clinton after the shock of the Republican capture of Congress in 1994. Morris has credited himself with persuading Clinton to adopt a strategy of "triangulation"[6]—Clinton presenting himself as the sensible, pragmatic alternative to both the radical right-wing Republican leadership in Congress and the allegedly liberal congressional Democrats. Although it is reasonable for Morris to claim credit for this positioning of Clinton since the first two years of the administration had confused Clinton's image, in fact Clinton's entire presidential career was an exercise in triangulation. From the primary campaigns of 1992 onward, Clinton had portrayed himself as a New Democrat. How did New Democrats differ from Old Democrats? The answer was never made clear positively but was defined negatively: New Democrats were not addicted to raising taxes. New Democrats were not addicted to deficit spending. New Democrats were not inclined to deny the responsibility of criminals for their acts or of citizens on welfare to return to the workforce. (One cannot but note, of course, how the new rhetoric of personal responsibility contrasted with the private behavior of the president himself.) New Democrats were not hostile to the family. New Democrats were not uncritical servants of their core constituencies, showing themselves willing to criticize African Americans as well as whites who used racist rhetoric. New Democrats were not unpatriotic. New Democrats, in short, were not susceptible to the pejorative labeling that had served Republicans so well in destroying the candidacies of Walter Mondale in 1984 and Michael Dukakis in 1988, when Democrats had been portrayed as the party of high taxes and deficits, flag-burning protesters, and alternative lifestyles. Clinton demonstrated to leaders of left-of-center parties in other democracies how to deal with attempts to portray their parties as outside the mainstream culture.

Whether the "third way" espoused by Clinton and his most avid follower, Tony Blair of Britain, had any positive content was less clear; the two of them were still searching for meaning in the term in a seminar in New York in September 1998. But political leaders are not elected to be political theorists; with the exception of a few awkward episodes over "gays in the military" and nominations such as his choices for head of the civil rights division of the Justice Department (Lani Guinier) and surgeon general (Joycelyn Elders) during his first two years in office, Clinton had shown how to deal with the attacks that Republicans had launched on Democratic candidates in the 1980s. Clinton's positioning was in a sense a posthumous creation of Lee Atwater, the designer of so many effective negative ads and wedge issues that Reagan and Bush had used against Mondale and Dukakis. Clinton showed that the center-left no longer had to accept ownership of the "counterculture" values of the 1960s but could itself invoke themes such as law and order, the family, and protecting children. It was a path followed by Tony Blair when he committed himself to policies that were, for example "tough on crime and tough on its causes." Blair, like Clinton, accepted that concern about crime need not be monopolized by the right.

In contrast to the apparent vulnerability of the left in the recent past on "social issues," Clinton demonstrated the advantage that the center-left could enjoy on other issues. Clinton recognized the continuing popularity of many, including the most expensive, aspects of "big government" even if the intellectual tides flowed against it. The political success of Clinton's insistence in 1997 and 1998 that the budget surplus be used "to protect Social Security first," rather than being devoted to tax cuts, illustrates the popularity of big government's most expensive program. In the context of right-wing ambitions to roll back growth in both the size and scope of the state that had occurred since the New Deal, Clinton offered the beneficiaries of its most popular (and not coincidentally largest and most expensive) programs reassurance that their programs were not in jeopardy. Older Americans could continue to count on the federal government to cover their medical bills, even if the children of mothers on welfare faced the risk of being pushed deeper into poverty by the so-called welfare reform act that Clinton signed. Clinton provided most Americans (other than the most needy) the assurance that they could continue to count on government in all the many ways to which they had become accustomed, from aid to their children in college to medical aid for their aging parents. Clinton proved to be a capable, defensive general who developed tactics that could be used to withstand the right-wing *blitzkrieg* that had seemed unstoppable in many advanced democracies in the 1980s and early 1990s.

What Clinton offered to the center-left was therefore a strategy that negated the effectiveness of the right's attacks on "social issues" by disavowing the "old" left while emphasizing his determination to defend popular (and expensive) aspects of the American welfare state such as Social Security and Medicare against right-wing radicals. The positioning strategy that Clinton used throughout most of his presidential career (triangulation) contained a strong element of criticism of his own party as well as of the Republicans. Republicans were too far to the right, argued Clinton, but Old Democrats—including the Democrats in Congress—were too far to the left, leaving Clinton as the sensible moderate center.

The parallels with Tony Blair are striking. Blair campaigned almost as strongly against the old left of the Labour Party as against his Conservative opponents. Blair seemed a better leader to most British voters during the 1997 election campaign than John Major, whose image should have been strengthened by his status as prime minister. But Blair was willing and able to defeat opponents of his policies in the Labour Party in a manner that Major could not replicate in the Conservative Party. This was triangulation, British style, with the occasional Old Labour left-wing candidate playing the role for Blair that congressional Democrats did for Clinton. We return later to consider whether this similarity of strategy was merely a coincidence or not. We should note, however, that the world of campaign consultants has become international. Just as the Conservative Party attempted to assist President Bush in 1992 by sending over advisers from its advertising agency, Saatchi and Saatchi, so James Carville and Stan Greenberg, Clinton's advisers, were on hand to assist Blair in 1997. Indeed, so close did this working relationship become that in 1997 National Opinion Polls announced that it had created a new company (Gould-Greenberg-Carville-NOP), linking Clinton's advisers with Blair's (Gould) to sell political consultancy services around the world.

Presentation

President Clinton was by no means the first American politician to employ campaign consultants, use focus groups, or commission opinion polls. Nonetheless, the Clinton presidency raised campaign techniques to a new level and made them a central part of governing as well as campaigning. It was not only that Clinton spent far more time, money, and energy on tracking opinion polls than previous presidents, but that specialists in public opinion and campaigning such as Morris were much more involved in policymaking than in the past, and policy initiatives were more thoroughly pretested on the public. While Morris's statements about the importance of his role might be discounted as self-promotion, the complaints by members of the administration such as Robert Reich (labor secretary during the first term) suggest that Morris's claims to a prominent role in policymaking were more than a figment of his imagination.[7] Drafts of the 1997 State of the Union message, for example, were tried out on cooperative shoppers who could be lured into watching them in stores rented in shopping malls; it was hardly a surprise, therefore, when the State of the Union message was voted a conspicuous success by a public on whom its popularity had been pretested so thoroughly. Similarly, while the White House Press Office has grown steadily over the years, the Clinton people were unusually forceful and proactive in "spinning" the media. Only during the early years of the Reagan administration was there a team in the White House more adept at spinning; Clinton characteristically expressed his admiration for this operation by bringing one of the Reagan advisers, David Gergen, onto his own staff for a time. Many center-left parties in advanced democracies had viewed opinion polls, advertising agencies, focus groups, and "spinning" as capitalist tools for manipulating the masses. Clinton showed how to use such techniques to protect the center-left from unrestrained, even unscrupulous attacks from the right.

Not surprisingly, the Clinton administration was also adept at the politics of symbolism. When the crisis of the Lewinsky affair struck, Clinton was able to count on the support of black and feminist organizations (see chapter 8), the latter of which came under fierce criticism because of apparent double standards for their tolerance of the president's sexual misconduct (in contrast to their strong criticism of the alleged sexual misconduct of Clarence Thomas, President Bush's Supreme Court nominee). The support of African-American and feminist interest groups was based in part on hard policy considerations such as the president's defense of affirmative action and abortion rights. It was also based, however, on appreciation of gestures the president had made, such as appointing large numbers of women and minority-group members to positions in his administration, his publicized friendships with African Americans such as Vernon Jordan, and his choice of Jesse Jackson to offer spiritual guidance at the height of the crisis.

Yet, past Democratic presidential candidates had not been thought indifferent to these core constituencies. Clinton's triumph was to show that it is possible to make real and symbolic gestures to core constituencies without offending the rest of the population. How was this achieved? In part through careful use of language so that, for example, white men could focus on the first part and African Americans on the second part of a promise to "mend not end" affirmative action. Clinton was also very careful (and in this Blair copied him closely) to make symbolic gestures that appeared to demonstrate sympathy toward "mainstream" values, to show that he "felt the pain" of ordinary families struggling to meet their commitments and instill moral behavior in their children in difficult times. Clinton's denunciation of Sister Souljah (a black rap singer who used racist words in her songs) spoke volumes to white Americans tired of what they felt were liberals' tendencies to blame whites alone for social problems. Whatever its failings as social policy, Clinton's signature of the welfare reform act sent a powerful message that virtues such as hard work and thrift were respected once again by Democratic politicians.

One might doubt the sincerity of many of Clinton's symbolic gestures. The president's much praised endorsement of sexual abstinence and responsibility for teenagers was not consistent with his own behavior. His support for school uniforms was irrelevant; America's schools are governed by thousands of elected school boards, not by the president or Congress in Washington. Clinton's return to Arkansas to supervise the execution of a mentally retarded murderer during the 1992 campaign was meant to demonstrate his commitment to being, in the language of Tony Blair, "tough on crime," though perhaps it illustrated better his ruthless determination to win. Yet whatever unease might be voiced by pundits or political scientists, there can be no doubting the extent of Clinton's success in transforming his party's image.

An interesting aspect of Clinton's skill in presentation that has also been copied by Blair is his use of stars from the entertainment industry to boost his own prestige. At one time, high government officials conferred celebrity on stars; in this era of diminished standing for government, stars confer celebrity on politicians. Clinton has been assiduous in surrounding himself with Hollywood stars, partly because they are a valuable source of contributions for his campaigns and legal defense fund, but mainly because of the glamor they provide. Kennedy had, of course, invited prominent performers to the White House, but he had mainly emphasized high culture in his invitations. Clinton, in contrast, surrounded himself with the stars of mass entertainment. Similarly, one of Blair's early guests at

10 Downing Street was Ian Gallagher of *Oasis*. Gallagher informed the press that he had not wished to accept the invitation but had done so to please his mother.

We should not exaggerate the potential of symbolic politics. In less favorable times, symbolic gestures may have counted for less. The president succeeded in avoiding the impression that he had given disproportionate attention to core constituencies such as African Americans or feminists by talking so much about—and appearing to have achieved—goals dear to white male Democrats, such as full employment and income growth. In the context of an expanding economy, which had been at the core of Clinton's campaign themes in 1992, gestures toward core constituencies such as African Americans were no longer perceived as threats to the rest of the population.

Governing in an Age of Constraints

Several factors combined to hinder the introduction of major new domestic programs in the 1990s. First, many democracies, including the United States, experienced resistance to tax increases on the part of citizens and increased willingness on the part of businesses to relocate in order to minimize tax liability. Second, the United States experienced a large budget deficit. Efforts to reduce the federal deficit, largely successful by 1998, included requirements that proposals that would increase public expenditure should be accompanied by proposals for compensating expenditure cuts. Finally, the intellectual climate in the early 1990s continued to stress enthusiasm for markets and a profound suspicion of government. The assumptions that government was inefficient, politicians and civil servants self-interested budget maximizers, and markets necessarily productive of the highest possible levels of public welfare were little challenged. Socialist alternatives to capitalism withered with the Soviet Union, and transformations in the world economy were alleged to have rendered the Keynesian welfare state outdated.

In this context Clinton launched, and his followers such as Tony Blair continued, the pursuit of a "third way" of governing. Those with long memories or historical background are likely to be cynical about talk of a "third way." After all, the search for a third way has been mounted ever since the conflicts between capitalism and socialism arose. The search for the third way has sometimes been conducted by vacuous politicians seeking little more than an era of good feelings; at other times the search has been conducted by demagogues and fascists. Perhaps the most successful searchers for a third way were the revisionists of social democracy in the 1950s, such as C.A.R. Crosland, who argued that social democrats could pursue greater equality successfully within the context of capitalism and without further extension of government ownership of industry.[8]

In the United States, where an explicit commitment to social democratic programs had never taken root, the third way was between the apparently callous neglect of those who did not succeed in the marketplace on the one hand and the apparently wasteful, possibly counterproductive social programs that had developed since the New Deal. For many Americans, welfare programs typified the problems of "big government." According to their many critics, the praiseworthy goal of trying to assist those in need had degenerated into a large bureaucracy administering programs with perverse incentives producing unintended consequences such as clients' unwillingness or inability (because of fear of losing such benefits as health insurance) to work. Similarly, the well-intentioned regulatory initiatives of the early 1970s undertaken by agencies such as the EPA and OSHA to counter serious problems of pollution, safety, and health had produced in practice an approach that maximized conflict and cost rather than solutions to the undoubted problems they were intended to address.

The Clinton administration tried hard to develop a third-way approach to governing, one that would combine a concern for social justice and equality with a repudiation of failed approaches of the past. Its efforts were fueled in part by conviction, in part by political or budgetary circumstance. Perhaps the largest third-way initiative was the commitment to "reinventing government" undertaken under the leadership of Vice-President Gore.[9]

The United States has always had a political culture critical of government in the abstract, even while strongly supporting many specific government programs. The antipathy toward "big government" and the strong though questionable belief of many Americans that the private sector does things better had long been a problem for Democrats. Democrats had often been attacked for defending vast bureaucracies that served their members rather than themselves, a perception encouraged by the increasing power of public-sector unions within the Democratic Party. There was a political imperative, therefore, for the administration to be seen to be doing something about the failings of "big government." Every government agency was required to create a "reinvention" office or unit. Management techniques such as total quality management that were intended to promote a more sympathetic approach to agency clients (now to be termed "customers") were propagated. Whether as a result government agencies did indeed become more efficient and attentive to customers is of course difficult to determine. The administration could certainly claim that its reinvention programs displayed its determination to seek better ways of pursuing desirable goals. Similarly, regulatory agencies such as the EPA were encouraged to expand programs that facilitated cooperation rather than conflict with industry, programs such as trading permits to pollute so that corporations could close down loss-causing sources of pollution rather than cutting production at profitable centers.

A second major third-way approach was in economic policy. To the consternation of many of the president's advisers such as James Carville, Clinton had given the highest priority in his early budgets to cutting the deficit.[10] Again, this was a demonstration of the administration's preparedness to break with allegedly Democratic toleration of high-spending deficit finance in the past—although of course the greatest increases in the deficit had been consequences of the policies of the Reagan administration. The president's support of the strictly anti-inflation policies of the chairman of the Federal Reserve Board, Alan Greenspan, and somewhat belatedly of the policies of the Bush administration on fostering freer trade through the North American Free Trade Agreement (NAFTA) and the World Trade Organization (WTO) promoted the impression that here was a Democratic administration that truly accepted the constraints of a capitalist economy. This was, of course, a pathway eagerly followed by Tony Blair in Britain, cultivating the goodwill of industrialists and financiers in opposition and daringly entrusting monetary policy to the Bank of England once in power.

The most dramatic attempt to follow a third way came in the Clinton administration's attempts to create a system of national health insurance. Again, this was partly a matter of necessity. Given the existence of a large budget deficit, the primacy given to reducing the deficit, and the absence of any will to do so through raising taxes, a means had to be found to seek health care for all without any additional government expenditure. The strategy chosen was based on the quintessentially third-way thinking of Alain Enthoven.[11] Large-scale health alliances would have combined elements of market-based approaches with elements that only government could provide (such as compulsory coverage) to insure that for the first time all Americans would have access to health care. Unfortunately, the ingenuity of the scheme was also a weakness; it proved too complicated to promote to the public, while its complexity provided ammunition for Republican opponents of universal health care.

One great danger of a third-way approach to governance is that by legitimating attacks on government programs, it opens up the danger of a political runaway train in which opponents of a government commitment are able to capitalize on critiques of the *methods* used in order to weaken a commitment to the very *purpose* of the program. The center-left might agree with an argument from the right that a particular program or agency is failing. The center-left might intend to reform and improve the policy or agency, but the fact that "everyone" has agreed that the policy or agency is a failure strengthens the hand of those who wish to abolish, not reform it, because they reject the goals of the policy or agency as well as the methods used.

This is what happened in the case of welfare reform. Clinton had come into office accepting the critiques of welfare programs that produced the call to "end welfare as we know it." Welfare reform comes in many forms, however. In some of the more progressive states such as Wisconsin, reform has actually resulted in increases in expenditure, as funds are needed to address barriers to employment such as lack of childcare, health insurance, and training. The federal welfare reform program, in contrast, was almost entirely punitive in character, and Clinton was ill-positioned to prevent its passage. Having accepted the need for welfare reform and having failed to articulate reforms of his own, he was unable to resist proposals from the Republican Congress for less generous, more punitive forms of welfare reform, and he signed the Republican bill into law, to the dismay of many Democrats, under the pressure of his reelection campaign in 1996. Welfare reform, however, was probably the only major example of a third-way approach spiraling out of control.

Did Clinton's third way have coherence? It is possible in these different policy areas to identify commonalities that it is perhaps not too grandiose to see as a strategy of governance. The elements of this strategy were as follows: First, the social obligations of government would not be reduced, with the exception of the commitment to the most needy through welfare reform. Second, the administration would pursue economic policies that could command the support of bankers more than unions or activists. Third, the respect for market mechanisms evident in economic policy would be extended into other areas (proposals for health care reform, reinventing government, and regulatory reform) wherever possible.

It is not clear, however, that these elements in a strategy of governance amounted to a philosophy of governance. In general, the administration's initiatives were more adept at accommodating to circumstances than at pursuing a political philosophy. Like many successful politicians, however, the president had no wish to be seen as acting purely on the basis of expediency. In September 1998, Clinton attended a seminar in New York with the Italian prime minister and his friend, Tony Blair, accompanied by Blair's house philosopher, Anthony Giddens.[12] Once again the band of political leaders attempted to define the third-way approach they shared. Overshadowed by the crisis of the Lewinsky affair, however, no one much noticed.

Clinton as a Role Model

Fashion among world leaders changes almost as rapidly as in *haute couture*. Today's vital model of leadership turns out tomorrow to have been strangely oblivious to problems and crises that we can now easily see were about to engulf the nation. Clinton's limitations as a leader will be more apparent as time passes. A president's reputation is often at its lowest just after leaving power, and one suspects that the stain of scandal will be more perceptible once Clinton can no longer claim credit for a robust economy. Nonetheless, certain memories and successes will endure.

First, and admittedly partly at the expense of his own party, Clinton did solve the fundamental problem that had plagued center-left politicians—how to gain and keep power. His two electoral victories, the first against an incumbent, were the greatest successes Democrats had achieved at this level since the 1960s. Twice aided by the economy, first by defeating Bush after a recession and then by enjoying the political rewards for presiding over the best performance by the American economy in forty years, Clinton could nonetheless plausibly claim that he deserved credit for these successes. In particular, he adroitly protected himself from the charge that he was another of those Democrats who were antifamily, pro-criminal, addicted to higher taxation, and hostile to the core values of mainstream America. Indeed, so successful was Clinton at avoiding the charge of extremism that it was the Republicans with their skepticism about popular government programs such as Social Security and their anti-choice rhetoric on abortion who were made to seem the extremists. For the first time in a quarter century, Clinton made the Democrats, not the Republicans, the sensible party that could be trusted with difficult issues.

Second, the president raised to new heights the techniques for reaching out to the nation beyond the political elites. Written off many times, Clinton showed a capacity to reach out to mass publics successfully. After enormous setbacks that might have overwhelmed a lesser politician (the failure of health care reform, the Republican capture of Congress, the Monica Lewinsky scandal), Clinton found ways not only to survive, and indeed to maintain extraordinarily high approval ratings, but also to make policy gains that infuriated his opponents. The humiliations of the Lewinsky affair were still in process when, in 1998, he won a budget agreement with the Republican congressional leaders that not only commentators but also many Republicans themselves regarded as a victory for the president.

Such successes were partly the result of personal skills and partly the result of institutional capacity. Clinton has been a supremely good speaker, in meetings and on television. But he has also completed a process, perhaps long in the making, of bringing experts on public opinion into the policymaking process. Consultants such as Dick Morris crossed the line between advising on policy and making it, as both Morris and less friendly observers such as Robert Reich have noted.[13] As Charles Jones has argued,[14] in the past we had a concept of passing from campaigning to governing in presidential transitions; the Clinton administration never made that transition, and under extremely difficult political conditions such as the Lewinsky affair, it thrived. It is hard to imagine successors reducing the capacity to run focus groups, conduct opinion polls, and pretest speeches that Clinton developed. Nor is it likely that heads of government in other countries will fail to emulate these techniques. Indeed, Clinton's visit to London in 1998 produced much mutual admiration and congratulation between the president's *spinmeisters* and their British counterparts, especially Alistair Campbell, Blair's press secretary.

We should note again, however, that the successful use of this strategy of permanent campaigning may work under only special circumstances. The soundness of the economy contributed powerfully to popular satisfaction with the president. The Republican majority in Congress spared Clinton expectations that he would make grand policy initiatives. In different circumstances, a president might need more support among the political elite. The Clinton administration, through its permanent campaign, remained well attached to the country as a whole, but it was curiously isolated from Washington. Three of the president's four short-lived chiefs of staff scarcely put down roots in the capital; the fourth, Leon Panetta, a highly experienced former congressman, was brought in to serve a brief term when Clinton was in difficulty after the 1994 midterm elections. The president was scarcely loved by congressional Democrats, whom he had been prepared to sacrifice in his triangulation strategy leading up to the 1996 reelection campaign. Even in 1998, when his need for supporters in the face of threatened impeachment was greatest, Clinton annoyed congressional Democrats by minimizing, through his spokespersons, their chances in the midterm elections in order to avoid the danger that Democratic losses might be seen as support in the country for his impeachment.

This distancing tactic was no doubt due in part to the need to negotiate with Republican leaders under conditions of divided government. Perhaps it reflected an attitude—also displayed by Tony Blair in Britain—that one's own party, rather than treated as a set of colleagues, was instead seen as an obstacle to be overcome or mastered. Neither Clinton nor Blair had much respect for the parties they led. Does this matter? The success of Clinton's cultivation of popular opinion invites emulation at home and abroad; whether a leader's distance from his own party would work quite as well under conditions of a less favorable economy or when divided government no longer exists remains to be seen.

The third claim that Clinton can make is that whether or not he developed a coherent "third way" philosophy, like Roosevelt, he encouraged a period of experimentation to deal with what Americans may, indeed did, believe to be genuine problems. Clintonism captured a fairly widespread public mood in the 1990s—that while socialism was dead and government programs often produced perverse unintended consequences, many aspects of big government, at least those serving middle-class Americans, were essential. Politicians should seek, to borrow Clinton's phrase about affirmative action, "to mend, not end" such programs. Scarcely heroic in their ambition, efforts to make environmental regulation more effective but less intrusive, the bureaucracy more efficient and responsive to users, and Social Security more actuarially sound represented a willingness to engage less in ideology and more in what had been called "relentless experimentation" in Franklin Roosevelt's administration. The purpose of that experimentation by the Clinton administration was not to extend the role of government, as in Roosevelt's day, but to restructure and reform the existing activities of government, acknowledging the truth of many criticisms of government while equally accepting the legitimacy of the expectations of government.

This approach recognized the central dilemma of governance in advanced democracies in the modern era. While many citizens and powerful interest groups have been scathing in their criticism of what in the United States is often called big government, very few in the United States or elsewhere really wish to reduce the size and scope of government responsibilities to the level of the 1950s, let alone the 1920s. While it is far too early to assess the success or failure of the reforms that have been instituted, the very attempt to grapple with this central problem of governance has deserved credit and, where center-left parties have come to power, has inspired emulation.

The Portability of the Model

Political leaders interact today more than ever before. They meet frequently in settings such as the G7, and they take a considerable interest in each others' domestic political problems, to the point of telephoning each other to sympathize over setbacks such as the Lewinsky affair, which prompted phone calls to Clinton from several heads of government, including the French president. Heads of government, as we have noted, even quietly dispatch their political advisers to help their ideological counterparts in other countries. This is not, as the American press often suggests, a one-way street. The interaction between the Labour Party and the Democratic Party, as between the Conservative Party and the Republican Party, has been very much a two-way street, with ideas and tactics being exchanged in both directions. Campaign consultancy has become an international business. While many political scientists continue to emphasize that every country is different in its institutions and cultures, politicians are increasingly willing to pay hard cash to obtain the advice of leading consultants from other countries. It is unlikely, therefore, that the Clinton model will go unnoticed by other leading politicians, particularly center-left politicians, around the world.

The reader will have noticed that the name of Tony Blair has occurred in this chapter with great regularity, far more so than, for example, the name of Lionel Jospin (the leader of the French Socialists.) While this may reflect, in part, the author's British background and knowledge, it is probably also the case that the similarities in style and strategy between Clinton and Blair, New Democrats and New Labour, are unusually strong. Just as Margaret Thatcher was a determined leader who imposed her philosophy on Britain more than Reagan imposed his on the United States, Blair will be a determined practitioner of the third way, and he is more likely to leave his mark on Britain than Clinton will on the United States. In his first two years in power, Blair changed Britain more than Clinton changed the United States in eight. But why should the parallels between Blair and Clinton, British and American politics, be so close in the late 1990s?

In spite of the significant differences between the United States and the United Kingdom in terms of institutions, culture, and public policy, some political scientists have suggested that there is a contrast also between the "Anglo Saxon" nations and continental European democracies. The Danish political scientist, Gøsta Esping-Andersen, for example, contrasts the British and American approaches to welfare with social democratic or conservative patterns found in the rest of Europe.[15] Perhaps the similarities between Clinton and Blair are but another manifestation of the links that bind Britain and the United States?

There are, however, two more obvious explanations. The first is that Britain, like the United States, passed through a similar political cycle preceding the advent of Clinton and Blair. Radical right-wing politicians who combined nationalism and commitment to market economics succeeded in demonizing the left-of-center party as extremist and dominated by special interests such as labor. The Democrats held onto the House of Representatives until 1994, but in presidential elections after 1976, they were thought almost certain to lose the White House to the Republicans, who were said to have a "lock" on the presidency. The center-left in Britain and the United States faced a very similar problem of reestablishing its credibility and electability, but this problem was not, as was often supposed, a universal phenomenon. The left did not lose ground everywhere. In terms of the balance of power between left and right in the legislatures of the major advanced industrialized democracies (though not in terms of the composition of cabinets), the left maintained its strength throughout the 1980s.[16] The decline of the left, in terms of electoral politics, was indeed primarily an Anglo-American affair, although some left-wing governments (most notably in New Zealand) implemented conservative shifts in policy. Clintonism was primarily a cure for left-of-center parties that had been losing badly; obviously its appeal was greatest for parties in such a predicament.

There are also some institutional prerequisites for the ability to follow the tactics of Clinton and Blair. We have emphasized the importance to Clinton (and to Blair) of image, and of promoting a favorable image through "spinning." Not all institutional arrangements facilitate symbolic actions or spinning the news. We might hypothesize that institutional prerequisites for success are that there be a prominent, centralized, and authoritative governmental position that can define *the* image of an administration or government. One is reminded of Lord Liverpool's famous advice to his cabinet: "It doesn't matter what we say, gentlemen, as long as we all say the same." Neither the American presidency nor the British prime ministership guarantees success in symbolic leadership and spinning. Presidents lose control over department secretaries, weak prime ministers such as John Major have trouble disciplining their parties and even their cabinets. Yet the presidency, with its large press office and ultimately unitary character culminating in a single individual, has a capacity to define and create an image that the office of Senate majority leader or even Speaker of the House inherently lacks.

One of Tony Blair's extraordinary achievements was to centralize power in his own hands as leader of the Labour Party even before winning the election. No leader of the Labour Party, usually thought of as a factious, divided party, has enjoyed as much authority. Blair set and maintained an image for the party in a way that predecessors might have wished to do, but lacked the power to do. Once in office, Blair strengthened the prime ministership by increasing the size of the politically appointed staff in Downing Street. He also entrusted his closest aide while in opposition, Peter Mandelson, with taking charge of the government information officers in different departments so that they would spin more actively to promote in a coordinated manner the image of the government. This produced the only serious tension between Blair and the permanent civil service to date; information officers, as permanent civil servants, disliked the idea of acting in as partisan a way as this strategy required. Those who were unwilling or unable to adopt the new style were forced out, however, and the new approach was implemented.

In contrast, many political chief executives around the world do not have the institutional capacity to profit from the Clinton example. Japanese prime minsters are usually sufficiently obscure officials immersed in the political world of the Liberal Democratic Party to be incapable of presenting the sort of strong clear image required by the Clinton approach. Prime ministers in parliamentary systems in which coalitions are the norm are equally unlikely to have the sort of opportunity that Clinton and Blair have had to establish such a strong public image. It is particularly interesting to note the attempts of Gerhard Schröder, the Social Democrat who became chancellor of Germany in 1998, to be "the German Clinton" (or the German Blair). Schröder had encouraged such comparisons before the election, and the apparent prominence of the chancellorship in the German political system seemed to make success likely. Once in office, however, Schröder found himself unable to spin his actions to the world because he lacked the centralized power to do so. The German chancellorship does not have the power or resources of the British prime ministership, let alone the American presidency. Within months, commentators were asking "Who's running Germany?"[17] and Schröder found that his third-way message was overwhelmed by the more traditionally left-wing views of the finance minister, Oskar Lafontaine. Perhaps the system where Clintonism as yet appears to have had no impact but where the institutional capacity is already in place is that in France, particularly if control of the presidency and the parliament are politically unified. Fortunately or unfortunately, we shall probably never have the opportunity of testing the capacity of

France for Clintonism because the political commitment to traditional welfare-state and labor-protection laws is too strong, and because there has been no prior period of radical right-wing rule that is a precondition for Clinton/Blair approaches.

The Limitation of Clintonism

Bill Clinton will receive a prominent mention in the history of the presidency for many reasons, some of which he would prefer to forget. His enormous success with the public, which far outstrips his impact to date on public policy, prompts many to wonder if his political style and strategies can be copied elsewhere. Clinton, as far as one can tell, is personally popular with many world leaders, and he may inspire other politicians to try to replicate his approach and style. It seems unlikely that many will do so, however. The number of countries having the crucial preconditions for Clintonism, namely emerging from a period of political domination by the right and having leadership institutions sufficiently centralized to emulate Clinton's style, is extremely limited. Few Americans recognize this limitation because, while the extent of their knowledge is easily overstated, they know more about Britain, one of the few examples of a country where a leadership style similar to Clinton's has been adopted, than about almost any other country. The frequency with which Tony Blair is compared to Clinton is ironically a reminder that few democracies share in full the conditions for Clintonism. Such a politically successful president of the United States is likely to have impressed his fellow leaders mightily, and to have prompted at least some modest attempts to copy his techniques everywhere. In the majority of advanced democracies, however, emulation of Clinton is both less necessary than in Britain and the United States because the right has not been so strong, and less likely because political institutions are less suited to his style.

12

Cutting *With* the Grain: Is There a Clinton Leadership Legacy?

BERT A. ROCKMAN

How do we come to grips with the nearly completed presidency of Bill Clinton? To pose this question reveals not only a presidency-centric outlook toward the American political system but also an individualized conception of leadership. It is plausible, after all, that the hard-charging Republican congressional class elected to the 104th Congress in 1994 may have had the largest leadership role of all in terms of setting a policy agenda, in later sealing the fates of two of their leaders (Newt Gingrich and Robert Livingston), and in trying ultimately, if unsuccessfully, to terminate Bill Clinton's presidency. The fact of the matter is that presidents are not always the whole story of political leadership,[1] perhaps not even the main story.

The odd coupling of prosperity and partisanship are the tag lines of the Clinton years. Alan Greenspan, chair of the Federal Reserve's Board of Governors, is reputed to have had something to do with the prosperity side of things, and a string of Republican leaders and backbenchers, as well as the ubiquitous independent counsel, Kenneth Starr, may have had something to do with the partisan side. Investors hung on Greenspan's words, while Clinton prayed that the sayings of Chairman Greenspan would not imperil his presidency. Although the sheer quantity of Newt Gingrich's words made each of them less consequential than Greenspan's, no one symbolized the clamorous partisanship of the Clinton years more than Gingrich, the mercurial rising, and now fallen, star of Republican aspirations to achieve a (Republican) party government in the aftermath of the 1994 congressional elections.

For at least half of Clinton's time in office, Speaker of the House Newt Gingrich was nearly as visible as Clinton and often no less important as a national political leader, though perhaps neither he nor Clinton was as influential as Alan Greenspan. Unlike Clinton, who coexisted uneasily with his party, Gingrich first mobilized his minions, leading them, as minority whip and prospective party leader, to do battle with the Clinton White House and the Democratic House majority, ultimately propelling his party into the majority in the House. In the long run, it could be that the major players of the period will prove to have been Gingrich and his fellow passionate Republicans. Together, they sought to provide clear direction to the country even as they overreached their warrant and ultimately were resisted—but not before *they*, rather than Clinton, left their imprint on policy. Ironically, the fervent congressional Republicans took the play away from the often innovative and more temperate Republican governors and, thereby, contributed to declining public assessments of their party.

In the American polity at the national level, powerfully contending political forces were afoot during the Clinton presidency. Gingrich's bombastic leadership style helped define the period and its politics, but it is notable that Gingrich's force has been spent, and so therefore may be the dreams of his followers for a sustained Republican majority. Gingrich has fallen; Clinton still stands. Gingrich's story is one of politics fueled by ideas and passions. Clinton's is a story of politics fueled by pragmatism and opportunism. Life is filled with ironic twists and turns. Gingrich's followers quickly turned on him even as he carried their creed. Clinton's supporters were often crossed by their highly adaptable principal, but they stayed with him and faltered hardly at all throughout his impeachment crisis.

Looking back upon the era, historians may say of this eight-year period that it continued the political wars that were stoked during the Reagan period.[2] But for most of the Clinton presidency the tables were turned. Instead of Republican presidents and Democratic congressional majorities (consistently in the House at least), the Republicans controlled Congress for six of the eight Clinton years, while the Democrats held the White House. For much of the Clinton presidency it was the Republican congressional majority rather than the Clinton White House that forced the issue. But if Gingrich went for the knockout blow, Clinton was the clever counterpuncher, eluding the main blows, frustrating his opponents, and sometimes tying them into knots. He will be remembered as a great technician of politics rather than as an innovator of policy. If this observation is correct, it also is likely to mean that aside from the impeachment crisis and the prosperity over which he presided, Clinton is apt not to be remembered much at all.

Presidents and Their Times

Stephen Skowronek's sweeping effort to explain the chances of presidential success and failure suggests how much presidents are captives of the times in which they seek to govern.[3] Obviously, a central question that anyone studying leadership must face is "what are the constraints imposed on, and opportunities open to, any particular leader?" To answer that question fundamentally means that the last thing, not the first thing, we should be looking at is the individual leader and that person's repertoire of aptitudes and deficiencies for the presidential role. These aptitudes and deficiencies are, in any event, likely to depend on which aspects of the role we choose to emphasize, a point nicely illustrated by Fred Greenstein's study of Eisenhower's distinctly anti-Gingrich, antipartisan definition of the role.[4]

Individual variation certainly has a place in leadership roles. But we also need to know about systems, situations, and incentives.[5] These elements define the likely range of possibilities open to any particular leader at any particular time. Political scientists differ widely on just how important individual variability is and, above all, whether it can have any systematic value in explaining the choices politicians, including presidents, make.

Two bodies of theory with wide currency in political science—*rational choice theory* and *bounded rationality*—suggest that individual variation is both marginal and idiosyncratic. Rational choice theory focuses on the role of incentives. With the right configuration of incentives you or I will behave similarly, at least if our utility functions are comparable. As one presidential scholar of the rational choice persuasion has put it:

> The presidency is also an institution, and the individual who occupies the office at any given time is an institutional actor, his role well specified by law and expectations, his incentives highly structured by the system. Some portion of presidential behavior, then, and perhaps a very large portion, is quite impersonal. All presidents, whatever their personalities or styles or backgrounds, should tend to behave similarly in basic respects.[6]

Another body of decision-making theory, known as bounded rationality, suggests that while we certainly respond to the incentives around us, these incentives are affected by our own pervasive cognitive limitations. We all have limited attention spans and are most likely to respond only to those matters that are essentially unavoidable. Moreover, we are unlikely to wrap ourselves up in many details unless they are specifically required by our jobs. We are, in short, apt to be *satisficers* (willing to do what is necessary to make our problem go away, but perhaps not what is necessary for its longer-term resolution).[7] We are, thus, more likely to be tacticians than strategists. We deal with the short run, whose problems are upon us, rather than the long run, whose problems are but dimly seen on the distant horizon. Bill Clinton, it is fair to say, reacted to his situations much as each of these theories would suggest. He, like other politicians, sought to optimize his own political prospects, and he often did so by signing on to options (such as welfare reform) that made immediate political problems disappear even as they stymied longer-term policy goals.

Although the ideas of rational choice and bounded rationality differ from one another—rational choice tells us that situations and institutions offer particular inducements to individuals, while bounded rationality tells us that we are likely to do just what is minimally needed to deal with our problem in the short term—they also have important similarities. Above all, each tells us that presidents will respond similarly when confronted with similar situations and contexts. They will do so in ways that enhance their political prospects and in ways that allow a tactical resolution of pressing problems. Such responses often complement one another.[8] If we have a general theory of incentives and attentiveness, the last thing we need to know is that individuals vary from one another because their variation is of little consequence. These general theories, of course, are quite overdetermined. They do, nevertheless have the virtue of leading us to look at the systemic forces driving the behavior of individual presidents, and in this particular case, that of Bill Clinton.

The study of individual leaders should begin with a recognition of the compelling contextual constraints and opportunities in which a leader plies his or her trade, and with a recognition that most everyone finds dealing with the short term more compelling than contemplating the long term mainly because one is known to us and the other is not. Yet, leaders differ in how they see opportunities and constraints. They differ, too, in their experiences and in the calculations they undertake and, in fact, in whether they undertake calculations at all. It is helpful perhaps to think in terms of counterfactuals. Would someone else have done the job differently faced with the same circumstances? Could someone else have done it differently under the same circumstances? And would doing it differently have made a difference in outcomes? These questions elude definitive answers simply because we cannot replay the same historical moment twice. But while we cannot definitively answer them, they offer insight into the range of possibilities that exist and, possibly, what the paths not taken might have revealed.

In the remainder of this chapter, I summarize various aspects of Bill Clinton's public personality and, more briefly, the periods of his presidency, the choices he consequently faced, and the decisions he made. I close by looking at Clinton's unique contributions of both a positive and negative sort, the environment within which he—and I believe other political leaders of his persuasion—have had to work, other paths he could have chosen, and what, in the more penetrating eye of history, he and his times add up to. Unlike the suspense required of a writer of mystery novels, one need not wait. I have already stated my conclusion. Clinton's legacy, such as it is, lies in politics, not policy. His style is to bob and weave and feint in the face of opponents whose messages have blared with coherence but no subtlety. He cushioned against the hardest Republican blows, deflecting some, but not all, of their shock. The Republicans got some of their way but little of the credit. Clinton's style wasn't pretty, but it was effective for him personally. He beat a path of least resistance. Whether Clinton's approach to finding the "happy medium" presages prospects for a longer-term political shift is harder to say (see chapter 1), but I think there is little to suggest that such a shift is probable. It is unlikely that a Clinton legacy will much outrun Clinton's own political longevity.

The Public Personalities of Bill Clinton: Policy Wonk versus Political Opportunist

Two conflicting images of Bill Clinton's style as a public leader were apparent from the outset. On the one hand, he is a much-touted *policy wonk*, someone whose mind runs to understanding and questioning policy details, to coordinating the impacts of various policies on one another, and to thinking about how what government does or makes possible can improve conditions in society.[9] From this perspective, the inquisitive and lively mind of Bill Clinton was welcomed by his fellow policy wonks within his party and among friendly interests.

The other dimension of Clinton's public personality, however, is his emphasis on finding the political center of gravity. In part this owes to his "New Democrat" credo and, in part, to the legacy of his governorship of a conservative, business-dominated state such as Arkansas, during which he also tried to shape a national image as a progressive, can-do governor. In this aspect of Clinton's public persona, he has been notable for being an adept practitioner of the art of the possible, maybe even of turning chicken waste into chicken salad, or at least selling the former as the latter. Clinton is not one to tilt at windmills. That much is certain. How, then, would these two sides of Clinton—the policy wonk and the astute, median vote–seeking politician be reconciled?

In one sense, of course, building support for policy requires effective politics and, therefore, leaders who are effective at politics. But a purely "splitting the difference" style of politics produces policy incoherence. The American system, even under unified government, is not kind to integrative policy plans. It is bound to dash the hopes of big-policy thinkers. When we add divided government and polarized partisanship to the equation, there is little hope that anybody's preferences will consistently gain the upper hand. (Colin Campbell refers to this in chapter 3 as "the governability gap.") James Madison may have thought that to be a good—and it may well be. But this inability to aggregate a coherent set of preferences also leads to an inability to sustain and integrate an attack on public problems, especially from the more interventionist (left-of-center) side of the political spectrum from which Clinton came.

So while it is entirely possible that political astuteness is the means by which a policy agenda may be greased, it also may be the altar on which it is sacrificed. Much depends upon who is committed to what and the intensity of their commitment. Here contexts and individuals interact. Newt Gingrich and his followers (fickle as they turned out to be) believed after the 1994 election that they had a mandate to follow their vision. Whatever the extent of the mandate, they soon outpaced it, though not before they left a mark. After the debacle concerning his health care initiative, Clinton knew he did not have a mandate and, in the face of the charged-up 104th Congress (elected in 1994), turned himself into a kinder, gentler Republican, signing onto, while softening the impact of, much of the Republican agenda (see chapter 2). Even after reelection, Clinton found ways to expropriate the most popular Republican issues. The Republican congressional majority, for example, hammered the Internal Revenue Service (IRS) as an agency too willing to employ police-state tactics to reach into the citizens' pockets. Since the IRS does not conjure up much sympathy from the nation's taxpayers, congressional Democrats found themselves unable to resist putting the clamps on the IRS as well. After initial opposition, Clinton jumped on board and proposed an overhaul of the IRS, including among other things, an outside board of overseers. Two *New York Times* reporters dazzled by Clinton's footwork noted:

> For a White House that is often defined by its agility at measuring the public mood and responding (or readjusting) accordingly, Mr. Clinton's reversal on the IRS measure was both remarkable and routine.
>
> Brazen as it was, the turnabout was a textbook example of the decision-making process in an administration where even senior officials concede that political considerations often eclipse policy commitments. . . .
>
> Once again, Mr. Clinton frustrated his foes by co-opting an issue that threatened him politically. . . .
>
> But the turnabout was reminiscent of his dramatic changes of course on issues as diverse as gay men and women in the military, grazing fees on federal lands, welfare overhaul, taming the deficit and a campaign to vaccinate children nationwide. . . .
>
> Though a few Clinton advisers groused that the episode demonstrated the triumph of politics over policy in the Clinton White House, most of those interviewed boasted that, once again, they had rescued the president from what could have been a debacle.[10]

In the aftermath of such maneuvering, it is hard to imagine that Clinton came into office with an integrated policy agenda requiring a careful sequencing of initiatives. With a then Democratic majority in both chambers of Congress, Clinton sought to deal with the budget deficit problem in order to make it possible to move on two broader initiatives, only one of which he actually sent forth as a legislative proposal. Clinton's health care plan was designed to alleviate a multiplicity of problems and ultimately to replace current programs (Medicare and Medicaid). The health care plan had three fundamental objectives: (1) to control the then soaring costs of health care; (2) to universalize coverage, thus widening the risk pool; and (3) to eliminate in the process Medicare and Medicaid, expensive programs whose viability was threatened and which, especially Medicare, faced serious adverse risk problems (because it consisted only of the elderly, whose health care expenses are greatest), thus guaranteeing high costs. By universalizing health care and removing it from the workplace, the administration could guarantee an important social protection presently unavailable to welfare families whose (usually female) heads the Clinton administration wanted to move off of the welfare rolls and into the labor market. From Clinton's perspective, welfare reform depended on health care universality and other support measures to move people (typically welfare mothers) into the labor force. Affording these discretionary expenditures would require deficit reduction. The lowered interest rates that presumably would result therefrom, in turn, could lower the deficit. Sequencing budgetary control, health care reform, and welfare reform was critical to Clinton's initial, very ambitious policy agenda.

The bill that eventually passed in 1993 to reduce the deficit not only did so without a single Republican vote in either chamber—a sure sign that trouble lay ahead for Clinton's policy ambitions—but it further constrained his ability to take policy initiatives requiring discretionary expenditures. The price of the package placed even greater pressures on the discretionary side of the budget than were already prevalent from the 1990 deficit reduction legislation that was enacted under Bush with the critical assistance of Democrats in both chambers and over the objections of the majority of Republicans in each chamber. Notably, these pressures on discretionary expenditures arose even before Republicans won control of Congress. They became still greater after the seven-year balanced budget legislation was enacted a few years later in the period of Republican congressional control.

The American system teaches hard lessons to would-be policy planners. The best-laid plans of mice and men (and presidents too) go oft awry, to paraphrase a famous line from the Scottish poet, Robert Burns. Clinton's own agenda lay in ruins—the policy wonk had met his match, defeated by the convoluted constitutional competition produced by Madisonian ideas. Yet, Clinton's ambitions were also ruined by the pressures on the federal budget, the antecedent budget bill of 1990, and the one sent forth from his own administration in 1993. These ambitions were further tattered by powerful partisan divisions, and the Republicans' belief that they had found a winning formula in placing the "big government, big spender, higher taxes" label on the Democrats. The environment was unfriendly to Clinton's ambitious policy plans, no matter how arduous or how desultory his pursuit of them.

After the 1994 election and the two subsequent elections, Clinton had little room for initiatives. His game was now defensive politics (see chapter 2). His mastery of this form of politics, aided of course by exactly the same features that defeated his policy ambitions, has been extraordinary. The American system favors defensive politics and hinders offensive politics, but even so, Clinton clearly mastered his domain. He was the critical veto point for Republicans to overcome, yet he proved time and again to be a moving target—holding off what seemed possible and caving in when that seemed necessary, but usually only after he had achieved a better (or at least less bad) deal.

Once the Republicans took over Congress, Clinton's game plan changed. Essentially, his strategic goals shifted from what he could achieve to what he could block or renegotiate and take credit for. Clinton was thus able to repackage himself as the New Democrat he had earlier claimed to be. It is less certain, though, whether this was a coherent posture or merely the median point between the initial preferences of the Republican congressional majority and those of the Democratic congressional minority. (On this point, see chapter 9.) Poised between the two party medians, Clinton could play a role that fit his sunny-sided political personality, namely to be the great political conciliator, reconciling Republican policy aspirations with the fears that these aspirations evoked among Democrats. He managed to pick off the most popular symbols of each party—the Democrats' identification with popular middle-class entitlement programs such as Social Security and Medicare, and the Republicans' identification with budget balancing, welfare reform, and tough-on-crime postures. Amid the party divisions on Capitol Hill, Clinton often appeared above the fray, urging reasonableness onto the contestants. This posture irritated his own party activists, whose dislike of the Republican congressional agenda was great, and frustrated the Republican activists, who were convinced that Clinton was nothing but a sheer opportunist, an immoral one at that, and, even worse, a successful one. It did help him, however, with the public at large, which contrasted him with the growling politics of the much aforementioned Newt Gingrich. And it certainly did not hurt him with key segments of the non–Washington based financial elite, who were happily watching the value of their securities rise to unprecedented levels.

In the face of much unreason, Clinton projected reasonableness, moderation, and, as he had in Arkansas, a knack for getting things done and for contributing to a favorable business climate. The role of Robert Rubin, initially the director of the National Economic Council and then secretary of the treasury in the Clinton administration, also loomed large. Rubin's knowledge of the Wall Street community, his good relations with Alan Greenspan, and, above all, his willingness to defend the positions of the financial community aided Clinton's relations with that community and perhaps contributed to the positive conditions of economic growth and stability.

In such a favorable economic climate, the demand for policy was not high. The strange combination of prosperity and partisan deadlock reduced demand for big initiatives. Policy would be focused on maintenance problems—for example, ensuring the viability of Social Security and Medicare in some form or other—and on numerous small and parceled initiatives, which Clinton liked to offer to show that his administration cared and was active, and which could be used to pay off some constituency, symbolically or otherwise.

Why did Clinton stir such deep animosity among his opponents in such a seemingly tranquil setting of peace and prosperity, especially after having bought big chunks of the opposition agenda? That is a puzzle. But there may be some answers in explicitly political factors. First, there is the increasing identification of the parties along the cultural war divide, and the intensity of convictions that cleave along this divide. Despite caving in to homophobia—signing the Defense of Marriage Act, for example—Clinton unstintingly supported the right to an abortion. His Hollywood constituency and his support from other groups on the Christian right's list of moral degenerates, not to mention his own frequently straying behavior, made him less than upright among the morally uptight. Second, there were Republican frustrations that Clinton, like the Grinch (not to be confused with the Gingrich), stole their Christmas. Why was Clinton getting the credit for what, after all, were mainly Republican initiatives? This frustration was perfectly summed up by the 1996 Republican presidential nominee, Bob Dole, who, having noted all of the Republican initiatives that Clinton had adopted as his own, wondered aloud and poignantly during his acceptance speech at the Republican national convention why Clinton himself was not there in San Diego at the GOP convention. Dole's joke was both funny and bitter; it reflected how tactically outfoxed the Republicans had been by the wily politician in the White House, despite actual Republican policy successes. Among Republicans, Clinton seemed to have stolen Reagan's formula—be upbeat and resilient, imperturbable and beyond sanction.

But for Democrats, the similarity with Reagan did not end there. One columnist noted acerbically that Republicans had a stronger stake in Clinton's presidency than did his own party since, in his view, Clinton had "done more for the GOP than Ronald Reagan." He noted as well that "it drives Republicans nuts that Mr. Clinton has claimed credit for GOP initiatives to reform welfare and balance the budget. But Mr. Clinton signed these bills, which a Democrat with stronger allegiances to his party's principles might have vetoed."[11] Clinton's claim to fame, in other words, is that his political tactics managed to antagonize the activists in *both* parties. Beyond these political and policy considerations, however, there were other elements to Clinton's public personality that seemed to create a near apoplectic state among many Republicans and even some of his own partisans. In the end, of course, his own partisans came to Clinton's rescue, much more because of their distaste for their Republican opponents than for any love between them and their amiably malleable and not terribly trustworthy president.

"Slick Willie"

A politician, like any of us, has a public side and a personal side, and the two do not always coincide. Nixon's public face was sanctimony; his private one vulgarity and prejudice. Eisenhower's reassuring smiles and avuncular presence in public contrasted with his legendary temper in private. Kennedy's Camelot turned out to feature a massively roving and indiscreet libido on the part of its principal. And so it goes. Clinton came into office suspected of numerous moral flaws, including a penchant for half-truths or untruths, possibly shady business deals, and an extraordinary sexual appetite. The sobriquet "Slick Willie" for Clinton was to the Republicans what "Tricky Dickie" for Nixon was to the Democrats—an expression of their confidence that the individual in question, regardless of any number of rebirths or apologies was, at bottom, an incorrigible cad.

The contemporary political environment does not draw a distinction between public and private life, although the public seems to have little difficulty in doing so.[12] The media are diverse and the bottom dwellers among them produce even undigested rumor instantaneously. Laws abound to ensnarl public officials over minor misdeeds and sometimes only the appearance of misdeeds. Opposition politicians are now the ones more often than not in control of congressional resources, and they stand ready sharpening their knives, cheered on, even impelled, by their party activists, regardless of which party is doing the head hunting and which is having its head hunted. Independent counsels have been frequently invested with limitless horizons and budgets to investigate any possible misdeeds of an individual rather than a specific allegation. It's a tough environment in which to survive, and an especially tough environment if there is much to reveal. Like most presidents, indeed like most politicians, in fact like most people, Bill Clinton is not above reproach if the threshold of reproach is set sufficiently low. Whatever his intelligence and perhaps desire to do public good and whatever his political acumen, Clinton's personal and perhaps even public life is scarred. His character is deeply flawed. He is, in fact, the much advertised Slick Willie.

All politicians stonewall and tell half-truths and sometimes complete lies. They do so not because politicians are an inferior breed of human being but because they are constantly in the public spotlight being asked questions (some of which are no one's business) to which truthful answers might be infelicitous or option-limiting. Franklin Roosevelt justified the lend-lease program as a way of avoiding sending American soldiers to the war in Europe. Lyndon Johnson said that American boys would not get sent to Vietnam. Richard Nixon claimed to have a secret plan to get out of Vietnam. (Strictly speaking, that may not have been a lie since no one could possibly know what it was.) Ronald Reagan, the only president for whom plausible deniability was a given, claimed to know nothing of Iran-*contra,* as did George Bush (when he was vice-president), despite evidence to the contrary. All of these presidents wanted to remain politically viable. Taking unpopular positions consistently and confessing that one broke the law for a higher purpose are generally not well-beaten paths to political survival. It is self-righteous in the extreme to expect that any of us operating under the same conditions would behave much differently.

It is also inevitable that politicians will be compared over time and under different circumstances to justify present behavior. In Clinton's case, the obvious comparison is with John F. Kennedy, since both men appear to have led lives of reckless sexual abandon. Kennedy's behavior was well-known in Washington circles, but it stayed there. There was no Internet then, no cable television, not even much talk (or shlock) radio. There were no sexual harassment laws or court rulings based on them, essentially requiring disclosure of an accused's past sexual behavior. And there were no independent prosecutors trying to push legal envelopes and rope in presidents, perhaps even to put a rope around them. This does not make the past better than the present, but it does make different the context, for now a president's private behaviors are apt to become publicly known and perhaps regarded as a fit subject for ridicule—or much worse. The Washington establishment forgave the sins of its members because its norms included reciprocity. J. Edgar Hoover, the FBI director in Kennedy's day, knew about Kennedy's liaisons with a Mafia leader's girlfriend and other questionable assignations, but Kennedy also knew about Hoover's peculiar sexual behavior as well, so reciprocity ruled. Kennedy's behavior may well have been reckless, but the context over which he presided was forgiving.

Clinton's behavior was obviously reckless, perhaps worse, but the context in which he presided was profoundly unforgiving, despite the fact that the general public did not seem much moved by Clinton's dalliances, or even his possible perjury,[13] and certainly did not think any of these actions warranted removal from office. Clinton's affair with Monica Lewinsky—given Clinton's testimony, one is hard put to know precisely what to call it—was essentially conducted in full public view, knowing that he was under investigation by Ken Starr's rabid team of prosecutors. Although we cannot be sure that Clinton committed perjury or conspired to obstruct justice, it was clear that he openly and publicly lied to the nation and to his associates. The reckless personal style contrasted ever so sharply with Clinton's own cautious political behavior, and with his unwillingness to take risks on behalf of either an appointee or a policy.

The reason for much of the religious right's contempt for Clinton was that he represented what the moralizers believed was a consummate blend of immoral politics and immoral character. What made it worse for them was that Clinton could manage to wiggle his way out of every crisis he faced. The moralizers on the right wondered why it was that Clinton could keep getting away with his deceptions, from his relationship with Gennifer Flowers to "I didn't inhale" to Paula Jones and all the way through the impeachment episode. In a moment of epiphany, however, the moralizers realized that the Clinton problem was really located in the American public. Paul Weyrich, one of the mainstay operatives of the right, concluded that the moral forces were out of step with the country as a whole and that the collapse of the impeachment effort resulted from the hostility, or at least apathy, of the public. Weyrich was quoted as saying that "we have to look at what we can do to separate ourselves from this hostile culture."[14] Other heroes of the right, noted for their sermonizing, also saw the Clinton acquittal as part of a degeneration of morality in the larger society. William Bennett, a former Reagan and Bush official, claimed "that ordinary Americans reacting to Mr. Clinton's conduct 'are complicit in his corruption,'" while Senator Robert Smith, a right-wing Republican from New Hampshire, declared that "the president's acquittal is a sad commentary on the prevailing values in America today."[15]

Clearly Clinton benefited from the fact that most of the public was now more like the old Washington establishment than the present one. Now it is Washington that moralizes while the public draws distinctions between public performance and personal life. Looking for an appropriate solution to the impeachment muddle, the public supported censure overwhelmingly, but the congressional Republicans refused to bite. The censure option generally ran at a 3:2 ratio with typically less than 5 percent "no opinion."[16] It is especially likely that the Republican members were responding to incentives within their party's electorate and its distribution of opinion rather than to the distribution of opinion in the public at large. Whatever the case, Clinton's opponents again overreached themselves in a political sense, reflecting a pattern of remarkable consistency since the government shutdowns of 1995 and 1996. Clinton was the beneficiary of the Republicans at the national level having turned themselves into the Democrats of a generation before, namely a party smug in the righteousness of its cause no matter how unhinged it became from majority sentiment. Clinton was a fortunate man to have the enemies he had.

Clinton's bubbly (perhaps even bubba-like) personality—in contrast to Richard Nixon's tormented and paranoid persona—helped him weather more crises than even Nixon had. But Clinton's effervescence hid a very hardball approach to politics. His ambition was to help level the disparity in campaign financing available to the parties, where the Republicans traditionally held a massive advantage over the Democrats. Clinton's aim was to campaign continuously to raise money and, as matters turned out, to auction off pieces of the White House on a temporary basis (allowing big donors to stay overnight in one of the White House bedrooms). Clinton especially cultivated Asian donors reputedly linked to the Chinese government, with few questions asked, convinced that where the money came from was less important than that it was there. His style of aggressive campaigning (getting messages out early and responding immediately) cost a lot of money, as did the continuous polling, originated initially by the Reagan campaign organization. Getting the money was vital. How it was attracted seemed less important to Clinton or to the finance people in the Democratic Party.

It did disconcert some Democrats who believed their party was being corrupted by such promiscuous fundraising, however, and, even more, it angered Republicans who believed that Clinton, once again, was getting away with something and beating the Republicans at what they did best, namely raising lots of money. To be sure, the Democrats still raised less than did the Republicans, but Clinton helped to narrow the gap. This produced a purist distaste for Clinton from within the Democratic Party and among journalists, who took him to be unprincipled and at least marginally corrupt. And Clinton's success on the money trail added further fuel to Republicans' distrust of him on virtually every score, from low character to his remarkable political adaptability and success to his virtually endless, and possibly corrupt, campaign. To many Republicans, Clinton appeared to be a slick version, with hair and without principles, of the rambunctious James Carville, his "good old boy" political adviser of the "take no prisoners" style.

Indeed, in the end, the Republicans' quest to impeach Clinton was predicated on the issue of his character as much as any factor, since the one matter that was undeniably not in dispute was Clinton's character defects. The statement delivered on behalf of the House Judiciary Committee majority by the committee's counsel, David P. Schippers, is quite revealing in this regard. Schipper's attack focused heavily on Clinton's character. Leaping upon Clinton's now infamous conditional about the meaning of the word "is" in his grand jury testimony, Schippers claimed

> that single declaration . . . reveals more about the character of the President than perhaps anything else in the record. . . . He also invents convoluted definitions of words or phrases in his own crafty mind. Of course he will never seek to clarify a question because that may trap him into a straight answer. Can you imagine dealing with such a person in any important matter?[17]

Whatever the validity of Schippers's case, among his political opponents, Clinton was clearly perceived to be as trustworthy as Richard Nixon and as buoyantly impermeable as Ronald Reagan had been perceived to be by Democrats—a low life with a high bounce.

The relevant question for the future is the impact of Clinton's character on his legacy. As the years go on and memory grows dim, the word "impeached" is likely to be the sound bite that will define the Clinton presidency, at least for the lay public. Does character matter is a big question. In a politics of reciprocities conducted in semiprivate among people who must repeatedly deal with one another, trust is an important ingredient for achieving political accommodation. But where politics is conducted by *spinmeisters* in an era of mass media, openness, and intense partisanship, character might actually get in the way. A remarkable facet of Bill Clinton's presidency is how well he fit the times in which he presided. He never let loyalty, principle, or sentiment get in his way (even as he exuded the latter quality for political profit). He has been the president of a rational choice theorist's dreams. And from that perspective, he has been a remarkably successful one. Yet, at the same time, Clinton was inherently an accommodating politician, who seemed to be concerned more about having a record than about its content—a clear indication that Clinton the politician has decisively triumphed over Clinton the policy wonk.

Governing with a Weak Hand

A few presidents have had significant resources to govern, at least for brief periods of time. Too often, these rare instances, along with crisis conditions, serve as our models of the conditions for presidential leadership. Franklin Roosevelt's first 100 days still resonate as a benchmark. But such circumstances are extremely unusual. More often than not, presidents, as Richard Neustadt told us they would, have to persuade, cajole, and bargain with others who have independent authority.[18] Under normal conditions, presidents are a part of the system, not the whole of it.

There is little doubt that, with the exception of rare moments of conclusive electoral results favoring their preferred directions, activist presidencies have even more formidable obstacles to overcome. Divided government is a big part of the story. Polarization across the parties, under conditions of divided government, makes life especially difficult for a president with an urge to do things. In addition, the uses of the filibuster and other delaying tactics in the Senate have risen meteorically in the past three decades.[19] When all of these conditions are put together, presidents are unlikely to get much of what they want from Congress if what they want is politically controversial, and especially if the controversy divides along party lines.[20]

Bill Clinton's saga is a familiar one by this point. He came to office in 1993 with big plans but with only 43 percent of the vote and a reduced Democratic majority in Congress. While he did get a budget bill passed that both raised taxes and decreased discretionary spending, he got it without a single Republican vote, and just barely. His marquee legislative package was the health care reform bill, which never even made it to the floor of the Senate. In his first two years in office, Clinton was more often below 50-percent approval than above it, and his party took electoral hits regularly until losing control of both chambers of Congress for the first time in forty-two years in the great Democratic debacle and Republican triumph of 1994.

After that, any effort to succeed on his own terms was hopeless. The Republican Congress, especially in the House under Newt Gingrich's leadership, hit the ground running and essentially controlled the agenda for at least a few years. As others have pointed out in this volume, once Clinton shifted to defense he became more successful and flourished politically. Tactically, the triangulation strategy devised by his political guru, Dick Morris, proved to be brilliant. This strategy helped put some distance between Clinton and his own party while it also allowed him to bask in the glow of popular position-taking. Moreover, indeed most especially, the triangulation strategy made the Republicans look petulant when they took umbrage with Clinton for stealing their best applause lines. So long as Clinton no longer had to commit great resources to enact an ambitious agenda, he was free to counterpunch, to look reasonable, and to make the Republicans look grumpy.

From the standpoint of traditional Democratic Party activists, the Clinton presidency now had more of a deterrent than an offensive capability. Expectations were accordingly lowered, and Clinton seemed to have massively benefited from that. This was not a time for big new programs, as leaders politically similar to Clinton have discovered in Canada, the United Kingdom and, most recently, Germany. Incremental adjustments might be possible, especially if they take the form of popular stances on issues of concern to many people, such as the "patients' bill of rights." Big new spending programs are out for the time being, and so too are traditional large unfunded mandates.[21] Boutique-size responses to public problems seem less complicated and more direct, and Clinton has shined at playing this game. New Deal issue alignments might still present the central lines of political cleavage (see chapter 1), but New Deal–size solutions are not likely these days. In this respect, Clinton appears to have discovered his New Democrat identity less as a coherent philosophy of governing than as a tenuous compromise based on what is presently doable and politically acceptable. The political center that Clinton discovered after 1994 was more a space than a philosophy.

The growth era of government has ended. Global markets and the need for competitiveness have in part seen to that. So too have the pressures imposed on budgets by entitlement programs with mandated expenditures. In the case of the United States, budget deals reached in 1990 and 1993 especially constrained discretionary expenditures, thus reducing the degrees of freedom with which to maneuver. *The bottom line in government increasingly has become the bottom line.* While that may be anathema to liberal Democrats, there is little reason for them to believe that they will soon be in a position to relive the glory days of the New Deal or the Great Society. Looked at through the traditional lenses of leadership typically preferred by liberal Democrats, Clinton cut a modest and opportunistic figure. The principal reason why is that he had few resources with which to govern, at least as liberals would have liked him to govern. Could he have done it differently? What, realistically, were the prospects of success if he had?

The Politics of Survival: Doing Better vs. Doing Well

Clinton's presidency remains to be completed. Clinton's judgment (to be generous) or his luck (to be less charitable) has held in the Balkans for now. The record of his presidency, however, is yet to be finalized, and we cannot be completely confident in what it leaves as its legacy. But we know much of the story to this point. The first and overwhelming theme of the story is context. That is so with all presidents, not just Clinton. Very rarely in the American context do presidents get a lot of resources to govern. In the past few decades, the problem of attaining sufficient presidential resources to govern has been especially difficult. The constraint on presidential power is especially troubling for Democratic presidents because they typically are being pushed by their party and its constituent members among the American chattering classes (intellectuals, academicians, and journalists) to do public good through public policy and programs. Expectations from the chattering classes are high mainly because they are themselves partial to the idea of using public policy to solve the nation's problems and ease its ills. While few from among this group were cheering Reagan on to fulfill his promises, their talk about unfulfilled promises haunts Clinton's presidency.

Given the politically inhospitable context in which the Clinton presidency was situated through most of its tenure in office, what could a president do? One could, as Clinton did, cut *with* the grain and try to appeal to the median voter, thereby increasing his prospects for political survival while, thus, decreasing his prospects (other than being impeached) for creating a significant legacy. Within a highly restrictive context, Clinton navigated his way with extraordinary adeptness and demonstrated remarkable political talent for making the best (aside from the Monica Lewinsky affair) of a bad situation. Certainly, two keys to Clinton's success were a booming economy and political opponents with a penchant for overreaching and even frightening elements of the population dependent upon middle-class entitlements as well as those who are socially liberal (even if economically conservative). His opponents helped make Clinton look good. He was clearly opportunistic, but what else could he have been? Furthermore, was the minimalist Clinton still a better deal for his followers than the Republican alternative?

What, however, if Clinton had cut *against* the grain? Is this a plausible model to contemplate? Imagine Clinton as a more steadfast leader—or, at least, if that is implausible, imagine someone else in Clinton's situation. It may be that such a leader would have caved less but also have been less likely to put the opposition into a tactical box. It also may be that such a leader might have articulated a defense for the "big government" that produced Social Security, Medicare, environmental protection, food and drug regulation, occupational safety, and so forth—public goods with broad appeal. Such a leader might also have sought to "keep hope alive" for national health insurance and for welfare reform connected to greater social protection as well as labor force entry. This sort of leader would have been unlikely to concur that "the era of big government is over" or to let national health insurance stay unremembered and, above all, unlamented. Such a leader would undoubtedly have projected a more aggressive partisan manner (perhaps much like that of Ronald Reagan) than the outwardly conciliatory style that Bill Clinton adopted. Aggressive leadership is less nuanced and more linear than the dazzling footwork that Clinton displayed in order to stay alive. It emphasizes persistence, principle, and rhetoric while looking for a favorable outcome farther into the future. But in the long term we're all dead, and Clinton, like most politicians, decided it was more important to keep himself alive than "hope." To be more generous, he also may have concluded that whatever he had to accede to, it would all be worse if he weren't there to blunt some of it. To cynics, this sounds a lot like rationalization. To pragmatists, it is important to distinguish between doing better and doing well.

History does not allow us to roll the dice again in order to contrast the two strategies. One could be properly skeptical, however, that under the prevailing circumstances much in the way of policy aspiration could be kept alive if the principal himself couldn't be kept politically alive. This justification, of course, is a familiar one for politicians with modest inner compass, easy principles, and temptations aplenty simply to survive. Clinton did, as Colin Campbell observes in chapter 3, choose the lectern rather than the bully pulpit.

Did he have a choice? Of course he did. Clinton could have chosen the path of greatest rather than least resistance. He might have fought harder, longer, and with more conviction to gain support for his party's ideas and to look at compromises as tactics for the larger strategy. That would have been heroic but probably also Quixotic. Clinton does not, to repeat, much like to tilt at windmills. What Clinton did is what most social scientific theory tells us a leader would do in similar circumstances. He tried to survive politically and do what seemed workable, especially for him. Health insurance was not about to be revisited *in toto*, but various parts, such as portability, would be revived when politicians of all stripes found it useful to claim they were solving a problem, however dubious the claim. Social science would tell us that Clinton acted in accordance with its norms. These may not be pretty, but at least they are predictable.

In the end, Clinton has been a brilliant political tactician but one without a strategy. Richard Neustadt's classic, *Presidential Power*, told us that without a strategy, presidents are likely to lose their way and to fail. But that assertion assumes that presidents know what they want and, above all, that what they want is something fundamentally deeper than political survival. That may be a hard claim to press in Clinton's case. At the very least, Clinton's counterpunching tactics reflect a philosophy of taking what is given. This may not be strategic in the grand sense, but the grand sense implies that a president has the tools to put a sweeping agenda or some substantial part of it into effect or, barring that, to discount the present for future possibilities (which may never arrive).

By definition, leadership cuts *against* the grain. It seeks to maneuver around the prevailing constraints. The way in which such leadership is exercised, however, carries with it controversy. Leadership may be linear, its goals reducible to a few good slogans. This form conjures up the bully pulpit. But leadership also may be nonlinear; Machiavelli suggested as much. And it may be focused more on preventing than on proposing. It may look opportunistic and even self-serving. It may also require redefining one's own appeals. Commentators on the presidency are obviously not likely to think that preventing the worst is better than optimal achievement. No one is likely to construct monuments around what did not happen. Clinton may have assimilated pieces of the Republican agenda, but he also required the Republicans to come to terms with him. The costs and benefits of that bargain remain open to debate, and how one calculates the cost-benefit ratio is apt to depend on how distant in either direction from the center one happens to be.

Clinton's like-minded colleagues of the left-center have come to power in governments where they had been shut out for a significant interval. Tony Blair in the United Kingdom and Gerhard Schröder in Germany, especially, have worked to redefine their parties closer to the political center, as Clinton has done in the United States with his party. The great mass of the electorate in advanced democracies is middle-class and is anxious neither to pay more nor to lose what it has. But there are large financial constraints to expanding or even sustaining at their present levels income-transfer programs. Globalized markets mean that politicians have to tread warily, lest they lose credibility in those markets. These conditions place special constraints on the parties of the left-center and have motivated them to develop a new look. Much of the new look is centered around developing a sustainable political coalition, which largely excludes appeals to the nonvoting "have-nots" in society and other unpopular or marginalized groups or causes.

Clinton did not instigate conservative policies, although he found their language to be politically appealing on, for example, welfare reform, the death penalty, and so on. When these policies seemed compelling or, perhaps more to the point, inevitable, Clinton chose them because his past words limited his present political options. Like Eisenhower, Clinton may be known for having put a tepid but confirmatory seal of approval on popular policies of the other party. Partly by doing so, he has positioned the Democrats to be viable presidential contenders. But the costs to the faithful are high. And these costs are most likely to be debated when the New Democrats go down to eventual defeat. In the meantime, we are left to consider whether Clinton, his other flaws aside, has been an unprincipled opportunist quick to shed ideas, commitments, and associates when they become inconvenient, or a pragmatic idealist who played a bad hand skillfully.

Notes

Introduction

1. *The Clinton Presidency: First Appraisals,* ed. Colin Campbell and Bert A. Rockman (Chatham, N.J.: Chatham House, 1995), 13–14.

2. Richard Rose notes that "presidential scholars do not divide politically like most Americans." They are more than twice as likely as ordinary voters to hold liberal opinions and much less likely to hold conservative views. In view of these facts, we note that it is generally the case that such scholars are keen to advise Republican presidents to accommodate to the Democrats' congressional majorities but are less keen on advising Democratic presidents to accommodate to the Republicans' congressional majorities (an admittedly more novel circumstance). Given the scholars' Democratic party preferences, compromise is good for Republicans but less so for Democrats. See Richard Rose, "Evaluating Presidents," in *Researching The Presidency: Vital Questions, New Approaches*, ed. George C. Edwards III, John H. Kessel, and Bert A. Rockman (Pittsburgh: University of Pittsburgh Press, 1993), 453–84.

3. Samuel Kernell notes that "just maybe survey respondents discriminate between the president as a public and private person, and they always have." See his "The Challenge Ahead for Explaining President Clinton's Public Support," *PRG Report* (Newsletter of the Presidency Research Group of the American Political Science Association) 21 (Spring 1999): 1–3.

Chapter 1: The Partisan Legacy

Two events shaped this essay, out of all proportion to any others. The need to think systematically about the New Democrats sprang from my association with the Oxford D.Phil. thesis by Kenneth A. Baer, "Reinventing Democrats: The Democratic Leadership Council and the Attempt to Change the Public Philosophy of the Democratic Party, 1981–1996"— soon to be a major book. And the opportunity to develop the entire argument came with a public lecture series at Oxford, entitled "The Two Majorities and the Puzzle of Modern American Politics," conducted with Edward G. Carmines and hugely facilitated by him.

Charles O. Jones then read the resulting draft with a reliably critical eye, catching many lesser errors and absolving himself of the larger ones. Having a cast of diverse and able colleagues like these is one of life's real pleasures.

1. The relevant literature is immense, but reasonably consensual on the policy highpoints. For social welfare in the earlier New Deal years, see William E. Leuchtenberg, *Franklin D. Roosevelt and the New Deal, 1932–1940* (New York: Harper & Row, 1963). For foreign affairs in this period, see James MacGregor Burns, *Roosevelt: The Soldier of Freedom, 1940–1945* (New York: Harcourt Brace Jovanovich, 1973). Social welfare in the later New Deal years is thoroughly covered in James L. Sundquist, *Politics and Policy: The Eisenhower, Kennedy, and Johnson Years* (Washington, D.C.: Brookings Institution, 1968). Foreign affairs is covered in Seyom Brown, *Faces of Power: Constancy and Change in U.S. Foreign Policy from Truman to Johnson* (New York: Columbia University Press, 1968).

2. For the forming of these two great social coalitions, see James L. Sundquist, *Dynamics of the Party System: Alignment and Realignment of Political Parties in the United States* (Washington, D.C.: Brookings Institution, 1973), esp. chaps. 10–12; and Everett C. Ladd Jr., with Charles D. Hadley, *Transformations of the American Party System* (New York: Norton, 1975), esp. Part I. See also Byron E. Shafer, "Partisan Elites, 1946–1996," in *Partisan Approaches to Postwar American Politics*, ed. Byron Shafer (Chatham, N.J.: Chatham House, 1998).

3. The "ownership" of these issues is documented initially in Angus Campbell, Philip E. Converse, Warren E. Miller, and Donald E. Stokes, *The American Voter* (New York: John Wiley, 1960), esp. chap. 5. On the electoral model developed to embody party competition in these years, see Angus Campbell, "Surge and Decline: A Study of Electoral Change," *Public Opinion Quarterly* 24 (1960): 397–418.

4. A great prologue to the breakup of the old order is Gareth Davies, *From Opportunity to Entitlement: The Transformation and Decline of Great Society Liberalism* (Lawrence: University Press of Kansas, 1996). For its valuational conflicts in particular, see Richard M. Scammon and Ben J. Wattenberg, *The Real Majority* (New York: Coward-McCann, 1970).

5. A contemporary overview of this general relationship is Byron E. Shafer and William J.M. Claggett, *The Two Majorities: The Issue Context of Modern American Politics* (Baltimore: Johns Hopkins University Press, 1995). A classic statement of the underlying possibilities for such a division is Seymour Martin Lipset and Stein Rokkan, "Cleavage Structures, Party Systems, and Voter Alignments: An Introduction," in *Party Systems and Voter Alignments: Cross-National Perspectives*, ed. Lipset and Rokkan (New York: Free Press, 1967).

6. The best single statement of this is Alan J. Ware, *The Breakdown of Democratic Party Organization, 1940–1980* (Oxford: Oxford University Press, 1985). The larger context is David R. Mayhew, *Placing Parties in American Politics* (Princeton: Princeton University Press, 1986).

7. By far the most comprehensive study of the New Democrats, and especially of the Democratic Leadership Council, is Kenneth Baer, "Reinventing Democrats: The Democratic Leadership Council and the Attempt to Change the Public Philosophy of the Democratic Party, 1981–1996," (D. Phil. thesis, Oxford University, 1998). See also Jon F. Hale, "The Making of the New Democrats," *Political Science Quarterly* 110 (Summer 1995): 207–32.

8. William Galston and Elaine Ciulla Kamarck, "The Politics of Evasion: Democrats and the Presidency" (Washington, D.C.: Progressive Policy Institute, 1989).

9. Democratic Leadership Council, "The New American Choice: Opportunity, Responsibility, Community," Washington, D.C., 1991.

10. Paul R. Abramson, John H. Aldrich, and David W. Rohde, *Change and Continuity in the 1992 Elections* (Washington, D.C.: CQ Press, 1994); *The Election of 1992*, ed. Gerald M. Pomper (Chatham, N.J.: Chatham House, 1993); *The Elections of 1992*, ed. Michael Nelson (Washington, D.C.: CQ Press, 1993).

11. David Butler, "The United States Election of 1992," *Electoral Studies* 12 (June 1993): 185–87. For the division by place of residence, compare *The Election of 1988*, ed. Gerald M. Pomper (Chatham, N.J.: Chatham House, 1989), table 5.2, p. 134, with Pomper, *Election of 1992*, table 5.2, p. 139. For the division by class among whites, compare Paul R. Abramson, John H. Aldrich, and David W. Rohde, *Change and Continuity in the 1988 Elections* (Washington, D.C.: CQ Press, 1990), table 5.1, p. 124, with Abramson et al., *Change and Continuity in the 1992 Elections*, table 5.1, p. 133. And for the division by self-described ideology, compare *The Elections of 1988*, ed. Michael Nelson (Washington, D.C.: CQ Press, 1989), table 3.2, p. 82, with Nelson, *Elections of 1992*, table 3.2, p. 78.

12. Pat Towell, "Campaign Promise, Social Debate Collide on Military Battlefield," *Congressional Quarterly Weekly Report* (*CQWR*), 30 January 1993, 226–29; Towell, "Nunn Offers a Compromise: 'Don't Ask, Don't Tell,'" *CQWR*, 15 May 1993, 1240–42.

13. See Mike Mills, "Road Work Ahead?" *CQWR*, 19 December 1992, 3884–89; Special Report, "Clinton's Bold Gamble," *CQWR*, 20 February 1993, 355–86; Special Report, "The Clinton Budget: White House Faces Reconciling Its Goals with What Congress Is Willing to Give," *CQWR*, 10 April 1993, 885–904; Special Report, "The Angst of Victory," *CQWR*, 7 August 1993, 2122–42.

14. See David S. Cloud, "The NAFTA Fix: Squeezed by Democrats and Other Allies, Clinton Inherits Mexican Trade Deal," *CQWR*, 28 November 1992, 3710–13; Special Report, "NAFTA Crucible: Undecided Members Weigh Voter Fears as Trade Pact Showdown Approaches," *CQWR*, 6 November 1993, 3011–33; and Cloud, "Free Trade Ethos: Clinton Forges New Coalition to Expand Nation's Commitment to Open Markets," *CQWR*, 20 November 1993, 3174–85.

15. The authoritative text, with a list of signatories and a forceful afterword from the man who became the Speaker-elect, is *Contract with America*, ed. Ed Gillespie and Bob Schellas (New York: Times Books, 1994). See also Haley Barbour, *Agenda for America: A Republican Direction for the Future* (Washington, D.C.: Regnery, 1996).

16. For health care, see Alissa J. Rubin, "Uncertainty, Deep Divisions Cloud Opening of Debate," and David S. Cloud and Beth Donovan, "House Delays Health Care Debate as Leaders Plot Strategy," *CQWR*, 13 August 1994, 2344–53; and Rubin, "Health Care Post-Mortem: Divided Democrats, United GOP Killed Overhaul Effort," *CQWR*, 1 October 1994, 2797–801. For crime, see Holy Idelson, "Clinton, Democrats Scramble to Save Anti-Crime Bill," *CQWR*, 13 August 1994, 2340–43; and David Masci, "$30 Billion Anti-Crime Bill Heads to Clinton's Desk," *CQWR*, 27 August 1994, 2488–93. But see especially Idelson, "An Era Comes to a Close," *CQWR*, 23 December 1995, 3871–73.

17. Byron E. Shafer, "The Mid-Term Election of 1994: Upheaval in Search of a Framework," in *The Republican Takeover of Congress*, ed. Dean McSweeney and John E. Owens (New York: St. Martin's, 1998). See also Tim Hames, "The U.S. Mid-term Election of 1994," *Electoral Studies* 14 (June 1995): 222–26.

18. For the initial translation of the Contract into legislation, see "House GOP Offers Descriptions of Bills to Enact 'Contract,'" *CQWR*, 9 November 1994, 3366–79. On their record for the self-imposed "100 Days," see Donna Cassata, "Republicans Bask in Success of Rousing Performance," *CQWR*, 8 April 1995, 986–1005. The complaint from the president came in response to a question at a press conference on 18 April 1995, as quoted in James W. Ceaser and Andrew E. Busch, *Losing to Win: The 1996 Elections and American Politics* (Lanham, Md.: Rowman & Littlefield, 1997), 42.

19. For these presidential preference polls, before and after the two governmental shutdowns, see Byron E. Shafer, "The American Elections of 1996," *Electoral Studies* 16 (September 1997): 395–396, figs. 1–2.

20. For the run-up to this event, see Jeffrey L. Katz, "Clinton's Quandary: All Eyes Turn to White House as GOP Prepares to Clear Big Welfare Plan," *CQWR*, 27 July 1996, 2115–19; for the signature itself, see Katz, "After 60 Years, Most Control is Passing to the States," *CQWR*, 3 August 1996, 2190–96.

21. Paul R. Abramson, John J. Aldrich, and David W. Rohde, *Change and Continuity in the 1996 Elections* (Washington, D.C.: CQ Press, 1998); *The Election of 1996*, ed. Gerald M. Pomper (Chatham, N.J.: Chatham House, 1997); The *Elections of 1996*, ed. Michael Nelson (Washington, D.C.: CQ Press, 1997); Ceaser and Busch, *Losing To Win*.

22. For reasonably typical reportage in the immediate aftermath, see CNN, "Democrats Enjoy a Big Night After a Hard-to-Read Election," www.cnn.com/ALLPOLITICS/stories/1998/11/03/election/overview. A comprehensive summary and analysis is Special Report, "Election 1998," *National Journal (NJ)*, 7 November 1998. For the composition of the Democratic vote, so central to analyses of the outcome as a "surprise," see especially Alan Greenblatt, "Re-Energized 'New Deal' Coalition Boosts Democrats for 2000," *CQWR*, 7 November 1998, 2983.

23. Labelling of the "six-year itch" is often credited to Kevin Phillips, though he very explicitly turned to other analytic yardsticks for interpretations in advance of the 1998 elections. See *American Political Report*, 16 October 1998. The notion of "surge and decline" is rooted in Campbell, "Surge and Decline."

24. For continuation of this underlying pattern through 1998, see esp. Thomas B. Edsall, "GOP's Own Successes Weaken Its Draw, Strategists Say," *Washington Post*, 25 November 1998, A4. See also Carl M. Cannon, "What Hath Bill Wrought?" *NJ*, 7 November 1998, 2621–22.

25. An upbeat interpretation of the prospects for New Democrats in the long run, from William Galston, coauthor of "The Politics of Evasion," is in Ben Wildavsky, "Monica and the New Democrats," *NJ*, 26 September 1998, 2334. For indications that the Clintons were worried that Vice-President Gore would undertake a deliberate attempt to blur distinctions between New and Old Democrats, see Joe Klein, "Learning to Run," *New Yorker*, 8 December 1997, 53–59. For indications that the Clintons were undertaking such an effort themselves, see Richard L. Berke, "Clintons Seek to Repair Rift for Democrats," *New York Times*, 19 July 1998, 1, 15.

26. For the immediate response among Republicans to the 1998 outcome, see Charles Pope, "Hollow 'Victory': A Chronology of Rebellion," *CQWR*, 14 November 1998, 3062–63. For a detailed analysis of the subsequent requirements for continuing a Republican Revolution, see Richard E. Cohen, "After the Riot," *NJ*, 14 November 1998, 2700–2706. But for indications that congressional Republicans had already begun to tend their own constituencies rather than some national movement, see Marc Birtel, "House: The Scandal Recedes," *CQWR*, 24 October

1998, 2873–75. More generally, see Burt Solomon, "Bill and Monica Who?" *NJ*, 31 October 1998, 2542–46.

Chapter 2: Campaigning Is Not Governing

1. See James David Barber, *The Presidential Character*, 4th ed. (Englewood Cliffs, N.J.: Prentice Hall, 1992.

2. See Samuel Kernell, *Going Public*, 3d ed. (Washington, D.C.: CQ Press, 1997).

3. Bob Woodward, *The Choice* (New York: Simon & Schuster, 1996), 344.

4. Ibid., 54, 126.

5. Elizabeth Drew, *Showdown: The Struggle between the Gingrich Congress and the Clinton White House* (New York: Simon & Schuster, 1996), 19.

6. See, for example, George C. Edwards III, *At the Margins* (New Haven: Yale University Press, 1989); and George C. Edwards III and Stephen J. Wayne, *Presidential Leadership*, 5th ed. (New York: St. Martin's, 1999).

7. "Interview with Clinton: Political Landscape," *New York Times*, 28 July 1996, 11.

8. "Democrats Look to Salvage Part of Stimulus Plan," *Congressional Quarterly Weekly Report*, 24 April 1993, 1002–3.

9. Bob Woodward, *The Agenda: Inside the Clinton White House* (New York: Simon & Schuster, 1994), 285. A CBS News/*New York Times* poll with before-and-after samples on 2 and 3 August found that support for the president's budget remained unchanged even in the immediate aftermath of the speech, but that opposition weakened.

10. "Switchboards Swamped with Calls over Tax Plan," *New York Times*, 5 August 1993, A18.

11. "Health Care Reform: The Lost Chance," *Newsweek*, 19 September 1994, 32.

12. Gallup poll of 15–16 August 1994.

13. Quoted in Alison Mitchell, "Despite His Reversals, Clinton Stays Centered," *New York Times*, 28 July 1996, 10.

14. Woodward, *Agenda*, 165.

15. Quoted in Mitchell, "Despite His Reversals," 10.

16. George C. Edwards III, Andrew Barrett, and Jeffrey Peake, "The Legislative Impact of Divided Government," *American Journal of Political Science* 41 (April 1997): 545–63.

17. CNN*USA Today* Gallup poll of 15–17 July 1994.

18. Cited in the *Wirthlin Quorum*, 5 June 1994, 2.

19. Gallup poll of 3–6 June 1994.

20. See George C. Edwards III, *Presidential Approval* (Baltimore: Johns Hopkins University Press, 1990), 130–34.

21. Charles O. Jones, *The Presidency in a Separated System* (Washington, D.C.: Brookings Institution, 1994), 294.

22. George C. Edwards III, *At the Margins: Presidential Influence in Congress* (New Haven: Yale University Press, 1989), chaps. 6–7.

23. Quoted in Jack Nelson and Robert J. Donovan, "The Education of a President," *Los Angeles Times Magazine*, 1 August 1993, 14. See also "The President at Midterm," *USA Weekend*, 4–6 November 1994, 4.

24. White House transcript of interview of President Clinton by WWWE Radio, Cleveland, 24 October 1994.

Chapter 3: Demotion? Has Clinton Turned the Bully Pulpit into a Lectern?

1. Richard E. Neustadt, *Presidential Power and the Modern Presidents: The Politics of Leadership from Roosevelt to Reagan* (New York: Free Press, 1990); Paul Charles Light, *The President's Agenda: Domestic Choice from Kennedy to Carter* (Baltimore: Johns Hopkins University Press, 1982), 7–9.

2. Walter Dean Burnham, "The Legacy of George Bush: Travails of an Understudy," 28–30, and Kathleen A. Frankovic, "Public Opinion in the 1992 Campaign," 111–13, both in *The Election of 1992*, ed. Gerald M. Pomper (Chatham, N.J.: Chatham House, 1993).

3. Paul J. Quirk and Joseph Hinchliffe, "The Trials of a Centrist Democrat," in *The Clinton Presidency: First Appraisals*, ed. Colin Campbell and Bert A. Rockman (Chatham, N.J.: Chatham House 1996), 262–89; Walter Dean Burnham, "Introduction—Bill Clinton: Riding the Tiger," 16–17, and Scott Keeter, "Public Opinion and the Election," 125–26, both in *The Election of 1996: Reports and Interpretations*, ed. Gerald M. Pomper (Chatham, N.J.: Chatham House, 1997).

4. Colin Campbell, *Managing the Presidency: Carter, Reagan, and the Search for Executive Harmony* (Pittsburgh: University of Pittsburgh Press, 1986), 18–19.

5. Ross K. Baker, "Sorting Out and Suiting Up: The Presidential Nominations," 57–59, and Gerald M. Pomper, "The Presidential Election," 142, both in Pomper, *Election of 1992*; Charles O. Jones, "Campaigning to Govern: The Clinton Style," 19, and Quirk and Hinchliffe, 263–64, both in Campbell and Rockman, *Clinton Presidency*.

6. Colin Campbell, *The U.S. Presidency in Crisis: A Comparative Perspective* (New York: Oxford University Press, 1998).

7. Walter Dean Burnham, "Realignment Lives: The 1994 Earthquake and Its Implications," in Campbell and Rockman, *Clinton Presidency*, 370.

8. See *Federalist Paper* No. 70.

9. John Kingdon, *Agendas, Alternatives, and Public Policies*, 2d ed. (New York: HarperCollins, 1995), 4, 24.

10. David R. Mayhew, *Divided We Govern: Party Control, Lawmaking, and Investigations, 1946–90* (New Haven: Yale University Press, 1991), 112.

11. Larry Berman, *The Office of Management and Budget and the Presidency, 1921–1979* (Princeton: Princeton University Press, 1979), 3; Daniel J. Palazzolo, *The Speaker and the Budget: Leadership in the Post-Reform House of Representatives* (Pittsburgh: University of Pittsburgh Press, 1992).

12. Clinton Rossiter, *The American Presidency* (New York: Harcourt, Brace, 1956).

13. "The Evolution of a Revolution," *The Economist*, 4 November 1995, 23.

14. Richard B. Cheney and Lynne V. Cheney, *Kings of the Hill* (New York: Simon & Schuster, 1996), 190.

15. Kinuko Y. Craft, "Can He Tame Washington?" *Newsweek*, 30 November 1992, 26.

16. Campbell, *U.S. Presidency*, 219. The term *boutique government* resonates with Evan McKenzie's *Privatopia: Homeowner Associations and the Rise of Residential Private Government* (New Haven: Yale University Press, 1994), as cited by Wilson Carey McWilliams, "Conclusion—The Meaning of the Election," in Pomper, *Election of 1996*, 245, in his discussion of a declining sense of civic community in the U.S.

17. Theda Skocpol, *Boomerang: Clinton's Health Security Effort and the Turn against Government in U.S. Politics* (New York: Norton, 1996), 16.

18. Bob Woodward, *The Agenda: Inside the Clinton White House* (New York: Simon & Schuster, 1994); Colin Campbell, "Management in a Sandbox: Why the Clinton White House Failed to Cope with Gridlock," in Campbell and Rockman, *Clinton Presidency*, 62; Ann Devroy, "Clinton Shuffles Staff to Return to 'Basics,'" *Washington Post*, 7 May 1993; Dana Priest and Ruth Marcus, "Key Clinton Health Ideas Face Major Opposition," *Washington Post*, 20 February 1994.

19. Larry Berman and Emily O. Goldman, "Clinton's Foreign Policy at Midterm," in Campbell and Rockman, *Clinton Presidency*, 291, 319.

20. Newt Gingrich, "Our Duty for 1994: Speech to the Republican National Committee."

21. Ibid.; Cheney and Cheney, *Kings of the Hill*, 201.

22. Newt Gingrich, *To Renew America* (New York: HarperCollins, 1995), 33–34.

23. Ibid., 119.

24. *TV Guide* advertisement, reproduced in John B. Bader, *Taking the Initiative: Leadership Agendas in Congress and the "Contract with America"* (Washington, D.C.: Georgetown University Press, 1996), 174–75.

25. Dan Balz, "The Whip Who Would Be Speaker: Gingrich Sees Role as 'Transformational,'" *Washington Post*, 20 October 1994.

26. Bader, *Taking the Initiative*, 178.

27. David S. Broder, "A Historic Republican Triumph: GOP Captures Congress; Sharp Turn to Right Reflects Doubts about Clinton, Democrats," *Washington Post*, 9 November 1994.

28. Burnham, "Realignment Lives," 363–85.

29. Kenneth J. Cooper and Eric Pianin, "GOP Rides Wave to Position of Power," *Washington Post*, 9 November 1994.

30. Joe Wallis and Brian Dollery, "Autonomous Policy Leadership," *Governance* 10 (1998): 17, quoting Roger O. Douglas, *Unfinished Business* (Auckland, N.Z.: Random House, 1993), 225.

31. Ibid.

32. Bader, *Taking the Initiative*, 36, 48.

33. Katharine Q. Seelye, "As a Model, Gingrich Takes Presidents, Not Predecessor," *New York Times*, 11 April 1995; Meg Greenfield, "The Gingrich Example," *Newsweek*, 4 November 1996, 80.

34. See McWilliams, "Conclusion," 259–60.

35. Ruth Marcus, "Clinton Reiterates Vow to Pursue New Democrat Agenda," *Washington Post*, 11 November 1994.

36. Federal News Service, "President Accepts Share of Responsibility for the Democrats' Shellacking," *Washington Post*, 10 November 1994.

37. Ann Devroy, "Panetta Holds Gingrich's Words against Him—and His Party," *Washington Post*, 6 December 1994.

38. Marjorie Randon Hershey, "Congressional Elections," in Pomper, *Election of 1996*, 213–16; Howard Kurtz, "Gingrich Plans to End Daily News Briefings," *Washington Post*, 3 May 1995; Dan Balz and John E. Yang, "Gingrich to Lower His Public Profile," *Washington Post*, 2 December 1995.

39. Ann Devroy, "President Struggling to Stake Out Strategy and Take the Offensive," *Washington Post*, 30 November 1994.

40. Elizabeth Kolbert, "The Stealth Strategist Refocusing Clinton," *New York Times*, 1 July 1995.

41. Burnham, "Realignment Lives," 384–85.

42. Ann Devroy, "Republican Adviser Stages a Quiet White House Coup," *Washington Post*, 18 June 1995.

43. Ann Devroy, "After Series of Moves to Center, Clinton Stakes Out Traditional Position," *Washington Post*, 20 July 1995; Christopher Edley Jr., "The Road to Clinton's Big Speech," *Washington Post*, 23 July 1995.

44. Terry Moe, "The Politicized Presidency," in *The New Direction in American Politics*, ed. John E. Chubb and Paul E. Peterson (Washington, D.C.: Brookings Institution, 1985), 258.

45. Campbell, *Managing the Presidency*, 269.

46. Jim Hoagland, "Candidate Against Change," *Washington Post*, 16 February 1995.

47. E.J. Dionne Jr., "The Big Idea," *Washington Post*, 9 August 1998.

48. David E. Rosenbaum, "Starting Point for Talks," *New York Times*, 14 June 1995; Eric Pianin and John F. Harris, "Hill Republican Leaders See Compromise as Possible While Some Administration Allies Perceive a Blunder," *Washington Post*, 15 June 1995; Alison Mitchell, "New Strategy Puts Clinton on His Own," *New York Times*, 15 June 1995; David Rosenbaum, "Both Sides of the Aisle Sense Capital's Unrest," *New York Times*, 21 October 1995; Ann Devroy, "Clinton's

Shifts Show Influence of Consultant," *Washington Post*, 3 November 1995; Ann Devroy and John F. Harris, "Clinton Says His Record Shows Remarkable Consistency," *Washington Post*, 31 January 1996.

49. David Broder, "Does Clinton Want to Govern?" *Washington Post*, 4 February 1996; Juan Williams, "Clinton's Morning in America," *Washington Post*, 12 November 1995.

50. Elizabeth Drew, *Showdown: The Struggle between the Gingrich Congress and the Clinton White House* (New York: Simon & Schuster, 1996), 131.

51. Former Clinton aide, interview by author, 23 December 1998.

52. Helen Dewar, "Despite Some Tensions, Hill Leaders Confident of Budget Agreement," *Washington Post*, 10 January 1997; Clay Chandler and Peter Baker, "Clinton Ponders Concessions on Medicare, Taxes," *Washington Post*, 9 January 1997; John F. Harris, "Retreat from the Methods of the Past," *Washington Post*, 12 January 1997; James Bennet, "In Evolution of Clinton, a Few Echoes Survive," *New York Times*, 2 February 1997; Alison Mitchell, "Clinton Seems to Keep Running though the Race Is Run and Won," *New York Times*, 12 February 1997; John F. Harris, "Clinton Finds It Tough to Shift Off Funds," *Washington Post*, 4 March 1997.

53. "Text of Newt Gingrich's Speech after being Reelected Speaker of the House," *Washington Post*, 8 January 1997.

54. Don Balz and John Yang, "Republicans Set Legislative Priorities," *Washington Post*, 7 March 1997.

55. Robert Pear, "Ex-Official Criticizes Clinton on Welfare," *New York Times*, 16 March 1997; Jerry Gray, "Gingrich Offers an Agenda, but the Christian Coalition Attacks Sharply," *New York Times*, 17 March 1997.

56. Eric Pianin, "Leaders Play Down Divisions as More GOP Strains Surface," *Washington Post*, 19 April 1997; Pianin, *Washington Post*, 2 May 1997; Eric Pianin and John E. Yang, "Gephardt Denounces Balanced Budget Plan," *Washington Post*, 21 May 1997.

57. John E. Yang and Eric Pianin, "Divisions Widen in House GOP," *Washington Post*, 18 June 1997.

58. Eric Pianin and Judith Havemann, "GOP Social Agenda Advancing in Hill Panels," *Washington Post*, 16 June 1997.

59. John F. Harris, "Clinton Rejects Hill Pressures on IRS, Promises 'Customer-Friendly' Agency," *Washington Post*, 11 October 1997; Richard L. Berke and Richard W. Stevenson, "Reversing Course on IRS, Clinton Takes the Wind out of Republican Sails," *New York Times*, 26 October 1997; John F. Harris, "'Outraged' Clinton Vows IRS Overhaul," *Washington Post*, 3 May 1998. The point about Clinton's betrayal of his reinvention rhetoric is made by Donald F. Kettl in *Reinventing Government: A Fifth-Year Report Card*, Center for Public Management Report 98-1 (Washington, D.C.: Brookings Institution, September 1998), 33.

60. John E. Yang and Terry M. Neal, "'Fast Track' Hits Brick Wall," *Washington Post*, 9 November 1997; John F. Harris, "President Takes Blame for 'Fast Track' Delay"; and Thomas B. Edsall and John E. Yang, "Clinton Loss Illuminates Struggle within Party," *Washington Post*, 11 November 1997.

61. Peter Baker, "Clinton Celebrates a Victory Made Possible by Reduced Expectations," *Washington Post*, 16 October 1998.

62. Richard Berke, "White House Acts to Contain Furor as Concern Grows," *New York Times*, 26 January 1998; John F. Harris, "Advisers Worry about Long-Term Implications of Ad Hoc Strategy," *Washington Post*, 11 February 1998.

63. Eric Pianin, "Breaking with Partner on Budget Deal," *Washington Post*, 3 May 1998; "Gingrich Wants to Tap Surplus for Tax Cuts," *Washington Post*, 9 May 1998.

64. As reported in David S. Broder, "The Real Scramble," *Washington Post*, 22 July 1998. See also Thomas B. Edsall, "GOP's Agenda Pleases Backers," *Washington Post*, 19 July 1998.

65. John F. Harris and Amy Goldstein, "Puncturing an AIDS Initiative," *Washington Post*, 23 April 1998.

66. Todd S. Purdum, "In Umbrage and Admission, It Was Vintage Bill Clinton," *New York Times*, 24 August 1998.

67. Robert Pear and Lizette Alvarez, "Federal Officials Shaken by President's Admission," *New York Times*, 24 August 1998.

68. Peter Baker, "Clinton Celebrates a Victory Made Possible by Reduced Expectations," *Washington Post*, 16 October 1998.

69. David A. Vise, "Clinton Plan to Tap DC Pension Fund," *Washington Post*, 16 October 1998; Linda Perlstein, "Budget's Modest Start on Teachers," *Washington Post*, 17 October 1998.

70. Melinda Henenberger, "Party Looks to Where It Went Wrong," *New York Times*, 8 November 1998; Katharine Q. Seelye, "Facing Revolt, Gingrich Won't Run for Speaker and Will Quit Congress," *New York Times*, 7 November 1998.

71. Confidential briefing, May 1998.

72. Joel Aberbach, "Sharing Isn't Easy: When Separate Institutions Clash," *Governance* 11 (1998): 149.

Chapter 4: The President as Legislative Leader

1. In addition to the sources cited, this essay is based on the author's interviews with participants. All unattributed quotes are from those interviews.

2. Randall Ripley, *Majority Party Leadership in Congress* (Boston: Little, Brown, 1969).

3. See Stephen J. Wayne, *The Legislative Presidency* (New York: Harper & Row, 1978); and Paul C. Light, *The President's Agenda: Domestic Policy Choice from Kennedy to Carter (with notes on Ronald Reagan)* (Baltimore: Johns Hopkins University Press, 1983).

4. Charles O. Jones, *The Presidency in a Separated System* (Washington, D.C.: Brookings Institution, 1994).

5. Samuel Kernell, *Going Public: New Strategies of Presidential Leadership* (Washington, D.C.: CQ Press, 1986).

6. Barbara Sinclair, *Majority Leadership in the U.S. House* (Baltimore: Johns Hopkins University Press, 1983); Sinclair, *Legislators, Leaders, and Lawmaking* (Baltimore: Johns Hopkins Univer-

sity Press, 1995); David Rohde, *Parties and Leaders in the Postreform House* (Chicago: University of Chicago Press, 1991).

7. For more detail, see Barbara Sinclair, "Trying to Govern Positively in a Negative Era: Clinton and the 103d Congress," in *The Clinton Presidency: First Appraisals,* ed. Colin Campbell and Bert A. Rockman (Chatham, N.J,: Chatham House, 1996), 88–125.

8. Pamela Fessler, "If People Get behind the President, Congress Is Likely to Follow," *Congressional Quarterly Weekly Report,* 20 February 1993, 380–81.

9. William Connelly and John Pitney, *Congress' Permanent Minority? Republicans in the U.S. House* (Lanham, Md.: Rowman & Littlefield, 1994).

10. Barbara Sinclair, *The Transformation of the U.S. Senate* (Baltimore: Johns Hopkins University Press, 1989).

11. David Hess, "100 New Faces Start in Congress Today," *Riverside Press Enterprise,* 5 January 1993.

12. Beth Donovan, "Clinton Reverses Directions: Battle Begins Anew," *Congressional Quarterly Weekly Report,* 23 January 1993, 182.

13. See Kernell, *Going Public.*

14. George Hager and David Cloud, "Democrats Tie Their Fate to Clinton's Budget Bill," *Congressional Quarterly Weekly Report,* 7 August 1993, 2122–29.

15. Haynes Johnson and David Broder, *The System* (Boston: Little, Brown, 1996).

16. Barbara Sinclair, *Unorthodox Lawmaking* (Washington, D.C.: CQ Press, 1997).

17. See Douglas Koopman, *Hostile Takeover: The House Republican Party 1980–1995* (Lanham, Md.: Rowman & Littlefield, 1996); and Dan Baltz and Ronald Brownstein, *Storming the Gates: Protest Politics and the Republican Revival* (Boston: Little, Brown, 1996).

18. Elizabeth Drew, *Showdown: The Struggle Between the Gingrich Congress and the Clinton White House* (New York: Simon & Schuster, 1996).

19. Dick Morris, *Behind the Oval Office* (New York: Random House, 1997).

20. Ibid., 79–88, 339.

21. See Blatz and Brownstein, *Storming the Gates.*

22. David Mayhew, *Divided We Govern* (New Haven: Yale University Press, 1991).

Chapter 5: Judicial Legacies

1. For further discussion of the legal policies and judicial appointments of the Reagan administration, see Charles Fried, *Order and Law: Arguing the Reagan Revolution—A Firsthand Account* (New York: Simon & Schuster, 1991); David M. O'Brien, "The Reagan Judges: His Most Enduring Legacy?" in *The Reagan Legacy: Promise and Performance,* ed. Charles O. Jones (Chatham, N.J.: Chatham House, 1988), 60–101; Sheldon Goldman, *Picking Federal Judges: Lower Court Selection From Roosevelt through Reagan* (New Haven: Yale University Press, 1997).

2. Quoted in O'Brien, "Reagan Judges," 62.

3. "Presidential Candidates Respond to AJS Questions About Justice System," *Judicature* 80 (1996): 93, 95.

4. See Richard E. Neustadt, *Presidential Power and Modern Presidents* (New York: Free Press, 1990). See also Rogelio Garcia, "CRS Report for Congress, Filling Policy Positions in Executive Departments: Average Time Required through Confirmation," 1981 and 1993 (Washington, D.C.: Congressional Research Service, 28 July 1998), 98–641 Gov.

5. For a further discussion, see David M. O'Brien, "Clinton's Legal Policy and the Courts: Rising from Disarray or Turning Around and Around?" in *The Clinton Presidency: First Appraisals*, ed. Colin Campbell and Bert A. Rockman (Chatham, N.J.: Chatham House, 1996), 126–62.

6. See O'Brien, "Reagan Judges"; and David M. O'Brien, *Judicial Roulette* (New York: Twentieth Century Fund/Priority Press, 1988), 49–65.

7. Eleanor Dean Acheson, interview by author, Washington, D.C., 1 December 1994.

8. For further discussion, see Sheldon Goldman, "Judicial Selection under Clinton: Midterm Examination," *Judicature* 78 (1995): 276.

9. See Sheldon Goldman, "Clinton's Nontraditional Judges: Creating A More Representative Bench," *Judicature* 68 (1994): 78.

10. Quoted by Naftali Bendavid, "Adding Diversity to the Bench," *Legal Times,* 27 December 1993, 7.

11. See O'Brien, "Reagan Judges"; and Barbara Hinkson Craig and David M. O'Brien, *Abortion and American Politics* (Chatham, N.J.: Chatham House, 1993), 157–96.

12. Quoted by Bendavid, 7.

13. Quoted by Joan Biskupic, "Despite 129 Clinton Appointments, GOP Judges Dominate U.S. Bench," *Washington Post,* 18 October 1994, A20.

14. Quoted by Neil A. Lewis, "Clinton Is Considering Judgeships for Opponents of Abortion Rights," *New York Times,* 18 September 1993, A20.

15. Quoted by Daniel Klaidman, "Just Like Old Times? Liberals Challenge President on Some Judgeships," *Legal Times,* 25 October 1993, 1.

16. Nan Aron, interview with author, Washington, D.C., 27 October 1994.

17. Quoted by David G. Savage and Ronald J. Ostrow, "Clinton's Big Bench: Judges of All Stripes and Colors Appointed," *Los Angeles Times,* 16 November 1994, A5.

18. Quoted by Stephen Labaton, "President's Judicial Appointments: Diverse but Well in the Mainstream," *New York Times,* 14 October 1994, A15.

19. Acheson, interview.

20. This section draws on the author's discussion in *Supreme Court Watch—1994* (New York: Norton, 1994), 3–5.

21. For an excellent analysis of Justice White's performance on the Court, see Dennis J. Hutchinson, *The Man Who Once Was Whizzer White* (New York: Free Press, 1998).

22. For further discussion, see David M. O'Brien, "How to Win Friends and Influence People: Life in the Supreme Court," *Los Angeles Times*, 13 June 1993, M1.

23. See Christopher E. Smith, Joyce Ann Baugh, Thomas R. Hensley, and Scott Patrick Johnson, "The First-Term Performance of Justice Ruth Bader Ginsburg," *Judicature* 78 (1994): 74.

24. See Stephen G. Breyer, *Regulation and Its Reform* (Cambridge, Mass.: Harvard University Press, 1982); and *Breaking the Vicious Cycle: Toward Effective Risk Regulation* (Cambridge, Mass.: Harvard University Press, 1993).

25. See Naftali Bendavid, "A Judicial Selection, Clinton Style: Avoiding the Big Fight," *Legal Times*, 11 September 1995, A1.

26. See Alliance for Justice, *Judicial Selection Project: Annual Report 1995* (Washington, D.C.: Alliance for Justice, 1996).

27. Ronald Stidham, Robert A. Carp, and Donald Songer, "The Voting Behavior of President Clinton's Judicial Appointees," *Judicature* 80 (1996): 16.

28. For further discussion, see David M. O'Brien, "The Courts: Diversity Hurts Liberals," *Los Angeles Times*, 5 February 1995, M1; and the discussion in the text at note 49.

29. See Terry Eastland, "If Clinton Wins, Here's What the Courts Will Look Like," *Wall Street Journal*, 28 February 1996, A15.

30. Quoted in James Bennet, "Judicial Dictatorship Spurns People's Will, Buchanan Says," *New York Times*, 30 January 1996, A1.

31. Quoted in Harvey Berkman and Claudia MacLachlan, "Clinton's Picks—Not So Liberal," *National Law Journal*, 21 October 1996, A1.

32. See David Rovella, "Judge Sarokin Decries Criticism of Bench, Quits," *National Law Journal*, 17 June 1996, A1.

33. For further analysis of the delays in the process of filling judicial vacancies, see Miller Center of Public Affairs, *Improving the Process of Appointing Federal Judges: A Report of the Miller Center Commission on the Selection of Federal Judges* (Charlottesville: University of Virginia, 1 September 1996).

34. For further analysis of Clinton's first-term judicial appointees, see Sheldon Goldman and Elliot Slotnick, "Clinton's First Term Judiciary: Many Bridges to Cross," *Judicature* 254 (1997): 80.

35. Quoted in Katharine Seelye, "Dole, Citing Crisis in the Courts, Attacks Appointments by Clinton," *New York Times*, 20 April 1996, A3. See also David Kairys, "Clinton's Judicial Retreat," *Washington Post*, 7 September 1997, C1.

36. See "Verbatim: Hatch Fires Warning Shot on Judges," *Legal Times*, 18 November 1996, 14.

37. See Bruce Brown, "Right Refocuses Aim at Judiciary," *Los Angeles Times*, 20 January 1997, A1, 6.

38. Edwin Meese III and Rhett Dehart, "Reining in the Runaway Judiciary," *Legal Times*, 20 January 1997, 22, 24.

39. See Harvey Berkman, "Hatch to ABA: You're Out. ABA: So What," *National Law Journal*, 3 March 1997, A1.

40. Quoted in Joan Biskupic, "Hill Republicans Target Judicial Activism," *Washington Post*, 15 September 1997, A1.

41. Alliance for Justice, *Judicial Selection Project: Annual Report 1997* (Washington, D.C.: Alliance for Justice, January 1998). See also Miller Center.

42. Quoted by Kirk Victor, "Bashing the Bench," *National Law Journal*, 31 May 1997, 10, 78.

43. See Peter Baker, "Clinton Says Republicans Are Threat to Judiciary," *Washington Post*, 28 September 1997, A23.

44. See Ed Henry, "His Power Being Judged, Hatch Beats Back Leaders, *Roll Call*, 1 May 1997, 25.

45. See Victor, "Bashing the Beach."

46. William H. Rehnquist, *The 1997 Year-End Report on the Federal Judiciary*, 31 December 1997.

47. See Orrin Hatch, "Judicial Nominees: The Senate's Steady Progress," *Washington Post*, 11 January 1998, C9; and Trent Lott, "Rehnquist's Rush to Judgment," *Washington Post*, 2 February 1998, A19.

48. See Thomas Edsall, "Clinton Plans Judicial Offensive," *Washington Post*, 16 January 1998, A1.

49. See "Controversial Nominee Withdraws," *Facts on File World News Digest*, 16 April 1998, 252, A3.

50. Quoted in Les Blumenthal, "Don't Select State Judge, Clinton Told; Group Says Chief Justice Durham Undeserving of Federal Judgeship," *The News Tribune*, 21 July 1998, B1.

51. See Justice Antonin Scalia's dissenting opinion in *Morrison v. Olsen*, 487 U.S. 654 (1988).

52. *Clinton v. Jones*, 117 S.Ct.1636 (1997).

Chapter 6: A Reinvented Government, or the Same Old Government?

The author gratefully acknowledges support from the Academic Senate and the Center for American Politics and Public Policy at UCLA, and the able research assistance of Klinton Miyao. Fred Kaiser and Roger Garcia of the Congressional Research Service graciously provided invaluable information and materials. Colin Campbell, Harvey Feigenbaum, Fred Kaiser, John Petrocik, and Bert Rockman generously provided helpful comments on the manuscript.

1. "I Have Striven to Achieve Excellence and Diversity," transcript of President Clinton's news conference, *Washington Post*, 21 December 1996, A16.

2. Martha Farnsworth Riche, "The Bean Count Is In!" *Washington Post*, 23 January 1994, C2. Similar figures were cited for the second term in an article on high-level appointees (apparently restricted to those requiring Senate confirmation) by Burt Solomon, "Claiming the Spoils," *National Journal*, 29 March 1997, 626.

3. See Janet M. Martin, "Women Who Govern: The President's Appointments," in *The Other Elites: Women, Politics, and Power in the Executive Branch*, ed. MaryAnne Borrelli and Janet M. Martin (Boulder, Colo.: Lynne Rienner, 1997), 51–72. The data are found in table 4.1, p. 58.

4. Rogelio Garcia, "CRS Report for Congress, Filling Policy Positions in Executive Departments: Average Time Required through Confirmation, 1981 and 1993" (Washington, D.C.: Congressional Research Service, 28 July 1998), 98-641 Gov; and Garcia, "CRS Report for Congress, Presidential Appointments to Full-Time Positions in Executive Departments during the 105th Congress, 1997–1998" (Washington D.C.: Congressional Research Service, 7 April 1998), 98-357 Gov. Appointments to positions in the military services, the uniformed civilian services, the foreign service, U.S. attorneys and marshals and like positions were excluded. My thanks to Klinton Miyao for his able coding of the data.

5. Both quotes are found in Burt Solomon, "Claiming the Spoils," *National Journal*, 29 March 1997, 626.

6. Ibid.

7. See Joel D. Aberbach, "The Federal Executive under Clinton," in *The Clinton Presidency: First Appraisals*, ed. Colin Campbell and Bert A. Rockman (Chatham, N.J.: Chatham House, 1996), 169, 176, for citations on the pragmatic, non-strident types Clinton generally appointed to cabinet and subcabinet positions in his first term. On the second term, see Jack W. Germond and Jules Witcover, "Fewer Thrills the Second Time Around," *National Journal*, 11 January 1997, 83. They note that while Clinton was still confined by his promise of "diversity" and of a cabinet that "looks like America," he got his new team in place faster in the second term than in the first term. Also see Dan Balz, "Clinton and Gore Have the Most Important Cabinet Chairs," *Washington Post*, 21 December 1996, A1, A16. Balz's story emphasizes that, as in selecting the first cabinet, "the interests of diversity dictated the final selections," and that diversity was more important than ideology in determining selection, in part because Clinton "largely reserved for himself the right to define domestic policy."

8. Ibid., 171.

9. Garcia, "CRS Report for Congress, Filling Policy Positions."

10. Ibid., 2.

11. See Aberbach, "Federal Executive under Clinton," esp. 175–76.

12. Garcia, "CRS Report for Congress, Presidential Appointments," 2. I could not find comparable data reported for the Reagan administration for days to confirm appointments at the beginning of its second term.

13. Rogelio Garcia, "CRS Report for Congress, Acting Officials in Positions Requiring Senate Confirmation in Executive Departments, As of February 1998" (Washington D.C.: Congressional Research Service, 11 March 1998), 98-252 Gov, 1.

14. For good summaries of the "administrative presidency" strategy, see Richard P. Nathan, *The Administrative Presidency* (New York: Macmillan, 1983); and Robert F. Durant, "The Administrative Presidency: Retrospect and Prospect," *PRG Report* 21, no. 2 (Fall 1998): 1–7. On the presidency in the complex American political system, see esp. Richard E. Neustadt, *Presidential Power and the Modern Presidents* (New York: Free Press, 1990); and Charles O. Jones, *The Presidency in a Separated System* (Washington: Brookings Institution, 1994).

15. See Kirk Victor, "Executive Branch End Run," *National Journal*, 16 May 1998, 1114.

16. Morton Rosenberg, "CRS Report for Congress, Legislative Proposals to Amend the Vacancies Act to Protect the Senate's Confirmation Prerogative" (Washington, D.C.: Congressional Research Service, 16 April 1998), 98-375 A, 1.

17. See John M. Broder, "Clinton, Softening Slap at Senate, Names 'Acting' Civil Rights Chief," *New York Times*, 16 December 1997, A1, A16.

18. Victor, "Executive Branch End Run," 1113.

19. Ronald J. Ostrow, "Not Just Acting," *Los Angeles Times*, 14 July 1998, A5.

20. Quoted in Victor, "Executive Branch End Run," 1114.

21. Ibid.

22. Durant, "Administrative Presidency," 3.

23. Ibid.

24. Ibid. Durant says that Clinton had issued a total of 248 executive orders during his first six years in office (up to 11 October 1998). An interesting paper by Christopher Deering and Forrest Maltzman suggests that Clinton issued more than this number. Deering and Maltzman's data record that Clinton issued 57 executive orders in 1993 rather than the 27 recorded by Durant. Their total for the years 1993–96 is 197. Deering and Maltzman used a corrected version of data reported in Lyn Ragsdale, *Vital Statistics on the Presidency: Washington to Clinton* (Washington, D.C.: Congressional Quarterly, 1996). The Deering and Maltzman paper contains a good discussion and empirical rebuttal of academic work suggesting little evidence that presidents use executive orders to circumvent a hostile Congress. See Christopher J. Deering and Forrest Maltzman, "The Politics of Executive Orders: Legislative Constraints on Presidential Power," paper presented at the annual meeting of the Midwest Political Science Association, Chicago, 22–25 April 1998. Figure 2 of the paper presents the data on executive orders.

25. Elizabeth Shogren, "Clinton to Bypass Congress in Blitz of Executive Orders," *Los Angeles Times*, 4 July 1998, A1, A14.

26. Robert Pear, "The Presidential Pen is Still Mighty," *New York Times*, 28 June 1998, WK3.

27. Alexis Simendinger, "The Paper Wars," *National Journal*, 25 July 1998, 1732–39.

28. Such actions also displease strong institutional loyalists in Congress. I thank Fred Kaiser for emphasizing this point in his comments on a draft of this chapter.

29. Cited in Pear, "Presidential Pen Is Still Mighty."

30. Cited in Simendinger, "Paper Wars," 1733.

31. See Nathan, *Administrative Presidency*, and Durant, "Administrative Presidency."

32. For an interesting treatment of the Bush administration's use of similar tactics, see Charles Tiefer, *The Semi-Sovereign Presidency: The Bush Administration's Strategy for Governing without Congress* (Boulder, Colo: Westview, 1994). Durant argues that Bush and later Clinton used the administrative presidency strategy in a less confrontational fashion than did Nixon and Reagan. See Durant, "Administrative Presidency," 1.

33. *William J. Clinton, President of the United States, et al., Appellants v. City of New York, et al.*, 118 S. Ct. 209 (1998).

34. Quoted in Robert Pear, "Justices, 6–3, Bar Veto of Line Items in Bills," *New York Times*, 26 June 1998, A1.

35. Guy Gugliotta and Eric Pianin, "Line-Item Veto Tips Traditional Balance of Power," *Washington Post*, 24 October 1997, A1, A6.

36. Quoted in ibid., A7.

37. Robert D. Reischauer, "Line Item Veto: Little Beef and Mostly Bun," *Washington Post*, 10 April 1996. Item reproduced on the Brookings Institution webpage: www.brook.edu/views/op%2Ded/reischauer/19960410.html.

38. Quoted in Gugliotta and Pianin, "Line-Item Veto Tips Traditional Balance of Power," A6.

39. "Justices, 6–3, Bar Veto of Line Item Bills," A16. See also Alexis Simendinger, "The Line-Item Veto and a Quarter...," *National Journal*, 5 July 1997, 1384, for a skeptical analysis of the effects of the law on spending and the budget process.

40. Like most reform efforts, reinvention has complex causes. The rising costs of the welfare state and pressure to remain competitive in the global economy are certainly two of the major reasons governments find reinvention (called the New Public Management in most of the internationally oriented literature) attractive.

41. Al Gore, *Creating a Government That Works Better and Costs Less: The Report of the National Performance Review* (New York: Plume, 1993), xxxviii.

42. This section draws on the excellent discussion in Donald F. Kettl, *Reinventing Government: A Fifth Year Report Card*, Center for Public Management Report 98-1(Washington, D.C.: Brookings Institution, September 1998), 2–6.

43. Ibid., 5.

44. Ibid.

45. Kettl cites a fair amount of the American literature on reinvention in the notes to his *Reinventing Government*. For a stimulating critique of the political theory behind the reinvention initiative, see Ronald C. Moe, "The 'Reinventing Government' Exercise: Misinterpreting the Problem, Misjudging the Consequences," *Public Administration Review*, 54, no. 2 (May/June 1994).

46. Kettl, *Reinventing Government, 5*.

47. Donald F. Kettl, "The Global Revolution in Public Management: Driving Themes, Missing Links," *Journal of Policy Analysis and Management* 16, no. 3 (1997): 449.

48. Both NASA contract management and management of IRS, the second agency discussed in this section, were identified by the comptroller general as "high risk" because of vulnerabilities to waste, fraud, abuse, and mismanagement. See United States General Accounting Office, *High Risk Series: An Overview*, February 1997, GAO/HR-97-1.

49. National Partnership for Reinventing Government, "High Impact Agencies: A Background Paper," September 1998, www.npr.gov/library/announc/hiapage3.html.

50. Chuck McCutcheon, "Lost in Space: NASA's Quest for a New Direction," *CQ Weekly* 56, no. 23 (6 June 1998): 1496.

51. Ralph Vartabedian, "Cost of New Space Station $3.6 Billion over Budget," *Los Angeles Times*, 15 February 1998, A1, A24, A26.

52. Warren E. Leary, "NASA Learns That Faster and Cheaper Isn't Always So," *New York Times*, 15 September 1998, B9.

53. According to a survey conducted by Princeton Research Associates in fall 1997 for the Pew Research Center for the People and the Press, the IRS was the federal agency least favorably rated

by the general public, with 49 percent of the sample expressing approval. In contrast, 89 percent gave favorable ratings to the Postal Service, 73 percent to NASA, and 51 percent to the Department of Housing and Urban Development. See the table "Change in Favorability of Federal Agencies," in "Deconstructing Distrust: How Americans View Government," www.people-press.org/trusttab.html. While the public may like the IRS least of all federal agencies, a 1998 poll by Louis Harris Associates found that 76 percent of Americans who had actually had direct contact with IRS employees said they had been treated fairly. The latter result was cited in Carol Marie Cropper, "Tangled Tale Of the Oilman vs. the IRS: What a Senate Panel Wasn't Told at Hearing," *New York Times*, 2 August 1998.

54. Kettl, *Reinventing Government*, 2.

55. Quoted in Graeme Browning, "Crashing Computers," *National Journal*, 1 March 1997, 414.

56. See Karen Kaplan, "CSC Wins IRS Contract to Update Systems," *Los Angeles Times*, 10 December 1998, C1, C2.

57. For a good summary of the legislation, see Richard W. Stevenson, "Senate Votes 96–2 on Final Approval for Changing IRS: Sweeping Legislation Seeks to Overhaul Management and Culture at Tax Agency," *New York Times*, 10 July 1998, A1, A11.

58. David Cay Johnston, "New IRS Law: A Guide to Shifting Burdens," *New York Times*, 26 July 1998, BU10.

59. Michael Hirsh, "Behind the IRS Curtain," *Newsweek*, 6 October 1997, 31. Also see David Cay Johnston, "Treasury Investigation Finds Little Evidence of IRS Abuse," *New York Times*, 26 April 1998, 19. The author notes that the audits of the poor were stepped up "in 1995 at the direction of Senator Roth and other Republican leaders who cut the IRS budget overall, but authorized more money to audit people claiming the Earned Income Credit."

60. David Hosansky, "Critics Say Hill May Overstep in Pressuring IRS to Ease Up," *CQ Weekly* 56, no. 23 (6 June 1998): 1505.

61. Ben Wildavsky, "A Hike in Complexity," *National Journal*, 23 August 1997, 1680.

62. Ibid., 1683.

63. "A taxpayer-friendly IRS?" CNN Interactive, 18 March 1998, www.cnn.com/US/9803/irs.customer.service.

64. Gregory F. Jenner, quoted in Richard W. Stevenson, "Waking Up to Reality of a Toothless IRS," *New York Times*, 28 June 1998, WK6.

65. Implementation of the act started in earnest in 1997. Agencies are required to "consult" with Congress in developing their strategic long-range plans. See Joel D. Aberbach and Bert A. Rockman, "Reinventing Government: Problems and Prospects," paper presented at the 1999 annual meeting of the Midwest Political Science Association, Chicago, 15–17 April 1999.

Chapter 7: Clinton and Organized Interests

1. Katharine Q. Seelye, "Long Fight Yields Hint of Victory," *New York Times*, 16 December 1998, A21.

2. Gregory L. Hager and Terry Sullivan, "President-Centered and Presidency-Centered Explanations of Presidential Public Activity," *American Journal of Political Science* 38 (November 1994): 1079–1104.

3. Alexis de Tocqueville, *Democracy in America* (Garden City, N.Y.: Anchor Books, 1969); Theda Skocpol, "America's Voluntary Groups Thrive in a National Network," *Brookings Review* 15 (Fall 1997): 16–19; Gerald Gamm and Robert Putnam, "Association-Building in America, 1850–1920," paper presented at the annual meeting of the Social Science History Association, New Orleans, 10–13 October 1996.

4. Kevin J. McMahon, "Altering Interpretation: Presidential Policy toward the Judiciary during the Administrations of Franklin Roosevelt, Richard Nixon, and Ronald Reagan," paper presented at the annual meeting of the American Political Science Association, Washington, D.C., 28–31 August 1997.

5. Mark A. Peterson and Jack L. Walker, "The Presidency and the Nominating System," in *The Presidency and the Political System*, 3d ed., ed. Michael Nelson (Washington, D.C.: CQ Press, 1990), 238–39.

6. Frank R. Baumgartner and Beth L. Leech, *Basic Interests: The Importance of Groups in Politics and in Political Science* (Princeton: Princeton University Press, 1998); Terry M. Moe, *The Organization of Interests: Incentives and the Internal Dynamics of Political Interest Groups* (Chicago: University of Chicago Press, 1980); Jack L. Walker, *Mobilizing Interest Groups in America: Patrons, Professions, and Social Movements* (Ann Arbor: University of Michigan Press, 1991); David W. Rohde, *Parties and Leaders in the Postreform House* (Chicago: University of Chicago Press, 1991); Kay Lehman Schlozman and John T. Tierney, *Organized Interests and American Democracy* (New York: Harper & Row, 1986); *The Social Divide: Political Parties and the Future of Activist Government*, ed. Margaret Weir (Washington, D.C. and New York: Brookings Institution and Russell Sage Foundation, 1998).

7. Baumgartner and Leech, *Basic Interests*, 103; Schlozman and Tierney, *Organized Interests*, 75; Walker, *Mobilizing Interest Groups*; James A. Smith, *The Idea Brokers: Think Tanks and The Rise of the New Policy Elite* (New York: Free Press, 1991); Andrew Rich and R. Kent Weaver, "Advocates and Analysts: Think Tanks and the Politicization of Expertise," in *Interest Group Politics*, 5th ed., ed. Allan J. Cigler and Burdett A. Loomis (Washington, D.C.: CQ Press, 1998), 235–53.

8. Walker, *Mobilizing Interest Groups*; Moe, *Organization of Interests*.

9. Baumgartner and Leech, *Basic Interests*, 111; Walker, *Mobilizing Interest Groups*.

10. Jean Stefaneic and Richard Delgado, *No Mercy: How Conservative Think Tanks and Foundations Changed America's Social Agenda* (Philadelphia: Temple University Press, 1998); Matthew C. Moen, *The Transformation of the Christian Right* (Tuscaloosa: University of Alabama Press, 1992), and *The Christian Right and Congress* (Tuscaloosa: University of Alabama Press, 1989).

11. See Walker, *Mobilizing Interest Groups*; Jeffrey M. Berry, *Lobbying for the People* (Princeton: Princeton University Press, 1977); Ken Kollman, *Outside Lobbying: Public Opinion and Interest Group Strategies* (Princeton: Princeton University Press, 1998); Kenneth M. Goldstein, *Interest Groups, Lobbying, and Participation in America* (New York: Cambridge University Press, forthcoming).

12. Margaret Weir, "Political Parties and Social Policymaking," in Weir, *Social Divide*, 1–45; U.S. Bureau of the Census, *Statistical Abstract of the United States, 1991* (Washington, D.C.: U.S.

Government Printing Office, 1991), 424–25; Alan Greenblatt, "Labor Wants Out of the Limelight after Glare of Probes, Backlash," *Congressional Quarterly Weekly Report*, 28 March 1998, 787–91; Richard Sammon, "Fall of Striker Bill Spotlights Doubts about Labor Lobby," *Congressional Quarterly Weekly Report*, 20 June 1992, 1810; Paul Starr, *The Social Transformation of American Medicine* (New York: Basic Books, 1982); Elton Rayak, *Professional Power and American Medicine: The Economics of the American Medical Association* (Cleveland: World Publishing, 1967), 2, 12.

13. Mark A. Peterson, "The Politics of Health Care Policy: Overreaching in an Age of Polarization," in Weir, *Social Divide*, 181–229.

14. Jimmy Carter, interview by author, Plains, Ga., 20 June 1984.

15. Greenblatt, "Labor Wants Out of the Limelight," 790; Theda Skocpol, "The Tocqueville Problem: Civic Engagement in American Democracy," *Social Science History* 21 (Winter 1997): 473; Skocpol, *Boomerang: Clinton's Health Security Effort and the Turn Against Government in U.S. Politics* (New York: Norton, 1996); Weir, "Political Parties and Social Policymaking"; Mark A. Peterson and Jack L. Walker, "Interest Group Responses to Partisan Change: The Impact of the Reagan Administration upon the National Interest Group System," in *Interest Group Politics*, 2d ed., ed. Allan J. Cigler and Burdett A. Loomis (Washington, D.C.: CQ Press, 1986), 163; Kirk Victor, "Asleep at the Switch?" *National Journal*, 16 January 1993, 131–34; Kollman, *Outside Lobbying*.

16. Mark A. Peterson, "Interest Mobilization and the Presidency," in *The Politics of Interests: Interest Groups Transformed*, ed. Mark P. Petracca (Boulder, Colo.: Westview, 1992), 221–41.

17. Peterson and Walker, "Interest Group Responses to Partisan Change."

18. Benjamin Ginsberg and Martin Shefter, "The Presidency, Interest Groups, and Social Forces," in *The Presidency and the Political System*, 3d ed., ed. Michael Nelson (Washington, D.C.: CQ Press, 1990), 335–52; Weir, *Social Divide*.

19. Dan Balz and Ronald Brownstein, *Storming the Gates: Protest Politics and the Republican Revival* (Boston: Little, Brown, 1996); David Maraniss and Michael Weisskopf, *Tell Newt to Shut Up!* (New York: Touchstone, 1996).

20. Stephen Skowronek, *Building a New American State: The Expansion of National Administrative Capabilities, 1877–1920* (New York: Cambridge University Press, 1982).

21. Elizabeth Drew, *On the Edge: The Clinton Presidency* (New York: Touchstone, 1994), 24; Richard Willing, "A Year of 'Highs' for African-Americans in Clinton's Cabinet," *Crisis* 101 (February/March 1994): 32–34.

22. Peterson, "Interest Mobilization and the Presidency," 232; Ginsberg and Shefter, "The Presidency, Interest Groups, and Social Forces."

23. Joseph A. Pika, "Interest Groups and the Executive: Presidential Intervention," in *Interest Group Politics*, ed. Allan J. Cigler and Burdett A. Loomis (Washington, D.C.: CQ Press, 1983), 298–323; memorandum to President Gerald R. Ford from William Baroody, 23 August 1974, quoted in Robert M. Copeland, "Cultivating Interest Group Support: Public Liaison in the Ford Administration," paper presented at the annual meeting of the Midwest Political Science Association, Chicago, 1985.

24. Mark A. Peterson, "The Presidency and Organized Interests: White House Patterns of Interest Group Liaison," *American Political Science Review* 86 (September 1992): 612–25.

25. For details on the typology, the approaches used by previous presidents, and an empirical analysis of President Reagan's use of liaison as governing party, see ibid.

26. Candidate Clinton used the phrase "end welfare as we know it" frequently during the campaign; see Drew, *On the Edge*, 394. He repeated it in his 1995 State of the Union speech, "Clinton Speech Envisions Local Empowerment," *Congressional Quarterly Weekly Report,* 28 January 1995, 302.

27. Peterson, "Presidency and Organized Interests."

28. *Federal Staff Directory* no. 2 (Mt. Vernon, Va.: Directories, Ltd., 1992, 1993); 1994, no. 2; 1995, no. 2; 1996, Fall; *Federal Yellow Book* (New York: Leadership Directories, Summer 1998).

29. For an example of this quote, see President Bill Clinton, "Remarks by the President to the Building and Construction Trades Union, AFL-CIO," Washington Hilton, Washington, D.C., 19 April 1993. For a general discussion of Clinton's programmatic approach, see Bob Woodward, *The Agenda: Inside the Clinton White House* (New York: Simon & Schuster, 1994).

30. Stephen A. Skowronek, "The Risks of 'Third-Way' Politics," *Society* 33 (September/October 1996): 33.

31. Bert A. Rockman, "An Agenda at Risk," *Society* 33 (September/October 1996): 26.

32. Haynes Johnson and David S. Broder, *The System: The American Way of Politics at the Breaking Point* (Boston: Little, Brown, 1996).

33. This section is based largely on Peterson, "Politics of Health Care Policy." For comprehensive assessments of the failure of health care reform in the 103d Congress, see Jacob Hacker, *The Road to Nowhere: The Genesis of President Clinton's Plan for Health Security* (Princeton: Princeton University Press, 1997); Johnson and Broder, *The System*, 511; Skocpol, *Boomerang*; and special sections in *Health Affairs* 14 (Spring 1995) and *Journal of Health Politics, Policy, and Law* 20 (Summer 1995).

34. Marie Gottschaulk, "The Missing Millions: Organized Labor, Business, and the Defeat of Clinton's Health Security Act," *Journal of Health Politics, Policy, and Law* 24 (June 1999).

35. Lawrence R. Jacobs, "The Politics of America's Supply State: Health Reform and Technology," *Health Affairs* 14 (Summer 1995): 143–57.

36. Charles O. Jones, *The Presidency in a Separated System* (Washington, D.C.: Brookings Institution, 1994), 20–21.

37. Hacker, *Road to Nowhere.*

38. Sources for quotations: memorandum to Ira Magaziner from Mike Lux, regarding "Memo We Discussed This Morning," 31 March 1993, 1, 2; memorandum to Hillary Rodham Clinton from Mike Lux, regarding "Politics of Remaining Major Health Care Decisions," 18 May 1993; memorandum to Hillary Rodham Clinton from Mike Lux, regarding "Interest Group Strategy on Health Care," 19 April 1993; memorandum to Hillary Rodham Clinton from Mike Lux, regarding "Organization of Strategy on Health Care," 9 March 1993, 2–3; memorandum to Hillary Rodham Clinton from Mike Lux, regarding "Positioning Ourselves on Health Care," 3 May 1993. Emphases are in the originals as presented.

39. Peterson, "Politics of Health Care Policy"; quotation from memorandum to the president from Mike Lux, 15 December 1993.

40. Memorandum to Hillary Rodham Clinton from Mike Lux, regarding "Positioning Ourselves on Health Care," 3 May 1993.

41. Peterson, "Politics of Health Care Policy"; Hugh Heclo, "The Clinton Health Plan: Historical Perspectives," *Health Affairs* 14 (Spring 1995): 92–93.

42. Based on data from a survey of 120 interest groups I conducted subsequent to the health care reform debate.

43. Jonathan D. Salant, "Alliance of Private Groups Pushes GOP 'Contract,'" *Congressional Quarterly Weekly Report*, 28 January 1995, 261–63; Alissa J. Rubin, "A Pressure Group Splinters," *Congressional Quarterly Weekly Report*, 27 May 1995, 1492; Alissa J. Rubin, "Spadework on Medicare Pays Off for GOP," *Congressional Quarterly Weekly Report*, 23 September 1995, 2895–97; Maraniss and Weisskopf, *Tell Newt to Shut Up!*

44. David S. Cloud, "Sound and Fury over NAFTA Overshadows the Debate," *Congressional Quarterly Weekly Report*, 26 October 1993, 2791–96; David S. Cloud, "Decisive Vote Brings Down the Trade Walls with Mexico," *Congressional Quarterly Weekly Report*, 20 November 1993, 3174–79.

45. Peter Kilborn, "The Free Trade Accord: Labor Unions Vow to Punish Pact's Backers," *New York Times*, 19 November 1993, A27.

46. Nathan Dietz, "Legislative-Executive Bargaining and the Vote on NAFTA: The Relative Impact of Pork Barrel Politics," paper presented at the annual meeting of the Midwest Political Science Association, Chicago, 18–20 April 1996, 5; Peter H. Stone, "Lobbyists Lend a Hand on NAFTA," *National Journal*, 30 October 1993, 2595–96; David S. Cloud, "As NAFTA Countdown Begins, Wheeling, Dealing Intensifies," *Congressional Quarterly Weekly Report*, 13 November 1993, 3104.

47. "Things Fall Apart," *The Economist*, 20 August 1994, 21.

48. Holly Idelson, "Clinton, Democrats Scramble to Save Anti-Crime Bill," *Congressional Quarterly Weekly Report*, 13 August 1994, 2340–41; Douglas Jehl, "Battle on Crime Bill Tests Clinton's Strategic Skills," *New York Times*, 23 August 1994, A1; "Forty-Six GOP Renegades Hand Clinton Big Victory," *Human Events*, 2 September 1994, 1–2.

49. Stephen Glass, "Anatomy of a Policy Fraud," *New Republic*, 17 November 1997, 22–25.

50. Based on a conversation with a White House official, 17 November 1998; "The State of the Union Address: Clinton Stresses Welfare, Health Care Reform," *Congressional Quarterly Weekly Report*, 29 January 1994, 197–98.

51. Rich Lowry, "Central Problem," *National Review*, 26 September 1994, 21–22.

52. Based on a conversation with a White House official, 17 November 1998.

53. David Mayhew, *Divided We Govern: Party Control, Lawmaking, and Investigations, 1946–90* (New Haven: Yale University Press, 1991).

54. Balz and Brownstein, *Storming the Gates*; Maraniss and Weisskopf, *Tell Newt to Shut Up!*; Seelye, "Long Fight Yields Hint of Victory."

55. See "Remarks by the President at the Democratic National Committee Plenary Session," Hilton Hotel and Towers, Washington, D.C., 21 January 1995, www.publications@clinton.ai.mit.edu.

56. *Federal Staff Directory* no. 2 (Mt. Vernon, Va.: Directories, Ltd., 1995); *Federal Yellow Book* (New York: Leadership Directories, Summer 1998).

57. Peterson, "Presidency and Organized Interests."

58. Peterson, "Politics of Health Care Policy"; Balz and Brownstein, *Storming the Gates*; Maraniss and Weisskopf, *Tell Newt to Shut Up!*

59. Jeffrey L. Katz, "After 60 Years, Most Control is Passing to States," *Congressional Quarterly Weekly Report*, 3 August 1996, 2195.

60. Grant McConnell, *Private Power and American Democracy* (New York: Knopf, 1967), 59; Walker, *Mobilizing Interest Groups*; J. David Greenstone and Paul E. Peterson, *Race and Authority in Urban Politics: Community Participation and the War on Poverty* (New York: Russell Sage, 1973); Ginsberg and Shefter, "Presidency, Interest Groups, and Social Forces."

61. John Ferejohn, "The Tale of Two Congresses: Social Policy in the Clinton Years," in Weir, *Social Divide*, 49–82.

62. Skowronek, "Risks of 'Third-Way' Politics."

Chapter 8: Race, Gender, and the Clinton Presidency

The authors want to thank Graham Wilson for his useful comments on earlier drafts.

1. Ideally, our focus on race should encompass the wide range of important racial/ethnic groups having an impact on politics today. Throughout this chapter, however, we focus primarily on African Americans as our racial case study. In selecting blacks and women as our specific subjects, we pinpoint groups that have stayed disproportionately in Clinton's corner, two with which the Democratic Party has built a substantial history of special relationships. Given that our assignment is to discuss race *and* gender, we also limit our discussion for practical reasons of space.

2. Katharine Q. Seelye, "Blacks Stand by the President in His Time of Need," *New York Times*, 16 February 1998, A11.

3. These formulations of identity politics cause many problems, but one, which we must acknowledge, is obvious: *women* and *African Americans* are overlapping sets of people. But we are dealing primarily with politically constructed categories and will point out some of the places where the confluence of racial and gender politics is most notable in this context. On this problem of identity and category, see Elizabeth V. Spelman, *Inessential Woman: Problems of Exclusion in Feminist Thought* (Boston: Beacon Press, 1988).

4. Robert D. Loevy, *The Civil Rights Act of 1964: The Passage of the Law that Ended Segregation* (Albany: State University of New York Press, 1997), 12.

5. Doris Kearns Goodwin, *No Ordinary Time: Franklin and Eleanor Roosevelt: The Home Front in World War II* (New York: Simon & Schuster, 1994). It is also important that some New Deal programs, such as Social Security, were biased against blacks. See Theda Skocpol, "African Americans in U.S. Social Policy," in *Classifying by Race*, ed. Paul E. Peterson (Princeton: Princeton University Press, 1995), 132–34. To the dismay of the black community (and Eleanor), FDR never threw his support behind the antilynching law. See Goodwin, *No Ordinary Time*, 164.

6. The partisan culture of the black community has changed so much that J.C. Watts Sr., the father of the only black Republican member of Congress, is reported to have said, "I'm not like my boy. . . . I told him that voting for the Republican ticket is like a chicken voting for Colonel Sanders." Quoted in Ron Jenkins, "New House Leader Fights Deadbeat Past," Associated Press, 23 November 1998.

7. Virginia Sapiro with Pamela Johnston Conover, "The Variable Gender Basis of Electoral Politics: Gender and Context in the 1992 U.S. Election," *British Journal of Political Science* 27 (1997): 497–523.

8. Carole Kennedy Chaney, R. Michael Alvarez, and Jonathan Nagler, "Explaining the Gender Gap in U.S. Presidential Elections, 1980–1992," *Political Research Quarterly* 51 (June 1998): 311–39.

9. Virginia Sapiro, "Feminism: A Generation Later," *The Annals* 515 (May 1991): 10–22.

10. Elizabeth Adell Cook, Sue Thomas, and Clyde Wilcox, eds., *The Year of the Woman: Myths and Realities* (Boulder, Colo.: Westview, 1994); Sapiro with Conover, "Variable Gender Basis."

11. Sapiro with Conover, "Variable Gender Basis."

12. EMILY's List functions primarily not just as a PAC (which would contribute money in its own name), but as an organization that "bundles" contributions, identifying candidates it favors and urging its members and supporters to send checks to EMILY's List, but made out to those campaigns. EMILY's List then "bundles" them together and forwards them to the campaigns, making clear, of course, who organized such large collective contributions. The Center for Responsive Politics lists EMILY's List's own contributions as thirty-second in the list of big contributors. It notes that the organization claimed to have bundled up to $6 million in total, a figure that "is impossible to verify, since much of it came in contributions under the $200 that need not be itemized by candidates." Larry Makinson and Joshua Goldstein, *Open Secrets: The Encyclopedia of Congressional Money and Politics* (Washington, D.C.: Center for Responsive Politics and Congressional Quarterly, 1994), 24–25.

13. David T. Canon, *Race, Redistricting, and Representation: The Unintended Consequences of Black-Majority Districts* (Chicago: University of Chicago Press, 1999), intro. and chap. 2. These minority-majority districts were struck down by recent Supreme Court decisions (*Shaw* v. *Reno*, 1993; *Bush* v. *Vera*, 1996; *Miller* v. *Johnson*, 1996), but the exact status of these districts is still to be determined by ongoing litigation.

14. Thomas Edsall, "Clinton Stuns Rainbow Coalition; Candidate Criticizes Rap Singer's Message," *Washington Post*, 14 June 1992, A1.

15. Clarence Page, "Clinton's Souljah Censure May Have Been His Salvation," *Orlando Sentinel Tribune*, 30 October, 1992, A19.

16. Ibid. Hispanic leaders were equally angered over their perception that Clinton ignored them and key issues such as immigration that were important to them.

17. Paul R. Abramson, John H. Aldrich, and David W. Rohde, *Change and Continuity in the 1992 Elections*, rev. ed. (Washington, D.C.: CQ Press, 1995), 38.

18. These numbers are from the Voter News Service exit polls. Figures from the National Election Study show that 92 percent of blacks voted for Clinton, while Gallup exit polls show that 82 percent of blacks voted for Clinton.

19. Abramson, Aldrich, and Rohde, *Change and Continuity,* 106; F. Christopher Arterton, "Campaign '92: Strategies and Tactics of the Candidates," in *The Election of 1992,* ed. Gerald M. Pomper (Chatham, N.J.: Chatham House, 1993), 102.

20. Tate, "Structural Dependence or Group Loyalty?" 184.

21. The tumble felt even steeper given that the Clinton presidential election year nudged the Democratic margin up to 54–46. "A Look at Voting Patterns of 115 Demographic Groups in House Races," *New York Times,* 9 November 1998, A20.

22. Ibid.

23. Associated Press, "GOP Victory Is Tied to White Male Vote; Polls Show Women Remained Loyal to Democratic Tickets," *Chicago Tribune,* 14 November 1994, 6.

24. This office is separate from the President's Interagency Council on Women, also formed in 1995, but with the express mission of implementing the Beijing Platform of Action, formulated at the United Nations Fourth World Conference on Women. It, too, helped trumpet the Clinton administration's accomplishments with respect to women and children.

25. ABC News poll, 3 January 1996.

26. Charlotte Grimes, "Women Want More than Words from GOP," *St. Louis Post-Dispatch,* 1 August 1996, 5B.

27. "The News Hour with Jim Lehrer," 13 August 1996, transcript 5632.

28. Gerald M. Pomper, "The Presidential Election," in *The Election of 1996,* ed. Gerald M. Pomper (Chatham, N.J.: Chatham House, 1997), 185.

29. Thomas B. Edsall, "Clinton Tailors Agenda to Suit Women's Needs," *Washington Post,* 21 October 1996, A1.

30. Pomper, "Presidential Election," 179.

31. Hohenberg, *Reelecting Bill Clinton,* 255–56.

32. Leonard Pitts Jr., "GOP Needs to Learn How to Talk to Black Voters," *New Orleans Times-Picayune,* 19 July 1996, B7.

33. Ibid.

34. Michael Allen, "Bob to Blacks: Sorry for NAACP Snub," *New York Daily News,* 24 August 1996, 2.

35. Howard Troxler, "Black Baptists Applaud Clinton," *St. Petersburg Times,* 7 September 1996, A4.

36. Rick Christie and Scott Shepard, "Race and the Election: Born-Again Politics," *Atlanta Journal and Constitution,* 6 October 1996, G1.

37. The Pew Research Center for The People and The Press, "Turnout Indicators Slightly Below '94 Level: GOP Congressional Lead Not Undercut by Backlash," 21 October 1998, http://208.240.91.18/oct98rpt.html.

38. Kevin Sack, "Democrats in Political Debt for Black Turnout in South," *New York Times,* 6 November 1998, A1.

39. Bill Maxwell, "Friends of Bill: Why Blacks Stand by Clinton," *St. Petersburg Times*, 4 October 1998, 1D.

40. Kevin Sack, "Blacks Stand by a President Who 'Has Been There for Us,'" *New York Times*, 19 September 1998, A1.

41. Sack, "Democrats in Political Debt for Black Turnout in South."

42. Ibid.

43. David Gergen, "The New Political Calculus: Democrats Have Figured Out the Future. Will Republicans?" *U.S. News & World Report*, 16 November 1998, 88.

44. Guy Gugliotta and Juliet Eilperin, "GOP Turns Attention to Contest for House Majority Leader," *Washington Post*, 10 November 1998, A1.

45. The statement is available at the NOW website, www.now.org/press/09-98/09-24b98.html.

46. Lyn Ragsdale, *Vital Statistics on the Presidency: Washington to Clinton* (Washington, D.C.: CQ Press, 1998).

47. Carl Tobias, "Judicial Appointments: Cautious Approach Advised," *National Law Journal*, 9 December 1996, A18.

48. Ruth Marcus, "Clinton Berates Critics in Women's Groups; President-Elect Assails Appointment 'Quota Games' as He Adds Riley, O'Leary to Cabinet," *Washington Post*, 22 December 1992, A1.

49. White House Office for Women's Initiatives and Outreach, "President Clinton and Vice President Gore: Supporting Women and Families." www.whitehouse.gov/WH/EOP/Women.

50. Martha Farnsworth Riche, "The Bean Count Is In! A Promise Fulfilled," *Washington Post*, 23 January 1994, C2.

51. Jeffrey Rosen, "Danny and Zöe: Ms. Baird and Mr. Quayle," *New Republic*, 1 February 1993, 28.

52. See, for example, Lani Guinier, "Groups, Representation, and Race-conscious Districting: A Case of the Emperor's Clothes," *Texas Law Review* 71 (June 1993): 1589–1642.

53. John Schwartz, "Blunt Talk, Sudden Exit; Surgeon General Outspoken from the Start," *Washington Post*, 10 December 1994, A1.

54. Ron Fournier, "No Regrets about Remarks, Defiant Elders Says," Associated Press, *Washington Dateline*, 9 December 1994.

55. Quoted in Joel D. Aberbach, "The Federal Executive under Clinton," in *The Clinton Presidency: First Appraisals*, ed. Colin Campbell and Bert A. Rockman (Chatham, N.J.: Chatham House, 1996), 172.

56. On first ladies, see "Symposium: First Ladies and the Presidency," *Presidential Studies Quarterly* 20 (Fall 1990): 677–790; Karen O'Connor, Bernadette Nye, and Laura van Assendelft, "Wives in the White House: The Political Influence of First Ladies," *Presidential Studies Quarterly* 26 (Summer 1996): 835–53; Robert Watson, "The First Lady Reconsidered: Presidential Partner and Political Institution," *Presidential Studies Quarterly* 27 (Fall 1997): 805–18. On Hillary Clinton, see Barbara C. Burrell, *Public Opinion, the First Ladyship, and Hillary Rodham Clinton* (New York: Garland Publishing, 1997).

57. Goodwin, *No Ordinary Time*.

58. Drew, *On the Edge*.

59. Francis X. Cline, "From Political Debit to Force: Hillary Clinton," *New York Times*, 22 November 1998, A1.

60. Toni Morrison, "The Talk of the Town," *New Yorker*, 5 October 1998, 32.

61. Peter Carlson, "It's Off to the Races Again, as Clinton Becomes Black," *Washington Post*, 29 September 1998, D2; Armstrong Williams, "Blacks Are Misguided in Their Support for Clinton," *USA Today*, 1 October 1998, 15A; Brent Staples, "Bill Clinton, the First 'Black' President," *Pittsburgh Post-Gazette*, 1 November 1998, E1.

62. See the White House website (www.whitehouse.gov/Initiatives/OneAmerica/accompreport.html) for a list of the various proposals.

63. The impact of websites is often overdrawn. But in light of our argument about the "two-step" nature of presidential influence with respect to women and African Americans, what is crucial is that journalists and interest group leaders use the web a lot for gathering basic information. Most important, it offers easy, direct access to the framing of the president's priorities and achievements as he would have them known.

Chapter 9: Clinton's Domestic Policy

1. Bill Clinton and Al Gore, *Putting People First* (New York: Times Books, 1992), 191.

2. Ibid., 14.

3. Ibid., 107.

4. Ibid., 94.

5. Bob Woodward, *The Agenda: Inside the Clinton White House* (New York: Simon & Schuster, 1994), 19.

6. Paul J. Quirk and Jon Dalager, "The Election: A 'New Democrat' and a New Kind of Presidential Campaign," in *The Elections of 1992*, ed. Michael Nelson (Washington, D.C.: CQ Press, 1993), 57–88.

7. Charles L. Schultze, *The Public Use of Private Interest* (Washington, D.C.: Brookings Institution, 1977).

8. Lawrence Mead, *Beyond Entitlement* (New York: Free Press, 1986).

9. Briefly, it is that a tax can create an economic incentive, as strong as policymakers wish, for firms to reduce pollution. Those firms that can reduce it at least cost to themselves and the economy (for example, those that need new equipment anyway) will reduce it the most. So the overall cost of any given amount of pollution control will be minimized. See Schultze, *Public Use*.

10. Sidney M. Milkis, "The Presidency and the Political Parties," in *The Presidency and the Political System*, 4th ed., ed. Michael Nelson (Washington, D.C.: CQ Press, 1995), 348–78.

11. James H. Kuklinski and Paul J. Quirk, "Reconsidering the Rational Public: Cognition, Heuristics, and Mass Opinion," in *Elements of Political Reason*, ed. Arthur Lupia, Mathew McCubbins, and Samuel Popkin (New York: Cambridge University Press, forthcoming).

12. Joseph Cooper and Garry Young, "Partisanship, Bipartisanship, and Crosspartisanship in Congress Since the New Deal," in *Congress Reconsidered*, 6th ed., ed. Lawrence C. Dodd and Bruce Oppenheimer (Washington, D.C.: CQ Press, 1997), 246–73.

13. Richard E. Cohen, "What Coattails?" *National Journal*, 29 May 1993, 1285.

14. In Helen Dewar, "Next President's Diplomatic Skill To Be Put to Test," *Washington Post*, 5 November 1992, A25, A32.

15. "With Democrat in the White House, Partisanship Hits New High," *CQ Almanac 1993* (Washington, D.C.: CQ Press, 1994), 14C–21C.

16. Woodward, *Agenda*, 181.

17. Since 1953, only Eisenhower and Johnson topped Clinton's 86.4 percent success rate for a first year in office. From "When Congress Had to Choose, It Voted to Back Clinton," *CQ Almanac 1993*, 3C–13C.

18. Michael Wines and Robert Pear, "President Finds Benefits in Defeat on Health Care," *New York Times*, 30 July 1996. (Citations of the *New York Times* refer to the national edition.)

19. See the website at www.gallup.com for a complete listing of Clinton's poll numbers throughout his term.

20. Walter Dean Burnham, "Realignment Lives: The 1994 Earthquake and Its Implications," in *The Clinton Presidency: First Appraisals*, ed. Colin Campbell and Bert A. Rockman (Chatham, N.J.: Chatham House, 1996), 363.

21. Newt Gingrich et al., *Contract with America* (New York: Times Books, 1994), 16–19.

22. David W. Moore, Lydia Saad, Leslie McAneny, and Frank Newport, "Contract with America: A Gallup Poll Special Report," *Gallup Poll Monthly*, November 1994. Two-thirds of respondents said they had not heard of the Contract (p. 20).

23. Remarks made on 11 November 1994, in *Contract*, 186.

24. Ibid.

25. Elizabeth Drew, *Showdown* (New York: Simon & Schuster, 1996), 189.

26. "Clinton Success Rate Declined to a Record Low in 1995," *CQ Almanac 1993*, 3C–7C.

27. *Weekly Compilation of Presidential Documents*, 18 April 1995.

28. In Drew, *Showdown*, 139.

29. Ibid., 213.

30. Ibid., 69.

31. *Weekly Compilation of Presidential Documents*, 13 June 1995.

32. Drew, *Showdown*, 236.

33. Polls listed in Drew, *Showdown*, 324.

34. "Clinton's Big Comeback Shows in Vote Score," *CQ Almanac 1996* (Washington, D.C.: CQ Press, 1997), C3.

35. "As Elections Loom, GOP Ardor Gives Way to Pragmatism," *CQ Almanac 1996*, 1–4.

36. Dick Morris, *Behind the Oval Office* (New York: Random House, 1997), 33.

37. Arguably, the public would have most preferred a more moderate reform, if it had fully understood the Republican bill. See Steven M. Teles, *Whose Welfare: AFDC and Political Elites* (Lawrence: University Press of Kansas, 1998), ch. 3.

38. Alison Mitchell, "Despite His Reversals, Clinton Stays Centered," *New York Times*, 28 July 1996, I28.

39. Francis X. Clines, "Gingrich, Role as House Leader Intact, Offers Clinton an Olive Branch," *New York Times*, 7 November 1996.

40. William Schneider, "A New GOP Tack: Bang, Bang. Kiss, Kiss," *National Journal*, 15 February 1997, 346.

41. Carroll J. Doherty, "Clinton Finds Support on Hill Despite GOP's Vocal Attacks," *Congressional Quarterly*, 3 January 1998, 14–15.

42. All from "States of the Union: Then and Now," *National Journal*, 24 January 1998, 154.

43. For an excellent overview of myriad economic indicators, see the website at www.whitehouse.gov/fsbr/esbr.html.

44. David E. Rosenbaum and Steve Lohr, "With a Stable Economy, Clinton Hopes for Credit," *New York Times*, 3 August 1996, A1.

45. Ibid., A8.

46. John T. Wholley, "Exorcising Inflation-Mindedness: The Transformation of Economic Management in the 1970s," *Journal of Policy History* 10 (1998): 130–52.

47. Schneider, "A New GOP Tack," 346.

48. "Pact Aims to Erase Deficit by 2002," *CQ Almanac 1997* (Washington, D.C.: CQ Press, 1997) 2–18.

49. Jonathan Rauch, "The Easy Way Out," *National Journal*, 10 May 1997, 930.

50. "Pact Aims to Erase Deficit," 2–18.

51. "Tone, Tenor of First Session Seemed Like Old Times," *CQ Almanac 1997*, 1–7; "Pact Aims to Erase Deficit," 2–18.

52. *Weekly Compilation of Presidential Documents*, 25 August 1997, 1225.

53. "Pact Aims to Erase Deficit," 2–20.

54. Jack W. Germond and Jules Witcover, "Much Ado about a Budget Nothing," *National Journal*, 10 May 1997, 947.

55. Ibid., 947.

56. Paul Starr, *The Logic of Health Care Reform* (Knoxville: Grand Rounds Press, 1991), 16. In contrast, health care spending accounted for only 5.9 percent of the GNP in 1965 and only 8.9 percent as recently as 1980. See the website at www.hcfa.gov/stats/nhe-oact/tables/t09.html.

57. Ibid., 22.

58. Clinton and Gore, *Putting People First*, 21.

59. Wines and Pear, "President Finds Benefits," B8.

60. These criticisms are reported in Theda Skocpol, *Boomerang: Clinton's Health Care Effort and the Turn against Government in the U.S.A.* (New York: Simon & Schuster, 1996), 10.

61. Wines and Pear, "President Finds Benefits," B8.

62. Skocpol, *Boomerang*, 108. Emphasis in original.

63. All from Adam Clymer, "The Clinton Plan is Alive on Arrival," *New York Times*, 3 October 1993, E3. Also in Skocpol, *Boomerang*, 5.

64. "Clinton's Legislative Strategy Falters," *CQ Almanac 1994* (Washington, D.C.: CQ Press, 1995), 29.

65. Wines and Pear, "President Finds Benefits," B8.

66. Lydia Saad, "Public Has Cold Feet on Health Care Reform," *Gallup Poll Monthly* 346 (August 1994): 2–9.

67. Alex Pham, "Health Care Outlay Seen Doubling," *Boston Globe*, 15 September 1998, D1.

68. "States of the Union: Then and Now," 154.

69. Jeff Schear, "Pulling in Harness," *National Journal*, 4 June 1994, 1286.

70. Peter T. Kilborn and Sam Howe Verhovek, "Clinton's Welfare Shift Ends Tortuous Journey," *New York Times*, 2 August 1996, A1.

71. Jeffrey L. Katz, "Clinton Urged to Slow Down," *CQ Weekly Report*, 22 January 1994, 119.

72. *Contract with America*, 66.

73. *Weekly Compilation of Presidential Documents*, 18 April 1995, 651.

74. Rochelle L. Stanfield, "Lots of Spin, But No Sign of Movement," *National Journal*, 1 June 1996, 1210–11.

75. Ibid., 1210.

76. Eliza Newlin Carney, "Is It All about Political Points?" *National Journal*, 16 March 1996, 620.

77. Jeff Shaar, "Looking for a Voice," *National Journal*, 16 March 1996, 594.

78. Ibid., 594.

79. Dick Morris claims that his polling data showed that a Clinton veto would turn a 15-point win into a 3-point loss in the November elections. Although the claim that a single issue could cause a swing of almost 20 points in a presidential election cannot be taken seriously, it indicates the importance Clinton's top political adviser placed on this issue. See Morris, *Behind the Oval Office*, 300.

80. Rochelle L. Stanfield, "This Reform May Not Be the Answer," *National Journal*, 3 August 1996, 1664.

81. Marilyn Werber Serafini, "A Quick Fix," *National Journal*, 16 November 1996, 2490–93; Peter Edelman, "The Worst Thing Bill Clinton Has Done," *Atlantic Monthly*, March 1997, 43–58. Edelman was Clinton's assistant secretary of health and human services.

82. Rochelle L. Stanfield, "Cautious Optimism," *National Journal*, 2 May 1998, 990–93.

83. Robert Pear, "Most States Meet Work Requirement of Welfare Law," *New York Times*, 30 December 1998, A1, A12.

84. Ibid., A1.

85. Kilborn and Verhovek, "Clinton's Welfare Shift," A18.

86. "Bill Clinton, Environmentalist?" *New York Times*, 5 January 1993, A14.

87. Norman J. Vig, "Presidential Leadership and the Environment," in *Environmental Policy in the 1990s*, 3d ed., ed. Norman J. Vig and Michael E. Kraft (Washington, D.C.: CQ Press, 1997), 104.

88. Clinton and Gore, *Putting People First*, 95–98.

89. *Weekly Compilation of Presidential Documents*, 21 April 1994, 868.

90. Mark Hertsgaard, "Global Warning," *New York Times*, 8 April 1995, 123.

91. *Weekly Compilation of Presidential Documents*, 14 June 1993, 1076.

92. Stephen M. Meyer, "Dead Wood," *New Republic*, 2 August 1993, 12.

93. John H. Cushman and Timothy Egan, "Battles on Conservation are Reaping Dividends," *New York Times*, 31 July 1996, A12.

94. Ibid. In principle it is reasonable to insist that regulations be cost effective (less costly than other methods of achieving the same goals), but demonstrating cost effectiveness rigorously can itself be exceedingly costly.

95. Todd S. Purdum, "Clinton Lashes Out at Congress," *New York Times*, 2 August 1995, A12.

96. Cushman and Egan, "Battles on Conservation," A12; and Drew, *Showdown*, 226.

97. Cushman and Egan, "Battles on Conservation," A12.

98. John H. Cushman, "Environment Gets a Push from Clinton," *New York Times*, 5 July 1995, A11.

99. Richard L. Berke, "GOP's Officials, Feeling Boxed In, Keep Looking for a Way Out," *New York Times*, 19 January 1999, A14.

100. Ronald Reagan came close in his 1981 tax and budget proposals, but only by appealing to highly unorthodox and wildly optimistic economic forecasts; and even Reagan called for cuts in domestic programs, though not in overall government spending.

101. Richard L. Berke, "Robertson, Praising Speech, Suggests GOP Halt Trial," *New York Times*, 21 January 1999, A1.

Chapter 10: Engaging the World

The authors want to thank the following individuals for their helpful comments: Bruce Jentleson, Robert Litwak, Miroslav Nincic, James P. Pfiffner, Bert Rockman, and Andrew Ross. For research assistance they thank Carlos Chavez, Erik J. Schelzig, and Curtis Simon.

1. See E.J. Dionne, "Running from Foreign Policy," *Washington Post*, 12 October 1993, A19; Linda B. Miller, "The Clinton Years: Reinventing Foreign Policy," *International Affairs*, October 1994, 621–34; Michael Mandelbaum, "Foreign Policy as Social Work," *Foreign Affairs* 75, no. 1 (January/February 1996): 16–32; Joshua Muravchik, "Carrying a Small Stick," *National Review*, 2 September 1996, 57–62; William G. Hyland, "A Mediocre Record," *Foreign Policy* 101 (Winter 1995–96): 69–74; and Richard H. Ullman, "A Late Recovery," *Foreign Policy* 101 (Winter 1995–96): 75–79.

2. Miller, "Clinton Years," 622.

3. Larry Berman and Emily O. Goldman, "Clinton's Foreign Policy at Midterm," in *The Clinton Presidency: First Appraisals,* ed. Colin Campbell and Bert A. Rockman (Chatham, N.J.: Chatham House, 1996).

4. Madeleine K. Albright, "The Testing of American Foreign Policy," *Foreign Affairs* 77, no. 6 (November/December 1998): 51.

5. John Gerard Ruggie, "The Past as Prologue? Interests, Identity, and American Foreign Policy," *International Security* 21, no. 4 (Spring 1997): 90.

6. Jacob Weisberg, "Bill Clinton's Legacy," *New York Times Magazine*, 17 January 1999.

7. John F. Harris, "A Changed President: More Focused, Less Quick to Anger," *Washington Post National Weekly Edition* 16, no. 33 (14 June 1999): 10.

8. Thomas Omestad, "Foreign Policy and Campaign '96," *Foreign Policy* 105 (Winter 1996): 39.

9. "Challenges Loom Abroad for President," *Congressional Quarterly*, 7 December 1996, 3344.

10. "Quayle Bashes Clinton on Issues," Associated Press, 12 January 1999.

11. Clinton address, World Affairs Council, 26 February 1999.

12. Richard Holbrooke, *To End a War* (New York: Random House, 1998).

13. John McCain, "Imagery or Purpose? The Choice in November," *Foreign Policy* 103 (Summer 1996): 20-35.

14. Moises Naim, "Clinton's Foreign Policy: A Victim Of Globalization," *Foreign Policy* 109 (Winter 1997–98): 34–35.

15. Ibid.

16. William Jefferson Clinton, "A Just and Necessary War," *New York Times*, 23 May 1999, 17.

17. James Kitfield, "Strategic Muddle," *National Journal* 29, no. 7 (22 November 1997): 2357.

18. Cited in "Foreign Policy Dreaming," *Washington Times*, 12 January 1998.

19. Albright, "Testing of American Foreign Policy."

20. Robert A. Manning and Patrick Clawson, "The Clinton Doctrine," *Asian Wall Street Journal*, 31 December 1997, 6.

21. Edward Mortimer, "Clinton Doctrine," *Financial Times*, 16 July 1997, 24.

22. Robert Worth, "Clinton's Warriors: The Interventionists," *World Policy Journal* 15, no. 1 (Spring 1998): 43.

23. E.J. Dionne Jr., "Limited Engagement: Defining the Clinton Doctrine," *Bergen County Record*, 29 December 1997, A13.

24. Andrew J. Bacevich, "The Clinton Doctrine: Don't Ask," *Washington Post*, 3 January 1999, C5.

25. Phyllis Schlafly, "Second Thoughts in the House about Funding IMF," *Las Vegas Review-Journal*, 22 April 1998, 9B; Dick Armey, "Clinton Doctrine: Indiscriminate Global Bailout of IMF Covers Others Peoples' Bad Debts and Undermines Free Market Processes," *Dallas Business Journal* 21, no. 35 (24 April 1998): 38.

26. Cokie Roberts and Steve Roberts, "Most Nations See United States as Honest Broker in World Conflicts," *Salt Lake Tribune*, 29 December 1998, A7.

27. Graham Evans, "The Vision Thing: In Search of the Clinton Doctrine," *The World Today* 53, nos. 8–9 (August/September 1997): 213.

28. Ibid.

29. In the military sense, one important purpose served by doctrine is to provide guidance for decisions in the absence of perfect information. Doctrine told the commander that if he did not have enough intelligence to make a situation-specific judgment, history suggested that a certain course of action was most likely the safest.

30. Scholars have served up various lists of "grand strategies" or "foreign policy paradigms" over the past several years. Barry Posen and Andrew Ross articulate four: neo-isolationism, selective engagement, cooperative security, and primacy; see Barry R. Posen and Andrew L. Ross, "Competing Visions for U.S. Grand Strategy," *International Security* 21, no. 3 (Winter 1996–97): 5–53. Terry Diebel offers at least five: containment, balance of power, collective security, hemispheric defense, and isolationism; see Terry L. Diebel, "Strategies before Containment," *International Security* 16, no. 4 (Spring 1992): 79–108. Robert Art suggests seven: selective engagement, dominion, global collective security, regional collective security, cooperative security, containment, and isolationism; see Robert J. Art, "Geopolitics Updated: The Strategy of Selective Engagement," *International Security* 23, no. 3 (Winter 1998–99): 79–113. Richard Haass proposes five purposes for foreign policy (Wilsonianism, economism, realism, humanitarianism, and minimalism) and three sets of means (unilateralism, neo-internationalism, and U.S. leadership); see Richard Haass, "Paradigm Lost," *Foreign Affairs* 74, no. 1 (January/February 1995): 43–58. A survey of U.S. foreign policy by historian Walter McDougall offers eight diplomatic traditions, which he calls canons or doctrines: exceptionalism, isolationism, Monroe Doctrine, Manifest Destiny, progressive imperialism, liberal internationalism, containment, and global meliorism; see Walter A. McDougall, *Promised Land, Crusader State: The American Encounter with the World Since 1776* (Boston: Houghton Mifflin, 1997). By conflating ends and means in generating their lists, academics further confuse dialogue on the issue.

31. See McDougall, *Promised Land*, 101–46. Also see Mark Shulman, "Institutionalizing a Political Idea: Navalism and the Emergence of American Sea Power," in *The Politics of Strategic Adjust-*

ment: Ideas, Institutions, and Interests, ed. Peter Trubowitz, Emily O. Goldman, and Edward Rhodes (New York: Columbia University Press, 1999): 79–101.

32. For a good overview of the genesis of the strategy, see Douglas Brinkley, "Democratic Enlargement: The Clinton Doctrine," *Foreign Policy* 106 (Spring 1997): 111–27.

33. James M. McCormick, "Assessing Clinton's Foreign Policy at Midterm," *Current History* 94, no. 595 (November 1995): 372.

34. Interventions in Haiti, Somalia, and Bosnia—all poor, weak countries on the international periphery—suggested non-selective engagement early on.

35. By homeland defense, the administration did not mean missile defense.

36. *A National Security Strategy for a New Century* (Washington, D.C.: The White House, October 1998), 6.

37. Richard Haass wrote in 1997 that the neo-Wilsonian vision represented by a strategy of enlargement "has had a negligible impact on day-to-day affairs. Enlarging the community of market democracies might look good on paper, but it has provided few policy-relevant guidelines for pressing foreign policy problems such as those presented by Bosnia, Iraq, North Korea, Rwanda, or Somalia." See Richard N. Haass, "Fatal Distraction: Bill Clinton's Foreign Policy," *Foreign Policy* 108 (Fall 1997): 112–22.

38. McCormick, "Assessing Clinton's Foreign Policy," 373–74. The McDonald's analogy is from Thomas Friedman, cited in Brinkley, "Democratic Enlargement."

39. Graham Allison, "Get Ready For the Clinton Doctrine," *New Statesman*, 8 November 1996.

40. John Stremlau, "Clinton's Dollar Diplomacy," *Foreign Policy* 97 (Winter 1994–95): 21; Gordon Wood, *The Radicalism of the American Revolution* (New York: A.A. Knopf, 1992).

41. For other critiques of this economic-centric approach to foreign policy, see Miller, "Clinton Years," 632.

42. It should be emphasized that at the onset of the Cold War, there were vigorous debates, such as that between George Kennan and Paul Nitze, on the pragmatic policy guideposts that flowed from the strategy of containment. See John Lewis Gaddis, *Strategies of Containment* (New York: Oxford University Press, 1982).

43. This brief overview of prospect theory is drawn chiefly from Jack S. Levy, "Introduction to Prospect Theory," *Political Psychology* 13, no. 2 (1992): 171–86; Robert Jervis, "Political Implications of Loss Aversion," *Political Psychology* 13, no. 2 (1992): 187–204; and Jack S. Levy, "Prospect Theory and International Relations: Theoretical Applications and Analytical Problems," *Political Psychology* 13, no. 2 (1992): 283–310.

44. Jervis, "Political Implications," 188–89.

45. Mandelbaum, "Foreign Policy as Social Work," 19–20.

46. Ibid., 21.

47. Ibid., 25.

48. Jervis, "Political Implications," 197.

49. Haass, "Fatal Distraction," 112.

50. Bruce W. Jentleson, "The Pretty Prudent Public: Post-Vietnam American Opinion on the Use of Military Force," *International Studies Quarterly* 36, no.1 (March 1992): 49–74; Bruce W. Jentleson and Rebecca L. Britton, "Still Pretty Prudent: Post–Cold War American Public Opinion and the Use of Military Force," *Journal of Conflict Resolution* 42, no. 4 (August 1998): 395–417.

51. See Miroslav Nincic, "Loss Aversion and the Domestic Context of Military Intervention," *Political Research Quarterly* 50, no. 1 (March 1997): 97-120.

52. Mandelbaum, "Foreign Policy as Social Work," 28.

53. "Unfinished Cold-War Business," *New York Times*, 26 February 1999, A20.

54. One of the biggest proponents of expanding NATO as a military alliance to prevent any future "loss of Europe" to Russia is Henry Kissinger. See, for example, Henry A. Kissinger, "Beware: A Threat Abroad," *Newsweek,* 17 June 1996, 41–43.

55. Peter Trubowitz and Edward Rhodes, "Explaining American Strategic Adjustment," in Trubowitz et al., *Politics of Strategic Adjustment*, 4.

56. Miller, "Clinton Years," 623. For an excellent discussion of cultural transformation in late-nineteenth century America and its impact on the evolution of a new foreign policy strategy, see Edward Rhodes, "Constructing Power: Cultural Transformation and Strategic Adjustment in the 1890s," in Trubowitz et al., *Politics of Strategic Adjustment*, 29–78. Quotation from page 62.

57. Jonathan Clarke and James Clad, *After the Crusade: American Foreign Policy for the Post-Superpower Age* (Lanham, Md.: Madison Books, 1995), 162.

58. Herbert Croly, *The Promise of American Life* (New York: Macmillan, 1909), 306.

59. George F. Kennan, "The Failure in Our Success," *New York Times,* 17 May 1994, A17.

60. Miller, "Clinton Years," 626.

61. For a good overview of the BEM strategy, see Stremlau, "Clinton's Dollar Diplomacy," 18–35.

62. Interview with Clinton administration official, Washington, D.C., February 1999.

63. Stremlau, "Clinton's Dollar Diplomacy," 31.

64. Interview with Clinton administration official, Washington, D.C., February 1999.

65. Ruggie, "Past as Prologue," 109.

66. Barry M. Blechman and Tamara Cofman Wittes, "Defining Moment: The Threat and Use of Force in American Foreign Policy," *Political Science Quarterly* 114, no. 1 (Spring 1999): 1–30; Barton Gellman, "Learning from Kosovo," *Washington Post National Weekly Edition* 16, no. 33 (14 June 1999): 6.

67. Jane Perlez, "The Terrible Lesson of Bosnia: Will It Help Kosovo?" *New York Times*, 1 February 1999, A11.

68. John F. Harris, "A Man of Caution," *Washington Post National Weekly Edition* 16, no. 30 (24 May 1999): 6

69. Charles A. Stevenson, "The Evolving Clinton Doctrine on the Use of Force," *Armed Forces and Society* 22, no. 4 (Summer 1996): 511.

70. Remarks by the president on foreign policy, 26 February 1999, White House press release.

71. Henry Kissinger, "No U.S. Ground Forces for Kosovo," *Washington Post*, 22 February 1999, A15.

72. Lee Hamilton, "Too Involved in Kosovo," *New York Times*, 1 February 1999, A27.

73. Eric Schmitt, "The Powell Doctrine is Looking Pretty Good Again," *New York Times*, 4 April 1999, A5.

74. The U.S. military throughout its history has been employed in noncombat, nonmilitary uses. See Samuel P. Huntington, "New Contingencies, Old Roles," *Joint Forces Quarterly* 2 (Autumn 1993): 38–43.

75. Charles William Maynes, "Squandering Triumph: The West Botched the Post–Cold War World," *Foreign Affairs* 78, no. 1 (January/February 1999): 20–21.

76. Barton Gellman and Steven Mufson, "Raising the Possibility of a New Internationalism," *Washington Post National Weekly Edition* 16, no. 33 (14 June 1999): 7.

77. See James P. Pfiffner, *The Modern Presidency*, 2d ed. (New York: St. Martin's, 1998), 160.

78. Robert O'Neill, "Looking Ahead: Uncertain World to Shape Foreign Policy, Trade Debate," Legislate News Service, 15 January 1999.

79. Ibid.

80. George Wilson and Richard Sia, "Budget 2000," Legislate News Service, 1 February 1999.

81. John Broder, "From Baptism of Fire to Kosovo: Clinton as Commander-in-Chief," *New York Times*, 18 April 1999, A8.

82. Fred Hiatt, "Applause is Cheap," *Washington Post*, 24 January 1999, B7.

83. Kissinger, "No U.S. Ground Force."

84. Bryan Bender, "KLA Action Fueled NATO Victory," *Jane's Defence Weekly* 31, no. 24 (16 June 1999): 5; "Air War's Damage Less Than Thought," *Sacramento Bee*, 28 June 1999, A1.

85. Interview with Clinton administration official, Washington, D.C., February 1999.

86. Posen and Ross, "Competing Visions for U.S. Grand Strategy," 44–50.

87. For further discussion on the challenges of making strategy in an uncertain world, see Emily O. Goldman, "Thinking About Strategy Absent the Enemy," *Security Studies*, 4, no. 1 (Autumn 1994): 40–85.

Chapter 11: Clinton in Comparative Perspective

1. By far the best of the biographies is David Maraniss, *First in His Class: A Biography of Bill Clinton* (New York: Simon & Schuster, 1995).

2. *Le Monde*, 22 September 1998.

3. For a rare and valuable attempt to place the U.S. presidency in comparative perspective, see Colin Campbell, *The U.S. Presidency in Crisis: A Comparative Perspective* (New York: Oxford University Press, 1998).

4. Lyn Ragsdale, *Vital Statistics on the Presidency: From Washington to Clinton* (Washington, D.C.: CQ Press, 1998), 169.

5. See Robert Kaplan, "The Fulcrum of Europe," *Atlantic Monthly*, 3 September 1998, 282.

6. Dick Morris, *Behind the Oval Office: Winning the Presidency in the Nineties* (New York: Random House, 1997).

7. Robert Reich, *Locked in the Cabinet* (New York: Vintage Books, 1997).

8. Anthony Giddens, *The Third Way: The Renewal of Social Democracy* (Malden, Mass.: Polity Press, 1998).

9. The approach was based on the ideas of David E. Osborne and Ted Gaebler, *Reinventing Government: How the Entrepreneurial Spirit is Reinvigorating the Public Sector* (Reading, Mass.: Addison-Wesley, 1992). For an early appraisal of the Gore reinvention initiative, see Donald F. Kettl, *Reinventing Government: Appraising the National Performance Review* (Washington, D.C.: Brookings Institution, 1994).

10. For discussions of this priority among Clinton's inner circle, see Bob Woodward, *The Agenda: Inside the Clinton White House* (New York: Simon & Schuster, 1994).

11. Alain Enthoven, *Health Plan: The Only Practical Solution to the Soaring Cost of Medical Care* (Reading, Mass.: Addison-Wesley, 1980). For analyses of the origins of the Clinton health care plan and its fate, see *The Problem That Won't Go Away; Reforming U.S. Health Care Financing*, ed. Henry Aaron (Washington, D.C.: Brookings Institution, 1996); and Theda Skocpol, *Boomerang: Clinton's Health Care Effort and the Turn Against Government in the U.S.A.* (New York: Simon & Schuster, 1996).

12. At least one of Giddens's books had crystallized the instincts of many New Labour politicians. See Anthony Giddens, *Beyond Left and Right: The Future of Radical Politics* (Stanford, Calif.: Stanford University Press, 1994).

13. Reich, *Locked in the Cabinet*.

14. Charles O. Jones, *Transitions* (Washington, D.C.: Brookings Institution, 1998).

15. Gøsta Esping-Andersen, *The Three Worlds of Welfare* (Princeton: Princeton University Press, 1990).

16. Geoffrey Garrett, "Capital Mobility, Trade, and the Domestic Politics of Economic Policy," *International Organization* 49 (1995): 657–87.

17. "Who's Running Germany?" *The Economist* 349 (5–11 December 1998): 8097.

Chapter 12: Cutting *With* the Grain

1. Charles O. Jones, *The Separated System* (Washington, D.C.: Brookings Institution, 1994).

2. See Alan I. Abramowitz and Kyle L. Saunders, "Ideological Realignment in the U.S. Electorate," *Journal of Politics* 60 (August 1998): 634–52.

3. Stephen Skowronek, *The Politics Presidents Make: Leadership from John Adams to George Bush* (Cambridge, Mass.: Belknap Press, 1993).

4. Fred I. Greenstein, *Eisenhower as Leader: The Hidden-Hand Presidency* (Baltimore: Johns Hopkins University Press, 1994).

5. Bert A. Rockman, "The American Presidency in Comparative Perspective: Systems, Situations, and Leaders," in *The Presidency and the Political System*, 5th ed., ed. Michael Nelson (Washington, D.C.: CQ Press, 1998), 62–87.

6. Terry M. Moe, "Presidents, Institutions, and Theory," in *Researching The Presidency: Vital Questions, New Approaches,"* ed. George C. Edwards III, John H. Kessel, and Bert A. Rockman (Pittsburgh: University of Pittsburgh Press, 1993), 337–85.

7. *Satisficing* is the term invented by Herbert Simon to suggest the limits of problem-related search and to draw a contrast with the assumption of optimality in classical economics. See Herbert A. Simon, *Administrative Behavior: A Study of Decision-Making Processes in Administrative Organization*, 3d ed. (New York: Free Press, 1976), xxviii.

8. See David R. Mayhew, *The Electoral Connection* (New Haven: Yale University Press, 1974).

9. A more elaborated version of this characterization may be found in Bert A. Rockman, "Leadership Style and the Clinton Presidency," in *The Clinton Presidency: First Appraisals*, ed. Colin Campbell and Bert A. Rockman (Chatham, N.J.: Chatham House, 1996), 325–62, esp. 345–48.

10. Richard L. Berke and Richard W. Stevenson, "Clinton Takes the Wind out of GOP Sails: Thinking of Politics Now and Later, He Reverses Course on IRS," *New York Times* (national edition), 26 October 1997, A14.

11. Jack Kelly, "More Than a Sex Scandal: Campaign-Spending Shenanigans Also Threaten to Unseat Clinton and Gore," *Pittsburgh Post-Gazette*, 30 August 1998, C3.

12. A consistent finding from national surveys, at least in the marginal distributions, has been the relatively low personal approval given to President Clinton along with a favorable evaluation of the conduct of his job as president. For example, immediately after public release of the referral to the House Judiciary Committee of Independent Counsel Kenneth Starr's report proclaiming at least eleven impeachable offenses relating to Clinton's behavior and testimony at the Paula Jones deposition and the OIC's grand jury, only 39 percent had a favorable personal opinion of Clinton while 62 percent approved of the way he was handling his job as president. Such findings were consistent throughout the impeachment process. See Richard L. Berke and Janet Elder, "Most in Poll Say President Should Remain in Office: Job Rating is Still High But Public View of His Moral Character Sinks to a Low," *New York Times*, 16 September 1998, A1, A24.

13. A survey taken on 13 December 1998, shortly before the House Judiciary Committee's vote on articles of impeachment, revealed that 80 percent of the public believed that Clinton had committed perjury about having an affair with Monica Lewinsky but 58 percent opposed his impeachment. And on 20 December, 67 percent of the public approved of Clinton's performance as president only a day after the House voted two articles of impeachment. See *"Post*-ABC News Poll: Beyond Impeachment," 21 December 1998, *Washington Post* Poll Archive, via www.WashingtonPost.com/wp-srv/politics/polls/vault/stories/data122198.htm.

14. Richard L. Berke, "The Far Right Sees the Dawn of the Moral Minority," *New York Times,* 21 February 1999, News of the Week in Review, 3.

15. Ibid.

16. See note 13.

17. "Excerpts From the Statement of Judiciary Panel Majority Counsel," *New York Times*, 11 December 1998, A22.

18. Richard E. Neustadt, *Presidential Power* (New York: John Wiley, 1960).

19. See Sarah A. Binder and Steven S. Smith, *Politics or Principle? Filibustering in the United States Senate* (Washington, D.C.: Brookings Institution, 1997), esp. 9, 10, and 86.

20. There are, however, some important caveats here. For example, Edwards et al. find that divided government most affects congressional initiatives rather than presidential ones, and Jones et al. note that declines in budget variability might reflect more political accord than gridlock. But it is the concurrence of division, partisanship, and the use of dilatory rules that may be more likely to influence presidential legislative capabilities than any one factor. See George C. Edwards III, Andrew Barrett, and Jeffrey Peake, "The Legislative Impact of Divided Government," *American Journal of Political Science* 41 (April 1997): 545–63; and Bryan D. Jones, James L. True, and Frank R. Baumgartner, "Does Incrementalism Stem from Political Consensus or from Institutional Gridlock," *American Journal of Political Science* 41 (October 1997): 1319–39.

21. In fact, Theda Skocpol argues that Clinton's health care plan, by avoiding the stigma of direct expenditure (the single-payer model) actually garnered opposition by imposing unfunded mandates on small businesses and also on health care suppliers in an effort to keep down the costs of health care. See Theda Skocpol, *Boomerang: Clinton's Health Security Effort and the Turn Against Government in U.S. Politics* (New York: Norton, 1996).

Index

A

abortion
    counseling gag rule, 77, 195
    litmus test for judicial appointments, 102–4
Aberbach, Joel, 68
Acheson, Eleanor Dean, 99–100, 104
administrative legacy
    controversies of, 123–28
    executive orders and, 128–30
    line-item veto and, 131–32
    personnel demographics and, 120
administrative presidency strategy, 130
affirmative action, 45, 59
agenda setting
    103d Congress and, 73–74
    Clinton's legacy in, 67–69
    domestic policy and, 205–7
    electoral mandate for, 52–54
    role of president in, 49, 51
Albright, Madeleine K., 227, 228, 233, 244
Alexander, Donald C., 135
Alliance for Justice, 103–4
Allison, Graham, 237
American Medical Association (AMA), 147, 156, 159
"angry white male," 178
appointments
    acting, 126–28
    compared to earlier presidents, 121, 122–24
    demographics of, 120
    gay and lesbian, 189
approval ratings, Clinton's, 39, 42
    compared to Eisenhower, 211
    compared to Reagan, 211
    and domestic policy, 211
    and government shutdown, 87
    and midterm elections of 1994, 207
Aristide, Jean Bertrande, 239
Armey, Richard, 55, 63
Aron, Nan, 103
Ashcroft, John, 110, 111
Asian Americans, 189–90
Asian economic crisis, 251
assault weapons ban
    crime legislation and, 83–84

gender and, 181
as gun control, 181
NAACP and, 181
NRA (National Rifle Association) and, 83
race and, 181
Astroturf mobilization, 146
Attali, Jacques, 231–32, 233
attorney general, Reno's appointment as, 99, 189
Atwater, Lee, 259

B

Babbitt, Bruce, 104, 106
Baird, Zöe, 36, 77–78, 189
Baker, James A., 61
Balkans crisis, 246, 290
Barber, James David, 33
Barkett, Rosemary, 104
Bauer, Gary, 111
Becerra, Xavier, 121
Becton, Charles, 107
Bennett, William, 286
Berger, Sandy, 228, 244, 245, 247
Big Emerging Market (BEM) Strategy, 243, 244
big government, ending, 24
Blackburn, Harry, 106–7
Blair, Tony, 258–70, 293
Bonior, David, 76
Boren, David, 206
Bosnia, 246, 247
Boxer, Barbara, 103
Brady Law, 195, 206
Breyer, Stephen G., 104–6
Broder, David, 57, 61
Brooks, Jack, 83
BTU tax, 79
"BTUed," 79
Buchanan, Patrick, 109
budget
    balancing, 209–10
    deficit and bully pulpit, 60
    strategy 1993–94, 39
bully pulpit
    and agenda setting, 67–69
    budget deficit and, 60
    and Clinton as synthesizer, 61
    and Clinton vs. 104th Congress, 51

and Contract with America, 62
divided government and, 50
and IRS reform, 63
and lack of mandate, 61–63
and Lewinsky scandal, 64–67
and needle exchange programs, 65
and permanent campaign, 59
and responsive competence, 59–61
and Franklin Delano Roosevelt, 49
and Theodore Roosevelt, 49
and survival politics, 59
and triangulation strategy, 59
and widening party gap, 63–64
Burnham, Walter Dean, 56
Bush, George, 13, 37
approval ratings of, 43
legacy of, 97
and organized interests, 153
Business Roundtable, 159
Byrd, Robert, 126

C

campaign strategies
opinion polls and, 260–63
and permanent campaign, 59, 268
"Campus Week of Dialogue," 194
Cannon, Joseph G., 57
Carter, Jimmy, 30, 75, 148, 153
Carville, James, 260, 265, 287
centrist leadership
as campaign strategy, 201
factors affecting, 204
as governing strategy, 202–4
integrative approach to, 203
opportunistic approach to, 203
with polarized Congress, 200
principled approach to, 203
prospects for, 222–26
split-the-difference approach to, 202
Chemical Weapons Convention, 233
child support collection, 194
Christian Coalition, 146, 160, 165–66
circumventing Congress, as administrative
legacy, 126–27, 129
China
engagement with, 227, 233, 245
technology transfers to, 249
citizen action groups, 146, 157
Clad, James, 242
Clarke, Jonathan, 242
Clean Water Act, 221, 222
Clinton, Hillary Rodham, 159, 191–92, 207,
216
Clinton v. *Jones*, 117
Clinton, William Jefferson
aggregate vote for, in 1992 election, 14
as chairman of Democratic Leadership
Council, 13
compared to John F. Kennedy, 285
links of, to black community, 174
as "our first black president," 193

as Peacemaker in Chief, 231
as policy wonk, 278–85
similarities to Tony Blair, 270–73
Slick Willie persona of, 284–88
as synthesizer, 61
cloture, 74
Cohen, Eliot, 233
Cohen, William, 228, 250
Committee on Party Effectiveness (CPE), 10
Comprehensive Nuclear Test Ban Treaty, 249,
251
Congressional Bastion, Myth of, 11
Congressional Black Caucus, 82, 169
Conservative Opportunity Society, 19
Consumer Price Index, revising, 215
Contract with America
and administrative legacy, 131
content of, 19
demise of, 56–57
deploying, 55–56, 67–69
divided government and, 22–23
guiding principles of, 54
public awareness of, 84–85, 208
Republican Revolution and, 18–20
Senate roadblocks to, 86
watering down, 62
and welfare, 219
"Creating a Better America for Ourselves and
Our Children," 63
crime control
103d Congress and, 83–84
assault weapons ban and, 83–84
domestic violence and, 198
gun control and, 195
Omnibus Crime Bill and, 20–21
organized interests and, 162–64
and violence against women and children,
195
Croly, Herbert, 242
Crosland, C.A.R., 264
Currie, Betty, 115
Cutler, Lloyd, 98

D

Dahrendorf, Ralf, 60
Danforth, John, 217
Daschle, Tom, 63
Dayton Peace Accords, 233
DeConcini, Dennis, 79
Defense of Marriage Act, 193, 196, 283
deficit reduction
and bully pulpit, 60
and divided government, 23–24
strategy 1993–94, 40
DeLay, Tom, 110
Democratic Leadership Council (DLC)
Clinton as chairman of, 13, 197
formation of, 11
demographics
administration personnel and, 120
judicial appointments and, 101, 114, 116

DiVall, Linda, 179, 186
divided government
    and bully pulpit, 50
    as Clinton's partisan legacy, 30–31
    Contract with America and, 22–23
    and deficit reduction, 23–24
    definition of, 9, 51
    and domestic policy, 207–10
    and election of 1998, 26–27
    and ending big government, 24
    and New Democrats, 9
    and organized interests, 164–66
    Republican control of Congress and, 25–28
    and shutting down the government, 23–24
    vs. unification after 1992 election, 15
Doherty, Carroll J., 228
Dole, Robert
    and Clinton's budget proposal, 50
    and Clinton's health care plan, 80
    and divided government, 24–25
    on Kosovo, 250–51
    on liberal judges, 108–9
    as leader of Republican opposition, 205–6
    and NAACP, 181–82
    as presidential candidate, 24–25
domestic policy, 263, 266
    aid to college students as, 215
    approval ratings and, 211
    and balancing the budget, 209–10
    defining agenda of, 205–7
    divided government and, 207–10
    economic policies and, 206, 214–16
    environmental issues and, 221–22
    government shutdown and, 211
    Lewinsky scandal and, 212–13
    limits on accomplishments in, 200
    obstacles to, 263–65
    triangulation and, 209
    uniforms for students as, 211
    veto power and, 208
domestic violence, 198
Douglas, Roger, 56
Downes, William, 104
Dukakis, Michael, 14
Dunn, Jennifer, 186
Durant, Robert, 127
Durham, Barbara, 115–16

E

Earned Income Tax Credit, 136, 179, 193, 209
Eckart, Dennis E., 162
economic policy
    103d Congress and, 79–80
    in 1993, 206
    accomplishments in, 214–16
    public support for, 80
    third-way philosophy and, 265
economic stimulus program, defeat of, 78–79
Edelman, Marian Wright, 166
Edelman, Peter, 63, 107, 220

Eisenhower, Dwight, 61, 276, 293
Elders, Joycelyn, 190, 259
Emanuel, Rahm I., 128
EMILY's List, 175
Employment Retirement Income Security Act
    (ERISA), 157
enlargement and engagement strategy
    description of, 235–38
    and entangling web strategy, 245
    implementing, 242–48
    loss aversion and, 239
    prospect theory and, 238–42
    selling to Congress, 238
entangling web strategy, 245
Enthoven, Alain C., 216, 265
environmental issues, 221–22, 42
Environmental Protection Agency, 222
Espy, Mike, 177
Era of Divided Government, 9, 14, 24, 27, 29–30
Esping-Andersen, Gøsta, 270
Evans, Graham, 234
executive action, 41
Executive Office of the President (EOP), 150
executive orders, 128–30

F

Family and Medical Leave Act, 77, 194
Family Research Council, 111, 146, 165
Federalist Society, 111
Federal Reserve System, 214
Feingold, Russell, 79
filibustering, 74, 82, 86
fiscal stimulus program, 38
fiscal surplus, 26
Fisher, Louis, 129
Fletcher, William, 115
Foley, Tom
    on assault weapons ban, 83
    on divided government, 75
    on NAFTA, 76
foreign policy
    in 1995, 230–31
    Big Emerging Market (BEM) Strategy and, 243
    Bosnia and, 248
    Clinton and Congress on, 249–50
    Clinton's doctrine of, 232–37
    Clinton's legacy in, 228–29
    enlargement and engagement strategy, 235–38
    five central challenges of, 232
    Grenada and, 239
    Haiti and, 239–40
    homeland defense and, 236
    International Monetary Fund (IMF) and, 246
    Israel and, 250
    Jordan and, 250
    military force and, 246–48
    National Economic Council (NEC) and, 243

national objectives in, 237
Palestine and, 250
Powell-Weinberger doctrine of, 247–48
previous president's doctrines of, 234
public interest in, 228–29
security strategy and, 237
strategic coherence and, 231
summary of, 250–53
Foster, Vincent, 207
fourth branch of government interest groups as, 140
framing issues, 37–38
France, resistance to Clintonism in, 272–73
Free Congress Foundation, 104, 111
free trade agreements, 40
Freedom of Access to Clinic Entrances Act, 195

G

Gaertner, Gary, 103
Gale, William, 136
Garcia, Rogelio, 122–23
GATT, 233
gay and lesbian appointments, 189
gays in the military
compromise agreement on, 53
lifting the ban on, 16, 207
media emphasis on, 78
Nunn's stand on, 78
gender, 182
and appointments, 101, 114–55, 186–87
assault weapons ban and, 181
in election of 1992, 175
in election of 1996, 178–82
historical context of, 170, 172
interest groups and, 185–87
issues, 192–96
judicial appointments and, 101, 114–15
and key to women's support, 180
Lewinsky scandal and, 169
midterm elections of 1994 and, 177–78
midterm elections of 1998 and, 182–85
opinion leaders and, 185
policies, 192–96
values and, 192–96
and voting patterns, 171
and women's group leaders, 186–87
women's roles and affiliations and, 174
Year of the Woman, 175
Gephardt, Dick, 63, 73, 76
Gergen, David, 184, 261
Giddens, Anthony, 267
Gingrich, Newt
and agenda setting, 67–69, 275
and bully pulpit, 50–51
and Conservative Opportunity Society, 19
and Contract with America, 18–20, 54–57
fall from grace of, 58, 274–275
history of, 52
opposition to health care reform by, 80
positioning for 1994 election by, 54
role of, in 1994 elections, 84
Ginsburg, Ruth Bader, 104–5, 188

Glenn, John, 126–27
Goldin, Daniel, 133
Goldman, Sheldon, 101
Gore, Al, 31, 131, 206, 220, 264
Gorton, Slade, 112, 115
governability gap, 50, 52, 53, 68–69
governing versus campaigning, 39–40, 45
government cutbacks, 138
Government Performance and Results Act, 138
government shutdown, 23–24, 86, 210–11
Gramm, Phil, 80, 112
Grassley, Charles, 110
Greenberg, Stan, 40, 260
Greenspan, Alan, 214, 251, 265, 274, 282
Greenstein, Fred, 276
Grenada, 239
gridlock, 73–74
Gugliotta, Guy, 131
Guinier, Lani, 125, 189, 259
gun control, 195

H

Haass, Richard, 240
Hacker, Jacob, 158
Haiti, 239–40
Hamilton, Lee, 248
Hargis, Billy Ray, 285
Harkin, Tom, 250
Hatch, Orrin, 104, 107, 110–11
health care reform
1993-94 strategy on, 36, 38–99
abortion counseling gag rule and, 77, 195
child support collection, 194
Clinton's policies on, 216–18, 280
copartisan approach to, 157
criticism of, 207
liberal synthesis approach to, 158
Medicaid and, 209, 215
medical research on fetal tissue and, 16, 77
national health insurance and, 265
organized interests and, 156–59
overshooting deadline on, 36
patients' bill of rights and, 195
public opinion on, 81–82
reasons for failure of, 35
and Republican Revolution, 16–17
health maintenance organizations (HMOs), 26, 224
Health Security Act, 155, 156, 167, 217
Health Insurance Association of America, 80, 156, 160
Heritage Foundation, 111, 146
Herman, Alexis, 153
Heymann, Philip B., 98
Hoagland, Jim, 60
Holbrooke, Richard, 231, 246
homeland defense, 236
Hoover, J. Edgar, 285
House Democratic Caucus, 10
Hubbell, Webster L., 98
Hussein, Saddam, 227, 228, 233, 245

I

Ickes, Harold, 58
IMF (International Monetary Fund), 246, 249
impeachment threat
    effects of, on judicial appointments, 116
    and organized interests, 155
    rhetorical presidency and, 43
impeachment trial, 141, 224
independent counsel law, 117
Independent Insurance Agents of America, 160
integrity, 42
interest group strategies, 140
interest groups, 140
    and Astroturf mobilization, 146
    Bush's approach to, 153
    character of, 145
    compromising with, 147
    and crime control, 162, 164
    Executive Office of the President (EOP) and, 150
    as fourth branch of government, 140
    growth of, 145
    and health care reform, 156–59
    Health Security Act and, 155
    impeachment threat and, 155
    and Jimmy Carter, 147, 153
    labor unions and, 156
    mobilizing support from, 150–55
    and NAFTA, 162
    organized labor and, 146
    party unity and, 147
    patronage and, 149
    and Republican takeover of Congress, 155
    reshaping, 149
    resisting, 152
    as social organization structure, 142–43
    strategies of influence of, 146
    summary of, 166–68
    third-way philosophy and, 154
    trade unions and, 147
    White House liaison with, 151–52
    women's, 165
interest group liaison, 150–53
    as consensus building, 151
    as governing party, 151
    as legitimization, 151
    as outreach, 151
    typology of, 152
Internal Revenue Service (IRS), 26, 45, 64, 92, 134–35, 139, 279–80
International Monetary Fund (IMF), 234, 246, 249
Iraq, 227, 228, 246
Ireland, Clinton as peace mediator in, 251
Ireland, Patricia, 188
Israel, 250

J

Jackson, Jesse, 176–77, 261
Jackson, Maynard, 177

Jefferson, William, 177
Jennings, Christopher, 66
Jervis, Robert, 239
Jipping, Thomas, 104, 111
Jones, Charles, 46, 158, 268
Jones, Paula, 109, 115, 286
Jordan, 250
Jordan, Vernon, 192, 261
Jospin, Lionel, 270
judicial activism, 109, 111–12
judicial appointments
    abortion
        litmus test and, 102–4
    Alliance for Justice and, 103–4
    comparisons with recent presidents', 117
    criteria for, 97
    demographics of, 101, 114, 116
    and diversity in lower federal courts, 99–105
    DoJ Office of Policy Development and, 100
    DoJ role in, 101
    effects of impeachment threat on, 116
    and failure to fill crucial positions, 98, 100
    Family Research Council and, 111
    Federalist Society and, 111
    Free Congress Foundation and, 104, 111
    Heritage Foundation and, 111
    judicial activism and, 109, 111
    litmus tests and, 102
    and midterm elections of 1994, 108–9
    NARAL (National Abortion Rights Action League) and, 103
    and number of judges appointed, 101
    and opposition to liberal appointees, 104–5, 109–16
    People for the American Way and, 103
    and position of attorney general, 99
    priority of, 97, 109, 112
    and problems with the DoJ, 98–99
    Reagan's legacy of, 97
    record number of vacancies and, 99
    Republican-controlled Senate and, 108–9
    and secret holds on nominees, 112
    selection process of, 101, 108
    success rate of, 110
    Washington Legal Foundation and, 104

K

Kasich, John R., 65
Kauffman, Bruce, 112
Kendall, David E., 66
Kennedy-Kassebaum bill, 94, 218
Kennan, George, 242
Kennedy, John F., 100, 256, 285
Kennedy, Robert, 192
Kerrey, Bob, 79
Key, V.O., 185
Kingdon, John, 51
Kissinger, Henry, 248
Klein, Joel, 101
Kohl, Helmut, 257

Kosovo, 227, 229, 242, 246–48, 251
Kyl, Jon, 112

L

labor unions, 156
Labour Party, 260, 270, 272
Lake, Anthony, 236
leadership
    bounded rationality theory and, 276–79
    Clinton and Gingrich, 274–76
    constraints and opportunities for, 277
    and end of government growth era, 290
    politics of survival and, 290–94
    rational choice theory and, 276–79
    and Republican control of Congress, 289–
        90
    resource constraints on, 288–92
    satisficing and, 277
Lee, Bill Lann, 127, 190
legislative leadership
    and budget agreement of 1997, 92
    changes in, since mid-1970s, 71–72
    and Clinton's reelection program, 90
    decentralized party system and, 71
    and electoral goals, 72
    evaluating, 94–97
    and minimum wage increase, 91
    and obstacles to compromise, 88–89
    and policy goals, 72
    and Republican attack on the IRS, 93
    and Republican strategic position, 93–94
    structural barriers to, 71
    three periods of, 72
    and triangulation, 89
    and welfare reform, 91
legislative leadership, 103d Congress
    and Clinton's policy agenda, 73–74
    and crime legislation, 83–84
    and economic program, 79–80
    and defeat of stimulus program, 79
    and filibustering, 74, 82
    and gridlock, 73–74
    and health care reform, 81–82
    and mood of the Democrats, 73
    and NAFTA, 76
    and New Democrat approach, 72
    policy accomplishments of, 77–78
    potential problems of, 73
    pressures of constituency on, 78–79
    and Republican cooperation, 74
    and Republican obstructionism, 84
    and third-way philosophy, 72
    and worst Congress in 50 years, 83
legislative leadership, 104th Congress, 274
    congressional majority party dominance
        in, 85–86
    and Contract with America, 84–86
    and filibustering, 86
    and government shutdown, 87
    as least productive Congress in history, 91
Leuchtenberg, William E., 109

Lewinsky scandal, 182
    British public opinion on, 256
    and bully pulpit, 64–67
    and domestic policy, 212–13
    and gender, 182
    and race, 169, 182
    and rhetorical presidency, 42–44
Lewis, John, 177, 183
Liberal Fundamentalism, Myth of, 11
line-item veto, 131–32
litmus tests for judicial appointments, 102
Livingston, Robert, 274
loss aversion, 239
Lott, Trent, 109, 112
Lowry, Rich, 163–64
Lux, Mike, 159, 160

M

Major, John, 255, 260, 271
McCaffrey, Barry, 66
McCain, John, 210
McConnell, Judith, 107
McFarlane, Robert C. (Bud), 61
Magaziner, Ira, 159, 207, 216
Mandelbaum, Michael, 239
Martin, Janet, 121
Massiah-Jackson, Frederica, 114
Matsui, Bob, 73
Mayhew, David R., 51, 164
Mead, Lawrence, 219
Medicaid
    capping, 215
    converting to block grant, 209
medical research on fetal tissue, 16, 77
Meese, Edwin III, 96, 110
Menendez, Robert, 121
Mfume, Kweisi, 181
Michel, Bob, 74
Michelman, Kate, 101
Middle East, Clinton as peace mediator in, 232,
    251
Mikva, Abner, 98
military force, 246–48
Milosevic, Slobodan, 227, 246, 248
minimum-wage increase, 91
Mitchell, George, 75, 106, 217
Mitterrand, François, 60, 257
Mobilization, Myth of, 11
Morris, Dick, 41, 61
    and agenda setting, 67, 87, 268
    triangulation strategy of, 59, 88, 209–10,
        258, 261, 289
Morrison, Toni, 193
motor voter legislation, 35, 37, 77
Moynihan, Daniel Patrick, 218
multilateralism, 245
Myth of Congressional Bastion, 11
Myth of Liberal Fundamentalism, 11
Myth of Mobilization, 11

N

NAACP, and ban on assault weapons, 181
Nader, Ralph, 148
Nash, Bob J., 121
National Abortion Rights Action League
    (NARAL), 103
National Aeronautics and Space Administration
    (NASA), 133–34, 138–39
National Association of Manufacturers, 159
National Economic Council (NEC), 243
National Federation of Independent Business,
    160
national health insurance, 265
National Partnership for Reinventing
    Government, 132, 133
National Performance Review (NPR), 131–33,
    134, 136
National Restaurant Association, 160
National Rifle Association (NRA), 83
National Security Strategy for a New Century,
    237
National Welfare Reform Act, 24
Native Americans, 189
needle exchange programs, 65
Neustadt, Richard, 140, 289, 292
"New American Choice:
    Opportunity, Responsibility, and
        Community, The," 12
New Deal era
    end date of, 6
    foreign affairs in, 4
    hallmark programs of, 4
    social coalitions in, 4–5, 167
New Democrats
    and 103d Congress, 72
    analysis of party defeats by, 11–12
    and changes in party structure, 7
    and Clinton campaign of 1992, 13–15
    definition of, 2, 258
    and divided government, 9–11
    on "ending welfare as we know it," 14
    and foreign affairs, 6
    main initiatives of, 12
    perspective of, on partisan legacy, 31
    and Ronald Reagan, 9–11
    and Republican Revolution, 15–16
    social coalitions of, 7
    and social unrest of 1968, 6–7
Nickles, Don, 212
Nixon, Richard, 71, 284, 287, 288
No Name Coalition, 160–61
North American Free Trade Agreement
    (NAFTA), 17–18, 35, 37, 64, 143, 265
    103d Congress and, 76
    Foley's stand on, 76
    opposition to, 76
    and organized interests, 161–62
    principled centrist leadership on, 206
    and Republican Revolution, 17
North American Treaty Organization (NATO),
    229, 236, 241, 246, 249

North, Oliver, 178
Nunn, Sam, 16, 78
Nussbaum, Bernard W., 98

O

Office of Public Liaison (OPL), 150, 154, 165
Omnibus Crime Bill, 20–21
"One America Conversation," 194
Operation Desert Fox, 234
organized labor, 146

P

Paez, Richard A., 103
Palestine, 250
Panetta, Leon, 55, 57–58, 67, 268
partisan legacy
    continuity of, 28–32
    divided government and, 30–31
    main elements of, 29
    New Democratic perspective on, 31
    Republican Revolution perspective on, 31
"patients' bill of rights," 195
patronage, 149
Paxon, Bill, 219
Paz, Samuel, 103, 107
People for the American Way, 103
Perot, Ross, 14, 16, 50, 202
Personal Responsibility and Work Opportunity
    Reconciliation Act of 1996 (PRWORA), 166
policy wonk, 278–85
"Politics of Evasion:
    Democrats and the Presidency, The," 11–
        12
Posen, Barry, 251
Powell-Weinberger doctrine, 247–48
President's Council on Sustainable
    Development, 222
presidential integrity, 42
presidential roles, 33
prospect theory, 238–42
public support
    limits of, 46
    obtaining, 38–39, 42–44
Putting People First, 201

Q

Quayle, Dan, 228

R

race
    affirmative action and, 181
    African-American group leaders and, 186–
        87
    angry white males and, 178
    appointments and, 101, 114–15, 186–87
    Asian Americans and, 189–90
    assault weapons ban and, 181
    and black vote in the 1992 primary, 177

and blacks in Congress, 176
and burning of black churches, 181
Campus Week of Dialog and, 194
and Clinton's links to black community,
    174
and election of 1992, 176
and election of 1996, 178–82
historical context and, 170, 172
interest groups and, 185–87
issues of, 192–96
judicial appointments and, 101, 114–15
Lewinsky scandal and, 169, 182
and midterm elections of 1994, 177–78
and midterm elections of 1998, 182–85
national conversation on, 193
Native Americans and, 189
One America Conversation on, 194
opinion leaders and, 185
policies on, 192–96
Republican landslide of 1994 and, 177–78
Statewide Days of Dialogue and, 194
values and, 192–96
and voting patterns, 171
Race Initiative, 194
Ragsdale, Lyn, 255
Rainbow Coalition, 176
Rangel, Charles, 176, 183
Rayburn, Sam, 57
Reagan, Nancy, 61
Reagan, Ronald, 61, 283, 288
    and defunding the left, 148, 167
    legacy of, 96
    and resisting organized interests, 148
    and rise of New Democrats, 9–11
Reed, Ralph, 63
Rehnquist, William H., 114
Reich, Robert, 261, 268
Reinhardt, Stephen, 103
reinventing government initiative, 118–19, 131,
    138
Reischauer, Robert, 130
Reno, Janet, 98, 189
Republican-controlled Senate, 108–9
Republican Revolution
    Clinton initiatives affecting, 16–18
    constraints on, 16
    and Contract with America, 18
    and foreign trade, 17–18
    and NAFTA, 17
    and New Democrats, 15–16
    and Omnibus Crime Bill, 20–21
    perspective on partisan legacy of, 31
Republican takeover of Congress, 155
responsive competence, 59
rhetorical presidency
    and budget, 39
    defensive strategy, cost of, 44–45
    executive action and, 41
    failure of partisan approach and, 34–35
    and fiscal stimulus program, 38
    impeachment threat and, 43
    and lack of resources for initiatives, 34–40

as leadership style, 33–34
Lewinsky scandal and, 42–44
limits of, 46–47
and potential sources of influence, 34–35
presidential integrity and, 42
and tobacco tax, 45
Robb, Chuck, 178
Rockman, Bert, 154
Roosevelt, Eleanor, 191
Roosevelt, Franklin Delano, 15, 70, 71, 144–
    45, 269, 285
Roosevelt, Theodore, 49
Rose, Richard, 227
Ross, Andrew, 251
Rossiter, Clinton, 51
Rubin, Robert, 244, 251, 282
Ruggie, John, 227, 245
Russia, 245

S

Sarokin, H. Lee, 104
"Save Social Security first," 213
Schippers, David P., 288
Schmoke, Kurt, 177
Schröder, Gerhard, 258, 272, 293
"senatorial courtesy," 99
Sessions, Jefferson, 111
sexual preference discrimination, 196
Shalala, Donna E., 65, 191
Sheppard, Lee, 135
Shelby, Richard, 21
Shogren, Elizabeth, 128
six-year itch, 27
Skocpol, Theda, 147, 217
Skowronek, Stephen, 154, 167–68, 276
Slick Willie persona, 284–88
Smith, Robert, 286
Souljah, Sister, 176, 262
Specter, Arlen, 113
Sperling, Gene, 64, 66, 128
spinning the media, 261, 271, 288
Starr, Kenneth, 43, 97, 109, 113, 115, 183, 212,
    274, 286
Starr Report, 43, 115
START treaties, 233, 251
"Statewide Days of Dialogue," 194
Stevens, Ted, 130
Sullivan, Michael J., 104
survival politics, 59

T

Taylor, Jeremy C., 128
third-way philosophy, 60, 263–67
    and 103d Congress, 73
    coherence of, 266, 269
    dangers of, 265
    elements of, 266
    and organized interests, 154
    and Tony Blair, 259–60
Thurmond, Strom, 104

tobacco tax, 45
Torricelli, Robert G., 250
trade unions, 147
Travelgate, 207
triangulation strategy, 209
    and bully pulpit, 59
    and legislative leadership, 89
    and political legacy, 258–60
Tyson, Laura D'Andrea, 214

U

United Nations, 245, 249
U.S. Chamber of Commerce, 159
U.S.S. *Harlan County*, 36

V

Vacancies Act amendment, 127–28
veto power
    and domestic policy, 208
    line-item, 131–32
Vietnam War, 6–7
violence against women and children, 180, 195
Violent Crime Control and Law Enforcement
    Act of 1994, 163

W

Walker, Edward, 285
Washington Legal Foundation, 145, 165
Watts, J.C., Jr., 186
welfare reform
    and Aid to Families with Dependent
        Children, 220
    Contract with America and, 219
    domestic policy and, 218–20
    family caps and, 219
    and legislative leadership, 91
    and National Welfare Reform Act, signing
        of, 24
Weyrich, Paul, 286
White, Byron, 105
Whitewater, 110, 113, 207
Will, George, 227
Williams, Alexander, 101
Wilson, James Q., 219
Wilsonianism, 238
women's groups, 165
Wood, Kimba, 36, 189
World Bank, 246
World Trade Organization (WTO), 265
Wye River memorandum, 250

Y

"Year of the Woman," 175

About the Contributors

Joel D. Aberbach is professor of political science and policy studies and director of the Center for American Politics and Public Policy at the University of California, Los Angeles. His books include *Keeping a Watchful Eye: The Politics of Congressional Oversight* and (with Bert A. Rockman) *In the Web of Politics: Three Decades of the U.S. Federal Executive* (forthcoming).

Larry Berman is professor of political science at the University of California, Davis. He is the author of (with Bruce Murphy) *Approaching Democracy* and *Lyndon Johnson's War: The Road to Stalemate in Vietnam.*

Colin Campbell is University Professor of Public Policy at Georgetown University, where he served as executive director of the Georgetown Public Policy Institute. His books include *The U.S. Presidency in Crisis* and *Managing the Presidency: Carter, Reagan, and the Search for Executive Harmony.*

David T. Canon is associate professor of political science at the University of Wisconsin–Madison. He is the author of *Race, Redistricting, and Representation: The Unintended Consequences of Black-Majority Districts* and (with Kenneth Mayer) of *The Dysfunctional Congress? The Individual Roots of an Institutional Dilemma.*

William Cunion is a doctoral candidate in political science at the University of Illinois at Urbana-Champaign. His research concerns several aspects of American national institutions, including presidential leadership of public opinion.

George C. Edwards III is Distinguished Professor of Political Science and director of the Center for Presidential Studies at Texas A&M University. His books include *At the Margins: Presidential Leadership of Congress* and *Presidential Approval*.

Emily O. Goldman is associate professor of political science and director of the International Relations Program at the University of California, Davis. She is the author of *Sunken Treaties: Naval Arms Control between the Wars* and coeditor of *The Politics of Strategic Adjustment*.

David M. O'Brien is the Leone Reaves and George W. Spicer Professor at the University of Virginia. He is the author of *Constitutional Law and Politics* and *Storm Center: The Supreme Court in American Politics*, as well as annual editions of *Supreme Court Watch*.

Mark A. Peterson is professor of policy studies and political science at the UCLA School of Public Policy and Social Research. He is the author of *Legislating Together: The White House and Capitol Hill from Eisenhower to Reagan* and the editor of the *Journal of Health Politics, Policy, and Law*.

Paul J. Quirk is professor of political science and the Institute of Government and Public Affairs at the University of Illinois at Urbana-Champaign. His books include *Industry Influence in Federal Regulatory Agencies* and (with Martha Derthick) *The Politics of Deregulation*.

Bert A. Rockman is the University Professor of Political Science at the University of Pittsburgh and coeditor of *Governance: An International Journal of Policy and Administration*. He is the author of *The Leadership Question: The Presidency and the American System* and (with Joel D. Aberbach) *In the Web of Politics: Three Decades of the U.S. Federal Executive* (forthcoming).

Virginia Sapiro is the Sophonisba P. Breckinridge Professor of Political Science and Women's Studies at the University of Wisconsin–Madison and Principal Investigator of the National Election Studies. Among her works are *Women in American Society: An Introduction to Women's Studies* and *The Political Integration of Women: Roles, Socialization, and Politics*.

Byron E. Shafer is the Andrew W. Mellon Professor of American Government at Oxford University and a Professorial Fellow at Nuffield College. He is the author of *Quiet Revolution: The Struggle for the Democratic Party and the Shaping of Post-Reform Politics* and (with William J.M. Claggett) *The Two Majorities: The Issue Context of Modern American Politics*.

Barbara Sinclair is the Marvin Hoffenberg Professor of American Politics at the University of California, Los Angeles. Her books include *Unorthodox Lawmaking: New Legislative Processes in the U.S. Congress* and *Legislators, Leaders, and Lawmaking: The U.S. House of Representatives in the Postreform Era*.

Graham K. Wilson is professor of political science at the University of Wisconsin–Madison, where he teaches in both the comparative and American politics programs. He is the author of *Only in America? The Politics of the United States in Comparative Perspective* and (with Colin Campbell) *The End of Whitehall: Death of a Paradigm?*